THE ARCHAEOLOGY OF EARLY CHINA

This volume aims to satisfy a pressing need for an updated account of Chinese archaeology. It covers an extended time period from the earliest peopling of China to the unification of the Chinese Empire some two thousand years ago. The geographical coverage includes the traditional focus on the Yellow River basin but also covers China's many other regions. Among the topics covered are the emergence of agricultural communities; the establishment of a sedentary way of life; the development of sociopolitical complexity; advances in lithic technology, ceramics, and metallurgy; and the appearance of writing, large-scale public works, cities, and states. Particular emphasis is placed on the great cultural variations that existed among the different regions and the development of interregional contacts among those societies.

Gideon Shelach-Lavi is the Louis Freiberg Professor of East Asian Studies at the Hebrew University of Jerusalem. He has conducted archaeological fieldwork in northeast China since 1995. He is currently heading the Fuxin Regional Archaeological Project. He has published many articles in leading academic journals. His most recent books include *Prehistoric Societies on the Northern Frontiers of China: Archaeological Perspectives on Identity Formation and Economic Change during the First Millennium BCE* (2009), *Chifeng International Collaborative Archaeological Project* (coauthor, 2011), and *The Birth of Empire: The State of Qin Revisited* (coeditor, 2013).

THE ARCHAEOLOGY OF EARLY CHINA: FROM PREHISTORY TO THE HAN DYNASTY

GIDEON SHELACH-LAVI

Hebrew University, Jerusalem

CAMBRIDGE
UNIVERSITY PRESS

CAMBRIDGE
UNIVERSITY PRESS

One Liberty Plaza, 20th Floor, New York, NY 10006, USA

Cambridge University Press is part of the University of Cambridge.

It furthers the University's mission by disseminating knowledge in the pursuit of education, learning, and research at the highest international levels of excellence.

www.cambridge.org
Information on this title: www.cambridge.org/9780521145251

First published 2015
Reprinted 2016

Printed in the United States of America by Sheridan Books, Inc.

A catalog record for this publication is available from the British Library.

ISBN 978-0-521-19689-5 Hardback
ISBN 978-0-521-14525-1 Paperback

To Professor Kathy Linduff

My teacher, mentor, and dear friend

CONTENTS

FIGURES

ACKNOWLEDGMENTS

The archaeology of any region is a cumulative process that builds upon the work of many individuals. This is all the more true for China, whose vast size and long history are uncovered by generations of committed Chinese archaeologists who often work in remote areas and at extreme conditions. All of us who are interested in the history and archaeology of China are indebted to these people, some acknowledged in this book and many others that I was unable to individually mention.

This book could not have been written without the help of many people and the generous support received from several institutions. I am grateful to all of them. My colleagues and friends: Francis Allard who was involved in defining the concept for the book and Yuri Pines who commented extensively (sometimes critically) on its historical parts. Kathy Linduff who connected me with Cambridge University Press and encouraged me to embark on the long journey of writing this book. The many colleagues I cannot name here who shared with me the results of their own work. I benefited immensely from the help of many Hebrew University students who gathered materials and worked on the illustrations for the book: Yitzchak Jaffe, Nir Horovitz, Amit Niv, and Tao Lumin. My student Chen Bo and my colleague and friend Teng Mingyu helped me locate materials unavailable in Israel and sent me new books from China. I am also grateful to all those who contributed pictures to this book, especially Gary Lee Todd for allowing me to use his extensive collection of photos and Xu Hong for his help and patience.

Most of this book was written while I was a resident at the Scholion Interdisciplinary Research Center at the Hebrew University. I am grateful to the center and to the Mandel Foundation that supports it for hosting me, and to members of my research group, especially Ronnie Ellenblum and Sharon Zuckerman, for many hours of informal discussions on a variety of topics that sometimes found their way into the pages of this book. I also spent extended periods of time at the Center for Frontier Archaeology at Jilin University, where I enjoyed a generous welcome, used their extensive collection of books and papers on Chinese archaeology, and benefited greatly from discussions with colleagues and students.

I am especially grateful for the assistance I have received over the years from the Louis Freiberg Chair of East Asian Studies. Support for the editing of this book was also received from the Faculty of Humanities at Hebrew University. Two gifted editors worked on different parts of the manuscript: Nicholas (Nik) John and Elana Chipman, and Dolev Rahat worked on the index. The book would not be what it is without their work.

Finally, I am also grateful to Beatrice Rehl, Anastasia Graf, Isabella Vitti, Minaketan Dash, and the staff of Cambridge University Press for their support and patience.

INTRODUCTION

This book covers a very long and enormously rich and complicated period in China's history. Beginning with the first peopling of the region some 1.6 million years ago, it pays special attention to the Neolithic and Bronze Age periods and concludes with the first imperial unification of China at the time of the Qin (秦) and Han (漢) dynasties.

When I first became interested in the archaeology of China as an undergraduate in the late 1980s, there was basically one book available in English on the subject – K. C. Chang's *The Archaeology of Ancient China* (Chang 1986). Even after my command of Chinese improved and I was able to read primary materials, the available data were not that extensive: preliminary reports in three major archaeological journals and a handful of textbooks, mostly published for local consumption by students in the few departments of archaeology that existed in China at the time. The illustrations of artifacts and sites in those publications were for the most part fuzzy black-and-white photos and drawings of poor quality. Today, the same field is almost unrecognizable: hardly a week passes without reports of new discoveries, and the numerous academic articles and books are accompanied by top-quality illustrations and data tables.

This flood of new publications is the outcome of the hundreds of archaeological excavations and surveys conducted in China every year. Consequently, our knowledge of Chinese archaeology

has dramatically expanded and our ideas about China's prehistory and early historic periods have been revolutionized. This very richness of new (and older) data, however, poses a real problem for the writing of a broad synthesis, such as this book. Selectivity is necessary and obvious, and our criteria for inclusion must be based not on how famous or spectacular a certain find is, but rather on how much it contributes to the specific issues we address.

Given China's antiquity, significant size, and ecological diversity, Chinese archaeology can make a vital contribution to our understanding of how societies develop, adapt to their respective environments, and interact with one another. For this reason, I focus on the development of local sociopolitical and cultural trajectories and the formation of local identities on the one hand, and on evidence for interregional interactions and the creation of shared cultural norms on the other. These themes populate the entire book and hold together its different chapters. But, for every period, I also include additional pertinent issues and analyze them from anthropological and historical perspectives. These themes guide my selection of the primary data included in the book. They also determine the spatial coverage of the book, which includes – but also extends beyond – the traditional focus on the Yellow River basin, and several chapters discuss the archaeology of China's northeast, northwest, southeast, and southwest. The archaeology of more distant regions within the borders of present-day China, such as Xinjiang, is also discussed, but only in cases where it is relevant to issues such as the development of long-distance contacts.

Although the book's time frame stretches from the earliest presence of humans in China through to the Han dynasty, it ranges primarily from the Neolithic to the Bronze Age, a period that spanned thousands of years and witnessed a series of significant formative events, transitions, and transformations. These include the emergence of agricultural communities, the establishment of a sedentary way of life, the development of sociopolitical complexity, advances in technologies such as ceramics and metallurgy, and the appearance of writing, large-scale public works, cities, and states.

The book is organized chronologically, although there is a degree of overlap between chapters that focus on different regions or topics during roughly the same time period. Each chapter (with the exception of the introduction and Chapter 1) is divided into two main parts (each of which is further subdivided): the first presents the relevant archaeological data with as little interpretation as possible, while the second uses these data to address various broader issues related to the main themes of the book, such as the development of economic adaptation, social trajectory, cultural change, the formation of local identities, and interactions between different regions of China.

A SHORT BACKGROUND TO THE HISTORY OF CHINESE ARCHAEOLOGY

China can boast of a long history of research into its material remains.[1] As in most other ancient cultures, sporadic mentions of ancient artifacts appear in early texts, but starting from the eleventh century CE they began to take on a much more systematic form. Under what is called "traditional antiquarianism," scholars of the Northern Song

(北宋, 960–1126 CE) and later dynasties classified collections of old artifacts, mainly bronzes and jades, dated them to ancient periods, identified their names and functions, and published their studies in elaborate catalogues.

Western-style modern archaeology arrived in China during the early years of the twentieth century, along with many other Western intellectual influences. The Swedish geologist J. G. Andersson, who was hired to work for the Geological Survey of China, is credited with many early discoveries of prehistoric remains, as well as with the introduction of modern archaeological methods to China. A number of other foreign archaeologists also worked in China during these early years. However, soon after Andersson's first discoveries, Chinese archaeologists such as Li Ji (李濟) and later Xia Nai (夏鼐) entered the field and became its leading figures. The first large-scale projects – such as the prehistoric excavations at Zhoukoudian (Chapter 2) and the excavations of the Bronze Age site at Yinxu (Chapter 8) – were conducted by Chinese archaeologists or carried out jointly with non-Chinese archaeologists. The dramatic discoveries made during this period, including, for example, the identification of the earliest documents in Chinese history, gave archaeology the high prestige it enjoys in China today.

After the Second World War and the Chinese Civil War, and with the rise of the Communist Party to power, archaeological research was incorporated into the state system. The field was now better supervised and the training of archaeologists in university departments and at the Academy of Social Sciences was regulated. During most periods, including the Cultural Revolution, field research continued uninterrupted, but the framework for interpretation was imposed from above to both fit the Marxist paradigm and serve nationalist goals (Tong 1995). After the death of Mao Zedong in 1976 and the ensuing reforms led by Deng Xiaoping, Chinese archaeology became increasingly open to the outside world. New methods and frameworks of interpretation were introduced and a number of international collaborations were established.

The legacy of this long intellectual history shapes the way archaeology is conducted in present-day China. For example, the names by which we identify different types of bronze vessels and the functions we assign to them are in most cases based on the work of imperial-era scholars from the traditional antiquarianism school. As in many other parts of the world, nationalist sentiments influence the interpretations of archaeological data, including their transformation over time. Nonetheless, such issues – which have been dealt with by previous research (e.g., Falkenhausen 1995; Tong 1995) – are beyond the scope of this book. Here, I transcend entrenched concepts and stale debates and look at the data with fresh eyes. Admittedly, my own models pervade this book, but I hope that by presenting some of the more raw data, you will form your own interpretations and perhaps even reject mine.

The themes that run through the chapters of this book are the local trajectories of economic, social, and cultural change and the interregional interactions among the local societies represented by these trajectories. While regional variation and interregional interaction may seem a natural framework for discussing a region as large and complex as China, serious discussion of these topics got under way relatively late in Chinese archaeology. In 1986, the fourth edition of Chang's seminal book, *The Archaeology of Ancient China* was published. This was not merely an updated version of the third edition, published almost ten years earlier, but rather a conceptual breakthrough in the understanding of China's ancient past and the development of Chinese civilization. Most notably, Chang argues in his book that the dominant mechanisms that catalyzed the development of Chinese civilization were contacts between different regional Neolithic cultures (Chang 1986: 234–42). Initially, this "Chinese interaction sphere" model was seen

by many as heterodoxy, but it has since become widely accepted, at least by researchers of the Late Neolithic period, although few researchers have attempted to apply Chang's model to regions beyond the basins of the Yellow and Yangzi Rivers and to periods later than the Neolithic.

Part of the reluctance to accept interactions as an important catalyst of social change and cultural development is the self-image of what constitutes "Chinese culture," including its sources and its development. This self-image, which evolved during the late preimperial and the early imperial eras, was projected back onto earlier periods as an elite-based description of a homogeneous Chinese culture superior to any other culture in its orbit. This anachronistic view was carried over to the modern era and perhaps even exaggerated by nationalist ideas imported to China from the West. It is probably not coincidental that the first challenges to this model were published in the mid-1980s during the chairmanship of Deng Xiaoping, whose reforms included the economic revitalization of selected regions throughout China and certain measures for regional autonomy.

The new "multiregional" approach should also be viewed in the context of the tremendous surge in archaeological discoveries in China over the past three decades, an increase partially explained by the close association between salvage archaeology and the tide of construction projects that has swept the country, including in many areas previously considered peripheral by Chinese archaeologists. These findings have highlighted the unique features of local cultures. Used to create local tourist attractions and to boost local pride, the new discoveries have been instrumental in what has been termed the "regionalist paradigm" of Chinese archaeology (Falkenhausen 1995).

A SHORT THEORETICAL FRAMEWORK

Awareness of interactions between prehistoric societies is not new in archaeological research. In fact, during the first half of the twentieth century, archaeologists devoted a great deal of effort to locating and identifying similarities in the shapes and styles of objects found in distant locations, and to speculating about the connections between the societies to which those objects belonged (Schortman and Urban 1992). A reaction against the simplistic "diffusionist" models that were often put forward to explain such similarities led archaeologists throughout most of the second half of the twentieth century to focus their research on local trajectories and the adaptation of local societies, almost completely disregarding evidence pointing to external contact. One critic termed this intellectual trend "the premise of calorific priority" (Sherratt 1995: 7). In recent years, however, this attitude has changed, and since the mid-1990s there has been renewed interest in cross-cultural interactions. Scholars who are part of this new movement address the interplay between local and supra-local processes to reconstruct and better understand the complexity of worldwide historical processes. Likewise, similar trends can be found in the discipline of history, with the growing popularity of so-called world history.

Archaeological studies of interregional interactions inevitably start with patterns of artifact distribution, but without a clear theoretical framework through which to study these patterns, we are unable to gain meaningful historical or anthropological insights. If we are not careful, "interaction" might easily become just a modern replacement for the term "diffusion" of fifty years ago, "which in causing everything, explained nothing" (Schortman and Urban 1992: 8). To avoid this we need to be explicit in our use of the term. In my view, interactions can arise from one of two processes (or from a combination of both):

1. The movement of people.
2. The movement of artifacts (and, to a lesser degree, materials).

In prehistoric societies, and especially among illiterate cultures, the transmission of information (including ideas, religious beliefs, etc.) should be viewed as the outcome of these mechanisms rather than as an independent mechanism. When analyzing archaeological data we should ask which of these two mechanisms was responsible for the patterns observed and what level of interaction was most likely to have created those patterns. The movement of people, for example, could consist of the large-scale migration of an entire population to a new territory, a one-time military invasion, the migration of a small group of people, or the travels of a handful of individuals from one place to another. Historical and ethnographic documentation of such movements should be used as analogies for findings from the archaeological record (Anthony 1990). Similarly, artifacts can be transferred from one place to another as part of large-scale trade, in exchange of "royal" tributes, in small-scale and down-the-line exchanges, through the occasional exchange of gifts, or through the transmission of religious relics and paraphernalia.

The two models of interaction that are most often proposed are those of migration and trade. Because migration and diffusion have often been used as synonymous terms (Trigger 1989: 150–74), archaeologists have in more recent years tended to altogether avoid the subject of migration. Nonetheless, there is little doubt that during historic periods – and presumably in prehistoric times as well – human groups of different sizes migrated over short, medium, and long distances (Anthony 1990). The movement of even a small number of people could, directly or indirectly, lead to meaningful social, political, or economic changes, but we must be extremely cautious in invoking the notion of migration. Clearly, there are different types and scales of migration, and we need to be specific about what exactly we mean when we employ the term "migration" as well as how a proposed model is supported or challenged by the archaeological data.

Unfortunately, migration is commonly understood in archaeology as the horde-like movement of an entire population and its replacement of the entire (or most of the) local population at the target destination. For example, Russian archaeologist Elena Kuzmina argued that in the Eurasian Steppes the late second millennium BCE was an epoch of large-scale migrations that "were necessitated by demographic causes – population pressure – and intensified by climatic crisis" (Kuzmina 1998: 72). Data presented in support of the existence of such migration and often associated with the spread of languages (such as the Indo-Iranian) are is often quite vague, yet descriptions of migratory waves that shaped the history of Eurasia nonetheless remain popular (e.g., Frank 1992: 9). In China too, large-scale migrations and population replacements are often evoked to explain changes in material culture (e.g., Fitzgerald-Huber 2003: 63; Wu 2002a: 60–1). When studying the archaeological record we must instead ask ourselves what the direct evidence is for such a cataclysmic event. Do we see a systematic destruction of sites, the total replacement of artifact styles and techniques, or a clear discontinuity in local developments? We should be more explicit about which aspects of the material culture changed and remained relatively stable. In many cases, the aspects of material culture that changed most rapidly were those associated with prestige objects and ritual practices. Therefore, migration, if it took place at all, was probably limited to small segments of the society such as the elite or specialists of various kinds (Shelach 2009).

Unlike the explanations based on diffusion and migration that fell out of favor for a time, research into ancient trade remained part of the archaeological agenda even during the heyday of the "new archaeology." Trade was perceived as a functional system – not unlike subsistence and adaptation systems – of the kind commonly studied by archaeologists. The most obvious advantage of the concept of trade over migration is the focus on objects and raw materials rather than on people, thereby enabling archaeologists to employ scientific methods such as trace element analysis in charting transmissions from one place to another. Thanks to scientific methodology, there is currently little doubt that transmissions through trade, sometime across vast distances, took place between human societies as early as the Neolithic period, if not earlier (Renfrew and Bahn 1996: 335–56). On a more theoretical level, trade is by nature a two-way interaction, and thus a focus on trade can help archaeologists escape some of the inherent biases and political implications of migration studies.

Despite their many advantages, studies of trade are rarely integrated into an anthropological model that addresses sociopolitical and economic processes. Discovering an exotic raw material or foreign object can indeed be exciting, but it does not provide an explanation of the socioeconomic impacts of trade. For that, we need to address issues such as the mechanisms and volume of trade, the impact of trade relations on the local economy, the ways different social groups and individuals used trade to elevate their socioeconomic standing, and the ways foreign objects or ideas were manipulated to produce social or political benefits. This kind of perspective compels us to examine the context in which the foreign object or material was found (e.g., mundane vs. ceremonial; elite vs. commoner). The types and quantities of artifacts may indicate whether we have found evidence of large-scale trade in commodities for daily use, small-scale trade in prestige items, or a down-the-line system of exchange in artifacts that have passed through many hands and have slowly percolated from region to region.

One insight suggested by recent studies of interaction is that we should imagine interaction not as something flat but rather as a multidimensional field made up of different types and levels of contact and exchange. Moreover, although different types of interaction networks tend to overlap, it is possible that a central node in one type of interaction network (e.g., a religious center) would be located on the fringes of another type (e.g., economic exchange) (Flad and Chen 2013). We should take such insights to heart when considering the function of a certain site or the position of one region vis-à-vis others.

Another theoretical perspective through which to study interregional interactions is political context. Under this heading are theories that analyze the domination of one region over another, interregional competition, and emulation. Chang's Chinese interaction sphere model (Chang 1986: 234–42), for example, does not explain how interactions were carried out but instead examines their sociopolitical and cultural effects. In fact, Chang's model may be seen as describing a specific manifestation of "peer-polity interaction," where sociopolitical evolution takes place in the context of interactions between polities of equivalent scale, power, and level of social complexity (Renfrew 1986).

If peer-polity interactions are those among equal partners, at the other extreme of the spectrum we find center-and-periphery models that describe imbalanced relations between polities of different scales. Such models, including Immanuel Wallerstein's "world system" model, are relevant only to the second part of this book and are described more fully in Chapter 9.

Rekindled interest in mid- and long-range interactions between societies located within the current borders of China and beyond has generated novel data and new interpretations of existing data. Unfortunately, however, these discussions tend to focus on issues of origin and the spread of cultural traits. Such discussions are often associated with nationalistic or patriotic sentiments and tend to produce more heat than light.

Another related practice in Chinese archaeology is correlating archaeological cultures in areas outside the so-called "core of Chinese civilization" with the names of people who, according to ancient Chinese texts, inhabited those regions. Two noteworthy examples include Wu En's identification of certain types of graves from northeast China containing bronze artifacts and dating between the ninth and the fifth centuries BCE with a group named the Mountain Rong (Shan-rong 山戎) (Wu 2002a: 60–1) and the common association between archaeological cultures from the Gansu-Qinghai region, such as the Siwa, Siba, and Kayue cultures, with the ancient Qiang (羌) people (cf. Li 1993: 119–20; Liu 2000: 25). Similarly, the prehistoric populations of the Sichuan basin are sometimes equated with the Ba (巴) and Shu (蜀) peoples, or the ancient inhabitants of Lingnan with the Yue (越) (Peng 2002). The problem is not merely that most of these analogies are anachronistic, but more fundamentally that they create the false impression that they provide an explanation while, at best, they simply label a material culture with a "historic" name. In the worst cases, such labeling infuses our understanding of the archaeological data with later biases regarding the lifestyle, political organization, and economic activities of the people who inhabited the peripheral regions in question.

I avoid this historical method as much as possible in this book and focus instead on the archaeological data and what they can tell us about ancient interregional contacts: What were the interaction mechanisms? What was moved by the interactions? How frequent and intensive were they? Which segments of society took part in these interactions, and how did contact with external groups affect the local society?

CHAPTER I

THE GEOGRAPHIC AND ENVIRONMENTAL BACKGROUND

This chapter provides the environmental framework necessary to understand the archaeological materials presented in the rest of the book. With its current borders, China is the fourth largest state in the world, a little larger than the contiguous United States, covering an area of some 9,330,000 km²,[1] across about 35 degrees in latitude and 75 degrees in longitude. Within this vast territory the climate ranges from humid subtropical conditions to extreme arid environments, and elevations range from the highest in the world to below sea level. This variation is highly relevant to this book because it is bound to have affected human adaptation across China as well as the nature of interactions among local societies.

This chapter considers significant topographic features – such as the main rivers, mountains, deserts, and plains – and describes their effects on the local environment in aid of a discussion on how they may have facilitated or hindered interregional interaction in ancient times. It continues with an overview of regional variation in climatic patterns, soils, and vegetation, and explains how subsistence activities and other adaptations continued to be constrained by local environmental conditions. Finally, it draws on results from paleoenvironmental studies in China to provide an overview of environmental change over thousands of years. Later chapters describe these changes in greater detail and illustrate how this information serves the important purpose of setting the environmental framework within which the issues of cultural change and other processes can be addressed.

DEFINING "CHINA"

Names by which the region at the focus of this book is currently known, such as Zhongguo (中國), China, and Kitaia, all appeared later than the periods described herein. The term "Zhongguo," usually translated as the "central state," was coined during the Eastern Zhou period (771–221 BCE). At the time it was understood in the plural form, the central states, and denoted the major states located in the central Yellow River basin. Even in the Qin and Han periods, the term had not yet acquired the all-inclusive meaning that it has today. In fact, throughout the imperial era, the Chinese and their Asian neighbors referred to themselves and to their state by the names of the changing dynasties (for example, the people of Han – 漢人 – or the people of Tang – 唐人). In Middle Ages Europe, China was known as Cathaya, a name driven from Khitan (in Chinese Qidan 契丹), the name of the non-Chinese tribe that founded the Liao dynasty that ruled north China and a vast area of the steppe between 916 and 1125 CE. The word "China" appeared in European languages only during the sixteenth or seventeenth centuries (Wilkinson 1998: 722–5).

More important than the formation of these later names, any kind of self-identification with a shared multiregional identity appeared relatively late in China. Only during the Western Zhou period (1047–771 BCE) did the Zhou elite exhibit what may be seen as symbols of a shared identity. Literary references to a shared identity, using terms such as Xia or Hua, Hua Xia, and Zhu Xia (夏, 華, 華夏, 諸夏), first appeared during the eighth century BCE, and it took several centuries for this collective identity to spread to wider segments of the population (Falkenhausen 2006: 166 and 402). A common identity became canonical only after the imperial unification of 221 BCE, when the political borders of the Chinese Empire were clearly demarcated and the cultural dichotomy between the Chinese and their neighbors, especially the nomadic people of the steppe, was highly emphasized (Di Cosmo 2002; Pines 2005: 90–1; Poo 2005). Even so, the process of identity formation and the dissemination of a Chinese identity to new regions and wider segments of the population continued throughout the imperial era.

In geographic terms, the borders of China are not a historically fixed reality. During some periods, such as the Tang (618–907 CE), political boundaries expanded, reaching beyond the current borders of the People's Republic of China (PRC) in some areas. At other times, such as during the Southern Song (1127–1279 CE), the area under the control of the Chinese Empire shrank dramatically, with some of the areas most identified with Chinese civilization falling into the hands of foreign dynasties. Moreover, some regions currently within PRC borders have only recently been incorporated into the Chinese realm, and their historic association with what can be defined as Chinese culture is negligible. Well-known examples include Xinjiang in the PRC's northwest and Tibet in the west.

How then can we discuss the archaeology of China for periods during which neither China nor any kind of Chinese identity existed or look at a region whose historical borders have constantly changed? One way of overcoming this problem is to focus on the area traditionally viewed as the "cradle of Chinese civilization" – the Yellow and Wei River basins – and ignore the majority of developments outside it. Another approach is to discuss the archaeology in China. This inclusive approach sees any archaeological data discovered within the borders of the PRC – regardless of their historical or cultural affinity – as the target of our study. In this book, however, I adopt an altogether different approach, based on the assumption that the origins of Chinese culture predate the explicit recognition of Chinese identity or identities by many millennia and that they coevolved across a relatively large region. In other words, I believe that Chinese identities were constructed from preexisting ways of life, religious beliefs, technologies, symbols, habits, and traditions that evolved in many different parts of China during the Neolithic and Bronze periods. As discussed in the following chapters, some of the most salient features of the region's prehistory are the constant interregional and intersocietal interactions and the gradual development of shared cultural elements. This stratum of shared culture was instrumental in the creation of some form (or forms) of shared identity and, finally, a unified political entity.

This approach does not lead me to a belief in the homogeneity of Chinese culture, or that it was predesigned during the Neolithic period. On the contrary, in this book I demonstrate that regional and interregional variation was one of the prominent features of the Neolithic and Bronze periods, and that this variability was inherited by the more formally defined Chinese culture of the late preimperial and imperial eras. This implies that, while I do not attempt to predetermine what should and should not be included in the definition of Chinese culture, the primary focus of the book is a wide geographic area inside of which societies were in relatively close contact with one another during prehistoric periods. Other regions, beyond this

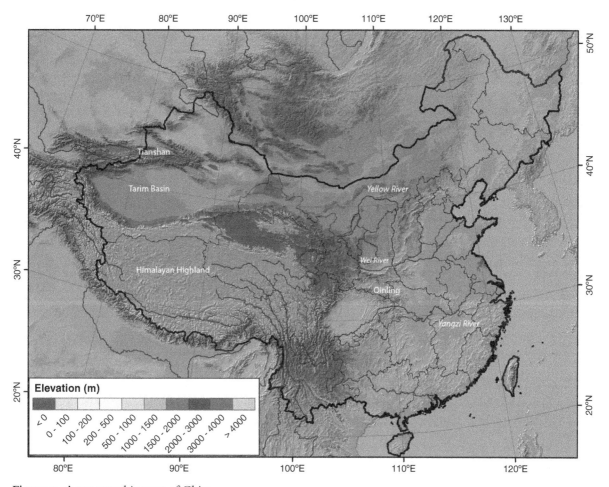

Figure 1. A topographic map of China.

core of interactions, are less frequently addressed, although their unique sociocultural trajectories, as well as contact between them and societies in the core area, are discussed.

THE TOPOGRAPHY OF CHINA

Based on the definition given earlier, the geographic focus of this book is determined neither by China's current or historical borders nor by traditional preconceptions, but rather by focusing on the areas in which Neolithic and Bronze Age societies coevolved. This area is centered in what is sometimes called "China proper," that is, the area around China's two largest river basins, the

Yellow River (黄河) and the Yangzi River (长江). But it also extends beyond their strict topographic limits, northward to the Liao River (辽河) basin, westward to the Wei River (渭河) basin and the Gansu corridor, and southward to the Nanling (南岭) mountain range (Figure 1). Regions beyond this core area are by no means culturally or ecologically unimportant to the content of this book. For example, we discuss contact with the more mobile populations of the steppe region to the northwest as well as with people living in the subtropical zone south of the Nanling range (a region known as Lingnan 岭南).

A broad overview of China's topography (Figure 1) reveals a meaningful pattern: The western parts are covered by mountains that decrease in height as we move eastward, while most of the wide valleys and plains are located in the east. Because the plains were more suitable for human habitation, especially once agriculture became the main economic base, the population has been unevenly distributed since antiquity, with the largest concentrations found in and around the wide valleys. By way of illustration, today some 90 percent of China's population is concentrated in those same valleys that constitute only one-third of the country's area (Figure 2). We can suppose that most of the human population in antiquity was also located in the east, while the mountainous western part of China was relatively sparsely populated. An exception is the Sichuan basin, located deep inland in western China. This region, highly suitable for agricultural production, was an ancient hot spot of population aggregation. Another exception is the Wei River basin, where population concentration also occurred early. This region remained an important cultural and political center during the entire period discussed in this book.

Another important general observation is that China proper is relatively isolated. It is surrounded by high mountains in the west, steppes and deserts in the north and northwest, an ocean in the east, and a tropical mountainous region to the south. It is commonly argued that these buffer zones that separated China from the centers of other great Old World civilizations are the reason Chinese civilization remained relatively isolated from external influences throughout its premodern history. While there might be a grain of truth to this argument, in the following chapters I demonstrate that even during early prehistoric periods long-range contact with societies in those so-called buffer areas and beyond played a meaningful role in the social, cultural, and technological changes undergone by societies in China proper.

The topography of China was shaped by the huge Himalayan massif to the west. The dramatic uplift of this area, which happened relatively recently in geological terms as a result of the tectonic collision of the Indian subcontinent with the Asian continent, is responsible for more than just the formation of the Himalayas (including the world's highest summits). The same process was also responsible for the formation of all the major mountain ranges in China, which run from west to east, perpendicular to the geological collision. These mountain ranges together with the rivers that run between them divide China into physiographic belts. Among these ranges, the Qinling (秦岭), which divides the Yangzi and Yellow River basins, is regarded as the boundary between north and south China. In the north, the Taihang (太行) and Yan (燕) mountains demarcate the plains of north China and separate them from the steppe and the forest zones to the north. In the south, the Nanling (南岭) range separates the Yangzi River basin from the subtropical regions to its south.

This topographic layout is an important factor influencing the nature of contacts between groups in different parts of China. Because in antiquity the long-range movement of people and the transportation of goods were facilitated by river navigation and land transport along modestly inclined river valleys, east-west movements were relatively convenient. North-south movements, in contrast, were constrained by the need to cross high mountains, wide rivers, and marshy areas. These conditions are thus highly pertinent to the theme of our book, since they shape interregional interactions. In the later periods, discussed in Chapters 10 and 11, constraints on large-scale north-south movements were one of the obstacles facing those who sought to unify China and, subsequently, those who wanted to stabilize unification once achieved. Under the Sui (隋, 581–618 CE) and Tang dynasties, this problem was partly resolved

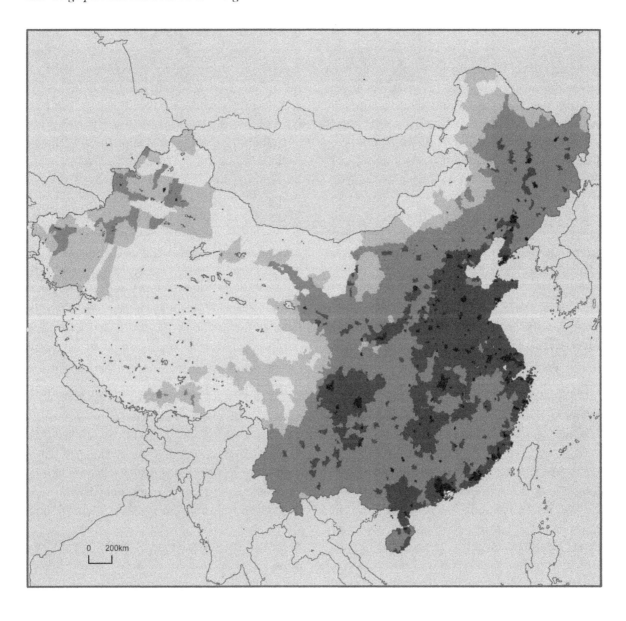

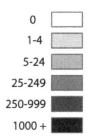

Figure 2. Distribution of human population in China at the beginning of the twenty-first century.

with the digging of the "Great Canal" that connected the Yangzi to the Yellow River basin and extended farther to the north, serving as the main transportation route for the imperial administration along which taxes, commodities, troops, and more were all moved.

The two main rivers of China, which from prehistory served not only as transportation routes but also as the focal areas of economic activity and population aggregation, acquired considerable symbolic status in Chinese culture. In classic texts the Yellow River is simply referred to as "The River," and its meandering curves were sometimes likened to the serpentine body of a dragon (an auspicious symbol in China). Prior to the twelfth century CE, most of the major capital cities were located along the Yellow River and its main tributary, the Wei River (渭河). For this reason, the Yellow River is often regarded as the "cradle of Chinese civilization" (a misleading term, as we shall see) and the political heart of ancient China.

The Yellow River is some 5,400 km long from its sources in the Himalayas to the Pacific Ocean in the east. Along this route, the river crosses the loess plateau, first flowing eastward and then changing course to move southward until it is joined by the Wei River and turns eastward again. During its progress through the loess plateau, the river's waters become saturated with loess (a fine grain soil), giving them their typical yellowish color and the name Yellow River. The river's soil concentration is the highest in the world, reaching up to 46 percent of its volume. Once the river enters the broad plains of east China and its currents slow down, some of this vast amount of soil is deposited. This constant supply of new soil contributes to the fertility of the plains, while at the same time it aggregates to block the river channel and cause occasional floods. The effects of these floods are usually only local – until the river meanders and finds a new route – but in some instances the scale of change is massive. Documented

historic instances of shifts in the Yellow River's route suggest that they sometimes caused huge devastation and numerous casualties. Past the plains, some of the soil carried by the Yellow River is deposited in the ocean, causing a gradual eastward shift of the coastline (Figure 3).

"Yangzi" is a Western version of the Chinese name, Changjiang (长江), or the "long river."[2] Some 6,300 km long, it is the longest river in Asia and the third longest in the world. Like the Yellow River, it flows from the Himalayas in the west to the Pacific Ocean in the east. However, it does not carry as much soil as the Yellow River and its channel is much deeper. As a result, the Yangzi has not been as prone to flooding and is much more suitable for navigation deep into the Chinese interior.

Other important rivers in the Chinese landscape include the Han River (漢江), which flows into the Yangzi from the north and whose valley serves as one of the natural routes between the Yellow and Yangzi River basins. The Wei River, mentioned previously, whose rich environment attracted populations from early times, and the Liao River, with its wide river valley and smaller tributaries, were also important focal points of human occupation northeast of the Yellow River basin. In south China, the Xi He (西河), whose lower part is known as the Pearl River (Zhujiang 珠江), was most important during China's modern history but has prehistoric significance as well.

THE CLIMATE OF CHINA

Climatic conditions in different parts of China are determined by three main factors: (1) latitude – the farther north a place is, the colder and dryer the climate tends to be; (2) distance from the ocean – the farther away a place is from the ocean, the dryer it is; and (3) altitude – the higher a place is, the colder its climate is. Given that China's west is higher than the east and is farther away from the

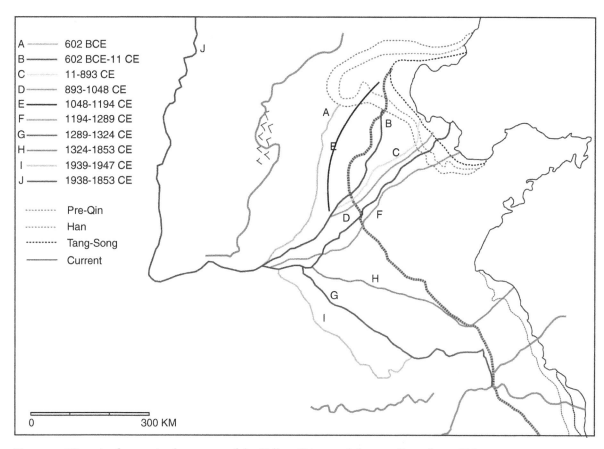

Figure 3. Historic changes in the course of the Yellow River and the coastline of east China.

ocean, a combination of these three factors results in climatic belts that run in more or less diagonal lines from northeast to southwest (Figures 4–6).

Precipitation in China is governed by the interactions of several major weather systems. In the winter, high pressure forming over north-central Asia pushes cold air southward along the eastern margin of the Tibetan Plateau and into north and central China, bringing with it cold and arid winds. In the summer, temperature differentials between the Indian and Pacific Oceans and the Asian land mass result in a flow of warm and moist air into the continent, where it interacts with the cooler air of the interior. The Indian monsoon brings heavy precipitation to southwest China and beyond, to the Himalayas and the

Tibetan/Qinghai Plateaus. The East Asian summer monsoon from the Pacific Ocean is the principal source of precipitation in south China and penetrates northward up to the Yellow River basin and beyond to the northeast (Figure 7). As a result of the Indian and East Asian monsoons, summer is the rainy season in China, with most precipitation falling between April and September.

To simplify the complex climatic mosaic of China, it is possible to divide the country into four climatic belts described in more detail later: (1) the northern forest, steppe, and desert zone; (2) the Yellow River basin; (3) the Yangzi River basin; and (4) the southern subtropical region.

The northern forest, steppe, and desert zone extends over the area from the northeastern

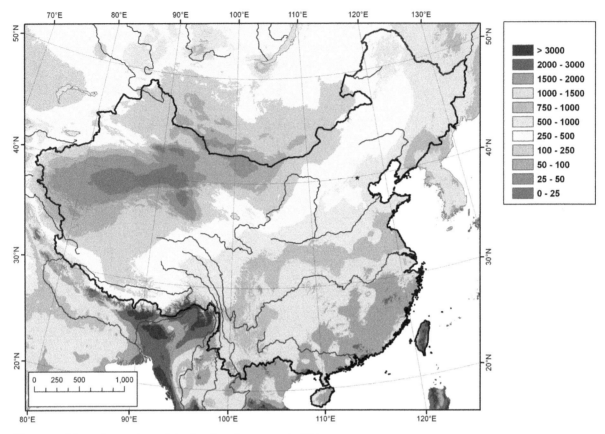

Figure 4. Map of annual precipitation (mm) averages in China.

provinces of Heilongjiang and Jilin (in the area formerly known as Manchuria), through Inner Mongolia, to Xinjiang in the west. This zone is located on the borders of China proper and has relatively harsh climatic conditions. Some of the world's driest deserts are located in this zone, and in most parts precipitation levels are below 200 mm a year. The area is also typified by extreme temperatures and wide differences not only between summer and winter temperatures, but also between day and night. In Heilongjiang, for example, there are areas where the average winter temperature is −32°C. In Xinjiang there are areas where average winter temperatures are below −10°C, while average summer temperatures are above 30°C.

The Yellow River basin is located at a relatively northern latitude − between 42 and 33 degrees

latitude north − and this clearly affects its climate. Winter temperatures are relatively low: along the Yellow River average winter temperatures are around freezing, and north of it they fall to −5°C. Average yearly precipitation varies between about 250 mm in the western parts to 750 mm in the eastern parts of this zone.

The Yangzi River basin covers an area between about 33 and 27 degrees latitude north. Its climate is much more moderate than the two more northern belts. Winter temperatures rarely fall below freezing, and the summers are not too hot. For example, in Zhejiang province, located in the eastern part of this zone, average temperatures are between 2 and 8°C in winter and between 27 and 30°C in summer. Average yearly precipitation in the Yangzi River zone is between 1,000 and 1,500 mm.

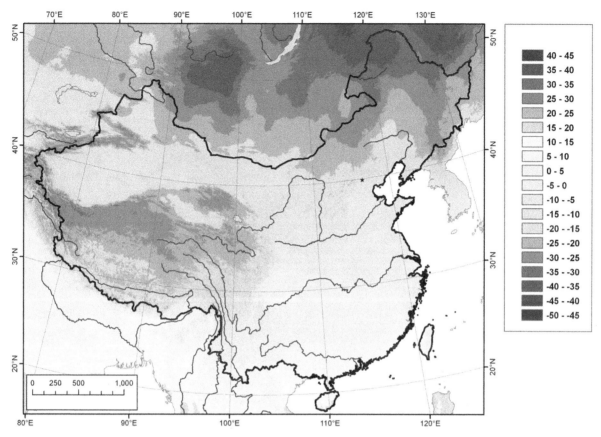

Figure 5. Map of minimum yearly temperatures (Celsius) in China.

The southern subtropical area lies to the south of the Nanling mountain range. It is a mountainous region dissected by many rivers and narrow valleys. Temperatures are quite stable, fairly consistently high during the winter and not particularly hot in the summer. In Guangdong, for example, the average temperatures are around 14°C in winter and around 29°C in summer. The summer monsoons carry large amounts of precipitation to the region. Most areas enjoy yearly precipitation levels greater than 1,600 mm.

VEGETATION AND ECONOMIC
POTENTIAL

Not just China's topographic and climatic conditions but also its natural vegetation is varied. From north to south it includes cold conifer forests, conifer and deciduous mixed forests, deciduous broad-leaved forests, mixed broad-leaved forests, evergreen broad-leaved forests, evergreen monsoon forests, and rain forests. Vast deserts and steppes dominate northwestern China, although conifer forests are also found in some of the high mountains there.

With the transition to agriculture, some of the natural vegetation was cleared to make way for agricultural fields, and the availability of arable land become an important factor in the development of human society. The availability of arable land and its fertility became increasingly crucial with the development of more complex forms of social organization and the concentration of large populations. Despite the enormity of China's

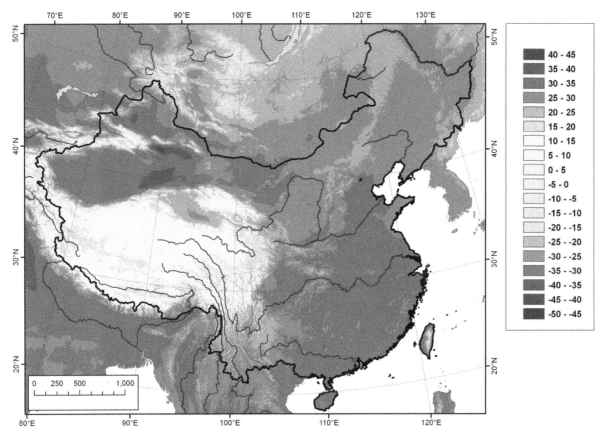

Figure 6. Map of maximum yearly temperatures (Celsius) in China.

territory, arable land resources are not that plentiful. Today, only 15 percent of the PRC's territory is suitable for agriculture (compared to 18 percent in the United States and 49 percent in India). In China proper the situation is somewhat better, but even in its most productive zones the percentage of arable land is relatively low compared to conditions in other major world civilizations.

Considerable disparities between the economic potential of China's different climatic belts existed in the past – and are still relevant today. The northern climatic belt is suitable for agriculture only in relatively few limited parts in the east and in oases that receive water from the melting snow of the Himalayan and Tianshan mountains in the west. In this zone, agriculture is limited not only by low levels of precipitation but also by the meager

accumulation of soil in many parts as well as by a very short growing season, which lasts only four months. During both prehistoric and historic times, the main economic activities here were hunting, mainly in the forests in the east, and the herding of animals (pastoralism) in the steppe and desert areas.

The Yellow River zone is much more suitable for agricultural production. The thick layers of loess soil that the river deposits are highly fertile and easy to cultivate. The moderate amount of rain and the relatively short growing season dictate the selection of plants that are drought resistant and mature quickly. The most important of these domesticates are millet and soy (see Chapters 3 and 4). The two plants, which complement each other well in dietary terms and contribute to the

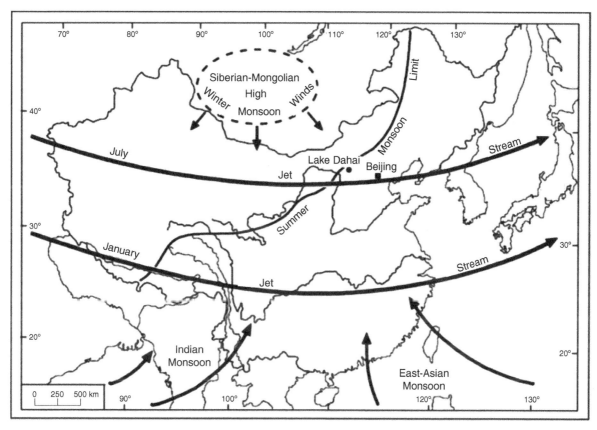

Figure 7. Meteorological factors affecting precipitation levels in China.

optimum exploitation of the fields, became the staple food of north China.

The conditions for agriculture in the Yangzi River zone are even more favorable than those in the Yellow River zone: although the soil that is brought down to the large valleys in the east is heavier than the loess soil, it is fertile and constantly renewed; rainfall is plentiful; and the growing season lasts nine months. Rice was first domesticated here and is the most important component of the agricultural system (Chapters 3 and 5). The cultivation of rice in paddy fields is particularly productive and, together with the farming of beans, vegetables, and fruits, yields a very agriculturally rich region.

Today the agricultural system of the southern subtropical zone is very similar to that of the Yangzi

River zone, specializing in the intensive cultivation of rice and other highly productive plants. However, agriculture started here relatively late, most probably as a result of input from the Yangzi River zone (Chapters 5 and 6). The region's mountainous terrain and narrow valleys, as well as the heavy rain and fast-growing natural vegetation, likely hindered the early development and rapid spread of agriculture.

ANCIENT CLIMATIC AND GEOGRAPHIC CHANGES AND THEIR EFFECTS

So far we have discussed China's current ecological conditions, but how similar are they to the conditions that prevailed during the periods addressed by this book? We know that climatic conditions have fluctuated quite dramatically over the past 20,000 years, and that these fluctuations might have affected the adaptation of human populations in China. The climatic sequence most relevant to the themes of this book began at the peak of the last Glacial Age, some 21,000 to 15,000 years ago. Temperatures at that time were six to nine degrees lower than they are today in north China and about four to five degrees lower in the Yangzi River basin. North China had at the time a cold steppe environment. Strong winter winds and weak summer monsoons caused the northern steppe conditions to extend south as far as the Yangzi River basin (Cohen 1998; Winkler and Wang 1993), creating an environment within the area of China proper that is considerably different from today's.

Around 13,000 years ago, the climate began improving. The Holocene, starting around 12,000 years ago, was typified by a relatively hot and humid climate with no extreme cold epochs comparable to those of the Glacial Age. However, even more modest fluctuations could have significantly impacted human adaptation. For example, sometime around 11,500 years ago, a period of dry and cold weather conditions, known as the "Younger Dryas" event, might have had such an effect, as could the warm and humid period known as the "Holocene (or Mid-Holocene) Climatic Optimum" that followed it (An et al. 2000; Zhou et al. 2001). Perhaps more than the long-term changes that affected the entire area covered by China proper, short-term yet intense fluctuations

on a regional scale may have had an even more drastic effect on local societies. One such event, discussed in Chapters 6 and 7, may have occurred during the late third millennium BCE and affected many societies in the eastern parts of central and north China.

In addition to climatic changes, the topography of China also underwent significant transformations. The rapid rise of the Himalayas affected ecologic conditions in many parts of China and impacted human adaptation during the Paleolithic period (Chapter 2). Sea levels, which were about 130 m lower than they are today at the peak of the last Glacial Age, rose with the increase in global temperatures and the melting of the polar ice sheets. This process resulted in a dramatic inland transgression of the coastline. More recent movements of the coastline include a slow regression resulting from the accumulation of deposits where the Yellow River enters the ocean, but also rapid inland transgressions followed by a regression during the late third and early second millennia BCE. Movements of the coastline could well have affected societies in the eastern part of China.

This brief discussion of geographic and climatic conditions (current and ancient) in different parts of China was presented not for its own sake but as a background to some of the main issues discussed throughout the rest of the book. In chapters where issues that are directly associated with ecological conditions are discussed, a more focused discussion is provided.

CHAPTER 2

BEFORE CULTIVATION: HUMAN ORIGINS AND THE INCIPIENT DEVELOPMENT OF HUMAN CULTURE IN CHINA

This chapter reviews the archaeology of the long period extending from the earliest presence of hominins in China almost two million years ago to the initiation of the socioeconomic processes that occurred during the last phase of the Glacial Age, some twenty-five thousand years ago, and that eventually culminated in the emergence of food production during the following period.[1] This long and crucial period in the history of humankind deserves treatment in an entire book, and indeed recent monographs on the subject have been published in China and elsewhere.[2] The focus of this book is the development of complex societies and the evolution of Chinese culture (or cultures), so we cannot delve into a more detailed discussion of the period. In the context of this book, a chapter on the Paleolithic period provides the background for the issues brought up in subsequent chapters. I do not, therefore, provide detailed documentation and analysis, but rather present an overview of important discoveries and a discussion of some of the more fundamental issues, such as the origins of humans in China and their economic adaptation. In keeping with the overall theme of this book, issues emphasized in the chapter include the regional variability of human society and evidence for intersocietal contact, even at such an early stage.

The first part of this chapter reviews some of the period's most important archaeological sites, including sites in northern China (Zhoukoudian, Nihewan, Lantian, and Dingcun), northeastern China (Jinniushan), southwestern China (Yuanmou, Longgupo), and southeastern China (Liujiang, Maba). This initial overview focuses on descriptions of artifacts (mainly stone tools) and the technologies used to produce them. The second section discusses the skeleton remains of the humans who presumably made these tools. These two sections provide the basic data for the subsequent discussion of the origins and evolution of humans in China and the development of their culture and technology.

ARCHAEOLOGICAL EVIDENCE FOR EARLY HUMAN OCCUPATION IN CHINA

Archaeological research into the earliest human inhabitants of China started relatively early: the French missionary, Emile Licent, had already identified prehistoric sites and stone tools by the 1910s. For many, however, the discovery of the Zhoukoudian (周口店) site by J. G. Andersson represents the turning point in Chinese Paleolithic archaeology. The large-scale excavations at this site, which started in 1921, are still regarded as one of the most important archaeological projects in China, and the human fossils, stone tools, and other evidence recovered at Zhoukoudian are still seen as the benchmark against which many of the more recent discoveries are evaluated. The excavations at Zhoukoudian and the analysis of the artifacts and human and animal bones found there attracted a large number of internationally acclaimed scholars, including the Austrian paleontologist Otto A. Zdansky, the Canadian paleontologist Davidson Black, and the French paleontologist and geologist Pierre Teilhard de Chardin. The Zhoukoudian excavation, and the Cenozoic Research Laboratory, which was set up to analyze the human fossils discoveries, were a hotbed for the first generation of Chinese paleontologists and Paleolithic archaeologists such as Li Jie, Pei Wenzhong, and Jia Lanpo.

Despite the early interest and the extensive and world-renowned discoveries made at the Zhoukoudian site, Paleolithic archaeology in China did not advance as fast or as far as other branches in the field. This relative neglect can be partly attributed to the fact that, historically, most research was carried out under the auspices of the Institute of Vertebrate Paleontology and Paleoanthropology (IVPP), which in effect inherited the position of the Cenozoic Research Laboratory. IVPP scholars were most interested in finding and analyzing human and animal bones, and paid little attention to archaeological sites and human-made artifacts.

Between the 1950s and the 1980s, knowledge of Paleolithic sites from different parts of China gradually accumulated, and in recent years Paleolithic archaeology has become one of Chinese archaeology's most rapidly developing subfields. Its prestige has been enhanced by advances in dating methods as well as discoveries of human fossils and human-made artifacts that have been successfully dated to the very early stages of world human history. These discoveries have also rekindled discussions about the "Chineseness" of early humans and their genetic and cultural links to the historic populations of China.

The Chronological Setting

Important sites discovered since the 1950s, such as Dingcun (丁村) in Shanxi province, the Nihewan basin (泥河湾) in Hebei, Lantian (蓝田) in Shaanxi, and Yuanmou (元谋) in Yunnan, have all highlighted the regional and chronological variation of sites and artifacts in China. However, despite these and more recent discoveries in Paleolithic archaeology, our knowledge of this long period remains rudimentary at best. In contrast to research in other parts of the world, most notably Europe, where Paleolithic stone tools are classified into temporal and regional traditions (or cultures) based on their style and manufacturing technology, in China it is still almost impossible to date artifacts and sites based on such parameters.

As a result, the overall perception of the Paleolithic in China is that of a very long and stable period with few technological or social changes. This perception might be the result of our partial knowledge and poor dating. In many sites, even the better known and more extensively excavated ones, the chronology is not well established, and it is therefore difficult to reconstruct the process of change. Many believe that the findings in China truly reflect a particularly stable stone tool technology, where the basic features of core-and-flake industries in the north and cobble-tool industries in the south endured throughout the Paleolithic period with little noticeable change. Clear "cultural markers" that elsewhere in the Old World are synonymous with specific periods, such as the hand axes (or bifaces) of the Acheulian culture (Lower Paleolithic) or the Levallois technique of the Mousterian culture (Middle Paleolithic), are much rarer and less regularly identified in China (Bar-Yosef and Wang 2012).

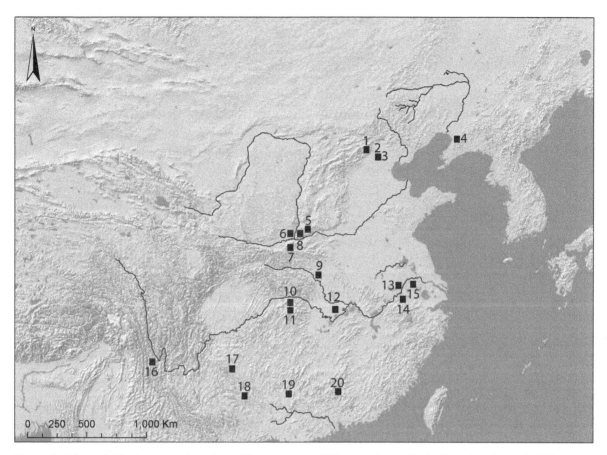

Figure 8. Map of all sites mentioned in Chapter 2: 1. Nihewan basin (including the sites of Majuangou, Xiaochangliang, Donggutuo, Cenjiawan, Maliang, Xujiayao, and Zhiyu); 2. Zhoukoudian; 3. Tianyuandong; 4. Jinniushan; 5. Dingcun; 6. Dali; 7. Lantian; 8. Xihoudu; 9. Bailongdong; 10. Longgupo; 11. Longgudong; 12. Jigongshan; 13. Longtandong; 14. Renzidong; 15. Tangshan Huludong; 16. Yuanmou; 17. Panxian Dadong; 18. Baise; 19. Liujiang; 20. Maba.

Currently, the earliest definitively dated sites in China are placed at around 1.7 or 1.6 million years ago (henceforth, MA), but, as discussed later, there are some as yet unconfirmed claims of sites predating 2 MA. To be on the safe side, we shall date the Paleolithic periods as following: the Lower Paleolithic is dated from ca. 1.7 to 0.78 MA for; the Middle Paleolithic is conventionally dated as ca. 0.78 to 0.13 MA (contemporaneous with the Middle Pleistocene); and the Upper Paleolithic is dated from ca. 0.13 to ca. 0.025 MA (or 25,000 before the present day – hereafter, BP). Sites dated from 25,000 BP to the end of the Glacial Age, around 10,000 BP, are discussed in Chapter 3, which deals with the transition from hunter-gatherer to sedentary agricultural societies.

The Earliest Sites

Recurrent arguments for very early dates of Paleolithic sites in China appear periodically in the archaeological literature. These claims are not unrelated to the more general debate about the origins of human populations in China (see "The Study of Hominin Remains and the Origins of Human Populations in China"). However, serious archaeological attention should also be paid to the individual sites, the evaluation of the artifacts found in them, and the methods used to date them.

One site that has recently attracted much attention as a candidate for the earliest evidence of human activity in China is Longgupo (龙骨坡), a large karstic cave located in Wushan county, Chongqing. The site was excavated in the late 1990s, and again more recently by a joint Sino-French team. The stone artifacts found there resemble the so-called core-and-flake industries known from other parts of China. Of the six hundred or more artifacts collected during the first phase of excavations, most tools are relatively small in size and classified as scrapers. Many artifacts have retained part of the cortex of the core from which they were produced (Figure 9) (Hou and Zhao 2010).

According to some estimates, the earlier strata at the site should be dated ca. 2.6 to 2.3 MA. The dates in these estimates are mainly based on paleomagnetic methods. A more recent study, using the electron spin resonance method, suggests a much later age of between 1.7 and 1.3 MA (Bar-Yosef and Wang 2012).

Another candidate for early hominin occupation in China is the Renzidong (人字洞) cave site located in Fanchang county, Anhui province. The site was discovered in 1998, and two seasons of excavations recovered stone artifacts and a large number of animal bones. Many of the animal skeletons found at this site are complete, suggesting that they were not killed or utilized by humans but rather entered the stratigraphy of the site during depositional episodes that are unrelated to human activity. Based on geological stratigraphy and the analysis of the Renzidong fauna, a date of ca. 2.4 MA has been suggested for the site. This early date, however, has yet to be corroborated by radiometric methods (Hou and Zhao 2010).

In north China, similarly early dates have been suggested for the Majuangou (马圈沟) site in the Nihewan basin, Hebei province. However, these dates are based primarily on similarities between the stone tools found at Majuangou and those from Longgupo. Recent research at the Nihewan basin suggests the much more conservative dates of ca. 1.7 to 1.6 MA for the earliest sites in the area.

Early Paleolithic Sites

The accumulated study of a relatively large number of sites dated to 1 MA or earlier is one of the foremost achievements of Chinese archaeology in the past thirty years. Even in the late 1980s, such early dates for the human occupation of China remained uncertain (Chang 1986), but today there is clear evidence from different parts of China, and the number of Early Paleolithic sites found continues to increase. The largest concentration and the best studied sites are currently those of the Nihewan basin. Nihewan is an elongated basin located in northwest Hebei and northern Shanxi. The basin is today centered on the Sanguan River (Figure 10), but during the Pleistocene the area included a lake (now extinct) and its tributaries. Strong erosion that cut the sediments by some 100 m has exposed the Pleistocene layers, thus making Nihewan one of the richest areas in China in terms of the ancient animal bones and stone artifacts found.

Although paleontological research at the Nihewan basin began in the 1920s, its first Paleolithic stone tools were identified only during the 1970s. In contrast to most of the well-known sites in central and southern China, which are mostly located in caves, sites from the Nihewan basin tend to be open-air occupations. Therefore, in many of these sites, the period of occupation was shorter and the artifacts less concentrated and fewer in number.

The oldest dated sites are found at the eastern side of the Nihewan basin. Important early sites in this cluster include Majuangou III, Xiaochangliang (小长梁), Donggutuo (东谷坨), and Banshan (半山) (Figure 10). Based on the average rate of sediment accumulation, the date of Majuangou III is estimated at ca. 1.66 MA., while

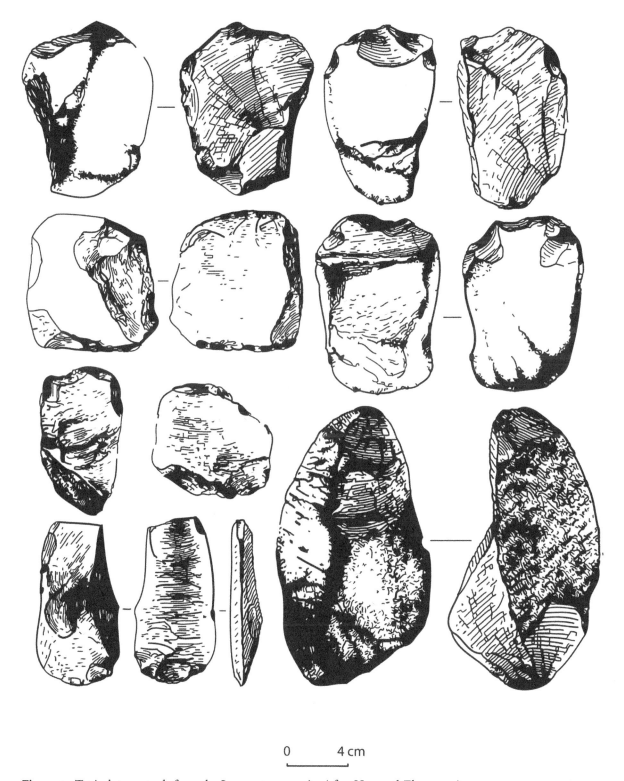

Figure 9. Typical stone tools from the Longgupo cave site (after Hou and Zhao 2010).

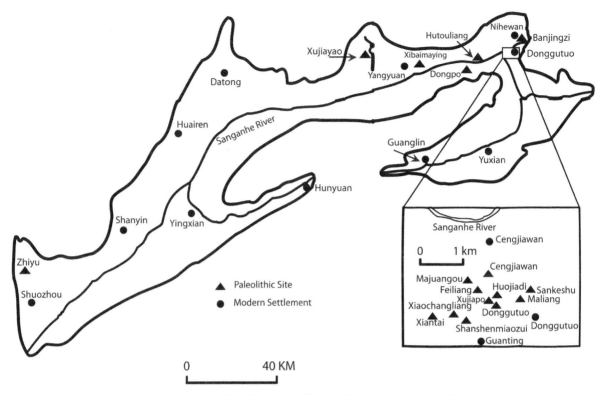

Figure 10. Map of the Nihewan basin and the location of Paleolithic sites in it (after Liu et al. 2012).

other sites in the cluster are dated to ca. 1.36 MA (Bar-Yosef and Wang 2012; Liu et al. 2012).

Majuangou III covers an area of some 85 m², and its occupation layer is only about 50 cm thick. According to the paleoenvironmental reconstruction, the site was located near the ancient lakeshore, in a marshy environment. Excavations carried out between 2000 and 2003 uncovered more than four thousand stone artifacts, including cores and flakes, but only a small number of tools, mostly scrapers. Most artifacts were made from quartzite, and the flakes were produced by direct hard hammering (Figure 11) (Dennell 2009; Keates 2010).

Donggutuo is another well-documented early site in the same vicinity. The richest site discovered in the Nihewan basin so far, it was also located close to the shore of the extinct lake. In seven excavation seasons during the 1980s and 1990s, more than 10,000 stone artifacts were found, along

with about 1,500 animal bones, inside deposit layers about 5 m thick. Most of these artifacts are classified as debitage, attesting perhaps to the poor quality of the raw materials. The artifacts classified as tools are relatively few (Keates 2010).

In sum, the stone artifacts in these two sites and in other nearby Early Paleolithic sites are quite similar. They are mostly small artifacts classified as belonging to the core-and-flake industry and made from the low-quality raw materials available locally, including flint, volcanic rock, chert, limestone, and quartz. The major method for flake knapping was direct hammer percussion, while the bipolar method used rarely. The tools are generally small, mainly scrapers, and simply retouched. Choppers or chopping tools were not recovered in these sites (Liu et al. 2012; Bar-Yosef and Wang 2012). According to one assessment of the industry, "the irregular shape of most cores and flakes implies that lithic technology was highly

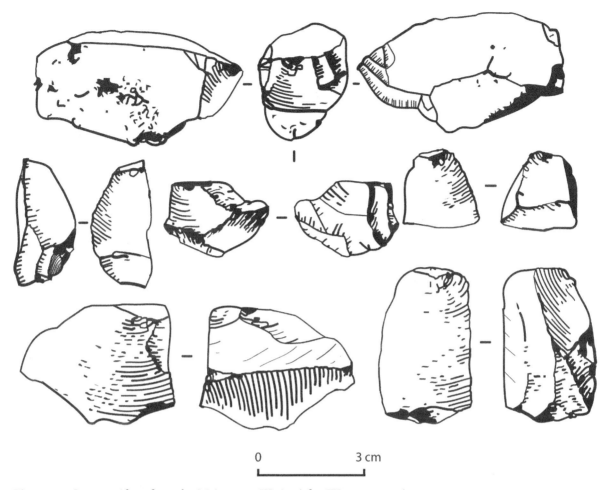

Figure 11. Stone artifacts from the Majuangou III site (after Wang 2005: 25).

expedient, with little foresight beyond the production of the next flake" (Dennell 2009: 182).

While no hominin remains have been found at any of the sites in the Nihewan basin, they have been found in other Early Paleolithic sites in north China such as Lantian. Lantian has been dated to ca. 1.15 MA, and another site, also in Shaanxi province, Xihoudu (西侯度), has been dated to ca. 1.27 MA. Both dates are tentative, and the tool assemblages collected at each of the sites are rather small. However, they furnish further evidence of human activity in this area during the Early Paleolithic period (Bar-Yosef and Wang 2012). These two sites are sometimes said to

represent the beginning of a "large-tool tradition" in north China (Figure 12), which is different from the "small-tool tradition" of the Nihewan basin. However, in reality, during this period, as well as in the Middle Paleolithic period, there is a great deal of overlap between the two supposedly distinct traditions. This distinction is further discussed at the end of this chapter.

South of the Qinling Mountains, Early Paleolithic sites are known at cave sites in central and eastern China, as well as at open-air sites in the southwest. We have already discussed the evidence from the two main cave sites: Longgupo and Renzidong. An important location farther to the

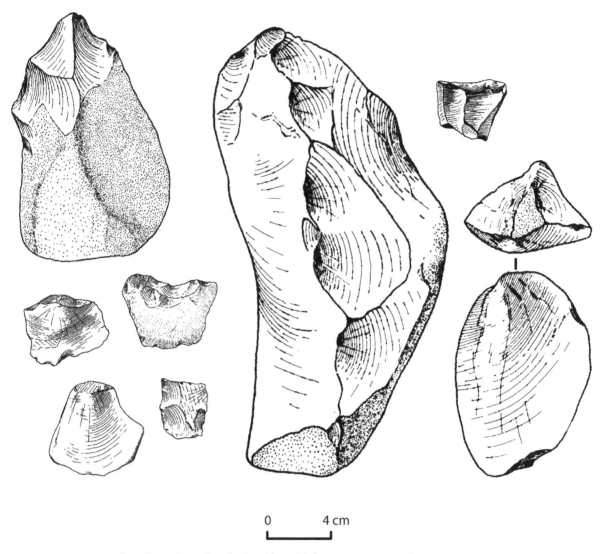

0   4 cm

Figure 12. Stone artifacts from the Xihoudu site, Shanxi (after Jia 1985: 137–9).

southwest is the Yuanmou basin (元谋), in Yunnan province. Like the Nihewan basin, the thick layers of Pliocene-Pleistocene deposits exposed here are rich in animal fossils and a few associated human-made artifacts. Archaeological and paleoanthropological attention was drawn to this area in 1965, when two incisors attributed to *Homo erectus* were found. Excavations at the same locality during the years following the initial discovery found twenty-two stone artifacts said to have come from the same geological layer. The artifacts are made from quartz

and quartzite, are relatively small in size, and have been classified as core, flake, scrapers, and choppers (Figure 13) (Hou and Zhao 2010).

The dating of the hominin fossils and stone artifacts found at Yuanmou is fiercely debated, as is the association between them. The age of the deposit from which they come has been variously dated to between 1.8 and 0.6 MA, based on the analysis of faunal remains and geologic stratigraphy (Wang 2005). Despite this uncertainty, many archaeologists nonetheless ascribe Yuanmou to the

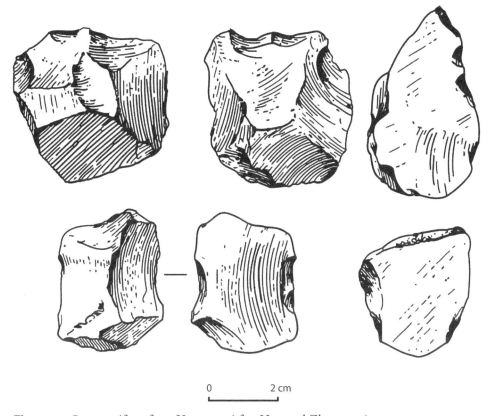

0   2 cm

Figure 13. Stone artifacts from Yuanmou (after Hou and Zhao 2010).

beginning of the Early Paleolithic period and correlate it with the Oldowan stone tool industry from Africa (Hou and Zhao 2010).

So far, no evidence of any modification of the environment to create a "camp" has been identified in any of the sites from the Early Paleolithic period in China. This accords with what we know about human behavior during this period from other parts of Asia: although similar locations may have been used repeatedly, each episode was short and did not leave behind any permanent marks aside from the stone artifacts and bones.

Middle and Late Paleolithic Sites

In comparison to the relatively small number of Early Paleolithic sites in China and the scant information on human society and adaptation that they have provided, there are many more known sites and much richer information for the Middle and Late Paleolithic periods. Although many new sites have been discovered in recent years, the scholarship for this period is still dominated by data from and analysis of one site: Zhoukoudian. As discussed in Chapter 1 and earlier in this chapter, Zhoukoudian was the site of one of the first large-scale, international, and multidisciplinary projects carried out in China. These excavations have been carried out at a scale much grander than at any other Paleolithic site in China, partly because the methods used during the 1920s and 1930s were cruder, but also because work at Zhoukoudian has been ongoing for some ninety years, right up to the present. The excavations at Zhoukoudian have exposed a long sequence of occupation, yielding about hundred thousand stone artifacts and an even

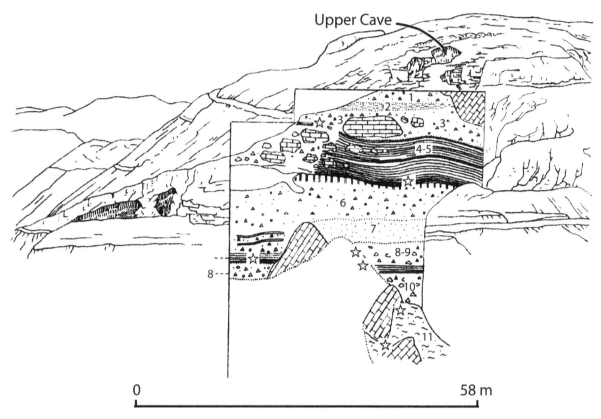

Figure 14. Drawing of the stratigraphic section of locality I at Zhoukoudian (after Zhang Senshui 1985: 156).

greater numbers of animal bones. The highlight of the early excavations was the discovery of human bones and skulls belonging to forty individuals, one of the largest samples of *Homo erectus* remains anywhere in the world. Zhoukoudian is thus considered one of the most important Middle Paleolithic sites in the world and figures prominently in any discussion of hominine evolution and the adaptation of early human groups.

Zhoukoudian is located in the Beijing area, some 20 km west of the city proper. It comprises several localities (or sites), the most important of which is locality I, where most of the hominin skeletons and other artifacts were found. The 45-m-deep stratigraphy of locality I is divided into seventeen layers from top to bottom, with the first evidence for human activity appearing in layer 13 (Figure 14). The hominin presence at locality I,

from layer 13 to layer 3, is dated from ca. 0.78 to 0.4 MA. During the first part of this sequence it was a cave site, but erosion and loss of stability caused the cave walls and ceiling to collapse, and in layer 5 it became an open-air site (Dennell 2009; Goldberg et al. 2001).

Of course, the occupation of Zhoukoudian by hominins was not continuous, and the site represents instead many unrelated episodes of human presence. However, the density of artifacts signifies the intensive repeated use of the locality over a very long period. The stone tool industry here was based on locally available materials, mostly quartz, but other types of stones as well. Recent studies have shown that relatively rare stones, such as rock crystal, were brought to the site from a distance of 2 km or more. It appears that the ability to select the most suitable materials for tool

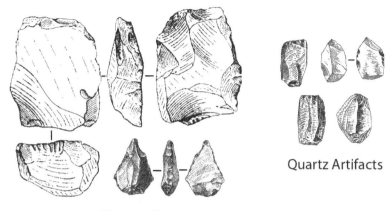

Quartz Artifacts

Flint Artifacts

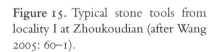

Figure 15. Typical stone tools from locality I at Zhoukoudian (after Wang 2005: 60–1).

Sandstone Artifacts

0   3 cm

production improved over the course of the Zhoukoudian occupation (Dennell 2009: 408–10).

Stone flakes made using the bipolar technique, and sometimes retouched, are the most common artifacts found at locality I. These flakes are relatively small in size (most are less than 5 cm long), hence the common classification of Zhoukoudian industry as one that produced small tools. Their shapes vary considerably, so much so that excavators have found it difficult to classify them into typological categories. Core choppers and tools made on cobbles are much less common (Figure 15). Aside from minor changes, it seems that throughout the long period of occupation the stone tool industry of Zhoukoudian remained relatively stable.

Some researchers have argued that animal bones found at locality I were modified by humans to serve as tools, but the evidence for this argument is scarce and inconclusive. Another contentious question is the intentional use of fire by the inhabitants of Zhoukoudian. Excavators of the site have cited burned bones, layers of ash, and even "hearths" as evidence in support of the hypothesis that they did indeed use fire (Zhang Senshui 1985: 156–7). Recent chemical and micromorphological analysis, however, has shown that much of what was originally identified as ashes is actually natural deposits (Weiner et al. 1998). Nonetheless, some of the animal bones examined by Weiner et al. and others were shown to have been burned, and given the more recent discovery of evidence for the use of fire at sites older than 0.5 MA in various parts of Eurasia, it remains plausible that the Zhoukoudian inhabitants did utilize fire.

Another debated issue is the source of the animal (and human) bones deposited at Zhoukoudian, and the position of hominins in the food chain that led to this accumulation. The idea that these bones represent, at least partly, hunting activities by the hominin population was challenged by Binford and Stone (1986). Their study of a small-scale sample of animal bones showed that a much larger percentage of the bones had marks of carnivores gnawing them than those with cuts made by stone tools. In a few cases, the stone tool marks were superimposed over the carnivore gnaw marks. They concluded that most of the bones found at Zhoukoudian were the remains of carnivorous activity, and that humans were primarily scavenging on those remains. Binford and Stone's conclusions are supported by a recent study of hominin remains from Zhoukoudian, which suggests that hominins were also hunted and brought to the site by carnivores (Boaz et al. 2004).

Sites dated to the same time period as Zhoukoudian's locality I were also identified at the Nihewan basin. Of these sites, Cenjiawan (岑家湾 ca. 0.900–0.970 MA) and Maliang (马梁, ca. 0.730 MA) are the best documented (Keates 2010). In comparison to earlier sites in this basin, at these sites the ability of humans to select good-quality raw materials for tool production seems to have improved. However, all in all, as was the case in Zhoukoudian, technological stability seems to be the salient feature of the local trajectory.

To the south of the Qinling Mountains, the most noteworthy sites of the era include Jigongshan (鸡公山) in the Yangzi River valley and localities in the Baise (百色) area in Guangxi province. Jigongshan is one of the only sites in China from this period where clear "living floors" have been excavated. Excavators at the site have identified two areas where stone tool production took place, and five circles of stones, each 1.5 to 2.5 m wide (Figure 16), have been identified as the remains of habitations (Wang 2005: 183–5).

At the Baise basin, more than ten localities where stone tools have been found are associated with tektites dated to ca. 0.8 MA.[3] Around a thousand stone artifacts found at these localities have been defined as part of a core-and-flake industry producing large tools (many longer than 10 cm). Some of these tools are extremely large; the largest is 38 cm long and weighs 7.5 kg (Wang 2005: 117–23). Many of the tools are bifaces shaped from large cobbles with rounded tips (Figure 17). Whether these can be defined as Acheulian hand axes is a matter of debate, but they clearly represent a different technocultural tradition from that of Nihewan and Zhoukoudian .

Sites belonging to the late Middle Pleistocene (~0.35–0.13 MA) continue the stone tool tradition of the earlier periods. The assemblages contain mainly core artifacts such as choppers and flakes. Examples of sites from this period include locality IV (also known as the New Cave) and locality XV at Zhoukoudian, Jinniushan (金牛山) Cave in Liaoning province, and Panxian Dadong (盘县大洞) Cave in Guizhou province (south

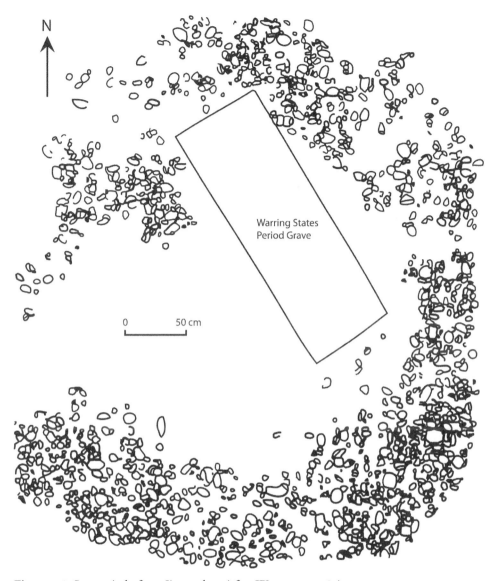

Figure 16. Stone circle from Jigongshan (after Wang 2005: 184).

China). Jinniushan Cave, dated to ca. 0.31–0.24 MA, is famous for a well-preserved skeleton of an archaic *Homo sapiens*. Although the collection of stone artifacts from this cave is rather small – comprising no more than two hundred flakes and some cores – analysis suggests that the stone tool industry at this site was very similar to that of locality I of Zhoukoudian. Clear evidence for the use of fire in controlled places ("hearths") has also been reported (Wang 2005: 62–9).

More than twenty thousand stone artifacts and thousands of animal bones have been found at the Xujiayao (许家窑) site in the Nihewan basin, also well known for remains of archaic *Homo sapiens* fossils. The lithic assemblage is still dominated by flakes made from locally available vein quartz and other raw materials. Direct percussion is still the dominant manufacturing technique, and most of the flakes are irregular in shape. Over 50 percent of the stone tools exhibit secondary retouch. The

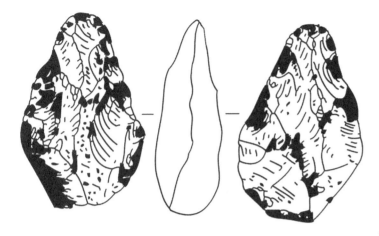

Figure 17. Bifacial stone tools from the Baise basin (after Wang 2005: 118).

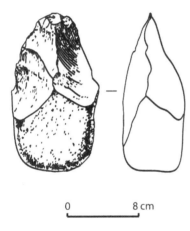

0   8 cm

relatively large number of spheroids is regarded as one of the unique features of this site (Liu et al. 2012), perhaps associated with hunting.

One of the most famous sites from the Middle Pleistocene is Dingcun (丁村), located in Shanxi province and dated to ca. 0.21–0.16 MA. Dingcun, in fact, comprises more than ten different localities spread along some 15 km of the Fen River's east bank. Large numbers of stone artifacts and faunal remains and three human teeth were collected from the surface of these localities, as well as some systematic excavations (Qiu 1985). The stone tool industry of Dingcun is considered by many to represent a continuation of the "large tool tradition," which is traced back to such sites as Xihoudu and Lantian. The production techniques

are mainly direct percussion. Flakes are the most common artifact, but core tools, including bifaces, are not uncommon. The most common tool types are choppers, heavy and light points, and scrapers. Many of the tools are highly regular, suggesting advancement in craftsmanship and cultural norms (Figure 18).

In south China, Panxian Dadong Cave in Guizhou province is dated to ca. 0.262 to 0.137 MA. The cave is about 250 m long and covers an area of about 10,000 m². It is particularly famous for the large faunal assemblage uncovered there. The stone artifacts found in the cave are made of local limestone, chert, and basalt. Greater numbers of retouched flakes are associated with the upper levels of this cave, suggesting an evolution

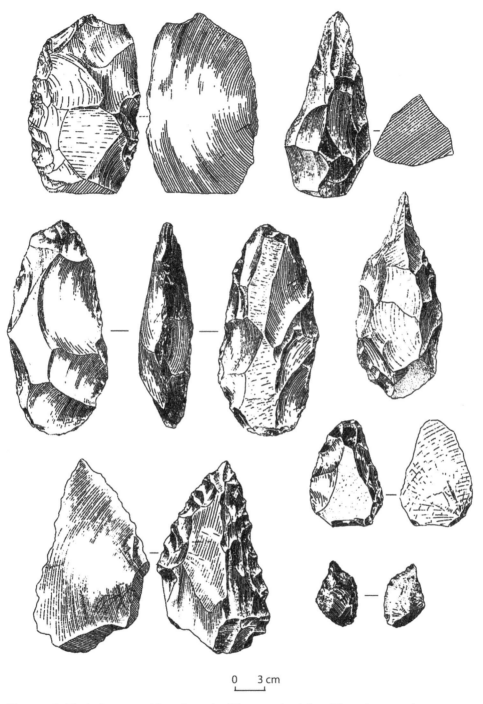

0   3 cm

Figure 18. Typical stone artifacts from the Dingcun site (after Qiu 1985: 191–5).

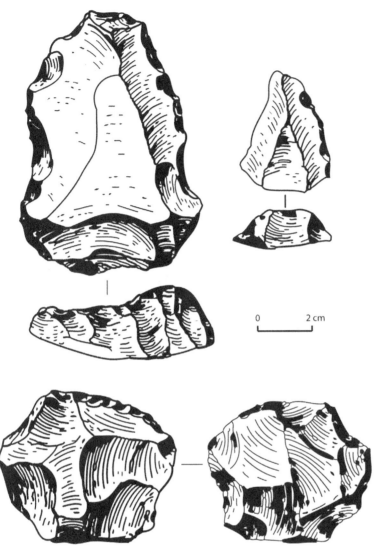

Figure 19. Stone tools from Panxian Dadong Cave in Guizhou province (after Wang 2005: 101).

0   2 cm

of stone tool technologies (Figure 19) (Wang 2005: 96–101).

It has been commonly suggested that the Levallois technique, one of the most characteristic features of the Middle Pleistocene ("Mousterian") industries in Europe and Western Asia, is absent from sites in China. In recent years, however, artifacts clearly produced by similar procedures have been identified at sites in north China, as well as at the Panxian Dadong Cave (Figure 19). The presence of artifacts made using the Levallois technique, while it was probably not a common

tool-producing technique in China, raises questions about long-range interactions and the transfer of technologies.

More rapid processes of technological (and perhaps social) change are apparent at sites from the Upper Paleolithic period. Methods for the more controlled production of flakes, and especially the more systematic production of blades, are typical to northern China. We know that a larger variety of materials, including bone, was used to produce artifacts, as well as ornaments. These changes, however, do not appear at sites in central and

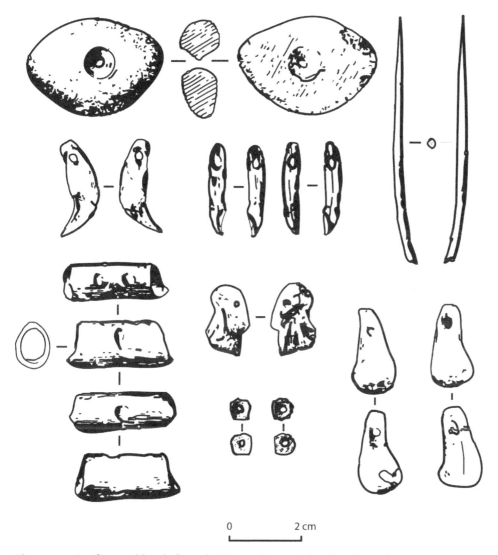

Figure 20. Artifacts and beads from the Upper Cave at Zhoukoudian (after Wang 2005: 219).

south China, where the core-and-flake industries continued.

The most famous and extensively excavated site of this period in China is the Upper Cave (Shanding Dong 山顶洞) at Zhoukoudian. The cave was discovered in 1930 and excavated in 1933 and 1934. It is best known for its human fossils. Deposits were divided into five layers, with the majority of the artifacts and human bones found in layer 4, which is variously dated to between ca. 34,000 and 27,000 BP (Norton and Gao 2008; Wang 2005).

Only a few flint and quartz tools were found at the site, but it contained other non-stone artifacts, such as polished antlers and bone tools. Among the most famed artifacts recovered are perforated animal teeth, shells, and calcareous stones, which were probably used as beads. Some of these beads were colored with red hematite (Figure 20).

Similar types of ornaments were recently dated to the same period at sites in Liaoning province. These findings reflect new types of cultural and social behaviors not seen in earlier sites. It has been

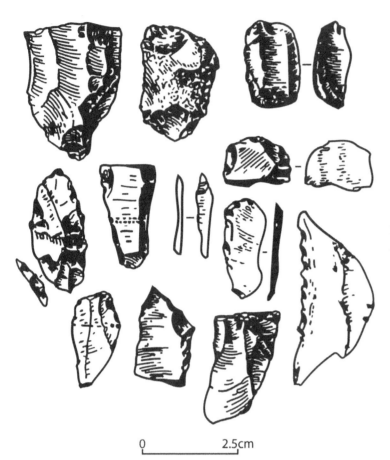

0   2.5cm

Figure 21. Stone artifacts from the Zhiyu site (after Wang 2005: 231).

argued that the humans found at the Upper Cave were intentionally buried, and that the beads were part of either their outfits or burial goods (Wang 2005: 205). If confirmed by additional systematic excavations, this reconstruction would represent evidence of another novel type of social norms and communal activity.

Some twenty Upper Paleolithic sites have been found in the Nihewan basin. One of the best known is the Zhiyu (峙峪) site, dated to ca. 29,000 BP. Roughly fifteen thousand stone artifacts and thirty-nine bone tools were recovered from an area of about 1,000 m² at the site. The artifacts are mostly small – less than 3 cm long. Analysis of the artifacts has revealed an evolved stone tool industry that utilized a variety of production techniques, including hard and soft hammer percussion, the bipolar technique, and indirect percussion

(Figure 21). Among the most renowned findings at the site are primitive types of microliths and evidence for the development of the microlith core shape, which remained typical for north China throughout subsequent periods (Liu et al. 2012). The technological and social developments revealed through findings at sites such as the Zhoukoudian Upper Cave and Zhiyu accelerated after around 20,000 BP and are discussed in further detail in Chapter 3.

THE STUDY OF HOMININ REMAINS AND THE ORIGINS OF HUMAN POPULATIONS IN CHINA

The study of hominin skeletal remains is a crucial part of our understanding of human evolution and the development of human culture and society in

TABLE 1. *Location, date, and skeletal features of some major discoveries of hominins in China*

Site	Skeleton parts	Attributed hominin type	Estimated date (in MA)
Longgupo, Chongqing	Mandible fragment, teeth	*Homo habilis* *Homo erectus* Ape (*Lufengpithecus*)	1.9
Yuanmou, Yunnan	Two incisors	*Homo erectus*	1.8–0.6
Lantian, Shaanxi	Calotte (skull part)	*Homo erectus*	1.15
Longgudong (龙骨洞), Hubei	Four teeth	*Homo erectus*	1.0
Bailongdong (白龙洞), Hubei	Eight teeth	*Homo erectus*	1.0
Zhoukoudian (locality I), Beijing	Skulls and bones attributed to 40 individuals	*Homo erectus*	0.78–0.4
Tangshan Huludong (汤山葫芦洞), Jiangsu	Two skull fragments and a tooth	*Homo erectus*	0.31
Longtandong (龙潭洞), Anhui	Skullcap, mandible, 11 teeth	*Homo erectus*	0.3–0.2
Jinniushan, Jilin	Well-preserved skeleton	Archaic *Homo sapiens*	0.31–0.24
Xujiayao, Hebei	Skull fragments and teeth	Archaic *Homo sapiens*	0.125–0.1
Dali (大荔), Shaanxi	Skull (well preserved)	Archaic *Homo sapiens*	0.2
Panxian Dadong, Guizhou	Five teeth	Archaic *Homo sapiens*	0.262–0.137
Maba (马坝), Guangdong	Skullcap	Archaic *Homo sapiens*	0.135–0.129
Dingcun, Shanxi	Three teeth	Archaic *Homo sapiens*	0.21–0.16
Liujiang (柳江), Guangxi	Cranial and postcranial remains	Modern *Homo sapiens*	0.05–0.04
Zhoukoudian (Upper Cave), Beijing	Three skulls, bones	Modern *Homo sapiens*	0.034–0.027
Tianyuandong (田园洞), Beijing	Mandible with six teeth, and some 30 bones	Modern *Homo sapiens*	0.042–0.039

The dates in this table are the best currently available estimates, but many of them are still disputed.

China. Central issues such as the effect of biological change (the evolution of modern humans) on hominin culture and technological skills can be studied only through the integration of paleoanthropological and archaeological research. The argument is the same for understanding the origin of humans and the spread of hominins to different parts of the world.

Identifying the hominin skeletal remains that correspond to the initial human habitation of China poses some problems. Currently the two main candidates for the earliest hominin fossils come from the southern part of China: Longgupo in the Chongqing region, and Yuanmou in

Yunnan (Table 1). A mandible fragment and several teeth found at Longgupo have been variously attributed to *Homo erectus* (*Wushanensis*), to *Homo habilis*, and even to ape, and are of unclear date (Dennell 2009: 180; Hou and Zhao 2010). The same problems also apply to findings at Yuanmou: it is unclear whether the two incisors found here belong to *Homo erectus*, their dating ranges considerably, and, moreover, the association between these teeth and the few stone tools found at the site is unclear (Hou and Zhao 2010).

More plentiful paleoanthropological data are available for the Lower and Middle Paleolithic periods, although the record is still fragmented and in some cases poorly dated. The presence of *Homo erectus* populations, as documented in Table 1, is clearly attested to in all parts of China. However, it is still unclear whether this occupation was continuous or intermittent. In north China in particular, where the climate tends to be cold and dry, hominin occupation may have been confined to the warmer interglacial periods, with the populations retreating southward during the cold and dry glacial periods (Dennell 2009: 183). A contrasting hypothesis argues that the onset of colder and drier conditions, which resulted in the reduction of tree coverage and the spread of an open savanna-like environment, actually facilitated the spread of populations out of Africa and into Asia's northern latitudes. According to this model, during interglacial periods, the thick forests and fauna of south China would have formed a barrier preventing the penetration of the savanna-adapted early humans southward (Ao et al. 2010: 477).

Research on the paleoclimate and paleoecology is essential for our understanding of the Paleolithic period. An example of such research is a recent study conducted at the Nihewan basin, which revealed a long-term trend toward colder and dryer conditions (Ao et al. 2010). The integration of data on overall trends and the more specific events of the glacial and interglacial periods, as well as their effects on the local environments in different parts of China, will shed brighter light on the processes of human colonization and adaptation. Another important component that should be integrated into such studies is the effect of geological processes and, especially, the uplift of the Tibetan Plateau by some 3 km (Dennell 2009: 204–17). This process had an enormous effect on the climate, wind regime, and geomorphologic environment of many parts of China. One of its most important effects was to lift the Qinling Mountains. As discussed in Chapter 1, the formation of the Qinling Mountains – stretching from west to east – created an ecological barrier between the regions to its north (especially the Yellow River basin) and to its south (especially the Yangzi River basin), thereby polarizing the climatic and ecological differences between north and south China.

The "Out of Africa" Model

Research into the early hominins of China should be positioned within the broader context of the origins and spread of our early ancestors. The most commonly held view supports the "Out of Africa" migration of *Homo erectus*, who went on to colonize most of the Eurasian continent. According to this model, tool-producing hominins originated in East Africa around 2.6 MA. *Homo erectus* appeared in the same region around 1.9 MA and, shortly thereafter, spread to Asia and Europe. Currently, the earliest dated *Homo erectus* fossils found outside of Africa are from Dmanisi in Georgia and are dated to ca. 1.75 MA (Dennell 2009: 84–98). The current dating of the earliest Paleolithic sites (but not hominin fossils) in China to ca. 1.7–1.6 MA is in line with the Dmanisi date and might support claims for the relatively rapid diffusion of hominins throughout the Eurasian continent. However, if we accept the arguments for much earlier dates for some of the sites in China – such as pre-2 MA for Longgupo and Majuangou – this would pose a serious challenge to the scenario and perhaps even to the entire Out of Africa model. While few scholars would explicitly suggest that *Homo erectus* evolved independently in China, the possibility is hinted at by statements such as "the evidence requires researchers to keep open minds in thinking of wider possibilities regarding early human evolution" and even "the 'Out of Africa' scenario may turn out to be just wishful thinking" (Hou and Zhao 2010: 17).

The simple, one-wave Out of Africa migration of *Homo erectus* has, in fact, been challenged from other directions as well. It has been suggested, for example, that the first wave of migration, typified by the Dmanisi population, whose stone tool technology is that of the core-and-flake industry, was followed by several later migrations of *Homo erectus* whose typical tools were the Acheulian bifaces (hand axes). According to this model, some of these populations may have even moved back to Africa. This modified version of the Out of Africa model would imply more complex networks of interactions, some spread throughout the African-Eurasian continent, and others more limited in scope (Bar-Yosef and Belfer-Cohen 2013; Dennell 2009: 186–202). Thus, even if it does not seem plausible to discard the Out of Africa model in favor of an Out of Asia one, a more multidirectional approach to the spread of hominin culture and genes is possible.

The Origins of Homo Sapiens *and Modern Human Population in China*

Homo sapiens remains have been recovered in China only since the 1950s, and although there are a fair number of sites where such remains have been found (see a partial list in Table 1), nothing that even closely resembles the richness of *Homo erectus* specimens found at locality I at Zhoukoudian is known. Not only is the number of individuals from each site very small, but the skeletons themselves, especially those of the earlier so-called archaic *Homo sapiens*, are highly fragmented. In fact, in most sites, only a few hominin teeth were found. So far, the best preserved fossils are the skeleton from Jinniushan and the skull from Dali.

Nonetheless, despite the fragmentary nature of the fossil record (or perhaps because of it), the origins of *Homo sapiens* and the development of modern human populations in China are another hotly debated question. According to the commonly held "Out of Africa 2" model, *Homo sapiens*, like *Homo erectus*, first evolved in Africa, whence a second wave of migration spread out to the rest of the world, replacing the existing populations of *Homo erectus*. This model is based on analyses of genetic variation (DNA studies) among current populations in different parts of the world.

Specifically, it puts forward the idea that present-day patterns of human genetic diversity were produced quite recently (in evolutionary terms), and that they reflect the history of the founding population: the longer a population evolves in relative isolation, the more diverse it becomes because of natural mutations. Thus, the African population is the most diverse, because it has evolved for the longest time, while populations outside of Africa, which were founded by a subset of the African population, have had less time to develop diversity (Figure 22a).[4]

Accommodating the hominin fossil records with the Out of Africa 2 model remains problematic. Although recent discoveries of hominin fossils in east Africa have pushed back the origins of *Homo sapiens* there to ca. 0.16 MA, it is still unclear if those are the earliest examples or whether fossils found in Southwest Asia are in fact earlier (Dennell 2009: 468–9). Like the current interpretation of the Out of Africa 1 model, it is now suggested that Out of Africa 2 was not a one-time event but, rather, a long-term process. An early group of a perhaps more archaic type of modern human may have emerged from Africa at about 0.22 MA, but the more widespread migration that carried with it the Upper Paleolithic tool kit from Africa occurred around 0.055 MA or thereafter (Bar-Yosef and Belfer-Cohen 2013).

A competing, multiregional hypothesis suggests that *Homo sapiens* evolved independently out of *Homo erectus* populations in different parts of the African-Eurasian continent. This model, also called the "candelabra model," argues that "the patterns of genetic diversity within and among human populations today were produced by a long history of predominantly short-range migrations, with infrequent longer ones, rather than a recent range expansion out of Africa" (Weaver and Roseman 2008: 69) (Figure 22b).

Many prominent Chinese archaeologists support this multiregional hypothesis, arguing that modern human populations in China evolved locally out of Middle Paleolithic populations of *Homo erectus* such as those known from Zhoukoudian. A series of so-called archaic *Homo sapiens* fossils are said to represent the local transition between *Homo erectus* and *Homo sapiens*. This model is supported by evidence of morphological traits that are shared by *Homo erectus* and *Homo sapiens* fossils from China, but not with populations elsewhere. For example, Wu Xinzhi and Wu Maolin (1985) identified the "shovel-shape" of the hominin incisor found at Dingcun and Xujiayao as a trait shared with both the *Homo erectus* fossils from Zhoukoudian and modern Mongoloid populations. Thus, these archaic *Homo sapiens* populations are seen as bridging the Middle Paleolithic and modern populations of China. Wu and Wu (1985: 105) identified other such traits, which they see as evidence for phylogenetic continuity in China, and which distinguish its *Homo sapiens* population from that of West Asia and Europe.

The continuation model presented by Wu and Wu is regarded by many Western scholars as reflecting a nationalist bias among Chinese archaeologists and paleoanthropologists (Sautman 2001). However, recent advancement in DNA analysis, and especially the ability to extract and reconstruct ancient DNA sequences, could offer a third model. This "admixture hypothesis" maintains the importance of African origins in the development of modern humans, but also allows for a certain genetic contribution from non-African populations (Weaver and Roseman 2008) (Figure 22c). For example, a comparative study of the recently completed draft sequence of the Neanderthal genome suggests that modern populations in Europe and Asia share between 1 and 4 percent of their nuclear DNA with Neanderthals. Modern African populations, however, do not share this Neanderthal genetic contribution (Green et al. 2010). This suggests that the specific genetic mixture occurred after *Homo sapiens* had migrated from Africa, as a consequence of interbreeding with the Neanderthal populations they encountered in Europe and Asia. Other related research found that, in addition to the Neanderthal genes that are shared by all Eurasian populations, Melanesians share genes with a ca. fifty-thousand-year-old skeleton from Denisova Cave from the Altai Mountains in southern Siberia (Reich et al. 2010).

A recent study of the DNA sequence from one skeleton of an archaic *Homo sapiens* from Tianyuandong suggests strong genetic connections to modern populations in China (Fu et al. 2013). In a global perspective, this individual, who dates to ca. 40,000 BP, postdated not only the divergence between African and Eurasian populations, but also the divergence between European and Asian populations. The scientists working on this skeleton concluded, however, that the "Tianyuan individual is most similar to the latter populations in carrying a genomic component related to the Neanderthal genome, but no Denisovan component is discernable with these analyses" (Fu et al. 2013: 2225). We do not have scientific proof for gene transfers from early hominins to modern populations in China, because comparable reconstructions of ancient DNA sequences of earlier hominin populations from China have not yet been conducted. Nonetheless, the discoveries of the Neanderthals' genetic contribution as well as the previously mentioned morphological similarities between *Homo erectus* and *Homo sapiens* skeletons in China suggest similar or perhaps even larger rates of genetic admixture (Shang et al. 2007).

STONE TOOLS AND THE SPREAD OF HUMAN CULTURE

The origins and spread of humans are, broadly speaking, related to one of the main themes of this book: the study of local variation and cross-regional interactions. Analysis of Paleolithic stone tool industries from various parts of China and their comparison with stone tool technologies from elsewhere in the African-Eurasian continent is even more closely related to this theme.

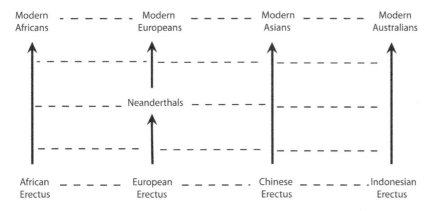

A. Multiregional

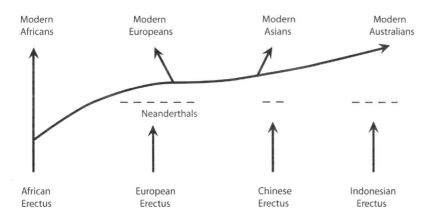

B. Out of Africa

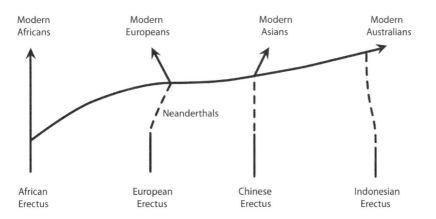

C. Out of Africa with Admixture

Figure 22. Three models of the evolution of modern humans: A. Multiregional; B. Out of Africa; C. Out of Africa with admixture (after Renfrew and Bahn 1996: 439).

In contrast to the analysis of human remains, the available data for the analysis of stone tools industries from different parts of China are much more plentiful and well documented. However, in this case, we lack the scientific tools, such as DNA analysis, that are available for the study of human skeletons.

One of the central questions in the study of stone artifacts (tools as well as tool manufacturing debris) is the existence of "traditions," or cultural attributes, and the spatial and temporal patterns of those attributes. As discussed earlier, the classification of stone artifacts into temporal and regional stone tool styles and manufacturing technologies is not well developed in China, nor is their dating. This is possibly due to the long-term continuity and slower rate of change in China as compared to other parts of the Eurasian continent. One exception is the common classification of Paleolithic assemblages from north China into two broadly defined traditions: one typified by relatively small artifacts, mainly irregular retouched flakes, the other by larger chopper-chopping artifacts and heavy triangular points. According to this model, the two traditions coexisted and coevolved in north China over a long period. The small artifacts tradition is associated with early sites such as Donggutuo (Early Pleistocene), Zhoukoudian locality I, and Xujiayao, and is ultimately also associated with the rise of the microlithic tradition during the Late Paleolithic and Early Neolithic. The large artifacts tradition evolved from early sites such as Xihoudu and Lantian (Early Paleolithic) and Dingcun, and culminated with the polished stone tools of the Neolithic period (Jia and Huang 1985).

While this broadly defined distinction between traditions is still used today (e.g., Liu et al. 2012), the significance of this dichotomy is unclear. Does it represent different types of economic adaptation or of stylistic norms? Were there two coexisting societies in north China and, if so, could they have maintained separate identities while living in the same region for such a long time? Even some of the original proponents of this distinction agree that it is simplistic and unrealistic to envision two unrelated lines of development in north China (Jia and Huang 1985: 224). More research into the classification of stone tools, as well as their manufacturing techniques and the functions they were used for, will probably dissolve this dichotomy.

Another well-established dichotomy is that of the core-and-flake industries of north China versus the cobble-tool industries of south China (Wang 2005). These two broadly defined traditions are assumed to have existed throughout the Paleolithic period, even persisting into the Neolithic. In this case, the different environmental conditions and availability of raw materials may have been contributing factors, but much more focused research on issues such as the selection of raw materials and the function of stone tools is needed to confirm this hypothesis.

On a much greater scale, the diffusion of typical Paleolithic traditions from Africa and Western Eurasia into China might reflect early instances of the spread of cultural norms and technologies. The best known debate focuses on the spread of hand axes (bifaces) to East Asia. In a seminal paper published in 1948, H. Movius argued that the Acheulian complex, typified by biface tools and well known from Africa and Western Eurasia, was not present in East Asia. This gave rise to the famous "Movius line," east of which bifaces were supposedly not found (Figure 23).

As discussed earlier, this theory was refuted by the discovery of bifaces at Baise and other locations north of it. However, it is also true that bifaces are quite rare in China and that most Middle Paleolithic sites in China have not yielded any. One explanation for this phenomenon is that the *Homo erectus* population that arrived in China belonged to an early wave of migration, represented also in Dmanisi (Georgia), while the somewhat later migrations that spread out of Africa and carried with them the Acheulian complex did not reach

Figure 23. Map of the Eurasian continent with the "Movius line" and location of sites east of it where hand axes are found.

China. If this explanation is accepted, then the hand axes found in China would have to be the result of an independent development in India, China, and East Asia, unrelated to the spread of populations from the west (Boëda and Hou 2004).

Another explanation for the scarcity of bifaces in China argues that although the technology was available to the Chinese population – whether through cultural contacts or local invention – it was not widely accepted because the natural conditions were not conducive. One sub-branch of this hypothesis, also used to explain the rarity of the Levallois technique in China, posits that the appropriate stone resources were unavailable. According to this hypothesis, the absence of good flaking material in China prevented the development of more advanced stone tool technologies (Gao and Norton 2002). However, this theory is sometimes challenged on the grounds that it is unclear whether good raw materials were indeed unavailable and, moreover, that in other parts of the world poor quality materials were used to produce bifaces and Levallois artifacts (Bar-Yosef et al. 2012; Bar-Yosef and Wang 2012).

It has also been hypothesized that in China, tools made of bamboo were used for many of the functions that elsewhere were performed with stone tools. Therefore, the argument goes, there was no need to invest as much energy in the production of sophisticated stone tools. This theory is especially relevant for our understanding of the underdeveloped and stable nature of stone tool technology in south China, where, even during later periods when microliths and other advanced tool-making techniques had appeared in the north, simple cobble-tool industries endured. South China is also the natural environment of bamboo, where it was readily available for the hominin population. A recent experimental archaeological study conducted in Hunan province demonstrated that replicated East Asian stone tools were quite effective in the production of various types of bamboo implements, and that these implements were suitable for a variety of tasks, including cutting meat and hide (Bar-Yosef et al. 2012). However, as the authors point out, while the study suggests that the "bamboo hypothesis" is possible, more direct evidence that Paleolithic stone tools from south China were extensively used to cut and shape bamboo would be needed to prove it. Microwear and edge damage research in Paleolithic stone tools from China may in the future provide this evidence.

In conclusion, it would seem that the debates about the presence or absence of well-known cultural markers in China, such as hand axes or the Levallois technique, have run their course and are no longer productive. In the future, we can expect to see more research attention paid not only to the classification of Paleolithic artifacts but also, and more important, to what such artifacts and the sites in which they are found can tell us about Paleolithic society in China and its economic and environmental adaptation. Even for this early stage in the development of human society, advanced analysis of artifact styles could lead to novel insights into matters of group identity and intergroup interactions.

The rapidly growing body of data on the layout of Paleolithic sites, the spatial distribution of artifacts and debris in them, the recovery of faunal and floral remains, and paleoclimatic signals will cer-

tainly enhance our ability to address more meaningful questions about the development of human society and culture in different parts of China. Our view of these processes is currently limited, but despite the overall stability of the stone tools industries in different parts of China, the development over time of more refined methods, the selection of more suitable stones for the production of tools, and the production of more standardized artifacts all attest to the evolution of stone tool technology and the incipient emergence of artifact styles. These changes are probably related to the improvement of economic adaptation. The use of fire – which may have started at such sites as Zhoukoudian locality I – became more commonplace in later sites, and at the Upper Cave of Zhoukoudian we may even be seeing the beginning of novel social phenomena such as the use of ornaments (perhaps to project identity) and the treatment of the dead (possibly burials). The rate of socioeconomic change and the development of these incipient traits accelerated during the next few thousand years, as we will see in Chapters 3 to 5.

CHAPTER 3

THE TRANSITION TO FOOD PRODUCTION: VARIABILITY AND PROCESSES

The transition to agriculture is one of the most significant events in the history of humankind, if not *the* most meaningful. It not only transformed the relationship between humans and their natural environment, but also profoundly and fundamentally altered human social relations and culture. Its significance lies not only in the fact that today – and for the past several thousands of years – the food we eat comes almost exclusively from a small number of domesticated plants and animals, but that human society as we know it could not exist without this reliance on agriculture. While a foraging economy is not without its advantages, it cannot support all of the attributes of the complex human societies that have evolved in different parts of the world. Dense populations and large sedentary settlements, food surpluses that support nonproductive activities and occupations, a stable social hierarchy, and craft specialization are some of the basic features that could develop only within the context of an intensive agriculture economy.

Small wonder, then, considering its monumental impact on humankind's history, that the transition to agriculture has been studied thoroughly. However, despite almost one hundred years of scientific research, many fundamental issues are still hotly debated: Was the development long and gradual, or was there a relatively rapid "revolution"? Is the transition to agriculture a single global process, or rather the result of many independent local developments? Were people pushed to "invent" agriculture because their living conditions were deteriorating, or were they motivated by the new opportunities it offered? What were the effects of climatic and ecological changes? Many of these questions refer to the interactions between humans and their natural environment: for example, the way that environmental conditions and climatic changes affected human adaptation, but also the way that humans' actions, such as plant and animal domestication and landscape modification, affected their natural environment. Equally important, though less often addressed directly, are the social preconditions that might have initiated the transition to agriculture or shaped its development. For example, it has been suggested that human experimentation with cultivation and domestication was catalyzed by social competition and the incipient development of social stratification rather than by economic needs.

China is recognized as one of the world's primary centers of independent agricultural development alongside Southwest Asia, Mesoamerica, and the Andes. Research here is therefore crucial not only for a better understanding of Chinese civilization, but also for understanding the broader history of humankind. In this chapter, we ask why, following an extended period during which hunter-gatherers successfully inhabited and exploited the rich and varied environment of China, some of these groups made the transition to agriculture, a change that did not always improve their quality of life or increase their life expectancy. As an introduction to a theme that is sustained throughout this book, this chapter also considers the nature and impact of interactions between different regions of China at this early time. We present a number of models, which alternately describe the development of agriculture and agricultural communities as a countrywide phenomenon; as a bipolar process with two centers, one in the north of China and one in the south; or as a process of interactions within a multicentered social landscape.

As with many archaeological issues, accurate dating is a crucial precondition for addressing questions about the development of agriculture in China. Without it we are unable to reconstruct the sequence of events and discuss causal relations among different variables. Without accurate dating, for example, we would be unable to determine if the decision by some societies to start living in permanent year-round sedentary villages was preceded by the transition to agriculture and was a result of it, or whether it preceded the transition to agriculture and was one of its prime movers. Likewise, we could not discuss causal relations between climatic changes and the development of agriculture without an accurate dating of both natural and the socioeconomic changes. In the following sections, we chart the chronology of the sites currently associated with the early phases of the transition to agriculture, describe the major discoveries made in those sites, and discuss the implications of these discoveries for our understanding of the transition to an agricultural and sedentary lifeway in China. Before we delve into the archaeological data, however, a clear definition of agriculture is in order.

WHAT IS AGRICULTURE?

For most of us agriculture is obvious but invisible. It is obvious because virtually all our food derives from agriculture and many other products we consume – from wool and cotton clothes to biofuel made from corn – are also agricultural products. Yet, it is invisible because most people living in developed countries encounter agriculture only in the form of finished products on supermarket shelves. We rarely get to see agriculture in action. Moreover, we seldom realize how profoundly our society depends on agriculture, not only for food, but for a great deal else as well: indeed, contemporary human culture as we know it – from technology, through political institutions, to art – cannot exist without agriculture. Because agriculture permeates every aspect of our society so deeply, we hardly ever stop to consider what it is exactly. We can all use the term, but ask someone on the street to define "agriculture" (I have tried this with my students many times) and you will not get a clear answer.

Webster's dictionary defines agriculture as "the science, art, or practice of cultivating the soil, producing crops, and raising livestock and in varying degrees the preparation and marketing of the resulting products." This definition contains two important elements: (1) agriculture has to do with *cultivation* and tending to plants and animals; and (2) agriculture is a *system of knowledge* ("science and art" in the Webster's definition) developed by people and transmitted among them. A crucial third element, however, is missing from this definition: *domestication*. The plants and animals that are part of the agricultural system have all been genetically modified and are now significantly different from their wild progenitors. Of course, cultivation, domestication, and the system of knowledge are not discrete or separate components of agriculture, but rather are interconnected.

Cultivation: Broadly defined, this term refers to all the ways in which humans intervene with nature in order to secure better harvests. In the cultivation of plants, this might include plowing, planting, weeding, fertilizing, and others. In the raising of animals, it includes building corrals and animal sheds, feeding the animals, helping

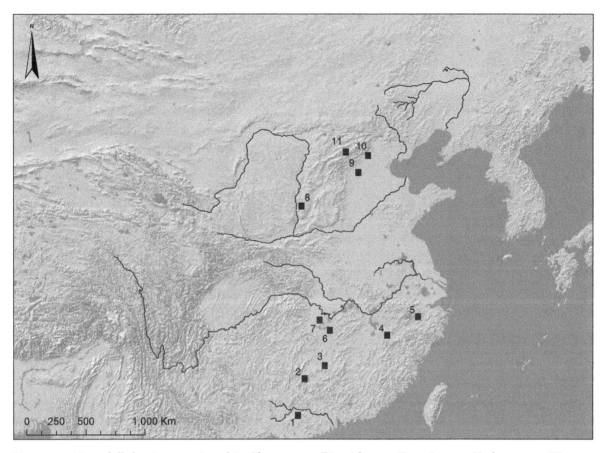

Figure 24. Map of all the sites mentioned in Chapter 3: 1. Dingsishan; 2. Zengpiyan; 3. Yuchanyan; 4. Xianrendong and Diaotonghuan; 5. Shangshan; 6. Bashidang; 7. Pengtoushan; 8. Longwangchan; 9. Nanzhuangtou; 10. Donghulin; 11. Hutouliang.

them breed, and so on. Most of these activities are archaeologically visible. For example, modifications to the landscape enable us to identify the location of agricultural fields, and architectonic remains have been identified with installations for raising animals. The chemical analysis of soil taken from ancient agricultural fields and corrals can identify the unique signature of such activities. Finally, the shape of stone tools, as well as microscopic analysis of their wear patterns, can confirm that they were used for agricultural activities such as plowing or digging.

Domestication: Domestication is commonly defined as a process "whereby humans modify, either intentionally or unintentionally, the genetic makeup of a population of plants or animals to the extent that individuals within that population lose their ability to survive and produce offspring in the wild" (Blumler and Byrne 1991: 24). Plants, for example, will often lose their effective seed dispersal mechanism and become dependent on humans for their reproduction. Domestic animals can also become dependent on humans for their reproduction and for defense against predators. Symbiotic relations are thus formed between domesticated plants or animals and humans. Domestication was probably not the outcome of an intended plan on the part of humans, but the selective forces behind such genetic changes came into play only with relatively intensive human intervention. For example, harvesting cereals with sickles selects for plants in which the ripe seeds do not disintegrate off the plant (nonshattering). It is pos-sible to identify domesticated plants and animals in archaeo-botanic and archaeo-zoological remains. In cereals such as rice, for example, the two com-mon traits associated with domestication are free-threshing and nonshattering. In the wild, free-threshing indicates that the seed is protected by a thick glume, while in domesticated plants this glume is more easily separated from the seed, and nonshattering means that when the seed is ripe the base of the spikelet that connects it to the ear or the stalk becomes fragile and the seeds are easily dis-persed. In domesticated plants on the other hand, the spikelet base remains solid even after the seed has ripened; this prevents the seeds from detach-ing from the stalk during harvesting. These traits, and especially the nonshattering spikelet base, can be detected through the microscopic analysis of the ancient plant remains found in excavations. Increased grain size and a change in the shape of the grain are additional traits associated with domestication, but because there is so much vari-ation among wild and early domesticated plants, this is not considered a reliable indicator (Fuller et al. 2007: 318). Similar changes are also found in domesticated animals, but because the selec-tive pressure in animals was directed at behavioral attributes – such as reduced aggression – morpho-logical changes are less clearly manifested during early phases of domestication (Zeder et al. 2006: 2–4). In both plants and animals, direct genetic evidence for domestication can be found by com-paring the DNA of domesticated species to that of their wild progenitors (Zeder et al. 2006: 5–7).

System of knowledge: Although discussions about agriculture tend to focus on the main staple foods of each region (for example, rice in central and south China and millet in north China) and on a select few domesticated animals (in China mainly pigs and water buffalo), agriculture is, in fact, a complex system encompassing numerous plants, animals, and techniques and where spatial and temporal coordination are crucial. For example,

while legumes are less important than cereals in terms of caloric input, they provide other nutri-tional values that are essential to the human diet. Moreover, soils that are depleted by many seasons of growing cereals can be revitalized by growing legumes, which have the capacity to restore nitro-gen from the atmosphere into the soil. Rotating different crops also helps avoid the build-up of pathogens and pests, so mixed cropping and crop rotation are essential for a functional agricultural system. Accumulated knowledge on scheduling and coordinating the different components of the agricultural system has to be transmitted from gen-eration to generation and from place to place. This is equally true for knowledge about the optimal environment for growing different types of plants, veterinarian expertise, techniques for the produc-tion of agricultural tools and storage facilities, and methods for preserving different foods and pro-cessing secondary products, such as wool, hide, and fibers, to give just a few examples. Some of the previously outlined activities, such as storage, leave behind traceable remains that we can identify in the archaeological record. Others, such as the scheduling of agricultural activities, are expressed thorough religious beliefs and rituals associated with the seasons and may be discerned from the analysis of art remains, religious artifacts, remains of religious structures, and graves.

HUNTER-GATHERERS VS. AGRICULTURALISTS: HOW DIFFERENT ARE THEY?

An assumption inherent in the previous discussion of the definition of agriculture is that these com-ponents identify agricultural communities because they are absent from societies prior to the transition to agriculture. However, archaeological research on preagricultural societies as well as ethno-graphic studies of current hunter-gatherers chal-lenge the accuracy of such a clear-cut dichotomy. For instance, it has long been known, but only emphasized more strongly in recent studies, that hunter-gatherers also engage in the modification of their environment so as to improve their yields. Sometimes termed "resource management" (Bellwood 2005: 12), such activities include the intentional burning of natural vegetation to stimulate the growth of desired weeds as well as other ways of reducing competition from nondesired species, such as weeding and landscape modification, selectively intervening in the populations of plants and animals (herd management), and others (Smith 2001). Such activities, it should be noted, are very similar to those of incipient agriculturalists. In addition, it has been shown that some social traits usually associated with agricultural societies, such as large group size, mechanisms for food storage and exchange, and even incipient social hierarchies, are also found among certain hunter-gatherer groups. The other side of the same coin is that some societies that are familiar with agriculture and consume domesticated food are, in fact, more dependent on wild food resources (Smith 2001). Thus, we should view the shift to agriculture *not as an event but as a process*, looking for the different phases, the decisions made, and the thresholds passed in the transition from hunter-gatherers to agriculturalists.

As noted earlier, the genetic and morphologic changes that we identify as correlates to the domestication of plants and animals evolved as a response to the selective pressure created by cultivation. Scholars disagree as to the rate at which such changes developed, with some arguing that it was a relatively rapid process, while others suggest a gap of a thousand or more years between the beginning of cultivation and the appearance of fully domesticated species (Fuller et al. 2007). This is an important issue, which we address later, but in principle, even if we envision a relatively fast process, clear morphological evidence for domestication would indicate that the process of transition to agriculture was well under way. In order to address the origins of agriculture and identify its causal

factors, we must look for earlier phases and explore the interactions between humans and wild plants and animals.

ARCHAEOLOGICAL EVIDENCE FOR THE TRANSITION TO AGRICULTURE IN CHINA

As should be clear, the archaeological data pertaining to the transition to agriculture ought to represent a long-term trajectory and not a single event. This trajectory should document, in a well-defined region, the progress from early experiments by hunter-gatherers in cultivating wild plants, modifying their environment, and raising wild animals to the appearance of domesticated plants and animals. One of the enduring problems of Chinese archaeology is that we are still unable to definitively document such a trajectory for any single region. In the words of one recent researcher, of the few locations in the world where agriculture is known to have evolved independently, China is the "only one where this development cannot be traced *in situ* out of a long hunter-gatherer tradition" (Bettinger et al. 2007: 83). This section summarizes what we do know about the crucial transition period and highlights the kind of data still missing and the kind of research needed to obtain it. For the sake of clarity, we shall discuss separately the evidence from north China (the Yellow River basin and north of it) and central and south China (the Yangzi River basin and south of it). This, however, should not be taken as an assertion that agriculture developed separately in these two broad regions. We address this question separately at the end of this chapter.

NORTH CHINA

Neolithic remains were first identified in the Yellow River basin during the early decades of the twentieth century by the Swedish archaeologist Johan Gunnar Andersson. Since then, subsequent researchers have provided ever earlier evidence for the beginnings of agriculture in north China. Indeed, pushing back the date of the *Yangshao* (仰韶) Culture and disproving Andersson's theory on the exogamous origins of the Chinese Neolithic was seen as a matter of national pride during the 1960s and 1970s (Fiskesjö and Chen 2004). After successfully dating the Yangshao Culture to the fifth millennium BCE, during the 1980s, Chinese archaeologists discovered the remains of even earlier sedentary communities in the region, pushing back the beginning of the so-called Neolithic era in the Yellow and Wei River basins to the seventh millennium BCE. At the same time, early sedentary sites were discovered in parts of China that had once been seen as peripheral to the development of Chinese civilization (Chang 1986: 87–95; Shelach 2000; Underhill 1997).

It is now clear that by the second half of the seventh millennium BCE, or some 8,500 years ago, sedentary agricultural societies populated most of the middle and lower Yellow River basin, as well as regions to its north. The archaeological remains of those societies are currently being sorted into regional cultures such as the Cishan (磁山) and Peiligang (裴李岡) in the middle reaches of the Yellow River, the Dadiwan (大地灣) in the Wei River basin, the Houli (后李) in the Shandong peninsula to the east, and the Xinglongwa (兴隆洼) in the Liao River basin to the northeast (Figure 25). These human societies, which we discuss in more detail in Chapter 4, represent an advanced, though by no means the final, stage in the transition to agriculture and sedentary ways of life. That remains of sometimes quite large quantities of domesticated plants have been identified at some of the sites suggests that at least a portion, and probably a substantial portion, of the human diet was derived from agricultural resources. The size of individual sites and the number of structures found in them indicate that each community was quite large; some are estimated to have housed up to two or three hundred people. Perennial residency and the long duration of a community in a single place are suggested by investments in permanent houses and public structures, as well as by well-defined cemeteries.

As mentioned earlier, we know practically nothing about the predecessors of these early villages and of the process of transition to agriculture in north China. This may suggest a rapid revolution accompanied by exponential population growth. However, it is more plausible that our lack of knowledge does not indicate a real break between the Late Paleolithic and Early Neolithic in north China, but rather that it is a product of the research that focused on the more visible remains of the larger Neolithic villages and did not pay enough attention to the more obscure traces left by hunter-gatherers of the Late Paleolithic (or what some call the Epipaleolithic) era. Recent discoveries may in fact suggest a very long and gradual transition to agriculture in China, which is comparable to or even longer than what is known for the better documented center of Southwest Asia.

Late Pleistocene Sites

Very little is known about the societies that populated north China during the peak of the last glacial era, between twenty and twelve thousand years ago. According to a survey carried out in the late 1990s (Lu 1999), fewer than twenty terminal Pleistocene sites were found in north China, and the situation has not changed much since. From the little we do know, however, it appears that certain meaningful technological and, perhaps, social changes occurred during this period. The best known evidence for such change is the transition from the production of pebble and large-flake tools typical of Paleolithic sites to the prominence of blade-based lithic industries. Most remarkable are tiny flake artifacts, usually no more than 2 cm

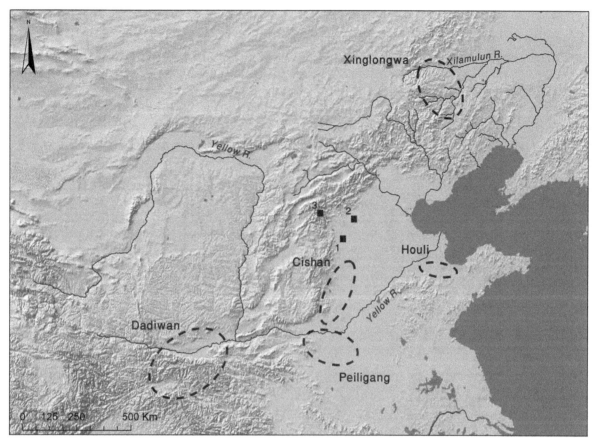

Figure 25. Distribution of Early Neolithic "cultures" in north China and the location of pre-Neolithic sites: 1. Nanzhuangtou; 2. Donghulin; 3. Hutouliang.

in length, known in the literature as microliths (*xishiqi* 细石器 in Chinese) (Figure 26).

Evidence of the existence of microlith industries during the Late Pleistocene and Early Holocene has been found in most parts of north China. For example, one study of sites associated with the *Xiachuan* (下川) Culture in southern Shanxi province, which dates to ca. 18,000 BCE, found that 95 percent of the stone tools are flaked blades and that the proportion of microliths among those tools is high. A similar trend is also well represented in sites from the Early Holocene period and in other parts of north China (Bettinger et al. 2007; Chen 2007: 8–20; Lu 1999). The ability to produce such tiny artifacts signifies the development

of sophisticated techniques of stone tool production. It also represents a more complex method of tool production, since the microliths were probably embedded in wood or bone handles to form the cutting edge of composite tools such as knives, sickles, or arrows.

There is no clear scholarly consensus on how these new tools are related to the economic strategies of Late Pleistocene societies. Some argue that increased proficiency in tool production reflects heightened economic specialization. According to this view, most microliths were used as arrowheads and the societies that produced them were specialized hunters (Bettinger et al. 2007: 96). However, most archaeologists associate microliths not with

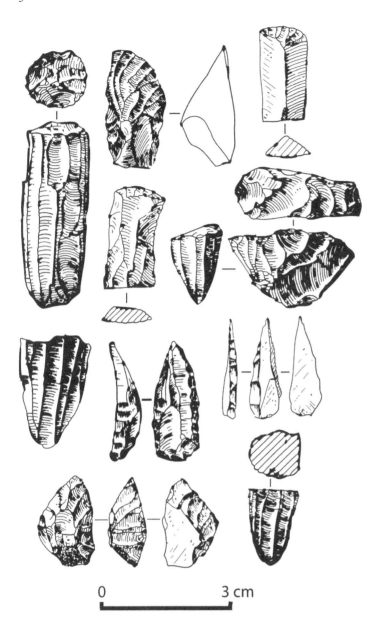

0   3 cm

Figure 26. Microlith and flint microlith cores of the Xiachuan culture, north China (after Wang et al. 1978).

a specialization in food procurement, but rather with a diversification of food sources and of collecting strategies (e.g., Aikens 1992: 102; Madsen et al. 1996: 227). According to this second interpretation, microliths were flexible, multifunctional artifacts. By fixing one or several microliths to a handle, tools were created that could be used for hunting (arrows), but also for gathering plants (ripping tools, such as sickles and knives) and other food gathering and processing tasks (such as skinning and hide processing). Moreover, as hunting implements, small microliths should be associated not with the specialized hunting of a single or a few types of very productive large animals, but rather with the opportunistic hunting of small game. This interpretation is closely associated with the "broad spectrum" hypothesis, which sees the expansion of the food resources utilized by hunter-gatherers,

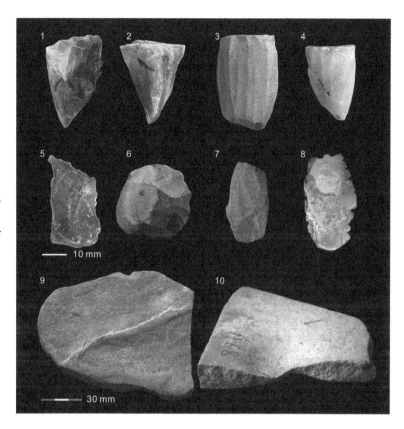

Figure 27. Artifacts from locality 1 at Longwangchan: 1–4. microblade cores; 5–7. microliths; 8. shell tool; 9. shovel; 10. grinding slab (quern) (after Zhang et al. 2011).

and especially the exploitation of secondary food sources such as seeds and nuts, as a crucial precondition for the development of agriculture.

Other types of artifacts, which made their first appearance in north China during the Late Pleistocene and became widespread during the Holocene, may also be associated with the broad spectrum hypothesis, in particular grinding stones, large polished stone tools, and ceramic vessels. Grinding stones, or querns (in Chinese, *mopan* 磨盘), are large flat stone slabs with one side, which is sometime slightly concave, smoothly polished. Grinding stones are traditionally associated with the processing of cereal grains into flour by agricultural societies, but a few such objects have been recently found in Late Pleistocene and Early Holocene contexts in north China. For instance, a quern was found at the Longwangchan (龙王辿) site, in Hukou, Shaanxi (Zhongguo 2007). The site is located in the heartland of the northern

Chinese loess plateau, on the second terrace above the Yellow River, and is dated to ca. 23,000 BCE (Zhang et al. 2011; Zhongguo 2007). Only a small part of the site has been excavated, but even so, archaeologists located the remains of some twenty fireplaces and recovered more than twenty thousand stone artifacts, as well as shells and a few animal bones. The stone artifacts are mostly flint and quartz microliths, but they also include a small number of grinding stones and polished stone axes. The quern that was reported in publication is made of sandstone and is 16.4 cm by 14.8 cm in size (Figure 27). Similar artifacts, including microliths and querns, are also known from Xiachuan sites in Shanxi (Wang et al. 1978) and from Shizitan (柿子滩) also in Shanxi province – dated more or less to the same period – and from other sites that might be slightly later and already associated with the transition to the Holocene (Liu et al. 2013; Shizitan 2010).

While grinding stones are intuitively associated with the dehusking and grinding of cereal grains, use-wear and residue analysis of three grinding stones from Shizitan (2010) suggests that they were used to process not only different types of weeds, including Paniceae grasses (the wild ancestor of millet), but also wild beans and tubers (Liu et al. 2013). Another recent study of grinding stones from an Early Holocene site suggests that they were used to process acorns (Liu, Field, et al. 2010). Later we return to discuss the food processed by grinding stones, but for now it is important to note that neither weeds nor acorns are first-choice foods: neither is particularly tasty, and both are difficult to digest, while acorns can actually be toxic. Grinding stones, though few in number, point to the consumption of secondary foods and to a strategy of diversified food exploitation. Polished stone axes, once viewed as the trademark of the "Neolithic Revolution," can also be seen as part of this strategy. Rather than being used exclusively for clearing fields and tilling land for agricultural production, they could also have been used for digging up roots and other activities associated with extensive gathering.

Early ceramic production predating evidence for the domestication of plants is a phenomenon now known across a wide region of East Asia (Kuzmin 2006; Shelach 2012). The unequivocal correlation between pottery and agriculture, a common presumption based on the chronology of ceramic production in Southwest Asia, does not hold true for East Asia. Nevertheless, the invention of ceramics is probably associated with cooking food. While it is possible to boil water and cook food in other types of containers – such as stone cooking in bark or basketry containers (Nelson 2010) – direct boiling in ceramic vessels is much more effective when lengthy cooking is needed to process tough foods or reduce toxicity. Considering that ceramics are easily breakable and more difficult to transport than baskets, the production of ceramic vessels makes sense only in the context of decreased mobility and the need to process tough and toxic foods, such as cereals, legumes, acorns, and so on.

Early Holocene Sites

If our knowledge of the societies that lived in north China during the Late Pleistocene is at best partial, our knowledge about societies that inhabited the same region during the Early Holocene is even scantier. In fact, our understanding of this crucial period, when the transition to agriculture might have occurred, is still based primarily on data from a very few sites, the best known of which are Hutouliang (虎头梁) and Nanzhuangtou (南庄头), both in Hebei province, and Donghulin (东胡林), in the Beijing area. All these sites are located north of the Yellow River basin and none have been extensively excavated and documented. Nanzhuangtou, the best known of the three, is dated to ca. 10,000 to 8000 BCE. The total size of the site is estimated to be about 20,000 m², but only a small portion has been excavated. As with earlier Pleistocene sites, archaeologists did not find structures at Nanzhuangtou, but excavations carried out in the 1980s and again in 1997 located the remains of fireplaces and recovered a small quantity of potshards, stone tools (including a few grinding stones), and bone tools (Figure 28) (Baoding 1991; Guo and Li 2002: 195–7; Hebei et al. 2010; Jin and Xu 1994). Large quantities of animal bones and shellfish were also found. Of the bones found during the excavations in the 1980s, 67 percent belong to different types of deer and the rest to wolves, dogs, pigs, and geese (Baoding 1991). Recent research identified some of the bones excavated from this site as belonging to domesticated dogs,qq thus representing the oldest evidence for animal domestication in China (Yuan Jing 2008). It was suggested that pigs had been domesticated as well (Guo and Li 2002: 203; Jin and Xu 1994: 36), but such claims have been refuted by specialized bone analysis (Yuan and Fled 2002).

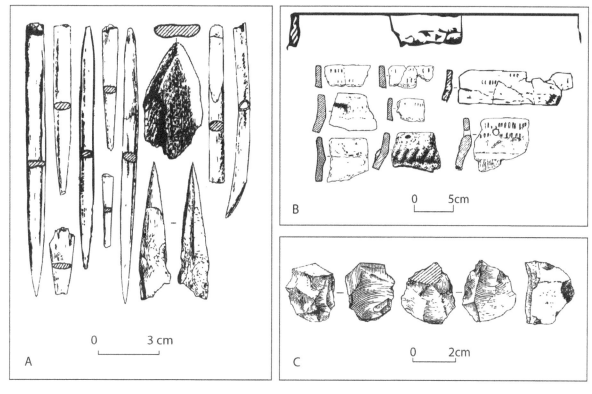

Figure 28. Artifacts from the Nanzhuangtou site: A. bone artifacts; B. potshards; C. stone tools (after Hebei et al. 2010).

The Donghulin site was recently dated to ca. 9000 to 7000 BCE. Here too, only a small portion of the approximately 3,000 m² site was excavated. Archaeologists located a few graves at the site, as well as hearths and ash pits, but no house structures were found. The artifacts excavated from Donghulin site include microliths, polished stone axes, adzes and grinding stones, bone implements, and a small quantity of potshards. Faunal and floral remains include bones, mostly of deer, a large quantity of freshwater shells, and two species of hackberry seeds (Hao et al. 2008; Liu et al. 2010a; Zhao et al. 2003). Residue and use-wear analyses conducted on two grinding stones (one flat "quern" and one long and narrow "hand stone") from Donghulin suggest that they were probably used to process acorns rather than cereals (Liu et al. 2010a). On the other hand, a differ-ent analysis of the starch residue extracted from potshards and grinding stones from Nanzhuang-tou and Donghulin identified it as millet (Yang et al. 2012). A bone handle into which microb-lades were inserted – one of which was found still intact (Beijing Daxue 2006) – may have been part of a ripping tool used to cut and collect weeds (Figure 29).

In conclusion, during the Late Pleistocene and Early Holocene we can identify in north China the emergence of a complex of artifacts that in most sites appear together. This complex includes microliths, grinding stones, and ceramic contain-ers. These objects can be correlated to changes in the economic behavior of the societies that pro-duced them, but we do not yet have evidence of the domestication of plants and animals (except for dogs) or of larger sedentary communities.

Fragmentary evidence, such as the graves found in Donghulin and the necklaces (Figure 30) found in one of the graves, may point to incipient social processes that accelerate in the following millennia (see Chapter 4).

The precise evolutionary transformation from these societies to the advanced sedentary agriculturalists of the seventh and sixth millennia BCE still eludes us. Not only is there a chronological gap of about one thousand years between Nanzhuangtou and Donghulin and the earliest known Neolithic villages in north China, but there is also a geographic gap between the two sites (and Hutouliang) and the areas where the earliest Neolithic cultures have been identified (Figure 25). In other words, while we can describe the socioeconomic background for the development of agriculture, we do not yet have an in situ trajectory for the transition to agriculture in north China.

This spatial and temporal gap is probably not real, but instead represents the shortcomings of the state of our knowledge today. In recent years, archaeological findings that could fill this gap have been uncovered in different subregions of north China. For example, in northeast China, local archaeologists have reported the discovery of a new culture, the Xiaohexi (小河西), which they claim is a transitional phase between local Epipaleolithic cultures and the developed sedentary villages of the Xinglongwa culture (Suo 2005; Suo and Li 2008). More extensive knowledge and a better understanding of this missing link are crucial for the reconstruction and analysis of the local trajectories that in different parts of north China represent the transition to sedentary, agricultural lifeways.

CENTRAL AND SOUTH CHINA

The transition to agriculture in the Yangzi River basin and south of it received little attention during the early years of archaeological research in China. It was assumed that domesticated rice was brought to this region from the south and that both agriculture and social complexity developed here much later than in the Yellow River basin from which they probably derived. The discovery, in the 1970s, of large quantities of rice dating to the fifth millennium BCE at Hemudu (河姆渡; see Chapter 5) suggested that rice was domesticated in the Yangzi River basin. This identification drew archaeological attention that has since led to several projects focusing on the origins of rice domestication. As a result, our knowledge about Late Pleistocene and Early Holocene societies in this region has increased dramatically and our reconstruction of the trajectory leading to agriculture here is more complete than that of north China.

Late Pleistocene Sites

The Late Paleolithic occupation of central and south China displays some broad differences in comparison with north China. In contrast to north China, where all the Late Paleolithic remains have

Figure 30. Shell and bone necklaces from Donghulin (photo by Zhao Chaohong).

been found in open-air sites, all evidence for human occupation in central and south China has been found inside caves. The most famous sites from this period include Xianrendong (仙人洞) and Diaotonghuan (吊桶环) in Jiangxi province, Yuchanyan (玉蟾岩) in Hunan province, and Zengpiyan (甑皮岩) in Guangxi province. The earliest open-air sites identified in the middle and lower Yangzi River valley, such as Shanghsan (上山) from Zhejiang province, and Pengtoushan (彭頭山) and Bashidang (八十垱) in Hunan province, are only found in the Early Holocene. Shell midden sites also first appear in southeast China during this period. Clearly, the late Pleistocene population of central and south China utilized the numerous caves that are scattered in the karstic landscape of the region for shelter. The good state of preservation at such sites makes them

ideal for archaeological exploration, but it is not yet clear whether early open-air sites also exist, if they have been destroyed, or if they remain covered.

Yuchanyan is a good example of a Late Pleistocene site in this region. It is a limestone cave site located in the Yangzi River basin (although it is some 450 km south of the river's main course). The cave is quite small in area – 12–15 m long and 6–8 m wide – suggesting that it was occupied by a small group of people. Excavators identified the remains of fireplaces in the space. The occupation of the site was dated to ca. 16,000 to 12,000 BCE (Boaretto et al. 2009).

Lithic assemblages at Yuchanyan, as well as in all other cave sites from central and south China, continue the older Paleolithic traditions. They are dominated by relatively large lithic fragments such as pebble choppers and other chopping tools (Figure 31). Flake tools are less common, but are, nonetheless, found along with bone and antler tools (Lu 2006). The almost complete absence of microliths at Late Pleistocene and Early Holocene sites in central and south China contrasts sharply with their popularity in north China (Chen 2007). Microliths were, in fact, commonly produced during this period by societies throughout the northern part of East Asia, including those in the Korean Peninsula, Japan, Siberia, and Mongolia (Kuzmin 2007). Their absence from the Yangzi River basin and regions to its south may, thus, signify a meaningful technoeconomic boarder.[1]

The most remarkable discovery at Yangzi River valley cave sites is early evidence for ceramic production. Evidence from the Yuchanyan cave was dated to between 18,300 and 15,400 BP (or ca. 16,000 to 13,500 BCE). In Xianrendong it was dated to ca. 20,000 BP (or ca. 18,000 BCE), making it the earliest evidence of ceramic production anywhere in the world (Boaretto et al. 2009; Wu et al. 2012). Complete vessels are difficult to reconstruct from the small potshards collected at

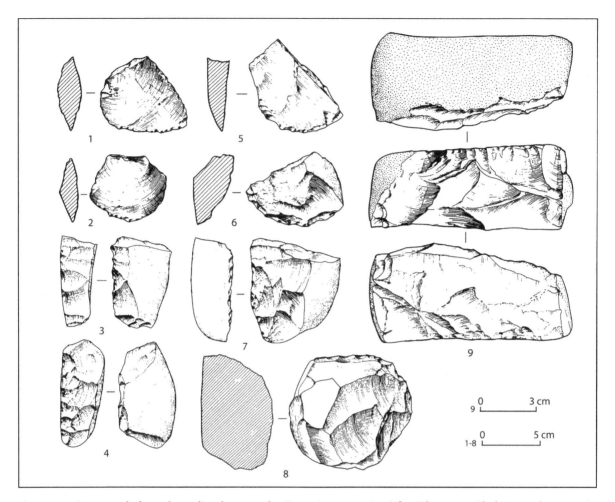

Figure 31. Stone tools from the earliest layers at the Zengpiyan cave site (after Zhongguo Shehui 2010b: 99–100).

these sites, but they represent coarse, soft, low-fired ceramics, usually tempered with quartz and charcoal and decorated with cord marks (Figure 32).

Because of the good preservation conditions inside the cave sites, archaeo-zoologists and archaeo-botanists have been able to recover large samples of animal bones and plant remains. For example, more than 40 species of plants and 45 species of animals and shells were identified by the excavators of the Yuchanyan site, while 108 species of animals and shells (including 20 bird types and 37 types of mammals) were found at the Zengpiyan site (Lu 2006: 133; Prendergast et al. 2009: 1034; Zhongguo Shehui 2003: 344–6). While it is possible that some of the animal bones were

brought to the caves by carnivores, examinations of animal tooth marks and of cut marks left on the bones suggest that most were probably hunted and consumed by the human occupants of the caves (Prendergast et al. 2009). Husks and phytoliths of wild rice found at Yuchanyan and in Xianrendong (Lu 2006: 133) also suggest that it was collected and consumed there.

Early Holocene sites

The occupation of some cave sites, especially in the south, continued during the Early Holocene. Most settlements starting from about 8000 BCE (10,000 cal BP), however, are at open-air sites.

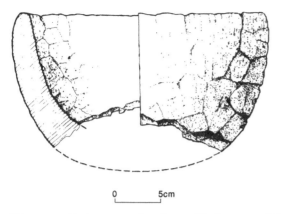

Figure 32. Early ceramic from Yuchanyan (after Zhongguo Shehui 2010b: 99).

This seems to signify a real shift in the occupation history of the region and in the structure of its local societies. Some sites, such as Pengtoushan, remain quite small and reflect societies that are comparable in size to those of the cave sites. Other open-air sites are much larger, representing a substantial expansion in community size. Bashidang, which is about 3 ha (30,000 m²) in size (Zhang and Hung 2008), is a good example of such a community. House structures are found at most of the sites in the Yangzi River basin, together with formal burial pits, suggesting a transition to full-scale sedentism and the incipient development of village life and the belief system that would later become typical of agricultural societies. Although they were apparently egalitarian societies, a few extraordinary discoveries – such as the ditch that may have enclosed the Bashidang community, as well as the somewhat larger structure found at Pengtoushan and the burial offerings found in some graves – might be indicative of incipient developments toward social complexity.

The lithic industry of these Early Holocene sites continues the local tradition of producing mainly pebble tools and large flake tools, although a few polished stone axes and grinding stones have also been found (Lu 2006). Pottery is much more common in these sites, and although it is still coarse and fired at low temperatures, it is more durable

than before, thereby allowing better reconstruction of vessel shapes. At Shangshan, for example, 85 percent of the vessels are flat-bottomed basins and the rest have either a round bottom or a low ring base. Some of the pots are decorated with cord marks, stamping, and incisions, and some are covered with red slip (Jiang and Liu 2006: 357).

At Shangshan and Pengtoushan, many of the ceramics are tempered with rice husks. This process has preserved the husks, or their imprint, and has made it possible to conduct morphological studies. Remains of rice have also been found in other contexts: in Bashidang, for instance, thousands of rice husks and grains were recovered in the course of one small-scale excavation (Hunan 2006: 508; Zhang and Pei 1997). Archaeologists and archaeo-botanists are debating whether the rice remains found at these sites are domesticated or wild, but it is clear that from ca. 8000 BCE rice was collected, consumed, and used for other purposes in much larger quantities than before. In addition to rice, plant remains and animal bones were also found at sites in the lower and middle Yangzi, which suggests that the populations of these communities were still intensely engaged in collecting wild plants (including nuts, fruits, legumes, and weeds) and hunted a wide variety of animals.

The situation in south China, south of the Yangzi River basin, is quite different from that in central China. Here too we observe a transition to open-air occupation during the Early Holocene, but most the most typical archaeological sites are shell middens (Chinese: beiqiu yizhi 贝丘遗址), rather than sedentary villages with house remains. Dingsishan (顶蛳山) in Guangxi province is a typical site (Zhongguo Shehui 1998). The site is a shallow mound, about 5,000 m² in size, made of an accumulation of layers of shells and other aquatic resources that were exploited by the local community. It is dated to ca. 8000 to 4000 BCE and subdivided into four cultural-chronological phases.

No structures associated with the earliest stratum have been found, but graves and ash pits were found in strata II and III, dated to ca. 6000–5000 BCE. Tools made of pebbles, bones, and shells, as well as coarse pottery tempered with calcite and decorated with cord marks and appliqués, were found in the middens.

The extensive exploitation of mollusks, found only rarely in Late Pleistocene sites, is a significant development that would continue to dominate the economic adaptation of societies in south China for millennia. Other wild plants and animals were also exploited, as is testified to by the identification at Dingsishan of more than twenty species of animal and plant remains. However, it is important to note that rice phytoliths are found at only the most recent layer, dated to ca. 4000 BCE (Zhao et al. 2005). At the Zengpiyan cave site, which continued to be occupied during the Early Holocene, micro remains of root plants and taro residue have been found (Lu 2006: 145). Some scholars have argued that pig bones found in this site belong to domesticated species, though this assertion remains controversial (Yuan and Fled 2002).

ARE WE THERE YET? PLANT AND ANIMAL DOMESTICATION DURING THE LATE PLEISTOCENE AND EARLY HOLOCENE

Dating the transition to agriculture is one of the most highly contested enterprises in Chinese archaeology. While archaeologists of China have commonly labeled every site with evidence for pottery production as Neolithic, a practice that may give the impression that the transition occurred during the Late Pleistocene,[2] others have pushed it to the Mid-Holocene period. The critical debate, however, is between those who see the earliest sites of the Holocene as representing the beginning of domestication and sedentary agricultural communities and those who date these phenomena to the sixth or even fifth millennium

BCE. The debate focuses on the morphology of plant remains and, to a lesser extent, on animal bones. Because, as we have seen, the pertinent data from north China are very scarce, the argument mostly centers on the domestication of rice in the Yangzi River basin, and in particular on the botanical remains from two sites: Bashidang, in the middle Yangzi River basin, and Shangshan in the lower Yangzi River basin, both dated to ca. 8000 BCE.[3] According to one study of grain phytolites from Bashidang, the rice consumed there was already domesticated (Zhang and Pei 1997). In a later paper, Jiang and Liu argued that the morphological traits of rice husks embedded in potshards from the Shangshan site indicate that rice was at "an early stage of domestication" (Jiang and Liu 2006: 358). A recent molecular study suggesting a single origin of rice domestication some 8,200 to 13,500 years ago (Molina et al. 2011) lends support to this view. In contrast, Dorian Fuller and his colleagues have argued that full rice domestication occurred only around 4000 BCE. They claim that fully domesticated nonshattering forms were not even present in Hemudu, a waterlogged site dated to ca. 5000–4000 BCE, where about twenty tons of rice husks were recovered (see Chapter 5) (Fuller et al. 2007). Furthermore, if the identification as millet of ancient starch grain extracted from artifacts from Donghulin and Nanzhuangtou (Yang et al. 2012) can be corroborated, it will be possible to argue that the domestication process of millet was equally long.

While I cannot decide here in favor of one side or the other of the debate, I suggest that by focusing on the biological attributes that differentiate domesticated species from their wild progenitors, we are overlooking the most important social and economic issues. When discussing the origins of agriculture and the cultivation of plants and animals (domesticated and wild), we should address the development of a system of socioeconomic knowledge within the broader framework of social changes, such as the transition to sedentism, the growth group size, and the incipient development of social complexity. In this sense, I agree with Fuller and his colleagues who argue that the process was very long. In fact, one of the main contributions of archaeological research in China is that it quite clearly demonstrates how long and gradual this process was: from the initial change in human adaptation at the height of the last Glacial Age some twenty thousand years ago to the final stabilization of relatively large sedentary agricultural communities some eight or nine thousand years ago. Looked at from this perspective, it becomes clear that the identification of rice (or any other species) that exhibits the full attributes of domestication is less important than the evidence for large-scale exploitation and consumption of wild rice – and perhaps its cultivation – which may have started thousands of years earlier. With this observation in mind it is time to turn to the crucial question: why did people in China become agriculturalists?

WHY AGRICULTURE? MODELS EXPLAINING THE TRANSITION TO AGRICULTURE IN CHINA

Why, after some two million years as successful hunters and gatherers, some human societies should change their subsistence strategy and become food producers is a conundrum that has been puzzling anthropologists for over a century. When anthropological and archaeological research was in its infancy in the late nineteenth and early twentieth centuries and the prevailing paradigm was that agriculture represented human advancement to a better, easier, and more secure lifeway, this issue was not problematized. Thus, the question was not why the transition took place, but rather how, when, and where people came up with the inventions that allowed them to improve their economic conditions.

Ethnographic and archaeological data collected since the 1950s forced the *why* questions to the forefront. Ethnographic research among contemporary hunter-gatherers in the world's most inhospitable places, such as the !Kong-San of the Kalahari Desert (Lee 1968), showed that they enjoyed a healthy diet, that their food resources were stable, and that they worked for only a few hours a day, spending most of their time pursuing leisure activities. Most anthropologists concluded that if this was the case in marginal areas, then the prehistoric hunter-gatherer, who lived in much more favorable environments, must have had an affluent existence. This assumption gained support from Harlan's famous experiment: using prehistoric harvesting methods he was able to collect a kilogram of clean wild wheat grains in one hour, which led him to estimate that prehistoric societies living in areas of dense wild wheat resources would have been able to harvest enough grain to feed themselves for the entire year in just three weeks (Harlan 1967).

More questions are prompted by the analysis of the bones and teeth of early agriculturalists, which suggests that the populations of early agricultural villages suffered from deteriorating health, especially tooth diseases related to their cereal-based diet, and an overall decrease in life expectancy as compared to hunter-gatherer populations. While the specific details of this reconstruction are still being debated (cf. Eshed et al. 2006; Eshed et al. 2010), it is clear that two of the common attributes of agriculture – the extensive exploitation and consumption of cereals and the formation of relatively large sedentary groups – were responsible for the deterioration in health conditions, at least during the early phases of this process.

Why, then, did people abandon their affluent lifeway in favor of a system in which, to put it somewhat simplistically, they would have to work harder for more hours a day, consume inferior foods, suffer from diseases, and have a shorter life expectancy? This is not the place to elaborate the many theories put forth to explain the transition to agriculture. For the purposes of this chapter it is sufficient to outline the three main groups of models that can be shorthanded as *push, pull,* and *social.*

The *push* models share the idea that people were forced to become agriculturalists because of external pressures beyond their control. Deteriorating climatic or environmental conditions and population pressures are the two sources most often cited in the literature as responsible for these pressures. As a consequence of these pressures, people were able to obtain fewer resources per capita and so, according to the model, were forced to produce more through cultivation and, eventually, domestication and agriculture. Exactly the opposite scenario is depicted by models in the *pull* set. Hunter-gatherers during the Early Holocene had ideal living conditions: the climate had become warm and humid, resources were abundant, and humans were few. Because food resources were plentiful, people could afford to experiment with cultivating plants and raising animals. Initially, those activities were not as productive as traditional hunting and gathering, but they enabled some people to travel less and thus become more sedentary. With sedentism or semisedentism, so this model suggests, efforts to "improve" the immediate environment of the community through cultivation intensified, eventually leading to agriculture.

The final set of models, labeled *social* models, focuses on group dynamics and interpersonal interactions. This theoretical perspective suggests that social dynamics, and especially competition for social prestige, compelled some people to invest energy in procuring and producing food. Hosting communal feasts or offering exotic or intoxicating foods, for example, could be a way for an aspiring leader to gain social prestige. According to these models, initial cultivation, and even full-scale domestication, came about as a result of efforts to gain more foods that were not essential for one's diet but would confer prestige, or even by tending plants and animals whose products would not be

used for food at all, but rather to produce prestigious items.

Testing these models is not as straightforward as one would like. It is difficult to directly asses the pressures that prehistoric groups are said to have experienced according to the push models or the affluence they are meant to have enjoyed according to the pull models, or to find archaeological correlates for the small-scale social competition crucial for the social models. Because of these difficulties, much of the discussion has revolved around variables that are more easily quantified, such as climatic changes and their effects on human adaptation.

Climatic Changes and the Transition to Agriculture

It is generally agreed that China was severely affected by climatic conditions during the peak of the last Glacial Age, ca. 21,000 to 15,000 years ago. Temperatures were probably six to nine degrees lower than they are today in north China, and about four to five degrees lower in the Yangzi River basin. In north China, a cold steppe environment is indicated by the bones of woolly mammoths and woolly rhinoceroses that were discovered in more than two hundred locations. Permafrost soils, found today north of the fifty-first parallel north, extended in some parts as far south as forty degrees north (Lu 2006: 130–1; Winkler and Wang 1993). Strong winter monsoons that pushed cold and dry air from the interior of the Eurasian continent south and eastward, and weak summer monsoons that did not bring much humidity from the oceans, caused the northern steppe environment to expand as far as the Yangzi River basin.

After ca. 13,000 BCE, the climate become warmer and more humid, until sometime around 9500 BCE, when a period of dry and cold climatic conditions, equivalent to what is known in other parts of the world as the Younger Dryas event, affected China. With the end of the Younger Dryas event, climatic conditions improved again until they reached an optimum peak of high levels of precipitation and warm temperatures between ca. 7000 and 2000 BCE (An et al. 2000; Lu 1999: 12–13; Zhou et al. 2001). In north China, those climatic changes precipitated the transition from a steppe grassland environment to one in which evergreen and broad-leaved deciduous forests thrived alongside patches of xerophytic herbs (Yi et al. 2003). During the same time, subtropical conditions developed in central and south China.

It should be noted, however, that this general schematic masks a great deal of interregional variation and short-term fluctuations. Recent studies suggest, for example, that as much as one to two thousand years may have separated the manifestation of these major climatic events in west and east China, and that there was much fluctuation in average temperature and precipitation within each of the broadly defined climatic periods (An et al. 2000; He et al. 2004). In order to correlate climatic change with archaeological findings, we need to reconstruct the climatic trajectory with much greater temporal and spatial resolution. Such a reconstruction is currently unavailable for most regions in China, so we have no choice but to discuss the broader trends without being able to test specific hypotheses.

Response to the stress created by the Younger Dryas event is one of the more specific push models put forward to explain the transition to agriculture in the Levant (Bar-Yosef and Belfer-Cohen 1992), and it has also been adapted to the Chinese setting (Bar-Yosef 2011; Bellwood 2005: 116–18; Chen Shengqian 2006: 528; Cohen 1998; Yasuda 2002: 137). According to this model, under the improving climatic conditions of the Early Holocene, hunter-gatherer societies were able to expand and become more sedentary. With the sharp onset of declining environmental conditions

caused by the Younger Dryas event, they were forced to develop new production methods. When climatic conditions improved once more, the full potential of these new methods was realized and full-scale agriculture emerged.

The application of this model to China is not yet sufficiently detailed. For instance, it is not clear that the Younger Dryas event impacted different regions in China in the same way and for the same length of time. Even if we assume that the climatic trend was similar, its effects on the living conditions for people residing in the Yangzi River basin, where current precipitation levels can exceed 1,500 mm per year and the temperatures hardly ever drop below zero, must have been very different from the effects on populations in the Yellow River basin and more northerly regions, where average yearly precipitation is 700 mm or less and the growing season is much shorter. Cohen's (1998) proposal that in both regions the transition to agriculture was triggered by the same climatic event seems unlikely.

One pull model, which many researchers apply to China, simply states that with the improving climatic conditions of the Holocene, especially during the optimum period (sometimes termed the Mid-Holocene Optimum), affluent hunter-gatherers were free to experiment with the cultivation of plant and animals. The increased importance of those cultivated resources and their final domestication were the result of a gradual process driven not so much by necessity or even by direct dietary needs as by convenience (distance to resources) and by the social processes that were initiated during this same time (increased sedentism, larger group size, etc.) (e.g., Liu 2004: 24–5; Lu 2006: 131; Price and Gebauer 1995: 6–8; Zhu 2001). A supporting argument, which has rarely been made in the context of China, but which may nonetheless be relevant, is that with an increase in atmospheric carbon dioxide levels during the Early Holocene plants became up to 60 percent more productive (Richerson et al. 2001: 393–4). This change could have triggered more extensive exploitation of grain-bearing plants, leading both to greater dependence on them and their cultivation as well as to their domestication.

Archaeologists are currently unable to reach a consensus regarding which of the conflicting scenarios better explains the transition to agriculture and sedentary lifeways in China. Because secure dates for the large-scale exploitation of cereals and the development of larger sedentary communities all postdate the Younger Dryas event, its relevancy for explaining the transition to agriculture in China is doubtful. This, however, does not mean that the pull theories are therefore accurate. In fact, attempts to label the environmental conditions of any given period as either favorable or unfavorable are problematic, not just because this presumes that different geographic regions were similarly affected by global conditions but, more important, because the terms "favorable" and "unfavorable" are not specifically defined. From the perspective of the human consumer, the same climatic change can have a positive effect on one food resource and a negative impact on another. For example, in north China, as in other parts of the northern hemisphere, the transition from the Pleistocene to the Holocene favorably affected the concentration of some plant resources (Richerson et al. 2001) while at the same time disrupting the migratory habits and concentrations of some mammalian species and decreasing the availability of large game (Song 2002).

Social and Economic Strategies and the Transition to Agriculture

Reconstructions of climatic trajectories and environmental conditions are important building blocks in forming a fuller understanding of the transition to agriculture, but reconstructions cannot *explain* this process on their own. An explanatory model, which builds upon their results, must address human motivations and decision making. One such model, which I believe can make sense of the Chinese data described earlier, is the so-called broad spectrum hypothesis (or broad spectrum revolution). This model, was first formulated by Kent Flannery in 1969, based on archeobotanic, archaeo-zoologic, and archaeological data from the Levant and Europe, and suggested that the transition to agriculture was rooted in a new economic strategy developed by Late Paleolithic societies. The new broad spectrum strategy included the exploitation of many more types of plants and animal species and a consequent decline in the consumption of first-rate food sources (such as large game and highly nutritious fruits) in favor of second-rate sources (such as small game and cereals that were more difficult to process). This dietary change was accompanied by technological developments, such as advances in hunting and fishing methods, tools to process the new foods (such as grinding stones), and better storage abilities (Flannery 1969; Stiner 2001).

The data presented earlier suggest that Late Pleistocene and Early Holocene societies in the Yellow and Yangzi River basins did indeed pursue a broad spectrum economic strategy: While the majority of animal bones at both Nanzhuangtou and Donghulin were identified as belonging to various deer species, less productive food resources, such as smaller animals and shellfish, were also found. The extensive use of microlith tools, grinding stones, and ceramic pots suggests the utilization of diverse animal and plant resources, including millet and acorns. Pits located at Donghulin may represent the development of storage facilities. Nonetheless, the absence of a more systematic recovery of plant and animal remains prevents a more thorough reconstruction of this strategy.

In the Yangzi River basin we find more direct evidence for the broad spectrum strategy. The diversity of plant and animal remains found at the Yuchanyan site is a good example: While the majority of animal bones found belong to deer species and water birds, a large variety of other animals, such as small carnivores, large rodents, tortoises, and fish, are also common. For instance, the bamboo rat represents 6 percent of the mammals (minimum number of individuals [MNI]) identified at the site (Prendergast et al. 2009). This diversity suggests that while the inhabitants of the site may have focused their attention on a few more productive animals – those with relatively large bodies, such as deer, or those found in larger concentrations, such as water birds – they did not refrain from hunting and trapping small animals that are less productive and more difficult to process.

While much attention has been paid to the exploitation of wild progenitors of the plants that were later domesticated – rice and millet, for example – the important trend, at least initially, was not the specialized exploitation of those exact species but the utilization of a wide variety of plant resources, many of them quite difficult and time-consuming to process – such as acorns. Acorns are nutritionally rich and sometimes found in high concentration, but because they are toxic and difficult to digest, they need to be extensively processed before consumption. As noted earlier, residue and use-wear analyses have suggested that one of the main functions of grinding stones found at some of the early sites in the Yellow and Yangzi River basins was to process acorns (cf. Liu et al. 2010a, 2010b). At the Tianluoshan (田螺山) site in the lower Yangzi River basin, dated to ca. 4,900–4600 BCE, quantities of acorns were found in storage pits alongside remains of rice, trapa (water chestnut) shells, and persimmon seeds. This suggests that acorns continued to be an important food resource well into the Neolithic period. It would seem that the consumption of acorns only decreased after domesticated rice agriculture had considerably intensified: at the earlier phases of Tianluoshan about 50 percent of the plant remains are acorns, while they drop to

about 10 percent during the most recent period of occupation. Over the same time span, rice remains increased from 8 percent to 24 percent (Fuller et al. 2009).

When considering the broad spectrum strategy from the perspective of human decision making, we should ask why at a certain point in time certain food resources were ignored, and procured and processed at another time. Such questions have been addressed by the human behavioral ecology (HBE) approach. Building on such theories as the optimization assumption model developed to explain animal predation, HBE simulates the costs and benefits of alternative courses of action under a range of environmental conditions. According to this model, when encountering a certain food resource, the forager decides whether or not to utilize it and considers the costs and benefits of pursuing other resources. Such considerations can include the likelihood of encountering a more beneficial resource, the time spent on finding and procuring each resource, the diminishing returns of continuing to harvest the same resource as opposed to looking for another, the time and effort spent on processing the resource, its ultimate nutritious value, and so on.

Studying the broad spectrum strategy while using the HBE perspective implies that we have to address both its short- and long-term advantages over strategies that primarily focused on fewer but more productive food resources. One way to account for this change in strategy is to deal not only with the overall productivity of the environment (better or worse), but also with its variability. When the environment is less predictable, a forager is more likely to use a greater number of resources than if he or she is certain that a more productive resource will be found. While the environment of the postglacial period may have been more productive overall, it was also less predictable. Greater seasonality and the disruption of the migratory routes of large game animals resulted in an environment where the most beneficial resources were less concentrated and more variable from season to season.

According to this approach then, the broad spectrum strategy helped the Late Pleistocene and Early Holocene hunter-gatherer groups mitigate their environmental uncertainty. It should be remembered that the broad spectrum strategy includes not only the hunting and gathering of a larger variety of food sources, but also the deployment of various techniques such as storage that help even out seasonal fluctuations in the availability of food. It is in this respect that some food resources, such as grains, but also acorns and nuts, gained added value, since they are more easily stored and less likely to spoil than other resources. Cultivating a certain number of annual plants, as well as tending wild animals such as pigs, may simply have been one more strategy aimed at increasing the predictability of the environment and evening out the disparities in available resources between seasons and between good and bad years. At the same time and as a result, all these methods also contributed to a decrease in mobility.

It is interesting to compare the trajectory in south China to developments in north and in central China. The fundamental processes observed are very similar in the three regions. In particular, there is evidence of the use of the broad spectrum strategy and the exploitation of secondary food sources. The extremely large variety of mammals, birds, fish, and shellfish identified at the Zengpiyan cave site (Zhongguo Shehui 2003: 344–5) represents this broad spectrum, and the widespread appearance of shell midden sites during the Early Holocene testifies to the intensive exploitation of resources that had not been used previously. The early production of pottery is another example of trends common to all regions in China. Nonetheless, despite these similarities, the transition to agriculture seems to have happened in the south at a much later date and was probably imported from central China (Zhang and Hung 2008: 312).

Asking why agriculture did not develop early in south China can help us understand why it did evolve in regions to the north. Perhaps, as some have argued, conditions there were too good and food resources too plentiful to provide any incentive to experiment with agriculture (e.g., Lu 2006). But it is possible that this "Garden of Eden" kind of explanation overemphasizes the affluence and idealness of tropical conditions. It is also possible that rapid vegetation growth in these areas meant that clearing fields for agriculture was more difficult, and that separating cultivated plots from naturally growing vegetation was almost impossible. Such conditions could have discouraged attempts at cultivating wild species and prevented the distinction between wild and incipient domesticated species. It is also possible that human occupation of the tropical areas of China was so sparse and communication among societies so rare that social processes such as internal and external competition, which might have encouraged people to start cultivating and selecting specific plants and animals, did not take place.

Another line of explanation focuses on the types of plants and animals that were the target of intensive exploitation during the Early Holocene in the south. For example, while shellfish were exploited intensively, they were not suitable for cultivation and domestication. Other food resources found at the Zengpiyan cave, namely root plants such as yam and taro, may have been domesticated in the south (Lu 2006: 145; Zhongguo Shehui 2003: 343). It is possible, however, that because root plants could not be gathered and preserved in the same way as cereals, this type of cultivation did not have the same social and economic impact that we find agriculture exerting in central and north China.

One Center, Two Centers, Multiple Centers: Geographic Diversity, Interregional Interaction, and the Transition to Agriculture

Comparing the socioeconomic trajectories of north, central, and south China can provide valuable insights into the variations within the regions and societies that underwent a transition to agriculture. It can highlight, for example, the development of different modes of human-nature interdependency and different types of social mechanisms that evolved in each region. At present, our ability to pursue this kind of cross-regional comparison is limited by the resolution of our archaeological and ecologic data, but the necessary data are fast being accumulated from different regions of China.

A related issue, which also pertains to one of the main themes of this book, is the nature and impact of interregional interaction at this early time. While some hypotheses have been put forward regarding the impact of such interactions on the development of new stone tool techniques in central and south China, for example (Zhang and Hung 2008: 300), scant concrete evidence for such interactions has been identified in the archaeological record. In fact, it is the contemporaneous development of agriculture and sedentary lifeways in different regions of China that constitutes the main "evidence," according to some scholars, for the development of such a network of interactions.

We have clear evidence for meaningful interregional contacts soon *after* the transition to agriculture. For example, rice grains found at the Jiahu site in Henan and dated to the seventh millennium BCE suggest early contact between societies in the Yangzi and Yellow River basins (Crawford 2006: 83–4). But can we push these types of contact to earlier periods? In the absence of concrete relevant data, most discussions of this question are theoretical. The accepted view, implicit in most writing on this subject, is that agriculture emerged in two distinct centers: millet-based agriculture in the middle and lower reaches of the Yellow River basin and rice-based agriculture in the middle and lower reaches of the Yangzi River basin. According to this model, interactions occurred mainly within these regions but rarely between them.

Two subsequent assessments have recently challenged this paradigm: one arguing for a unified sphere in which both millet- and rice-based systems evolved, the other for a much more fragmented process and the development of agriculture in a multicentered landscape. The model that sees agriculture as a unified countrywide phenomenon was most explicitly presented by David Cohen (1998), who argued that the simultaneous development of agriculture in the Yangzi and Yellow River basins could not be coincidental. Rather, this coevolution occurred because of similar climatic trends (the effects of the Younger Dryas event) as well as through interactions and the exchange of ideas. Microliths found in Bashidang (Hunan 2006: 276–85) may suggest interactions between the middle Yangzi River region and regions to the river's north. However, the absence of microliths at most other Yangzi River sites, especially the earlier cave sites, seems to be evidence against the importance of such contact at the earliest stages of the transition to agriculture.

At the other end of the theoretical spectrum, researchers working outside the so-called core regions in the middle and lower reaches of the Yangzi and Yellow River basins have recently argued for a multicentered understanding of the origins of agriculture (Bettinger et al. 2010; Shelach 2000). This model is based on the identification of early domesticants in those "peripheral" regions and on the unique features of the local trajectory and local cultural attributes. It argues that rather than looking for one or two major centers in which agriculture developed and from which it spread to other regions, we should instead reconstruct the local trajectories and observe the indigenous experiments with plant and animal cultivation, even in cases when such experiments did not lead directly to the development of fully fledged agricultural adaptation. These models encourage us to systematically explore the local trajectories in different subregions of China and to continue looking for concrete evidence for both local developments and external contacts.

CHAPTER 4

THE DEVELOPMENT OF AGRICULTURE AND SEDENTARY LIFE IN NORTH CHINA

Starting at around the mid-seventh millennium BCE, north China witnessed one of the most dramatic social, economic, and cultural changes in its history. For hundreds of thousands of years the human occupation of this region had consisted of small groups of mobile hunter-gatherers. Then, within a short period of less than a thousand years, the entire region became populated by much larger sedentary agricultural communities. This change is reflected both in a dramatic increase of the region's population density and in the size of individual communities. During the same period, the economic strategies of the Early Neolithic societies became much more dependent on food production, they adopted far more complex forms of social organization, and interpersonal relations were transformed. These trends were accompanied by meaningful cultural changes – the development of art forms, new types of belief, the careful treatment of the dead, and so on.

Archaeological remains from the very first societies of the Early Neolithic period – those dating to the seventh and early sixth millennia BCE – show a clear departure from the Paleolithic traditions in this region. For example, even the earliest sites from this period are compact villages, where unmistakable remains of houses and other permanent structures can be identified. This is in sharp contrast to the absence of such features at the earlier sites discussed in previous chapters, such as

Nanzhuangtou and Donghulin. This is not to say that the findings imply a complete break between the two periods; on the contrary, I believe that the processes described in Chapter 3 carried through into this period and were responsible for much of what happened during the Early Neolithic age. Nonetheless, the pace of change accelerated and many new material expressions emerged.

Perhaps our incomplete knowledge of the developments during the Late Pleistocene and Early Holocene contributes to our view that changes of the seventh and sixth millennia BCE were "revolutionary." It is probable that new discoveries and more thorough explorations of archaeological sites dating from the twelfth to eighth millennia BCE will shed light on the gradual development of agriculture and sedentism in north China. Nevertheless, even if we assume that the actual gap between the Paleolithic and Neolithic occupation of north China was not as wide as it currently seems, the social, economic, and cultural transformations of the Early Neolithic period are still very dramatic.

This chapter discusses the sedentary agricultural communities that flourished in different regions of north China from the seventh to the fourth millennia BCE. Throughout this and the following chapter, this period is called the Early Neolithic. It is not my intention to enter the debate about the suitability of the term "Neolithic" (lit. the

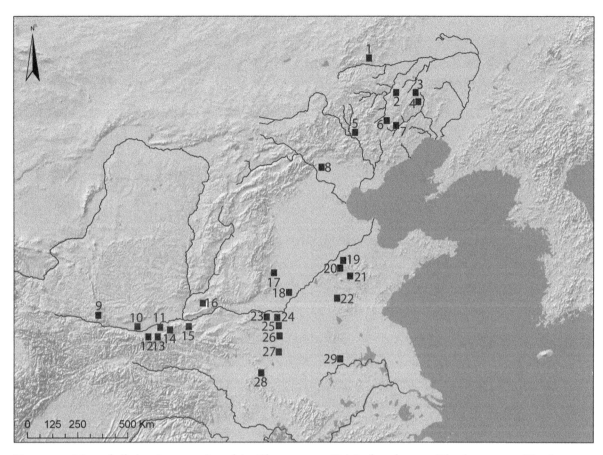

Figure 33. Map of all the sites mentioned in Chapter 4: 1. Baiyinchanghan; 2. Zhaobaogou; 3. Xinglonggou; 4. Xinglongwa; 5. Houtaizi; 6. Niuheliang; 7. Dongshanzui; 8. Shangzhai; 9. Dadiwan; 10. Anban; 11. Shijia; 12. Banpo; 13. Jiangzhai; 14. Yuanjunmiao; 15. Xipo; 16. Xiyincun; 17. Cishan; 18. Xishuipo; 19. Xiaojingshan; 20. Yuezhuang; 21. Dawenkou; 22. Wangyin; 23. Xishan; 24. Dahecun; 25. Peiligang; 26. Tanghu; 27. Jiahu; 28. Xiawanggang; 29. Yuchisi.

"new stone age"), nor do I mean to take a stand on the subdivision of the Chinese Neolithic into subperiods.[1] Rather, the term is used as a shorthand in order to avoid repeating what would otherwise be a rather lengthy definition.

In this chapter I discuss the cultural attributes of societies that populated north China during the Early Neolithic and analyze their economic adaptation, social makeup, and culture. Archaeological discoveries in China are typically classified into "cultures" (wenhua 文化) and "subcultures" (or "types"; leixing 类型), spatiotemporal units that aggregate all the archaeological

remains from a given area at a given period. This classification system has analytical advantages and disadvantages. For the purpose of the following discussion I find it more useful to examine general trends, which tend to transcend "cultural" boundaries and are often incongruent with the geographical or temporal boundaries of any single "culture." However, because the names of cultures are so commonly used to label sites, it is impossible to avoid using them altogether. Throughout this book, these names are therefore of necessity mentioned in the text and also presented in comparative chronological tables.

TABLE 2. *Early Neolithic archaeological cultures of north China*

Date BCE	Northwest (upper Yellow River)	Wei River basin	Middle Yellow River	Lower Yellow River	Northeast
6500 6000		Dadiwan 大地湾 (6200–5400)	Peiligang 裴李岗 (6500–5000) Cishan 磁山 (6500–5000)	Houli 后李 (6500–5500)	Xinglongwa 兴隆洼 (6200–5400)
5500		Shizhaocun 师赵村 (5400–5000)		Beixin 北辛 (5500–4300)	Zhaobaogou 赵宝沟 (5400–4500)
5000		Early Yangshao 仰韶早期 (5000–4000)	Early Yangshao (5000–4000)		
4500				Dawenkou 大汶口 (4300–2600)	Hongshan 红山 (4500–3000)
4000	Middle Yangshao (4000–3500)	Middle Yangshao (4000–3500)	Middle Yangshao (4000–3500)		
3500	Late Yangshao (3500–3000)	Late Yangshao (3500–3000)	Late Yangshao (3500–3000)		
3000					

THE MATERIAL CULTURE OF EARLY NEOLITHIC SOCIETIES IN NORTH CHINA

This section presents an overview of the main archaeological data pertaining to the societies of the Early Neolithic period. By definition, this perspective requires generalization, and I will necessarily gloss over some of the variation between sites and between different regions. The variations between sites will be discussed in a separate section. When reading the following description of the material culture of Early Neolithic north China, the reader should also keep in mind that our knowledge of this period in different regions of north China is far from consistent: for some regions (such as the middle Yellow River basin or the northeast of China) it is quite comprehensive and includes data about a variety of social and economic aspects; but for other regions, such as the lower Yellow River, our data are based primarily on excavations of graves.

Settlement Patterns and Village Organization

Increased population density is one of the variables most commonly associated with the transition to agriculture. It is related to increased economic productivity, as well as to a range of social transformations. In north China at the beginning of the Early Neolithic period, regional population densities were quite low. For instance, within the 219 km² surveyed at the Yiluo River valley in Henan (Liu 2004; Liu et al. 2004; Qiao 2007), only five Peiligang settlements were located, representing a combined total area of 2.3 ha. In northeast China, the Chifeng survey project, which covered an area of 1,234 km² in eastern Inner Mongolia, identified fewer than twenty Xinglongwa sites, covering a total area of 28 ha (Chifeng 2011). The occupation density in these two systematically surveyed regions was 1 ha of occupation per 44 to 95 km². While this ratio represents a low population density, it is nonetheless much higher than it was during any previous period in these regions. Occupation density increased dramatically in both regions toward the end of the Early Neolithic period: in the Yiluo River valley, the number of Middle Yangshao sites increased to ten, and then tripled during the late Yangshao. The area of occupation increased to 46 ha and 76 ha in the two periods, respectively, reaching a ratio of 1 ha of occupation per 2.9 km² at its peak. In the Chifeng area, occupation during the Hongshan period covered an area of 298 ha, or 1 ha of occupation per 4.1 km².

The compact nature of Early Neolithic sites, the size of their population, and their planning suggest that these were true villages and not just small hamlets or scattered households. The earliest sites in the Yellow River and Wei River basins and in the northeast were usually 1 to 2 ha in size, but occasionally as large as 8 ha. The smallest villages comprised only a few households, but it is estimated that the larger ones were home to between 100 and 300 people (Neimenggu 2004). Early Yangshao communities from the middle Yellow River basin and Zhaobaogou (赵宝沟) communities from northeast China were not much larger: based on a surface survey and a sample of excavated houses, it was estimated that the population of the Zhaobaogou site numbered between 236 and 388 people (Shelach 2006: 334), and the population of Jiangzhai (姜寨) has been estimated at between 300 and 400 (Lee 2007; Peterson and Shelach 2012).

A significant change occurred during the latter part of the Early Neolithic, when much larger communities appeared and the hierarchy between small and large communities became much more pronounced. The largest later Yangshao settlements, which seem to have functioned as the central nodes of the local settlement system, ranged from 40 to 90 ha in size (Gansu 2006; Liu 2004: 93; Ma 2005), and are estimated to have had populations of more than one thousand (Qiao 2007). The Xipo (西坡) site in Henan province, dated

to the middle Yangshao period, was about 40 ha in size (Ma 2005). The size of Dadiwan (大地湾), in the Wei River basin, increased from about 8 ha during the earlier phases of the Early Neolithic to about 50 ha during the late Yangshao period (Gansu 2006: 397). The contemporaneous Anban (案板) site, located farther east, but also in the Wei River basin, was about 70 ha in size (Liu 2004: 86–93). Although there was also population growth in northeast China, it seems that no Hongshan site was as large as the biggest sites in the Yellow and Wei River basins.

Most Early Neolithic sites seem to have been carefully preplanned: houses and domestic structures are coordinated with each other; there also seems to be a clear separation between private and public spaces, production sites, ritual areas (including cemeteries), and so on. At several of the Early Neolithic sites, the borders of the residential area are delineated by a ditch. The earliest evidence of such features is found in sites in northeast China, such as Xinglongwa (兴隆洼) and Baiyinchanghan (白音长汗) (where two such enclosures were found). The ditches at these sites are not very large – they are 0.55–1.00 m deep and 1.5–2.0 m wide (Guo et al. 1991; Neimenggu 2004: 41; Shelach 2000: 395–403; Zhongguo Shehui 1985; Zhongguo Shehui Kexueyuan Kaogu Yanjiusuo Neimenggu Gongzuodui 1997) – which suggests that they represent a way of demarcating the site rather than constituting a real defensive barrier (Figure 34). Similar ditches, though not as well preserved, are also known from Peiligang (裴李岗) sites in the middle Yellow River basin, such as Jiahu (贾湖) and Tanghu (唐户), and from the lower Yellow River basin at the Xiaojingshan (小荆山) site (Henan 1999: 128–30; Henan et al. 2008; Shandong 2003). More substantial ditches were found at early Yangshao sites (Figure 35). At Banpo (半坡) and Dadiwan, the ditches are up to 8 m wide and 5 m deep, while at Jiangzhai a smaller ditch averages 2.2 m wide at ground level and 1.0 m wide at its bottom, and is 1.7 m deep (Chang

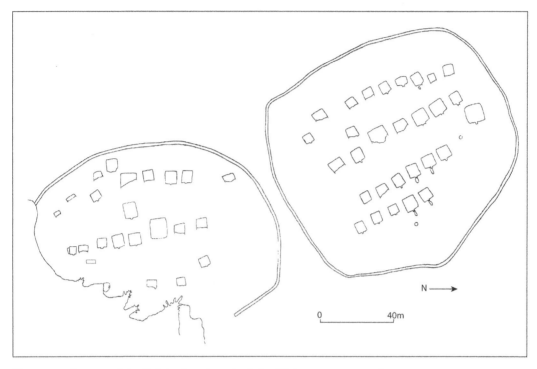

Figure 34. Layout of the Baiyinchanghan site (after Neimenggu 2004: 4).

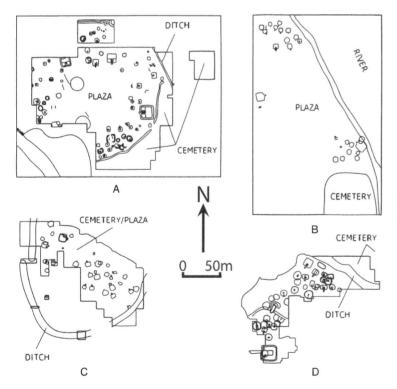

Figure 35. Plans of the Early Yang-shao period villages of Jiangzhai (A), Beishouling (B), Dadiwan (C), and Banpo (D) (after Peterson and Shelach 2010: 254).

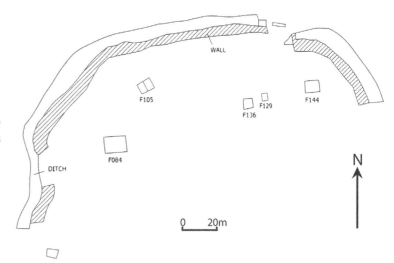

Figure 36. Plan of the Late Yangshao period wall at Xishan (after Peterson and Shelach 2010: 254).

1986: 116; Xian 1988: 51–2, 67). In a few sites dated to the later part of the Early Neolithic both ditches and walls were found. The late Yangshao Xishan (西山) site in central Henan is 25 ha in size, which is smaller than Xipo, Dadiwan, and Anban. However, similar to these sites, it was probably a central node in the local settlement hierarchy. A portion of the Xishan site is enclosed by a roughly circular ditch and a pounded earth wall (Figure 36). The wall, now mostly destroyed, was originally 3 to 5 m wide, 2.5 m high, and about 200 m in diameter, with two gated entry points. The surrounding ditch varied from 4 to 11 m in width and was 4.5 m deep in places (Liu 2004: 93–4).

Another feature common to many Early Neolithic sites is "plazas," or open areas located between the houses, which were presumably used for public activities. The basic layout of an Early Neolithic village is exemplified by Jiangzhai, probably the most completely exposed site from this period. The basic layout of phase I at Jiangzhai can be described as a set of three concentric circles: (1) the innermost open courtyard or plaza; (2) a band of residential structures and storage pits; (3) and a ditch, beyond which lay cemeteries. Two animal pens and two night soil (manure) sheds were located at the periphery of the plaza; five kilns were located on the outer side of the

ditch and two were located inside the village (Figure 37a).

The excavated segment of the residential area of phase I at Jiangzhai (about 70 percent of the total residential area) contains 65 contemporaneous houses and 121 storage and ash pits (Peterson and Shelach 2012). The doorways of all houses opened toward the central plaza, and the pits seem to cluster around individual houses. Some archaeologists have identified five distinct clusters of buildings that divide the Jiangzhai community into five residential sectors. Each cluster consists of several smaller structures grouped around a larger one and separated from the adjacent sectors by narrow zones of unoccupied space (Figure 37b) (Lee 2007; Xian 1988: 67–8; Yan 1999: 136–7). Similar village segmentation has been identified at many other Early Neolithic sites, though these characterizations are by no means universally agreed upon (Peterson and Shelach 2010). In the northeast, sites associated with the Xinglongwa and Zhaobaogou periods do not have central plazas. Instead, houses are organized in orderly rows with their doorways all facing the same direction and a clear separation between private and public spaces (Shelach 2006).

Some sites from the late phases of the Early Neolithic not only are larger than anything seen before, but their organization contains new

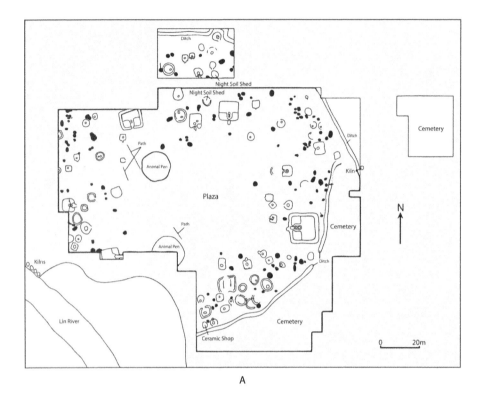

A

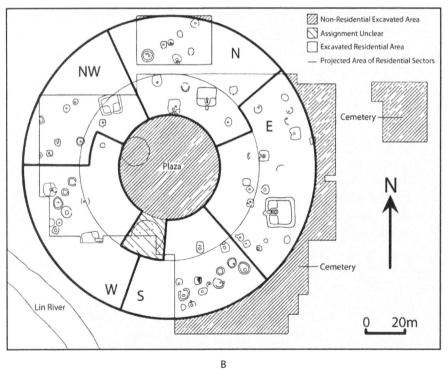

B

Figure 37. A. Layout of Jiangzhai phase I; B. Division of Jiangzhai village into five residential sectors (after Peterson and Shelach 2012).

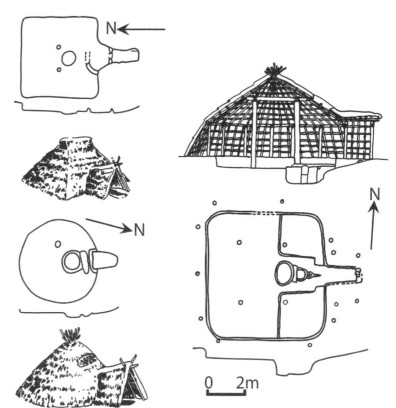

Figure 38. Typical (left) and larger and more elaborate (right) Early Yangshao period dwellings (after Peterson and Shelach 2010: 256).

elements as well. The Xipo site, for example, is centered around a cluster of larger structures constructed on layers of pounded earth foundations (Ma 2005). At Dadiwan, the organization of the early Yangshao village is very similar to that of Jiangzhai, but it was replaced during the late Yangshao by a much more segregated layout: the flat lower area, where the earlier village was located, became occupied by smaller dwellings, installations, and graves, while much larger and more elaborate houses were located on the higher terraces that overlook it (Gansu 2006).

Domestic Structures

House remains dated to the Early Neolithic period reflect a substantial investment of labor. The earliest were single-room, surface-built, or semi-subterranean structures, with timber frame wattle-and-daub walls and thatch roofs. Most houses had pounded earth floors, with shallow hearths for cooking and heating excavated in their centers. Early Yangshao houses found at sites such as Banpo and Jiangzhai are either round or square in shape, and most are between 10 and 30 m² in size with minimal or no internal divisions (Figure 38). A few much larger (up to 100 m² in area) and more elaborate structures have sometimes been interpreted as public and/or ritual facilities, or as the residence of lineage heads (Lee 2001b: 335; Liu 2004: 79–81; Peterson and Shelach 2012; Xian 1988; Yan 1999).

Rectangular semi-subterranean houses are typical to the Xinglongwa and Zhaobaogou periods in northeast China. Houses range between 20 and 80 m² in size, with some larger houses up to 140 m² also reported. At the Zhaobaogou site, houses included shallow rectangular hearths lined with flat stones, and some houses also had niches dug into the back wall and storage pits in the floor. A few

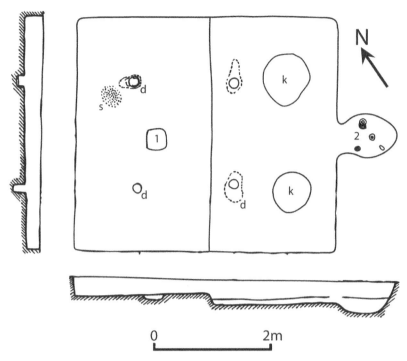

Figure 39. House F6 from the Zhaobaogou site. 1. Hearth; 2. Concentration of artifacts in the niche; d. Posthole; k. Shallow pit; s. Concentration of ashes (after Zhongguo 1997: 29).

of the structures were divided in two, with the floor of the front half slightly elevated and creating a shallow step down to the rear of the house (Figure 39).

During the late phase of the Early Neolithic, single-room houses continued to be the norm, but larger multiroom rows or "apartment blocks" have been found at some late Yangshao sites (Figure 40). Examples of such multiroom structures can be seen at Xiawanggang (下王岗) in southeastern Henan, where a single house measuring 45 m by 5–10 m contained a dozen or more two- to three-room units, as well as several single-room units (Gong 2002: 131–2). At Dahecun (大河村), near Zhengzhou, in north-central Henan, at least three such rows have been identified (Chang 1986: 126–34). Similar structures have also been found in the lower Yellow River region at places such as the late Dawenkou (大汶口) site at Yuchisi (尉迟寺), where fifteen row houses were excavated inside the 2 ha area enclosed by the site's ditch. The shortest structures have only two rooms, but the larger ones

have as many as twelve (Figure 41) (Gao and Luan 2004: 107–9; Zhao 2009). Although they shared common walls, each room had its own entrance, hearth, and separate set of domestic artifacts, suggesting that each was home to a single nuclear family. Some of the small single-room units may have been used as storage facilities (Lee 2001b: 335–46; Zhao 2009; Zhengzhou 2001).

The latter part of the Early Neolithic also witnessed the appearance of special-purpose houses that were probably associated with social stratification and the early emergence of local elites. A few unusually large structures dating to phase IV at Dadiwan have been described by some as "palatial" and are thought to have been the residences of community elites (Liu 2004: 86–8; Yan 1999: 139–40). The largest of these structures (F901) was a multiroomed building covering an area of 290 m² (420 m² including affiliated structures). Its layout included a main room in the center and several small rooms on the two sides and at the back. This main hall was supported by sixteen large posts and

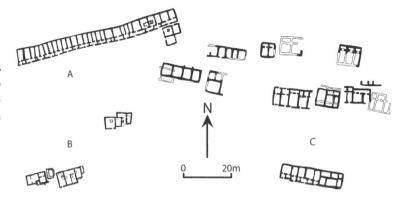

Figure 40. Plans of multiroom houses of the Middle and Late Yangshao period at A. Xiawanggang; B. Dahecun; and C. Baligang (after Peterson and Shelach 2010: 258).

had a big hearth dug into the floor. The building was fronted by a covered porch and a large open plaza of compacted earth (Figure 42) (Gansu 2006: 414–28). At Xipo, each of the central buildings was also quite large (ca. 80 m²). They were constructed atop subsurface pounded earth foundations and had a very long and narrow entrance; their floors and walls were plastered with red pigment (Ma 2005: 29–36).

Other than houses, storage pits are the only type of domestic structure commonly found at Early Neolithic sites. The shape and size of the pits vary considerably, and it is not always easy to tell whether they were used to store food or for garbage disposal. At the Cishan (磁山) site, dated to the beginning of the Early Neolithic, 474 pits were discovered. These pits vary considerably in shape and size. Most are circular or oval and have straight walls, but their depth varies between 0.5 m and more than 5 m (Hebei 1981). Layers of grain were found at the bottom of 88 such pits, suggesting that their main function was indeed the storage of food (Tong 1984). Animal bones and other artifacts found in other pits suggest that some either were originally dug to contain refuse, or were given over to this function after they were no longer considered suitable for grain storage.

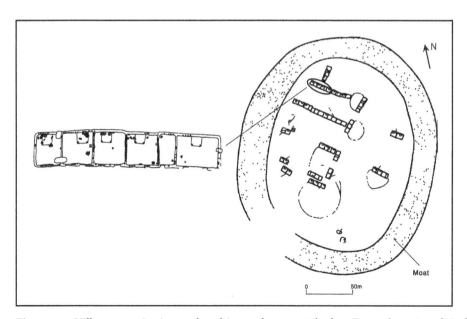

Figure 41. Village organization and multiroom houses at the late Dawenkou site of Yuchisi (after Yang 2004: 69).

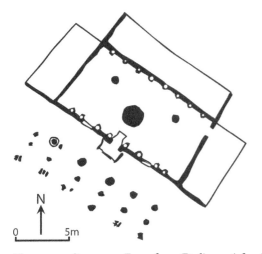

Figure 42. Structure F901 from Dadiwan (after Peterson and Shelach 2010: 256).

The variation in shape and size of the storage pits identified at Cishan is typical of most Early Neolithic sites. The same types of pit, for example, were found at periods 1 to 3 at Dadiwan (Figure 43). At Jiangzhai, the volume of 121 contemporaneous storage pits assigned to the earlier phase varies between 0.23 m³ to 16.75 m³, averaging 2.9 m³ (Peterson and Shelach 2012). Some storage pits from the latter part of the Early Neolithic period have a bell-shaped cross-section (narrow mouth, wider bottom) (Figure 44).

Storage pits are usually found clustered around residential structures, though in some places, such as Cishan, many pits are not associated with any particular house. In northeast China, while some

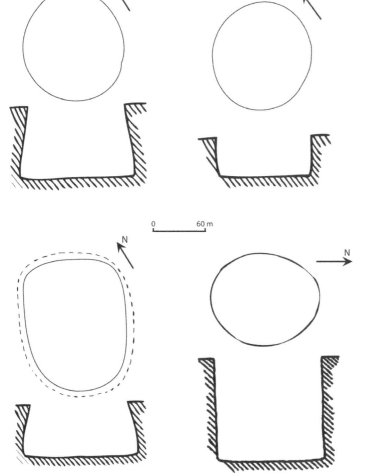

Figure 43. Storage pits from period II at Dadiwan (after Gansu 2006: 117–18).

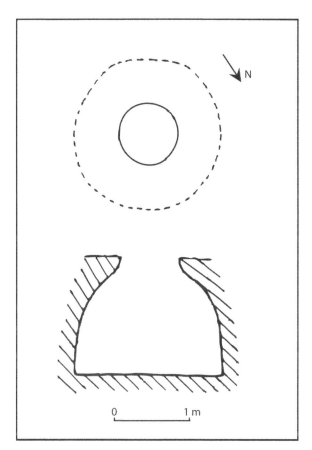

Figure 44. "Ball-shaped" storage pits from period IV at Dadiwan (after Gansu 2006: 454–5).

pits are scattered between the houses, some were excavated inside the houses (Neimenggu 1997; Zhongguo 1997).

Cemeteries, Burials, and Religious Structures

Beliefs about the afterlife as well as some treatment of the dead were probably part of the human experience before the Neolithic period, but evidence for such activities is extremely scarce. This changed dramatically during the Early Neolithic period, from which graves are found at almost every site. In some early sites graves are scattered among the houses, but even at this early phase some sites have a formal cemetery. One of the earliest cemeteries excavated is at the Peiligang site (Li 2003: 112–14). The 114 graves that have been excavated so far are arranged in an orderly fashion: all are oriented more or less in the same direction, and only in a very few cases are newer graves dug into older ones (Figure 45).

The designation of a special area to serve as a cemetery is one of the most interesting developments associated with the beginning of the Neolithic period in north China, since it may imply a clear cognitive distinction between the realms of the living and the dead. This separation is made even clearer during the Yangshao period, when cemeteries are located outside the ditch encircling the habitation area (Figure 35). The orderly placement of the graves and the fact that they do not intrude on one another suggest that they were marked above ground, and that graves were visited by relatives of the

Figure 45. Layout of the cemetery at Peiligang (after Zhongguo Shehui 2010b: 140).

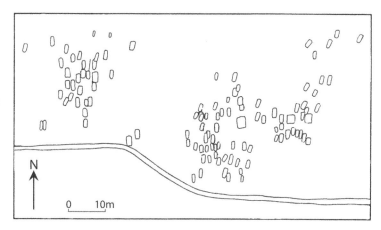

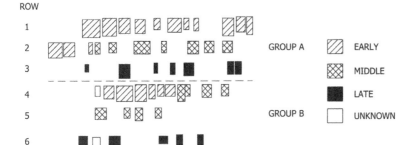

Figure 46. Schematic plan of the Early Yangshao–period cemetery at Yuanjunmiao (after Peterson and Shelach 2010: 258).

deceased not only during the funeral, but during later periods as well. Children, who were often buried under the floor of the house rather than in the formal cemeteries, may have been seen, in this respect, as a separate category, which, even after death, was more closely associated with the living.

Some villages from the Yangshao period have more than one cemetery, and it has been argued that each cemetery was designated for a specific segment of the village population. At Jiangzhai, for example, it is commonly assumed that each cemetery corresponds to the village segment that it faces on the other side of the ditch. At Yuanjunmiao (元君庙), the cemetery is organized in parallel rows.

Based on the artifacts found in graves, archaeologists were able to sort them into three periods (early, middle, and late) and to divide the cemetery into two parts. In each part, the arrangement of the graves is orderly, from the earlier to the later (Figure 46), and it has been suggested that each part of the cemetery belonged to a different segment of the village population (Zhang Zhongpei 1985).

Pre-Yangshao and early Yangshao graves from the Wei and middle Yellow River basins are usually simple shallow pit graves, each containing a single adult interred in the extended position (Figure 47). In northeast China, graves at Xinglongwa sites are shallow pits that are sometimes lined with stone

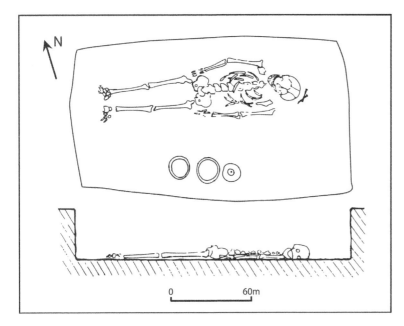

Figure 47. Pit grave from period II at Dadiwan (after Gansu 2006: 271).

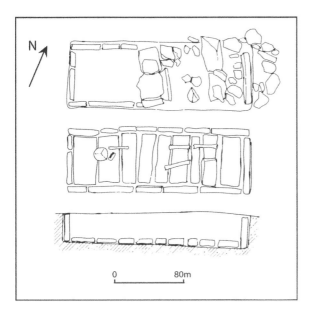

Figure 48. Stone-lined pit grave from the Baiyinchang-han site (after Neimenggu 2004: 31)

slabs and covered with stones (Figure 48). Infants and young children were commonly buried in urns that were interred inside residential areas, between buildings or under house floors (Figure 49).

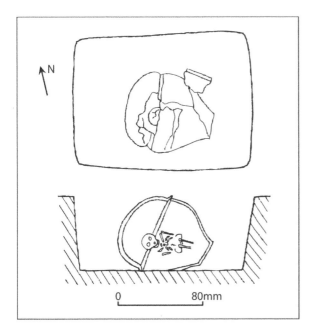

Figure 49. Urn burials of infants from period II at Dadiwan (after Gansu 2006: 273).

Early Neolithic graves usually contain a small number of grave goods, typically a few ceramic vessels, stone tools, and ornaments. For example, among fifty-one pit graves at one of the Jiangzhai cemeteries, forty-one contained grave goods. Altogether, 251 artifacts were found inside these graves: 146 were ceramic vessels, while the rest were smaller stone and bone artifacts (Xian 1988: 53).

Graves from the early phases of the Early Neolithic are largely undifferentiated. Most are of roughly similar size and elaboration, and there is little variation in the quantity or quality of grave goods found inside them. Of the 349 graves excavated at Jiahu, for example, only 2 percent are longer than 2.5 m and only 6.3 percent are deeper than 71 cm (Henan 1999: 139–43). Because most of the relatively large graves contain more than a single interment, the actual variation in size is even smaller. No single interment grave contained more than four ceramic vessels (Henan 1999: 656–701).

Some graves from the beginning of the Early Neolithic contain bones of more than a single interment. The examination of human bones recovered from these graves provides evidence that, while sometimes the individuals found in them were buried immediately after their death, in other cases they were interred as part of a secondary burial – that is, they were first buried elsewhere and then, after their flesh had decayed, the bones were collected and reburied. A few collective burials are found in most sites from this period, but at some sites they are the majority (Figure 50). At Yuanjunmiao, for example, two-thirds of the graves are collective and they contain 92 percent of all the individuals buried in this cemetery. The number of individuals buried in each of the collective graves ranges from two to twenty-five (Zhang Zhongpei 1985).

During the late phases of the Early Neolithic, burial variability increased dramatically, both within each cemetery and between cemeteries.

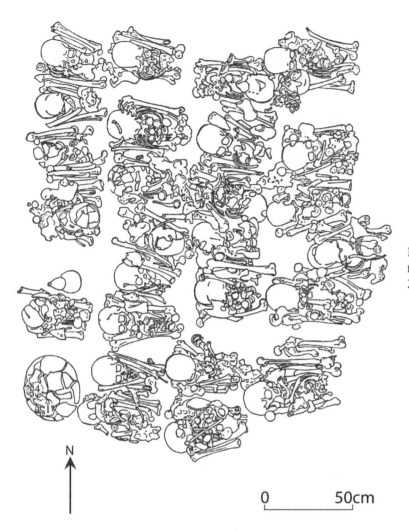

Figure 50. Collective burial M25 from the Shijiacun cemetery (after Zhongguo Shehui 2010b: 256).

N

0   50cm

While simple pit graves containing just a few burial goods remained common, other, much larger, more elaborate, and richer graves also appeared. In many graves a secondary ledge (*ercengtai* 二层 台), upon which offerings were placed, was constructed along the walls of the earth pit. The quality and the number of offerings found in the richer graves far exceed anything seen in this region before. For example, at Xipo, all graves contain a single interment in the supine extended position. Most graves have a secondary ledge, but they vary considerably in terms of size and the amount of goods placed in them (Figure 51). Among a group twenty graves excavated recently, the smallest are 1.8–2.2 m long, 0.6–1.2 m wide, and about 0.6 m deep; the biggest are almost 4 m long, 3.5 m wide, and more than 2 m deep. The quantity and type of grave goods found in these graves, however, are less varied than the differences in size between them. Five of the graves contained no burial goods at all, while the richest grave contained eight ceramic vessels, a large jade axe, and a bone tool (Henan et al. 2008).

We find even more pronounced variation in graves from the Dawenkou period in the lower Yellow River region. At the beginning of this period, in cemeteries such as Wangyin (王因),

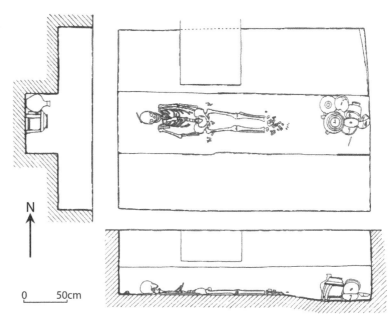

Figure 51. Two graves from Xipo (after Henan et al. 2008: 8).

N

0   50cm

where 789 graves have been excavated, variation is still minimal (Underhill 2002: 92–3). By the late phases of the Dawenkou, however, large differences emerge in terms of the labor invested in the construction of graves and the artifacts placed in them. At the Dawenkou site, graves belonging to the middle Dawenkou period range in size from 0.42 to 8.12 m². While the smaller burials are simple pit graves, larger ones contain a secondary ledge and a wooden coffin. The number of artifacts placed in these grave ranges from none to 106, and the size of the grave tends to correlate with the number of artifacts placed in it (Liu 2004: 138–42; Underhill 2002: 104–13). Variation among graves is expressed not only in terms of size, structure, and the number of grave goods, but also in the quality of the grave goods. Prestige artifacts found mainly in richer graves include expensive ceramic vessels such as tall-legged cups and stemmed dishes with cutout designs, jade objects, carved cylinders made of ivory or bone, and pig mandibles. Grave M10 at the Dawenkou site, 4.2 by 3.2 m with a secondary ledge and a wooden coffin, is a prime example of a prestigious burial: its occupant is an old female, and it contained ninety-three vessels,

many of which were prestige items, as well as a large jade axe, jade ornaments, four pig mandibles, and other animal bones (Figure 52).

Uncommonly large and elaborate graves have also been found in the middle Yellow River region. The most famous example is grave M45 from the Xishuipo (西水坡) site in Henan (Figure 53) (Puyang 1989). The grave measures 4.1 by 3.1 m and has a keyhole shape. The main occupant, a tall adult male, lies in the center of the grave surrounded by the remains of three adolescents (two males and one female), who appear to have been killed so as to accompany him in death. In addition, hundreds of clam shells are arranged on either side of the principal's body to form representations of a tiger and a dragon. A third pictograph, sometime identified as the "celestial Big Dipper ladle" or as representing an axe, was drawn using two human tibiae placed perpendicular to a smaller triangular pile of shells at his feet.

Secondary burials were not common during the latter part of the Early Neolithic, with the exception of a unique burial tradition typical to the Luoyang area (in the central Yellow River region) during the middle and late Yangshao period,

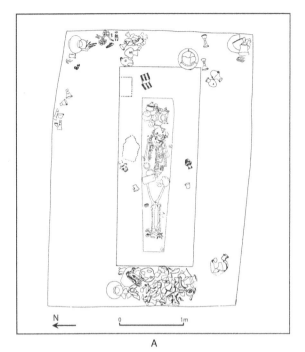

A

B

Figure 52. A. Grave M10 from Dawenkou; B. Grave goods found inside grave M10 from Dawenkou (after Gao and Luan 2004: 123–4).

namely, the secondary urn burial of adults. The urns, which were probably specially made for this purpose, are fairly tall (30 cm or more), with some decorated with unique polychrome paintings (Ding 2008; Liu 2004: 132–3).

In northeast China, formal cemeteries are not known from the Hongshan period, and most individual graves either form parts of larger ceremonial structures or are located in stone piles (or "cairns"). Some of the burials in this region are secondary, but most are single primary burials. Each structure includes one central interment and additional, smaller graves surrounding it. The burial chamber is made of stone slabs, and even the biggest graves are quite small: only just big enough to contain their occupant in the extended position (Figure 54). Each grave contains few, but very expensive burial goods; mostly exquisite jade artifacts, some of which had probably been used by the deceased either as necklaces or as ornamentation on their clothes (Guo 1995a: 33–6; Liaoning 1997).

Northeast China is the only region where there are clear indications of the construction of ritual structures during the Early Neolithic period. Some structures date to the Zhaobaogou period (Zhongguo 1997: 127–8), but most are from the Hongshan period. The most famous Hongshan ritual structures are located at sites such as Niuheliang (牛河梁) and Dongshanzui (东山嘴), which have been identified as ritual centers. However, the division between ritual and domestic functions at these sites is not as clear-cut as some would have it: domestic activities, including habitation, probably took place at the so-called ritual centers, and ceremonial structures are also found at domestic sites (Peterson et al. 2010).

The Niuheliang complex, in western Liaoning province, has more than ten related sites within a 50 km² area, at the center of which stands the so-called Goddess Temple, an elongated structure of irregular shape, 25 m long and 2–9 m wide, constructed on a large earthen platform nearly

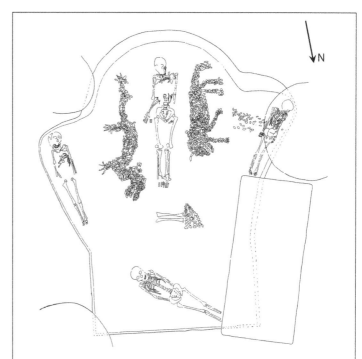

Figure 53. Xishuipo grave M45 (after Yang Xiaoneng 2004: 2:54).

Figure 54. A Hongshan grave from Niuheliang (courtesy of Liaoning Institute of Archaeology and Cultural Relics).

Figure 55. The Goddess Temple at Niuheliang (courtesy of Liaoning Institute of Archaeology and Cultural Relics).

3 ha in size (Figure 55). The remains of life-size clay sculptures of humans and animals, probably originally attached to its walls, have been found inside the "temple" structure. One of the sculptures is a well-preserved female figure, hence the structure's name (Figure 56) (Barnes and Guo 1996; Liaoning 1997).

There are some thirty ritual structures in the area surrounding the Goddess Temple. The largest cluster is at locality 2, which contains three large circular structures, one rectangular and one square structure, as well as a few smaller ones (Figure 57). All these structures are made of stone and earth, and their external diameter is about 20 m at the base. Hundreds of bottomless, painted pottery cylinders, each 50 cm high, were placed around each of the structures (Figure 58). Those structures are sometime identified as altars, and those in which burials are incorporated as cairns (Guo 1995a; Liaoning 1997).

The Production of Artifacts

Artifacts found at Early Neolithic sites and graves provide evidence for a rapid growth in technological capabilities and in the scale of production. Artifacts such as ceramic vessels, stone tools, and ornaments made with semiprecious stones are important evidence for the development of the socioeconomic system of Early Neolithic

Figure 56. The Goddess statue from the Goddess Temple at Niuheliang (courtesy of Liaoning Institute of Archaeology and Cultural Relics).

villages and suggest the incipient development of craft specialization, division of labor, and exchange networks.

Although, as discussed in Chapter 3, ceramic production had already gotten under way in China during the Late Pleistocene, the quantity and quality of shards found at sites from the Late Pleistocene and Early Holocene suggest a relatively low level of production. In contrast, even very Early Neolithic sites from different regions have yielded large quantities of ceramic vessels and potshards. The large number of kilns found at Early Neolithic sites also suggests production on a larger and much more systematic scale than before. At the Jiangzhai site alone, remains of seven kilns have been located (Xian 1988: 48–9), and their clustering in areas outside the village ditch suggests that production was regulated.

In comparison with earlier periods, Early Neolithic ceramics were of much better quality, and continued to improve throughout the period. While the shape and style of ceramic vessels vary considerably from region to region, the general trajectory is similar: throughout the Early Neolithic the firing temperature increased, producing much less crumbly wares; improved control over the firing atmosphere was attained, resulting in vessels of more homogeneous color and quality; and the quality of clay and the techniques for shaping it both improved, producing more elegant and complex types of vessels.

The earliest ceramic vessels of the Early Neolithic were molded by hand and were usually simple in shape. Within each of the regional "cultures," the number of vessel shapes is relatively small: While some legged vessels were found in the middle Yellow River region, most vessels have flat bases, straight walls, and a simple mouth. Incised and stamped decorations are common (Chang 1986: 93–5; Shelach 2000) (Figure 59). The most notable development of the early Yangshao period is the appearance of colored decorations, which were achieved by oxidizing iron minerals, which required a high degree of control over the atmosphere inside the kiln. While the vessels retained their simple shapes, the red and black decorations of some vessels are quite sophisticated (Figure 60). Similar colored decorations at this time are unknown at other regions, but other decorations were seen, and to some extent shapes of vessels were becoming more sophisticated as well.

During the late phases of the Early Neolithic an overall increase in the diversity, quality, technological sophistication, and dimensional standardization of ceramic vessels all suggest the beginnings of more specialized pottery production. Color decorations were by now far more widely spread, appearing in northeast China (Hongshan), in the lower Yellow River region (Dawenkou), and in the Wei River region (Underhill 2002). More significant perhaps, vessels took on much more

Figure 57. Locality 2 at Niuheliang (courtesy of Liaoning Institute of Archaeology and Cultural Relics).

elaborate shapes, and production techniques, which included the use of molds and the early use of the potter's wheel, became more sophisticated. Middle and late Dawenkou vessels, with their elaborate shapes and sometimes composed of multiple pieces, offer a prime example of this increased sophistication (Figure 61), but similar developments have been documented in other regions as well.

During the Early Neolithic, stone tool production continued in the tradition of earlier periods in north China. Microliths and stone blades are quite common in early sites. Ground stones are also commonly found, including large tools now identified as spades and hoes. Indeed, agricultural tools in China continued to be made of stone, wood, and bone, up until they were replaced by iron tools during the late-first millennium BCE. At the earlier sites of the Early Neolithic, grinding slabs (or querns) became even more common than before (Figure 62).

One of the most interesting developments in Early Neolithic craftsmanship is the production of items laboriously carved from hard semiprecious stones such as jade and turquoise. Small jade ornaments first appear in graves of the Xinglongwa period in northeast China, but the carving of jade and other hard stones reached its peak in

Figure 58. One of the stone structures at locality 2 and a typical ceramic cylinder found near it (courtesy of Liaoning Institute of Archaeology and Cultural Relics).

this region during the Hongshan. Many Hongshan graves contain jade objects, some quite large and labor-intensive. They were carved in the shape of real and mythological animals, or as geometrical plaques and tubes. Many of them have holes, suggesting that they were used as pendants or were stitched to their owner's clothes (Figures 63A and 63B) (Guo 1995a).

Although less common, evidence for the production and consumption of artifacts made from hard stones can also be found in other regions of north China. At the Xipo site, for example, six of

Dadiwan   Houli

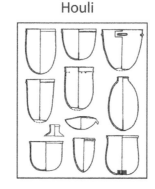

Cishan

Figure 59. Comparison of ceramic vessels from the Peiligang, Cishan, Dadiwan, Houli, and Xinglongwa sites (after Zhongguo Shehui 2010b: 116; 152; 143; 131; 159).

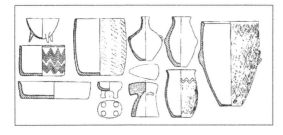

Peiligang

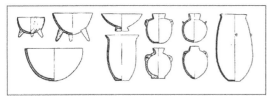

Xinglongwa

twenty-two graves contained jade artifacts. Some of them are quite large, including a large polished jade axe (*yue* 钺) measuring 17 by 6 cm (Figure 63C) (Ma et al. 2006).

THE ECONOMIC ADAPTATION OF EARLY NEOLITHIC SOCIETIES IN NORTH CHINA

Agriculture, as defined in Chapter 3, was widespread in north China by the beginning of the Early Neolithic period. Morphological evidence for domesticated plants and animals has been found at sites in all of the different subregions of north China, alongside tools that suggest the systematic cultivation of agricultural fields. However, it should not be assumed that once agriculture existed it become the only viable economic mode. This section also addresses evidence regarding the socioeconomic organization of early villages.

Domesticated Plants

The traditional staple food of north China was millet, and it is assumed that the two species of

Figure 60. Early Yangshao vessels decorated with colored patterns (photos by Gideon Shelach).

millet, foxtail millet (*Setaria italica*) and broomcorn millet (*Panicum miliaceum*), were both domesticated in this region. Earlier evidence for broomcorn

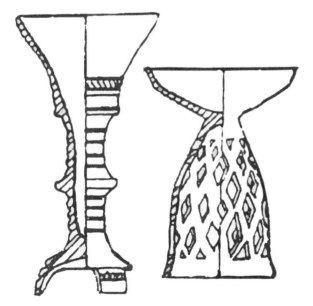

Figure 61. Elaborate Dawenkou vessels (*gu* cup and *dou* stemmed dishes) (after Gao and Luan 2004: 60).

millet is dated to the seventh or early sixth millennia BCE. Grains of broomcorn millet were recovered from the Xinglonggou (兴隆沟) site, in eastern Inner Mongolia, the lower strata at Dadiwan in the Wei River basin, at the Yuezhuang (月庄) site in the lower Yellow River region, and at Peiligang sites in the middle Yellow River basin (Barton et al. 2009; Liu and Chen 2012: 82–5; Zhao 2004). A recent study of phytoliths recovered from the earth inside the storage pits at Cishan suggests that broomcorn millet was cultivated there from around 8000 BCE, and that foxtail millet appeared in small quantities after about 6500 BCE (Lu et al. 2009).[2] If confirmed, these would be the earliest domesticated plants in China, but the dating accuracy in this study is still being debated. Grains of these two types of millet have been found in large quantities at sites dated to the fifth millennium BCE and later throughout all regions of north China.

Soybean (*Glycine max*) is another important food in north China. Although not actually a cereal, it is

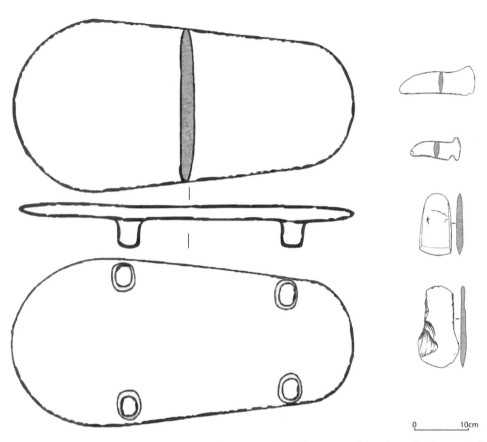

0   10cm

Figure 62. Grinding stones, agricultural stone tools, and stone sickles from Peiligang (after Zhongguo Shehui 2010b: 133).

one of the "five grains" (or basic food) celebrated in the classic Chinese texts. Because it is difficult to distinguish between domestic and wild varieties, the date and location of soybean domestication remain contested. Wild soybean seeds have been found at Early Neolithic sites, such as Jiahu (Zhao and Zhang 2009), but most scholars believe that it was not domesticated until the Late Neolithic and that it became widely used only during the Bronze Age (Liu and Chen 2012: 85–91). Hemp (*Cannabis sativa*) may also have been domesticated and used in Yangshao communities for the production of oil and fibers, but evidence of its domestication is scarce (Crawford 2006: 81).

Early rice remains have also been found at the Jiahu site (Zhao and Zhang 2009), representing the northernmost extension of rice exploitation at this early date, but it is unclear whether this was fully domesticated rice (see Chapter 5). Wheat (*Triticum* spp.), barley (*Hordeum vulgare*), and oats (*Avena* sp.) were introduced to north China from West Asia, but not before the Late Neolithic and Early Bronze age period (Crawford 2006: 78–80; Flad et al. 2010; Lee et al. 2007).

Domesticated Animals

Animal domestication went hand in hand with the domestication of plants in north China. Dogs had already been domesticated to serve as guarding and hunting animals in previous periods; however, the main food producing animals in China were

Figure 63. Early Neolithic jade artifacts: A. Typical Hongshan artifacts; B. Jade axe (*yue*) from the Xipo site; C. Dawenkou artifacts (photos by Gideon Shelach [A and C] and Gary Lee Todd [B]).

domesticated during the Early Neolithic period. Among these animals, the pig (*Sus domesticus*) was the most important, both as a source of meat and as a status symbol. It is probable that pigs were domesticated simultaneously in more than one place (Flad et al. 2007), including in the Yangzi River basin and north China. In north China, the oldest evidence for domesticated pigs comes from the Jiahu and Cishan sites (Yuan Jing 2008), but it is likely that domesticated pigs were raised in contemporaneous sites as well. By the early Yangshao period there is plentiful evidence for the importance of pigs, including the animal sheds constructed at the Jiangzhai site and the numerous pig bones found at various sites. By the later part of the Early Neolithic, pig bones, including complete skulls or mandibles, are found in graves and pig figurines and statues are also known, indicating the ritual significance and prestige attached to the animal (Kim 1994)).

Data on the domestication of other mammals in north China are not as complete as we would like. Domesticated cattle (*Bos taurus*) bones have been tentatively identified at Jiangzhai, but these findings are disputed, and it is unclear whether cattle were domesticated locally or originated from West Asia or India (Flad et al. 2007: 192–3). Sheep and goats were probably introduced to China from West Asia. It is unclear when they first appeared in north China, but it was probably either during the late stages of the Early Neolithic or, more likely, during the Late Neolithic (Flad et al. 2007: 193). Domesticated horse and camel were introduced to China at an even later stage.

In addition to mammals, other types of animals were also important components of the agricultural complex of north China. One such animal is the domestic chicken (*Gallus gallus domesticus*). Like the pig, the chicken was most likely domesticated in several different places simultaneously, including in China (Liu et al. 2006). Bones of domesticated chicken have been identified at Cishan (Zhou 1981), but the extent to which they were exploited during the Early Neolithic is debated. Another important animal was the silkworm (*Bombyx mori*). Remains of a silkworm cocoon found at Xiyincun (西阴村), in Shanxi province, suggest that silkworm domestication and the production of silk started in north China during the Early Neolithic period (Chang 1986: 113).

The Economic Base of Early Neolithic Societies

The identification of domesticated plants and animals has traditionally been viewed as evidence that the transition from hunter-gathering to agriculture was complete by the Early Neolithic. The Cishan site is seen as one of the prime examples of this transition. The capacity of the eighty-eight excavated storage pits, with their thick layers of millet remains, has been estimated at around 70,000 kg

(Tong 1984: 197). This quantity of grain could easily have fed the entire population of the village, thus suggesting a heavy reliance on agriculture. Stone tools identified as sickles, spades, and axes are interpreted as representative of the agricultural orientation of the Cishan and Peiligang villages. The more than two hundred grinding slabs and hand stones found at Cishan, as well as similar artifacts found in other contemporaneous sites, are all associated with the processing of domesticated cereals (Chang 1986: 88–93; Tong 1984).

This idealized view of Early Neolithic village economy being predominantly based on agriculture has been challenged in recent years. Large quantities of wild animal bones and wild plants have also been recovered from Cishan and contemporaneous sites in all regions of north China. For example, plants such as wild walnuts (*Juglans regia*), hazelnuts (*Corylus heterophylla*), and hackberry (*Celtis bungeana*) have been recovered from pits at Cishan (Hebei 1981); and of the twenty-three animal species identified at that site by their bones, deer are the most numerous. Other wild animals include boar, cattle, hares, fish, turtles, and shellfish (Zhou 1981).

Similar findings are reported from other sites dating to the beginning of the Early Neolithic period. At Jiahu, for example, a systematic floatation of earth samples from the 2001 excavation season recovered the charred remains of twenty-four types of plant. These included rice, wild soybean, wild fruits (such as grapes), tubers (such as lotus), nuts (such as acorns), water plants (such as water chestnut, *Trapa spp*), and weeds (Zhao and Zhang 2009). In addition, the bones and shells of thirty-eight animal species, including mammals, birds, fish, shellfish, and turtles, were also found at the site (Henan 1999: 784–805). Based on the large quantity of fish bones and the relative quantity of rice in the flora assemblage, a recent analysis concluded that the village of Jiahu subsisted mainly on fishing, hunting, and gathering, with agriculture and animal husbandry playing only a secondary role (Zhao and Zhang 2009).

It appears, then, that the economy of the earliest Neolithic villages was still largely based on wild resources, with domesticated food gaining importance only gradually. Grinding tools, once seen as evidence of the prominence of domesticated cereals, could actually have been used for processing wild nuts such as acorns. This is the case not only for pre-Neolithic sites, as discussed in Chapter 3, but also for Early Neolithic communities. For example, the most abundant remains of plant starch recovered from grinding stones at the Shangzhai (上宅) site, near Beijing, were from acorns, while millet was only the second most common (Yang et al. 2009).

Scientific studies of human and animal bones lend support to this alternative reconstruction of Early Neolithic economy. For example, a study of fifty-three human skeletons from the Xinglongwa site found a relatively low incidence of the pathologies that are usually associated with the transition to agriculture – iron deficiency, for example, or anemia, periosteal reactions, and dental cavities – thereby suggesting a relatively low level of reliance on agriculture (Smith 2005). An analysis of carbon (δ^{13}C) and nitrogen (δ^{15}N) isotopic composition in human and animal bone collagen from the Dadiwan site suggests that, during its earlier stage, the occupants' diet was based primarily on wild resources, with very little consumption of millet (Barton et al. 2009). Similar results are also reported from an analysis of human bones recovered at Houli period sites in the lower Yellow River basin (Hu et al. 2008).

By the Yangshao period, the proportion of domestic food in the human diet seems to have increased considerably. Although hunting did not altogether cease, isotopic analysis of human bones from such sites as Jiangzhai, Shijia (史家), and level 2 at Dadiwan shows that millet provided up to 80 percent of the human diet. Not only humans but also pigs and dogs consumed millet in large quantities (Barton et al. 2009; Pechenkina et al. 2005). These findings are also supported by the signs of stress, disease, and malnutrition found in human bones from Shijia (Smith 2005).

THE SOCIOPOLITICAL AND ECONOMIC ORGANIZATION OF EARLY NEOLITHIC VILLAGES IN NORTH CHINA

In all regions of north China we can identify the gradual process of transformation from a relatively egalitarian society and more or less autonomous villages during the early part of the Early Neolithic, to a more complex and stratified society and the initial emergence of social and economic formations that transcended the local community by the latter part of it. To avoid biases, I prefer not to use loaded terms such as "tribe" or "chiefdom" to describe Early Neolithic society. Instead, I use the more neutral expressions of "stratification" and "social complexity." Stratification refers to the vertical gaps between individuals in terms of their prestige, political power, and wealth, while social complexity connotes the horizontal diversification and specialization of individuals and social institutions. The developments of stratification and social complexity are related, but are not identical processes. Especially during the initial phases described here, a society could be quite complex – with evidence for craft specialization and a differentiation of the society into subgroups according to kinship, age, gender, and so on – while disparities in wealth and political power remained minimal.

Archaeological correlates for stratification are found in domestic contexts or in graves. Differences in house size, the quality of materials from which they were built, and the quality and type of artifacts (including food remains) found in them suggest wealth and power differentials between families and individuals. Although graves have ritual contexts, archaeologists assume a correlation between the power and prestige people enjoyed during their lifetime and the treatment they receive after death. We cannot assume, of course, that it is a straightforward one-to-one correlation. As we know from both historical and ethnographic studies, some societies tend to highlight differences, while others tend to downplay them; nonetheless, we assume that every society has certain norms that govern social relations and their mortuary expressions, and that the systematic study of a large enough sample of graves from a given prehistoric society will reveal its rules. The differences between graves can be quantified in terms of the labor invested in their construction and the artifacts placed in them, but also in terms of the presence of unique artifacts or symbols that represent political or religious authority. The analysis of human bones found in graves can point to signs of malnutrition and the effects of hard labor, thus providing direct evidence for economic and political disparities.

The most common correlate for social complexity is evidence of full-time craft specialization. A society in which some people devote all of their working hours to the production of a single type of artifact such as ceramic vessels or jade ornaments must have systems that support the exchange of these products for food. In many instances it also entails the existence of other institutions and specialists who use those products. However, determining whether an artifact was produced by a full-time specialist can be a particularly tricky undertaking. The identification of workshops, production tools, and manufacturing debris, and their association with specific households, may be another indication of craft specialization.

Hierarchy and Social Complexity during the Early Part of the Early Neolithic Period

Little evidence is found in the archaeological data for either vertical gaps or the horizontal diversification of societies in north China during the beginning of the Early Neolithic. In the early villages there are only minor differences in the size of houses and their associated storage facilities. Differences in the size of graves and the labor invested in their construction and furnishing are also minor. The development of a ceramics industry can be seen as evidence for increased technological knowledge, but it is improbable that it required full-time (or even part-time) specialization. The enclosure of some communities by ditches may have required village-wide coordination. However, the construction of ditches of the kind discovered at Baiyinchanghan, Jiahu, Tanghu, and Xiaojingshan would not have necessitated a great deal of labor and, therefore, we should not assume that permanent social institutions would have been needed in order to support it.

As a whole, in villages from the second phase of the Early Neolithic – those identified with the early Yangshao, Zhaobaogou, and early Dawenkou periods – the architecture, patterns of community settlement, and mortuary practices suggest the continuation of an earlier, fundamentally egalitarian form of social organization. Some of the attributes defined as representing the beginning of the Early Neolithic became more pronounced, suggesting the inception of social complexity. For example, the ditches at sites such as Banpo and Dadiwan are much more impressive, requiring more work to construct, and perhaps a more stable division of labor and a coordinated workforce. Findings related to ceramics production – the sophisticated colored decorations of early Yangshao ceramics, the identification of special areas for the firing of pottery and, perhaps, for ceramic production – at such sites as Jiangzhai also suggest the development of some degrees of craft specialization.

At early Yangshao sites such as Banpo and Jiangzhai, a few of the houses are much larger and more elaborate than the rest. The prevalent interpretation is that these houses served as public and/or ritual facilities (Lee 2001b: 335; Liu 2004:

79–81; Xian 1988), thereby signifying the emergence of social complexity. However, domestic features located inside the houses, such as hearths, and the mostly domestic artifacts excavated from their floors identify these structures as the residences of lineage heads or other important persons (Peterson and Shelach 2012). These findings, then, might support the argument for the development of social complexity – the division of the community into several subunits, such as large lineages – but could also be interpreted as evidence of the initial development of stratification.

There is scant mortuary evidence suggesting differences in social status between individuals during the early Yangshao period in the middle Yellow River basin and the Wei River basin, or in the Beixin and early Dawenkou periods in the lower Yellow River basin. Adult graves exhibit only minor variation in the quantities of utilitarian goods among the offerings, while objects that could plausibly be interpreted as prestige goods were rarely interred with the deceased. The interment of a few children or adolescents with large numbers of beads has been interpreted as signaling a status that was ascribed at birth rather than being achieved during the lifetime of the deceased (Xian 1988). Given the larger social context, however, it is more likely that they received this treatment as a result of ceremonial considerations unrelated to their status in life.

The Economic Organization of Villages during the Early Part of the Early Neolithic

If we take the extensively studied Jiangzhai site as an example, the Early Neolithic village, as a whole, seems to be a self-sufficient economic unit. The combined volume of the 121 contemporaneous storage pits ascribed to phase I is 345.7 m^3. It has been estimated that even if only a part of this storage capacity was used at any given point in time, it would have contained more than enough grain to feed the entire community for a whole year

(Peterson and Shelach 2012). However, the manner in which these and other resources were produced and distributed among different households in Jiangzhai is an equally important question.

According to one assessment, the production, accumulation, and redistribution of resources in the early Yangshao communities were regulated at the level of the village residential sector, by the lineage heads. Differences in the proportional composition of the artifact assemblages in the various sectors are seen as indicative of differential sector-level participation in certain kinds of economic activity (e.g., farming, animal husbandry, or stone tool manufacture), the products of which were then exchanged for those of other sectors (Lee 2001b: 336; Liu 2004: 8, 113–14; Yan 1999: 137). This view suggests the emergence of a complex economic system with a very low level of economic stratification.

An opposing view holds that production, resource pooling, and consumption were all organized primarily at the household level (Peterson and Shelach 2012). Differences in the proportional composition of household artifact assemblages and patterns of refuse disposal indicate that some households had begun to focus on particular economic activities. The tight clustering of storage pits around individual homes in Jiangzhai also implies the privatization of household resources, or "restrictive sharing," while differences in household storage capacity (which do not correlate with household size) suggest disparities in resource accumulation. These differences suggest greater economic interdependence, and thus a level of economic complexity unrelated to purported village segmentation. They also suggest an incipient level of economic stratification. This initial stratification may have been intensified by families who sought to exploit (however modestly) new economic opportunities within the village, or to provide themselves with a greater degree of economic security. Similar trends of incipient accumulation of wealth by individualized households have also observed in societies of the Zhaobaogou period in northeast China (Shelach 2006).

THE EMERGENCE OF STRATIFICATION, SOCIAL COMPLEXITY, AND REGIONAL POLITIES DURING THE LATE PHASES OF THE EARLY NEOLITHIC

The shift to greater stratification and more complex forms of social organization seems to have accelerated during the late phases of the Early Neolithic, as represented by findings from the middle and late Yangshao, the middle and late Dawenkou, and the Hongshan periods. In some regions of the middle Yellow River basin and the Wei River basin, the clustering of smaller sites around one or two particularly large sites suggests the formation of a settlement hierarchy and polities that transcended the individual village (Liu 2004: 164–8). The clustering of the Hongshan population around large ritual sites might represent similar processes among societies in northeast China (Drennan and Peterson 2006). Such processes, while still at their incipient stage, paved the way for the emergence, during the Late Neolithic and the Bronze Age, of much larger and much more stratified regional polities and, eventually, states (Chapters 6, 7, and 8).

The construction of expensive public structures, such as the earthen walls found at some late Yangshao and Dawenkou sites, or the temples found at Hongshan sites, required the pooling of resources and coordination by leaders or persons of higher status who resided in the central nodes of the settlement clusters. Extraordinarily large and elaborate single houses, such as F901 from Dadiwan (Figure 42), could have been the residences of these newly emergent leaders. The organization of the village also reflects the transition from a group-oriented and more or less egalitarian society to a more centralized and hierarchical social system. This can be seen at Dadiwan in the transition from the concentric, community-oriented layout of the

early Yangshao village to one in which larger and more elaborate houses are located on higher terraces (Gansu 2006).

The exceptionally large, complex, and rich graves that have been found in cemeteries dated to this period are probably the burial sites of community leaders and elite. Grave M10 from the Dawenkou site, which was much larger than the average Dawenkou grave and contained more than a hundred burial goods and remains of animal offerings (Figure 52), is a prime example. Certain burial goods, like the large polished jade axes found at a few graves at the Xipo site, are seen by scholars as representative of the authority of the emerging leaders.

Xishuipo grave M45 (Figure 53) has often been taken to be a "shaman's" grave (Liu 2004: 155; Underhill and Habu 2006). However, James (1993) has persuasively argued against the reading of symbols it contains as supernatural and celestial: The "dragon," for example, is more likely a common alligator. Similarly, she argues that the interpretation of the shells and human bones found at the feet of its main occupant as representing the ladle of the Big Dipper is equally tenuous, and that they are just as likely to represent an axe. This grave, therefore, is more likely to have been the resting place of a sociopolitical leader. The presence of other individuals in the grave, probably killed to accompany the main occupant in death, represents the ability of such leaders (in this case, not the occupant of the grave, who was already dead, but his successor) to rule over the lives and deaths of the common people.

Increasing indications of interpersonal and intercommunity violence are probably also related to the hierarchical nature of society. The earthen walls that surrounded central settlements suggest that rival regional polities conflicted with one another. However, the fact that in Xishan, for example, only a small portion of the site is enclosed by a ditch and a pounded earth wall may suggest that internal conflicts were no less endemic. At the same site, several mutilated (including decap-itated) skeletons found in abandoned storage pits are direct evidence that violence was not only a threat, but a reality. Similar evidence has also been found in other late Yangshao sites (Liu 2004: 46; Yang 1997; Zhengzhou 1979: 341).

The growing economic interdependence of later Yangshao households is inferred from their amalgamation into the long multiroom houses. Each row of dwellings seems to represent an eco-nomically cooperative multifamily household, and new apartments appear to have been built directly on to the ends of rows as needed. In other words, these additions represent the expansion of multi-family households over time (Peterson and Shelach 2010).

Craft specialization is suggested by the time-consuming production of jade artifacts such as those found at Hongshan ritual sites (Figure 63), as well as by the technically challenging production of tall cups and other ceramics of the Dawenkou period (Figure 61). Another indication of special-ization and exchange is found at the Xipo site, where some households have been identified as engaging in the production of cinnabar powder, a relatively rare mineral pigment used throughout the middle Yellow River valley in funerary rites and in decorating pottery (Liu 2004: 83–5; Ma 2005).

Skeletal indicators of diet and physical stress from the later Yangshao period through to Late Neolithic Longshan times (2800–1900 BCE) indi-cate an increase in manual labor. This may be related to agricultural intensification, or it may sig-nify increased stratification and the pressure now exerted by the elite on the common population to produce more. Likewise, stratification is also sug-gested by evidence for growing differences in the quality of foodstuffs consumed by individuals dur-ing the latter part of the Early Neolithic (Pechenk-ina et al. 2002; Pechenkina et al. 2005; Smith 2005). All of this evidence indicates an increase in the complexity of the economic system as well as

more restricted access to prestigious products and foods.

REGIONAL VARIABILITY AND INTERREGIONAL INTERACTIONS DURING THE EARLY NEOLITHIC PERIOD IN NORTH CHINA

In the earlier discussion on the advent of agricul-ture, a village way of life, and the development of socioeconomic complexity and stratification, the data were presented as if belonging to a single tra-jectory shared by societies from all the subregions of north China. However, this apparent homo-geneity masks much variation between the differ-ent regions. This variability is best exemplified by "cultural" attributes such as the shape and deco-rations of ceramic vessels. However, it also goes much deeper, and in some cases, we can identify meaningful variations in modes of socioeconomic organization. At the same time, it is important to note that Early Neolithic societies did not develop in isolation, and it can be demonstrated that by this period regional and interregional interactions had become more frequent.

Broadly speaking, three main ceramic traditions of the Early Neolithic period can be distinguished: the Yangshao tradition of the Wei River and mid-dle Yellow River, typified by relatively simple forms and colored decorations (Figure 60); the Dawenkou tradition of the lower Yellow River with its emphasis on elaborate forms (Figure 61); and the Xinglongwa-Hongshan tradition of the northeast, whose typical vessels are simple in shape and have incised or stamped decorations. We can find a similar regional variation in other industries, such as jade artifacts production, as well.

On the one hand, our ability to track a tradi-tion (with modifications) in the same region over thousands of years surely means there was some kind of cultural continuity. We might be unable today to decipher the meaning ascribed to a cer-tain motif, or the significance of a vessel's unique

shape, but the fact that it was copied and reproduced by generation after generation suggests that
it was nevertheless meaningful, and that this meaning was shared by people who lived in a certain
region, but not by people in other regions where
that particular motif or vessel were not found.

On the other hand, however, we know that
each of these broad regions was inhabited by hundreds and maybe thousands or more village communities, each of which constituted a more or
less independent socioeconomic unit. Archaeological classifications sometimes lead us to view those
independent units as belonging to a single over-
arching "culture," but in reality contact between
those societies, and especially between those more
than a day's walk apart, could not have been very
intensive. This rather autonomous nature of small-
scale societies is sometime reflected in variation
within broadly defined "cultures." Clear examples
are the unique decorations of ceramic urns from
the Luoyang region or vessels decorated with elaborate colored and incised patterns, found only in
one region of the Zhaobaogou culture (Shelach
2000).

Identifying more meaningful differences in the
social organization and core values of societies
in different subregions requires a more thorough
analysis. Although such debates are often spec-
ulative, they raise interesting ideas and questions
for future research. One example of this kind of
research is a comparison of Early Neolithic societies in northeast China with those of the Yellow and Wei River basins, which revealed meaningful social differences between the two regions
(Shelach 2006). In Zhaobaogou and Xinglongwa,
for example, villages houses were organized in
rows (Figure 34) that did not face each other.
Consequently activities carried out inside or in
front of each house were not visible to people in
other houses. This kind of arrangement seems to
emphasize the individual space of each house and
is therefore quite different from the arrangement
of Early Neolithic villages in the Yellow and Wei

River basins, where the community is much more
nucleated and all houses face each other and open
to a common public space (Figure 35). This particular spatial arrangement, also found elsewhere
in the world, places more emphasis on the shared
commonality of the group than on the individual
households (Byrd 1994; Rautman 2000).

The placement of storage facilities may also
suggest a contrast between the more "group-
oriented" society of the early Yangshao and the
"individualized" Xinglongwa and Zhaobaogou
societies. In northeast China, most houses had
internal storage facilities. At the Zhaobaogou site,
for example, of the sample of fourteen undisturbed
excavated houses, eleven had such facilities. In
contrast, at sites such as Jiangzhai, all storage facilities were located outside the houses.

Religion may be another field in which societies from northeast China differ from those of
the Wei and Yellow River basins. Religious beliefs
and ritual activities were important in all Neolithic
societies, but their relative sociopolitical significance was different. Ritual structures (or "temples"), which are found only in northeast China,
along with the graves associated with these structures, might suggest that religious ideas and specialist practitioners (priests) were more important to
the sociopolitical integration of societies in northeast China than in other parts of north China during the Early Neolithic period.

The roots of these socioreligious configura-
tions may be traced back to earlier periods in
northeast China. A relatively large number of figurines, especially anthropomorphic figures, have
been excavated at Xinglongwa and Zhaobaogou
sites and represent a larger concentration of early
anthropomorphic figurines than anywhere else in
China. Small clay figurines excavated from Xinglongwa period sites represent the beginnings of this
local tradition. Much more impressive are larger
anthropomorphic statues made of stone, most of
which have been dated to the Zhaobaogou period.
One such statue was found at the Baiyinchanghan

Figure 64. Anthropomorphic stone figurine from Houtaizi (h. 34 cm) (photo by Gideon Shelach).

site, and a group of six stone statues, some as tall as 35 cm, was found at the Houtaizi (后台子) site (Figure 64) (Chengde 1994: 61–3).

The production of anthropomorphic figurines continued in northeast China throughout the Hongshan period (Guo 1995a: 38–40), the period from which artifacts indicating the flourishing of other religious activities, including a life-size statue from Niuheliang, were also recovered. Zhaobao-gou and Hongshan figurines have commonly been interpreted as representing pregnant women and, thus, as being related to a cult of fertility (Chengde 1994). However, while it may be impossible to decipher the specific meaning assigned to these artifacts by the ancient societies that produced and used them, the fact that this was a unique and long-term regional tradition is in itself meaningful. We may even speculate that because of the more

"individualistic" nature of Neolithic societies in the northeast, religion was a more important integrative mechanism there than it was for the more "group-oriented" societies located to the south in the Yellow and Wei River basins.

Internal interactions within each of the broadly defined subregions of north China are strongly implied by similarities in the shapes and decorations of ceramic vessels and other artifacts. The relative cultural homogeneity and rapid spread of new forms surely implies regular contact between villages. Evidence for specialized local crafts, such as the production of cinnabar powder at the Xipo site, suggests an activity that was primarily geared toward exchange with other communities, particularly during the latter part of the Early Neolithic.

The development of a system of exogamous marriage, which is at least suggested by the analysis of human bones from a few Early Neolithic cemeteries (Gao and Lee 1993), could be responsible for an increase in the frequency and intensity of intersocietal interactions. The intensity and directness of such contact declined in proportion to the distance between two villages, but it was not limited by the artificial "cultural" boundaries we now impose upon the archaeological data. For example, the techniques and styles of earthen wall and large "corridor" house construction spread during the latter part of the Early Neolithic throughout a large region, from the Wei River basin in the west to the lower Yellow River basin in the east. Further indirect evidence for interregional interaction is provided by the appearance of colored decorations on Hongshan ceramic vessels. It is assumed that the technique (but probably not the style) for producing ceramics with colored decorations spread during this period from the Yellow River basin to northeast China.

Evidence for even longer range and less direct contact may be found in the relatively rapid spread of domesticated plants and animals. This sphere of long-range interactions transcends the boundaries of north China to include the Yangzi River basin and perhaps other regions as well. Rice grains found at the Jiahu site in Henan and dated to the seventh millennium BCE are the earliest evidence for contact between societies in the Yangzi and Yellow River basins. Rice was more common, though still not a major food source, at sites of the late phases of the Early Neolithic in north China. This slow trickle of rice in small quantities suggests very infrequent and probably indirect interactions. We cannot preclude the possibility that, during this period, other types of domesticated plants and animals spread out slowly from their initial place of domestication to a very broad region. Such processes have cumulative effects on socioeconomic organization, but they do not involve intense and regular interactions.

CHAPTER 5

THE SHIFT TO AGRICULTURE AND SEDENTISM IN CENTRAL AND SOUTH CHINA

Between the seventh and the fourth millennia BCE, central and south China witnessed a transition from mobile hunter-gatherer to sedentary agricultural societies. Similar to the transition in north China described in Chapter 4, this process engendered dramatic social, economic, and cultural changes. While the processes in north and central China and, to a lesser extent, south China are similar in their general outline, there are also meaningful differences among them. It seems, for example, that the transition in central China was much more gradual than that in the north.

This chapter is similar in structure to the previous one. It reviews the archaeological evidence for the occupation of the Yangzi River valley and regions south of it from the seventh to the fourth millennia BCE and then addresses the issue of homogeneity and variability in the nature and rate of the developmental trajectories in different subregions. Because this chapter addresses regions with diverse climatic and ecological conditions, the data provide ample illustrations of the variation both within and between each of the larger subregions.

Because of the complexity of the region under discussion in this chapter, it is subdivided into four subregions: the eastern (lower) parts of the Yangzi River basin, the middle part of the Yangzi River basin (including the Sichuan basin), Lingnan or mainland south China, and the southeast coastal region. The archaeological "cultures" collected in Table 3 are used throughout the chapter as spatiotemporal reference points.

THE MATERIAL CULTURE OF EARLY NEOLITHIC SOCIETIES IN CENTRAL AND SOUTH CHINA

Settlement Patterns and Village Organization

The geography and ecology of central and south China present major obstacles to regional studies. Ancient sites are often difficult to locate since they are covered by paddy fields, and thus our knowledge of prehistoric settlements is based on chance findings and unsystematic recovery. A recent project carried out in the western part of the Sichuan basin attempted to overcome this obstacle through extensive and systematic coring (Chengdu 2010). This approach can provide a statistically sound sample of the buried sites, and although the data it provides differ from those offered by the surface surveys that are suitable for most regions of north China, it does deliver a comparable map of settlement distribution, site hierarchy, and so on.

Currently, the only region for which we have any detailed knowledge of settlement patterns is the Liyang (澧阳) plain in northwest Hunan province near Dongting Lake, in the central Yangzi region. Although no systematic regional survey has

TABLE 3. *Early Neolithic archaeological cultures from central and south China*

Years BCE	Lower (eastern) Yangzi	Middle Yangzi	Lingnan	Southeast coast
7000	Xiaohuangshan 小黄山/ Kuahuqiao 跨湖桥 (ca. 7000–5000)	Pengtoushan 彭头山 (ca. 7500–6000)		
6500		Chengbeixi 城背溪 culture (ca. 7000–5000)	Dingsishan 顶蛳山 (ca. 7000–5000)	
6000		Lower Zaoshi 皂市下层 (ca. 5800–4800)		
5500	Hemudu 河姆渡 (ca. 5500–3300)			
5000	Majiabang 马家浜 (ca. 5000–4000)	Tangjiagang 汤家岗 (ca. 4800–3500)		Keqiutou 壳坵头 (4700–3000)
4500		Daixi 大溪 (c. 4500–3300)[a]		
4000	Songze 松泽 (ca. 4000–3300) Beiyinyangying 北阴阳营/ Xuejiagang 薛家岗 (ca. 4000–3300)		Dingsishan 顶蛳山 phase IV (ca. 4000–3000)	Xiantouling 咸头岭 (ca. 4000–3000)

In each of the subregions some archaeological cultures may chronologically overlap with one another because their spatial distribution is not identical. The Sichuan basin is not included in this table because sites in its eastern part – the Three Gorges area – are affiliated with cultures of the middle Yangzi, while few Early Neolithic sites are known from the Chengdu basin, to the west.

[a] Daixi is often transliterated as Daxi.

been carried out in this region, a large number of Neolithic sites are known, including famous sites such as Pengtoushan (彭头山), Bashidang (八十垱), and Chengtoushan (城头山). Within an area of some 500 km² researchers have identified 222 sites dating from the eighth to the third millennia BCE (Pei 2004).

As one would expect, the earliest Neolithic occupation of the Liyang plain is sparse, and the sites dated to the eighth and seventh millennia BCE are quite small. Altogether eleven sites were dated to this period, with an accumulated size of 9 ha. The best known sites, Pengtoushan and Bashidang, are estimated to be about 1.5 and 3.4 ha in size, respectively. Although some public works, such as the ditch at Bashidang, have been identified, no settlement hierarchy or political clustering of sites was found. Each site seems to have

functioned as an autonomous community. During the next period – the so-called Lower Zaoshi (皂市下层) culture dated to the sixth and early fifth millennia BCE – the number of sites found increases to seventeen and their accumulated area to 23 ha. The largest site from this period is 4 ha in size, but there is still no apparent hierarchy or clustering. A more substantial transformation of the regional system occurred during the late fifth and the fourth millennia BCE – the so-called Daixi (大溪) culture – when the number of sites increased to forty-six and their accumulated size reached 73 ha. More significantly, the sites now seem to form two clusters, with the western cluster forming a hierarchical pattern around one prominent site – Chengtoushan – which is 8 ha in size and enclosed by a wide ditch and a wall. The clustering and hierarchy of sites in this region

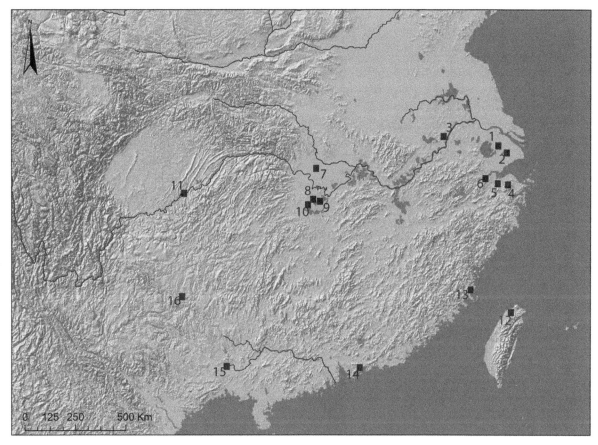

Figure 65. Map of all sites mentioned in Chapter 5: 1. Caoxieshan and Chenghu; 2. Chuodun; 3. Lingjiatan; 4. Hemudu, Tianluoshan; 5. Xiaohuangshan; 6. Kuahuqiao; 7. Hujiawuchang; 8. Chengtoushan; 9. Bashidang; 10. Pengtoushan; 11. Daixi; 12. Dapenkeng; 13. Keqiutou; 14 Xiantouling; 15. Baozitou; 16. Dingsishan.

continued to evolve during the Late Neolithic period (Chapter 6).

Some of the early sites show signs of preplanning similar to those identified in the north. For example, the Bashidang site is enclosed on two sides by the river, while the other sides are bounded by a ditch that varied in width from less than 2 m to more than 5.5 m. The earth excavated from the ditch was piled to form a low earthen wall (Hunan 2006). The construction of these structures was likely to have been motivated by considerations of flood control rather than defense. Furthermore, this marking of the village borders is also a sign of communal integration.

During the fourth millennium, some of the sites in the middle Yangzi region were enclosed by wider moats and by earthen walls. One of the best known examples is the Chengtoushan (城头山) site: It is located on a low mound, some 2 m above the surrounding plain. The moat and wall that enclosed this circular shape site were rebuilt and expanded four times between ca. 4000 and 2800 BCE. At the final stage, the moat was 35–50 m wide and 4 m deep, and the walls were 5 m high, 27 m wide at the bottom, and 16 m wide at the top. During the two earlier phases of the site, however, the ditch and the walls were much less impressive: the ditch was only 3 m wide and 2.5 m deep, and the walls were 11 m wide at the bottom and 1.5 m high (Hunan 2007: 84–7) (Figure 66).

We lack comparable data for sites in the lower Yangzi region. Although the preservation of organic materials, including house remains, at sites such as Kuahuqiao (跨湖桥) and Hemudu (河姆渡) teaches us much about the daily life of the Early Neolithic communities in the region, we know very little about regional patterns of settlement distribution. It seems that sites from the sixth and fifth millennia BCE were autonomous and that only minimal public works were carried out here. However, because only a small portion of the overall area of any site has been excavated, we know little about the overall site layout. The large public structure found at the Lingjiatan (凌家滩) site suggests the development of more complex sociopolitical systems during the fourth millennium BCE, but because the excavations specifically focused on ritual structures, we know little about the residential area of the site, its overall organization, or the regional settlement patterns.

For Early Neolithic south China, evidence of settlement continued to be located mainly at cave sites and shell middens. Because many of these sites are not well dated, and because no systematic regional survey has been carried out, it is hard to discern patterns of occupation or to address trajectories of population densities. Typical open-air sites such as Dingsishan (顶蛳山) and Baozitou (豹子头) are known in the southern part of Guangxi province (Zhongguo et al. 1998; Zhongguo Kexueyuan Kaogu Yanjiusuo Guangxi Gongzuodui et al. 2003). No habitation structures were identified at these sites, though graves and a few ash pits were found together with ceramic vessels and shell, bone, and stone artifacts. Human occupation of the many karstic caves in Guangxi and Guangdong provinces continued from earlier periods. Some early caves sites, such as Zengpiyan (甑皮岩), continued to be occupied during this period, with no noticeable changes between the different periods of occupation. After ca. 5000 BCE, the occupation of caves became much less common, possibly indicating the socioeconomic transformation of local societiess.

Little is known about the occupation of the eastern coast of south China prior to ca. 4500 BCE. A few sites from the fifth millennium BCE are known in this region, with Keqiutou (壳坵头) being the most famous. It is located on Haitan Island, off the coast of Fujian. It is a site of large shell middens some 3 ha in size, where large quantities of potshards and stone tools were found along with shell debris. Structural remains at the site include twenty-one shell pits (probably used for food debris), some one hundred postholes, and one grave (Jiao 2007: 45–54).

Domestic Structures

Two different traditions of house construction can be identified in central China during the Early Neolithic period: in the middle Yangzi region houses were constructed on the ground level or were semi-subterranean and quite similar to houses found at Early Neolithic sites in the north. A different type of construction that emerged during this period is typical mainly in the lower Yangzi region, where houses were constructed from wood, with their floors raised above the ground on poles.

In the middle Yangzi region six houses and fifteen pits were excavated at Pengtoushan, and twenty-two houses and eighty pits were excavated at Bashidang (Hunan 2006). Most houses are rectangular in shape and constructed on the surface level, although circular and semi-subterranean houses are also known. Postholes indicate a wooden structure that probably supported wattle-and-daub walls. The houses are quite small, ranging in size from about 8 to 40 m².

More elaborate house structure techniques from the sixth millennium BCE were found at the Hujiawuchang (胡家屋场) site in the middle Yangzi region, where house floors are covered with packed layers of burned clay, sand, and fragments of lithics and pottery (Hunan 1993). Postholes dug inside the house floors are very

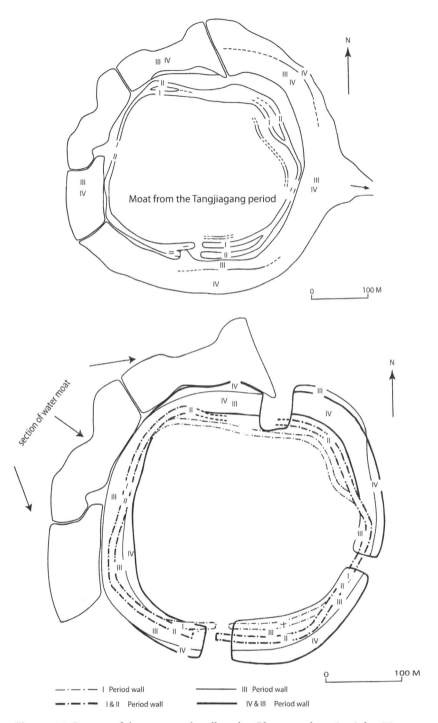

Figure 66. Layout of the moat and wall at the Chengtoushan site (after Hunan 2007: 1:162–3).

small, indicating that they may have supported a roof but not a second living floor. Houses dated to the fourth millennium from the Chengtoushan site are similar in shape and construction methods to those from earlier periods, though they are larger. Among the twenty-eight houses excavated in this site, five are larger than 50 m² and one (no. 104) is about 200 m². Here too the floors of some houses are surfaced with burned clay, sand, and fragments of lithics and pottery (Hunan 2007: 168–89).

During the same period, a new tradition of house construction emerged in the lower Yangzi River region. At the waterlogged Kuahuqiao site, dated to ca. 6000–5000 BCE, the superb preservation of organic materials has allowed the recovery of wooden structures that seem to have supported houses in which the living floors were raised above ground (Zhejiang 2004). These so-called *ganlan* (干栏), or pole houses, are well adapted to a swampy and often flooded environment, thereby becoming one of the most common types of dwelling in central and south China (as well as in regions of Southeast Asia) during the prehistoric and historic periods. Constructing the living floors on poles high above ground helped avoid the harmful effects of moisture and floods.

Remains of *ganlan* constructions are even better preserved at the Hemudu site, dated to the fifth millennium BCE. The wooden posts and planks, and especially the technique for joining them together (called mortise and tenon joints), indicate a high level of carpentry skills (Figure 67). Some of these houses were very large, reaching 23 m long and 7 m wide (Chang 1986: 208–11).

Unfortunately, little if anything is known about Early Neolithic domestic structures in south China. That no permanent habitation structures have been found at most of the open-air sites – such as Dingsishan and Baozitou in Guangxi or at sites such as Xiantouling (咸头岭) in the southeastern coast region – may suggest that these were seasonal sites that developed around the exploitation of shellfish resources. The so-called "shell-

pit" and postholes discovered at Keqiutou are interpreted, in contrast, as evidence for the permanent or semipermanent occupation of this site. These postholes are small, between 15 to 35 cm in diameter and about 30 cm deep, and are clustered in two groups – the first of thirty-one and the second of sixty-nine holes. It was hypothesized that wooden posts inserted into these holes supported two houses, but it is impossible to reconstruct the shape of those structures (Jiao 2007: 49).

Storage pits have been found at many sites in the Yangzi River basin. In the middle Yangzi region, pits are usually round or irregular in shape. Most are quite shallow, but in Bashidang some are at least 0.5 m deep. Layers of burned ash and potshards were found inside some of the pits (Hunan 2006: 252–60). Similar pits have also been found at Chengtoushan (Hunan 2007: 209–33), and the ceramic vessels found in some of them may have been used to store food. In the lower Yangzi River some storage pits have a wooden frame and are rectangular in shape (Figure 68), a feature not known from sites in north China or the middle Yangzi River. The large quantities of acorns found in some of the pits at Kuahuqiao are the clearest indication that the pits were indeed used to store food (Zhejiang 2004). As mentioned earlier, storage or garbage pits are also known from sites in south China.

Cemeteries, Burials, and Religious Structures

Formal graves appeared early in the Yangzi River basin, but burials during this period are relatively simple and contain few grave goods. At Pengtoushan, twenty-one graves were found. They are all simple, small pit graves, some rectangular and some oval. The graves contain up to six ceramic vessels and ten small beads and ornaments. Although the human bones are badly preserved, based on the size of the graves and the remaining bones it is assumed that most were secondary burials (Hunan 2006: 39–44). The ninety-eight graves

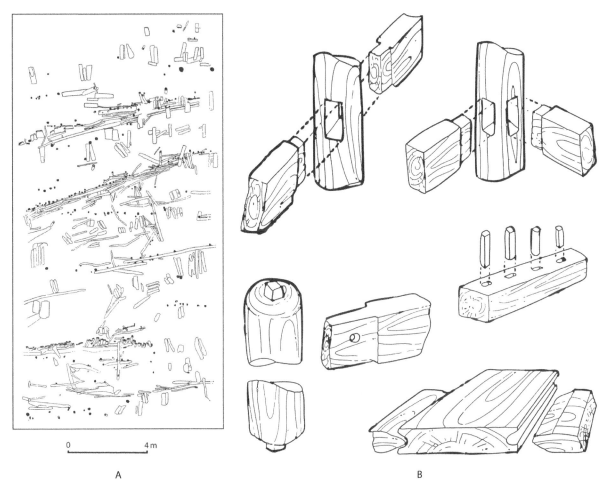

Figure 67. A. Wooden structure of houses from the Hemudu site; B. Details of the mortise and tenon joints (after Zhejiang 1978b: 45).

found at Bashidang are more or less similar to those at Pengtoushan (Hunan 2006: 261–75).

More diversity is evident among graves from the late phases of the Early Neolithic. The 130 graves excavated at the Daixi site are mostly simple pit graves that were dug along a north-south axis, and bodies were placed with their head facing south. Most graves contain a single body, but a few are a joint burial of an adult and a child (Wang 1990a). A small number of graves contain no grave goods at all, while most had at least a few items. The richest contained between thirty and forty items, including ceramic vessels and stone and bone artifacts for everyday use. The average number of grave goods increased over time, and ceramic vessels become the favorite type of grave goods during later part of the Daixi period. Wang Jie has argued that, because female graves are on average richer than male graves, Daixi was a matriarchal society (Wang 1990a). However, it would seem that regardless of the gender of the grave's occupant, the differences between graves are not very pronounced, suggesting a relatively egalitarian society with no gender biases.

At Chengtoushan, some 215 pit graves and 95 urn graves are dated to the Daixi period (Hunan 2007: 286–308). The graves are located within the area enclosed by the moat and wall, but are

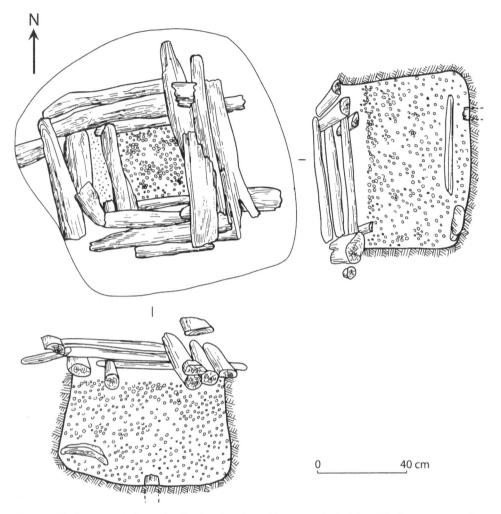

Figure 68. Storage pit from the Kuahuqiao site with acorns in it (after Zhejiang 2004: 27).

concentrated in three small clusters or cemeteries, each containing both pit and urn graves. The pit graves vary in size and in the amount of grave goods placed in them. The smallest graves, such as M766 (Figure 69), are only 1 m long, 50 cm wide, and 14 cm deep. The body was placed in a flexed position with no grave goods. Larger pit graves, such as M678 (Figure 70), are 2.5 m long, 1.1 m wide, and 20 cm deep. In addition to the body of the main occupant, M678, for instance, contains the skull of a child, twenty-four ceramic vessels, and two jade ornaments. Of the 215 pit graves, 47 had no grave goods in them, while the

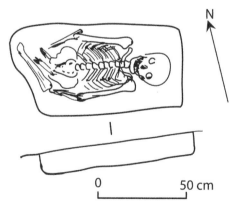

Figure 69. Grave M766 at Chengtoushan (after Hunan 2007: 291).

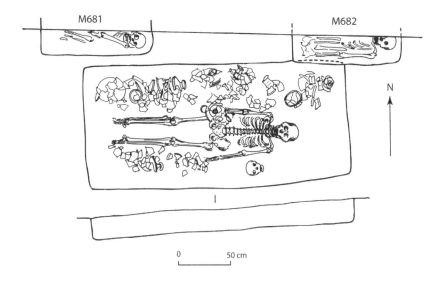

Figure 70. Grave M678 at Chengtoushan and the artifacts found in it (after Hunan 2007: 294).

remaining 168 graves contained between one and thirty items, mostly pottery.

Urn graves are small circular pits about 50 cm wide and 30 cm deep, inside which a large vessel containing the deceased's bones would be placed. The larger vessel is usually covered by a second smaller vessel, without additional grave goods (Figure 71). It is difficult to analyze the diverse findings of the Chengtoushan graves because of the poor preservation of the human bones. We do not know even if the deceased placed in the small pit graves and in the urn graves were children or adults, or whether they were primary or secondary burials.

A somewhat different mortuary tradition is found at the Lingjiatan site, located in Anhui province, in the lower Yangzi region, and dated to the fourth millennium BCE. At the center of this site, the prehistoric population erected a large platform made of layers of soil and pebbles and several stone altars. More than fifty tombs were dug into this platform. The graves vary considerably in terms of size and especially in the wealth of their contents. While the poor graves contain few grave goods, if any, richer graves contain hundreds of artifacts, including labor-intensive jade artifacts. The richest grave excavated from this site thus far (labeled 07M23) is 3.45 m long, 2.1 m wide, and 0.55 m deep and contains the remains of a wooden coffin. A total of 330 artifacts were found in this grave, including 214 jade objects, 98 stone tools, and 16 ceramic vessels (Figure 72) (Anhui 2008).

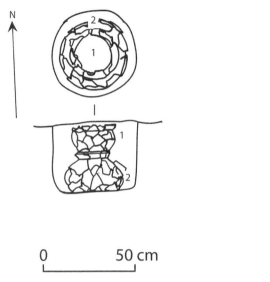

Figure 71. Urn grave M719 at Chengtoushan (after Hunan 2007: 308).

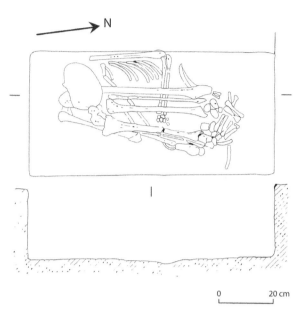

Figure 73. Grave M116 from the Dingsishan site (after Zhongguo 1998: 14).

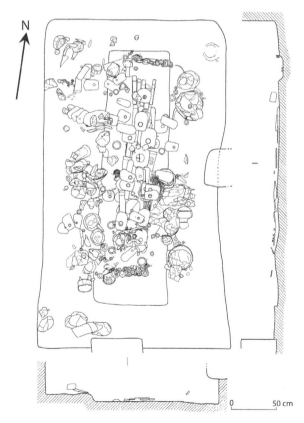

Figure 72. Grave 07M23 from the Lingjiatan site.

A relatively large number of graves was found in south China, at shell midden sites such as Dingsishan. They are all small, simple pit graves containing only a few grave goods (mostly stone tools) or no grave goods at all. Grave M116, for example, is 1.1 m long, 50 cm wide, and 25 cm deep. It contains the bones of an adult male in the flexed position, accompanied by one stone tool, one shell tool, and five stones (Figure 73). Many of the deceased are buried in the flexed position and some are dismembered. As noted, there is minimal variation among the graves. Altogether 149 graves are dated to the second and third phases of the Dingsishan site: most had no grave goods at all, only a few had one to three tools made of stone, bone, or shell, and a very few contained potshards (Zhongguo et al. 1998: 14–22).

The archaeological identification of religious structures is often quite difficult. The clearest evidence of such structures existing in central China during the Early Neolithic is provided by the earth and rubble platforms found at sites such as

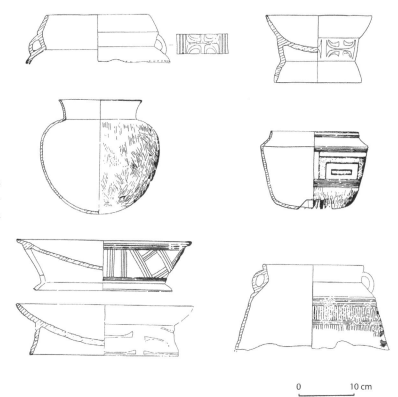

Figure 74. Ceramic vessels from sites of the lower Zaosi cultures, middle Yangzi River basin (after Hunan 1993).

0   10 cm

Chengtoushan and Lingjiatan. At Chengtoushan, the excavators identified three such platforms, the largest of which is dated to the Daixi period. It is about 200 m² in size and made of clean yellow soil. Similar to the platform at Lingjiatan, pits and graves were also dug into this platform. The sites' excavators identified the layers of ash and potshards that covered the platforms as remains of the rituals that would have taken place on and around it (Hunan 2007 266–79).

The construction of platforms into which graves were dug and the rich jade inventory found at Lingjiatan are well-documented phenomena from the third millennium across the lower Yangzi River basin (Chapter 6). It is quite possible that these ritual complexes denote the emergence of societies that were more stratified and in which sociopolitical prestige was symbolized thorough the accumulation of labor-intensive jade artifacts.

The Production of Artifacts

Ceramics found at the earliest Neolithic sites in the middle and lower Yangzi River regions are coarse and were fired at a low temperature; their walls are uneven in thickness; they are tempered with plant fibers; and their shapes are simple. The lithic assemblage at these sites also shows a clear continuity from the regional chopping tool tradition of the Late Paleolithic. Over the following two thousand years most ceramics produced in the middle Yangzi River basin continued to be quite coarse and simple, but some more elaborate forms, including ring bases, as well as more elaborate engraved decorations and red slip, were found at sites associated with the Chengbeixi (城背溪) and lower Zaoshi cultures (Figure 74).

Higher-quality pottery vessels were also found at the Kuahuqiao site in the lower Yangzi River region (Zhejiang 2004). Many of the vessels

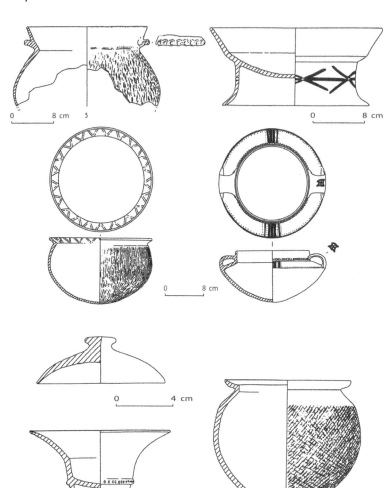

Figure 75. Ceramic vessels from the Kuahuqiao site (after Zhejiang 2004: 81, 88, 98, 109, 124, 137, 144).

excavated there have walls of uniform thickness, and their shapes are more elaborate than anything previously seen in the region. While round bases are the most common, ring bases and high pedestal bases are also common. Incised and appliqué decorations are most common, though some color decorations and black burnish are also known (Figure 75). Ceramic production from the subsequent Hemudu period seems to represent a continuation of this tradition (Liu 2006).

In the middle Yangzi region, the development of more sophisticated craft technology is attested to by the pottery and stone industries of sites asso-

ciated with the Daixi period. Particularly during the late phases of this period, stone tools are polished and drilled and ceramic vessels were made on tournettes (slow wheel). Some vessels have a low ring base or pedestal, while others have short legs. The most distinctive Daixi culture pottery is red on the outside and black on the inside, and some vessels have painted decorations (Wang 1990a, 1990b) (Figure 76). Sophisticated kilns for ceramic production excavated at the Chengtoushan site (Figure 77) are further evidence for the advancement of pottery production technology (Hunan 2007: 257–64).

Figure 76. Ceramic vessels of the Daixi culture (photo by Gary Lee Todd).

The excellent preservation of organic materials in some of the waterlogged sites of the lower Yangzi region provides a unique opportunity to observe the types of craft that are not otherwise often visible in archaeological sites. The most striking examples are wooden objects, found at sites such as Kuahuqiao and Hemudu, which attest to a very high level of carpentry skills. The remains of wooden house structures found in these sites, including the signs of the mortise and tenon joints technique, are one such type of evidence. Wooden tools, such as digging sticks and hoes, offer further evidence, as does a dugout canoe made of pine, and rowing paddles (Figure 78). Evidence for a very developed bone working industry is also found abundantly at sites of the Hemudu period (Figure 79).

Another unique discovery at the Hemudu site is the earliest archaeological evidence of lacquer

artifacts (Liu 2006: 102–4). Lacquer artifacts are produced by applying many thin layers of tree resin varnish on a core made from wood or cloth. The varnish is mixed with minerals to produce shiny colors (usually red and black). The production of lacquerware is a very time-consuming and specialized craft that requires knowledge of the processing and refinement of a specific tree resin, the treatment of coloring minerals, and the application of the varnish onto the wooden base. Scattered finds document continued low-level use of lacquer throughout the Late Neolithic and early Bronze Age, until it developed into one of the most characteristic industries of central China.

Some of the most impressive evidence for emerging craft specialization in the lower Yangzi region comes from the Lingjiatan site, where a large number of sophisticated jade artifacts have been found. During one recent excavation, for example, 214 jade artifacts, some quite large, were recovered from four tombs and the platform into which they were dug (Anhui 2008). The large number of jade objects found in this ritual context suggests the existence of jade-carving specialists. Some of the graves at Lingjiatan also yielded evidence of the jade craft, including a sandstone drill and jade debris. This may indicate the high prestige of jade producing artisans (Zhang and Hung 2008).

Lingjiatan jade types include *yue* axes, *bi* discs, *huang* pendants, and *jue* earrings, most of which continued to be manufactured in this region during the third millennium BCE. The most outstanding finds are a small number of human and animal figurines, including six jade human figures (ranging in size from 7.7 to 9.9 cm high), a jade bird with an octagonal star carved on its chest, and the so-called jade dragons and turtles, made of two pieces of jade with a jade plaque inserted between its shells.

As noted, although the ceramics industry emerged in south China at more or less the same time as it did in central and north China, over the

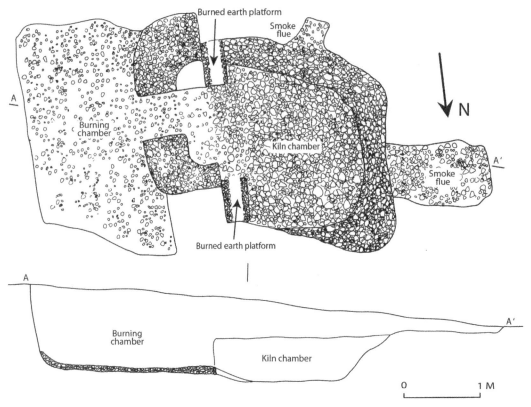

Figure 77. Kiln for ceramic production from the Chengtoushan site (after Hunan 2007: 260).

next few thousands of years it did not evolve to the same extent as in regions to the north. Ceramics found at the shell midden sites are sand and shell tempered, and most vessels have simple shapes and round-bottomed bases. Some of the vessels are decorated with cord marks and shell impressions. Other common artifacts include shell tools as well as chipped and polished stone tools (Jiao 2007: 49–58; Zhongguo et al. 1998; Zhongguo Kexueyuan Kaogu Yanjiusuo Guangxi Gongzuodui et al. 2003).

THE ECONOMIC ADAPTATION OF EARLY NEOLITHIC SOCIETIES IN CENTRAL AND SOUTH CHINA

At a very general level, the trajectories of transition from hunting and gathering to agriculture are similar to those described for north China. However, a much more varied picture emerges when the data are examined at a higher resolution. Indeed, one of the main contributions of research carried out in central and south China is that it highlights the varied pathways to agriculture. In the future, research not only should focus on identifying a few specific domesticated species, but also should adopt a more quantifiable approach that would enable us to discuss the relative importance of each economic resource, be it domesticated or wild. This approach accords with our understanding of agriculture as a process, as discussed in Chapter 3. It is also instrumental in understanding the development of mechanisms of economic organization, resource procurement, and exchange.

Domesticated Plants

Rice, the staple food of central and south China, is the main target of most research carried out in these regions. As already discussed in Chapter 3,

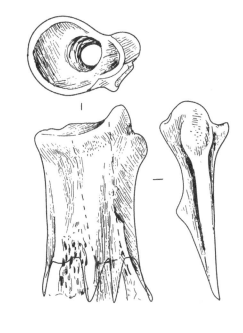

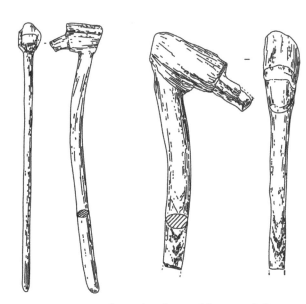

Figure 78. A spade made of animal bone and digging sticks made of wood from the Kuahuqiao site (after Zhejiang 2004: 177).

the dates and the processes of rice domestication are hotly contested by archaeologists. While thousands of rice husks and grains were recovered at Bashidang (Hunan 2006: 508; Zhang and Pei 1997), archaeologists and archaeo-botanists are still debating whether the rice remains found here

and at other sites from the eighth and seventh millennia BCE are domesticated or wild. Some view the morphology of rice grains from Bashidang, and from the probably contemporaneous site of Shangshan (上山) in the lower Yangzi basin, as evidence that domestication was already under way during the seventh millennium BCE. Others, though, such as Dorian Fuller, are pushing the date of rice domestication forward to the late fifth millennium BCE. It seems that the genetic transformation of rice from the wild progenitor to the domesticated species took a longer time and was much more gradual than previous models have suggested (Fuller et al. 2007; Zheng et al. 2009).

Rice grains have been found at several additional sites dated to the seventh and sixth millennia BCE, such as Hujiawuchang in the middle Yangzi and Kuahuqiao in the lower Yangzi region (Hunan 1993; Zhejiang 2004). At Kuahuqiao alone, excavations yielded more than a thousand grains of rice. It would appear that even if rice was not yet domesticated, its cultivation was already under way. For example, a spade made of animal bone and digging sticks made of wood that were probably used for tilling fields were found at Kuahuqiao (Figure 78). However, remains of a large number of plants and animals, most of them not yet domesticated, indicate that at both sites rice was probably not the main food source.

This situation probably changed during the Hemudu period. The large quantity of rice husks found at the Hemudu site (some estimates are as high as twenty tons) is seen by many as evidence of rice cultivation and domestication. The large number of bone spades found at Hemudu (Figure 79) is likewise clear evidence of the development of paddy field cultivation (Zhejiang 1978a, 1978b). Rice paddies and associated irrigation systems were found in the early deposits that predate the moat and walls at the Chengtoushan site, dating to ca. 4500 BCE (Hunan 2007). Small paddy fields with irrigation ditches and wells were also found at other contemporaneous sites, such as Tianluoshan (田螺山) as well as Caoxieshan 草鞋山, Chenghu

澄湖, and Chuodun 绰墩 in Jiangsu province, confirming the spread of this method during the fourth millennium BCE (Fuller et al. 2007; Zheng et al. 2009).

In south China, rice is found only at relatively late strata. For example, at the Dingsishan site, plant phytoliths from the lower three strata, dated ca. 7000 to 5000 BCE, contain wild species. Domesticated rice phytoliths were identified only at the most recent stratum, dated to ca. 4000 BCE (Zhao et al. 2005). Although domesticated rice, as noted, was probably imported to this region from the north, it is possible that tubers, such as yam and taro, were domesticated in south China, where they have been exploited for a long time. Lotus, whose roots and seeds have been found at such sites as Hujiawuchang, could also have been cultivated and perhaps even domesticated there, but more research is needed to confirm these hypotheses.

Domesticated Animals

Pigs and dogs, both of which may already have been domesticated (or were in the process of domestication) during the Early Holocene, are the primary domesticated animals found at Early Neolithic sites in central and south China. Pig bones in particular are quite common at sites in both the middle and lower Yangzi regions such as Chengtoushan, Kuahuqiao, and Hujiawuchang (Yuan et al. 2008). In south China, it is possible that domesticated pigs were being raised at a relatively early stage and complemented a diet that was based mainly on tubers, shellfish and wild animals. Some scholars argue that the pig bones found at the Zengpiyan cave site belong to a domesticated species, but this claim remains controversial (Yuan and Fled 2002). It is not even clear whether pig bones found at strata from earlier than the fourth millennium BCE at sites such as Dingsishan and Baozitou come from domesticated species (Zhao et al. 2005). Thus, although the progenitor of the pig – the wild boar – was common in south China,

it is possible that, like rice, pigs were not domesticated locally, but were brought to the region from the Yangzi River basin during the late fifth or early fourth millennia BCE.

Aside from dogs and pigs, the other candidate for domestication in central and south China is the water buffalo, the animal also most commonly identified with the agricultural system of central and south China. The water buffalo's primary utilization as the draft animal of the rice paddy fields is, however, a very late development, which probably started only during the first millennium BCE. Nevertheless, water buffalo bones have been found in large quantities at Early Neolithic sites in this region. At Hemudu, for example, not only were water buffalo bones found in garbage deposits, but they also constituted the raw material for the production of agricultural tools. Because only one species of water buffalo (*Bubalus mephistopheles*) was identified at these sites, the common assumption has been that this particular species was first domesticated in the Yangzi River region around 5000 BCE (Chang 1986: 211). However, more recent research, including analysis of ancient DNA, suggests that the bones from Hemudu and other contemporaneous sites belong to wild water buffalo, and that the domesticated water buffalo was introduced into China from south Asia only during the first millennium BCE (Liu et al. 2006).

The Economic Base of Early Neolithic Societies

As discussed in Chapter 3, communities inhabiting central and south China during the Late Pleistocene and Early Holocene pursued a broad spectrum economic strategy. It is very interesting to note that the beginning of agriculture did not cause any immediate changes to this strategy. For thousands of years after the cultivation of plants and animals began in this region, and even after fully domesticated species were available, local communities continued to exploit wild resources on a relatively large scale. This is true not only for south

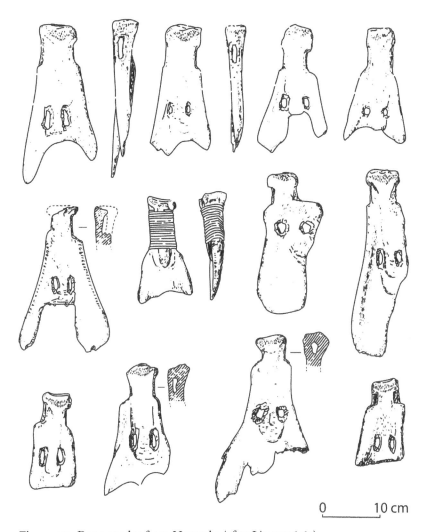

Figure 79. Bone spades from Hemudu (after Liu 2006 65).

China, where, as we have seen, agriculture started late, but also in the Yangzi River basin, considered to be one of the world's primary centers for the development of agriculture.

At Chengtoushan, for example, remains of seventy-five plant species were identified. Rice was the most abundant among them, but many other edible plants were also found, including water caltrop, Job's tears, gorgon fruit, purple perilla, winter melon, chestnut, peach, and plum (Hunan 2007) . Similar varieties of plants were also identified at Hujiawuchang, Hemudu, and Tianluoshan. The excellent preservation condi-

tions at Kuahuqiao make possible a comprehensive analysis of the economy of the community that resided there. Botanic remains there are mostly of wild species, including water caltrop, acorn, water chestnut, Job's tears, knotweed, and rice (Fuller et al. 2007; Zhejiang 2004). It is worth noting that the wooden frame storage pits excavated at the site were filled with acorns (Figure 68), illustrating the importance of wild food resources for the local community's economy.

The proportion of wild plants to domesticated ones seems to have changed during the fifth and fourth millennia BCE, when rice grew in importance as the staple food of societies in the Yangzi River region. The quantity of rice found at the Hemudu site as well as the discovery of paddy fields remains at sites such as Chengtoushan suggest that as time progressed societies in this region devoted more energy to the cultivation of rice and their diet became more dependent on it. However, even then, Hemudu and contemporaneous communities continued to consume a large variety of wild plants, which remained an important source of food (Fuller et al. 2007).

Grain starch extracted from shards of ceramic cooking pots excavated at the Kuahuqiao site were identified as belonging to at least eight different genera, the most common being rice, Job's tears, beans, and acorns (Yang and Jiang 2010). This constitutes direct evidence of the variety of plants *cooked* and consumed by the Kuahuqiao community. An analysis of starch extracted from grinding stones at the Xiaohuangshan (小黄山) site located in the lower Yangzi River region produced very similar results. The most prevalent plants identified in this analysis were Job's tears, beans, chestnuts, acorns, tubers, and rice (Liu et al. 2010b).

Patterns of meat consumption here are very similar to patterns of plant consumption in the Yangzi River region. Although domesticated pigs had been raised in this region since the beginning of the Neolithic period (probably even before rice was fully domesticated), hunting and fishing remained the main source of meat throughout the Early Neolithic. At the Kuahuqiao site, researchers unearthed more than five thousand animal bones from thirty-two species, including fish, shellfish, crab, turtle, alligator, swan, crane, dolphin, dog, badger, raccoon, dog, pig, tiger, leopard, cat, rhinoceros, sika, antelope, and water buffalo (Zhejiang 2004). More or less the same variety was discovered at Hujiawuchang (Hunan 1993), Chengtoushan (Hunan 2007), and Hemudu (Chang 1986: 211; Zhejiang 1978b).

A tentative analysis of the numbers of individual animals belonging to each of the spices found at these sites suggests that most of the meat consumed came from wild animals. At Kuahuqiao, for example, mammals' bones constituted between 40 percent and 70 percent of the animal bones found at different strata, but only 9 to 27 percent of those were from pigs, while deer bones made up 38 to 46 percent, and bones from other wild mammals 38 to 46 percent (Yuan et al. 2008). Even at sites from the late fourth and early third millennia BCE, bones from domesticated animals rarely reached 50 percent of the mammal bones found (Yuan et al. 2008). Moreover, given that hunting birds, fishing, and collecting shellfish were also important, we can be confident that wild resources continued to be far more economically significant than domesticated ones.

More research on the regional variations between societies in the Yangzi River basin is needed. For example, it has been argued that in the western part of Hubei province, sites identified with the Chengbeixi culture were occupied by groups of hunter-gatherers who practiced seasonal mobility and did not occupy permanent villages (Yang 1991). It is possible that during the sixth and fifth millennium BCE the Yangzi River basin was settled by a mosaic of groups with different types of economic strategies: some were more mobile and heavily dependent on hunting and fishing, while others were more sedentary and focused intensively on the collection and cultivation of rice and other plant resources.

The trajectory in south China must have been quite different from that in north or central China. As indicated previously, domesticated rice was exploited in this region only from the fourth millennium BCE and onward, and it was probably imported from the north (i.e., from the Yangzi River basin). Prior to this period, even wild rice, which must have been locally available, was not exploited intensively and was certainly not cultivated (Zhao et al. 2005). Instead, the local communities relied mainly on collecting various tubers, water caltrop, and other wild resources. Patterns of meat consumption point to the same conclusion. Even at relatively late phases of the Early Neolithic, faunal remains at sites such as Dingsishan and Baozitou consisted mainly of wild animals such as bovines and deer, as well as of aquatic resources (species of fish and shellfish) and birds. This is indicative of an economy that was still largely based on hunting, fishing, and collecting shellfish (Zhao et al. 2005).

It is probable that the high availability of tubers such as yam and taro, as well as the plentiful and year-round availability of wild animal resources, inhibited the extensive exploitation of other food resources. Such reliance on locally available wild plants and animals shaped the economy of south China for thousands of years until – and to a certain extent, even after – rice cultivation entered the region.

Alongside sites such as Dingsishan, where there is evidence of the exploitation of a wide variety of plants and animals before the slow transition to agriculture, findings at other sites, such as Keqiutou, seem to indicate a focus on the intensive exploitation of shellfish and fish. It is possible that sites on the eastern cost of south China in particular adopted a marine-based economic strategy and, by the late fifth or fourth millennia BCE, started to develop seafaring capabilities that enabled them to expand the variety of marine resources they exploited.

THE SOCIOPOLITICAL AND ECONOMIC ORGANIZATION OF EARLY NEOLITHIC VILLAGES IN CENTRAL AND SOUTH CHINA

As with north China, the trajectory in central and south China began with societies where horizontal gaps (complexity) and vertical diversification (stratification) were minimal. From this common starting point the three regions diverged into somewhat different trajectories. Archaeological limitations aside, it seems safe to say that while

the trajectory of societies in the north represents a relatively rapid transition to agriculture and a gradual but steady development of stratification and social complexity, the transition to agriculture in central China was much more gradual and the economy remained mixed until the end of the Early Neolithic. At the same time, the growth of stratification and social complexity was much slower and had not yet matured to the same degree as in the north by the end of the Early Neolithic. South China represents what seems to be a completely different kind of trajectory where, although domesticated plants (rice) and animals (pigs and dogs) were available at least from neighboring societies in the Yangzi River, if not locally, their initial adaptation into the local economy began only at the end of the Early Neolithic. At the same time, during the three to four millennia defined here as the Early Neolithic, we have little if any archaeological evidence for even the incipient development of either stratification or social complexity among societies in south China.

Settlement Hierarchy and Social Complexity

Although we do not have systematic settlement data for central and south China in the same way we do for some regions in north China, a trajectory of transformation from a sparse and more or less egalitarian pattern during the early part of the Early Neolithic to a more dense, centralized, and hierarchical pattern during the latter parts is suggested by findings from at least one region in the central Yangzi region. As discussed earlier, in the Liyang plain we can observe the change from undiversified small sites during the sixth millennium BCE to the development of a system in which sites varied in size, as well as the probable development of site hierarchy, during the fourth millennium BCE. It appears that similar processes occurred in other regions of central China, including the lower Yangzi region, though we currently lack the data to support such a conclusion.

In sites of the early period, such as Bashidang, preplanning of the community layout and small-scale public works indicate communal integration. Larger-scale works at sites such as Chengtoushan from the fifth and fourth millennia BCE suggest regional integration, as well as the pooling and controlling of the workforce. The ritual platforms into which graves were dug, found at sites such as Lingjiatan, may have been the focal points of some emerging regional polities. However, because we know so little about the domestic occupation of Lingjiatan and other sites in this region, it is impossible to reconstruct the settlement patterns that would support such a hypothesis.

Similar processes of regional hierarchy and the emergence of more elaborate and larger sites as central nodes of local hierarchies have *not* been identified in south China. While this lack of data may be a function of insufficient archaeological attention, it nevertheless seems to reflect the persistence of egalitarian and less complex societies up to the end of the Early Neolithic period. Even at relatively large sites such as Dingsishan and Keqiutou, which have seen large-scale excavations, there are no indications of the kinds of structures associated with the development of a settlement hierarchy or of other evidence for regional or even local stratification.

Economic Organization, Stratification, and Social Complexity

The archaeological data suggest that the trajectory in central China moved toward more stratified and complex societies, as it did in the north. Evidence for the organization of craft production and labor organization is not as plentiful as we would like, but we do have some indications of specialization and a division of labor. For example, the mortise and tenon joints of *ganlan* houses at Hemudu, as well as the large-scale and complex nature of other wooden artifacts found there and

at other similar sites, attest to a high level of carpentry skills. Evidence of lacquer production from Hemudu, although not very intensive, suggests the development of a craft that is not only very labor-intensive, but also requires a high level of skill and knowledge. As in the north, the development of a jade industry, which flourished toward the end of the Early Neolithic in the lower Yangzi region, suggests both specialization and the exchange of raw materials and finished objects. A few elaborate ceramic vessels and sophisticated kilns used in ceramic production found at the Chengtoushan site suggest the emergence of ceramic specialists at central sites in the settlement hierarchies of the middle Yangzi region.

At the social level, remains of religious structures and ritual activity at sites such as Lingjiatan might reflect the existence of religious specialists who initiated the construction of the structures and presided over the ceremonies conducted in them. Such developments probably go hand in hand with the emergence of social and political authority, but this is an issue that requires further study.

Unlike for northern China, where we have archaeological data that shed light on the organization of craft production at the levels of the household and the community, no similar data are available for central China. The only indication of related processes is the large *ganlan* houses from Hemudu. Some of these houses are up to 23 m long and 7 m wide, possibly suggesting the emergence of extended families or multifamily households. Such processes, similar to those we saw in the long multiroom houses of north China, suggest the pooling of resources and the creation of larger and more diversified economic units. Integration of this type might lead to the specialization of certain household members in crafts such as carpentry or jade curving. A number of larger than average houses dated to the fourth millennia BCE at Chengtoushan might indicate the beginning of stratification between households

Analysis of mortuary data supports the notion of a gradual development of social and perhaps economic stratification in central China. While early graves in both the middle and lower Yangzi River basin regions are undifferentiated – all are relatively small and unelaborate and contain few burial goods – greater diversity is evident in some of the later cemeteries. Although the state of preservation of the graves at Chengtoushan is not ideal, it is clear that some graves are larger than others and contain many more burial goods. The diversity between graves is even greater at Lingjiatan, in the lower Yangzi River, where the richest grave not only is much larger than the average, but also contains a wooden coffin and a large number of artifacts, including two hundred that are made of jade (Figure 72). However, because all of the graves at Lingjiatan were excavated into a ritualistic platform, it is possible that the varying degrees of elaborateness of the graves reflect not only differences in wealth, but also differences in social and religious prestige.

Nonetheless, it seems that, even at the end of the Early Neolithic period, the differences in size, elaborateness, and richness between graves were not as great as they were in some societies of north China during the same time. We can suggest, perhaps, that societies in central China were more group-oriented, to the extent that even the emerging stratification was expressed in common monuments (the ritual structures). This is quite similar to the Hongshan culture of northeast China, where rich graves were also part of larger communal monuments.

As already noted, very little evidence exists to support the development of similar social or economic hierarchies in south China. We have no indication of settlement hierarchies or public architecture, and although a large sample of graves from sites in this region was excavated, the graves were all found to be small and unelaborate and contained very few or no burial goods.

This, combined with the very rudimentary nature of the pottery and artifacts discovered at southern sites, suggests an egalitarian society with little differentiation in wealth or prestige and with no craft specialization.

REGIONAL VARIATION AND INTERREGIONAL INTERACTIONS DURING THE EARLY NEOLITHIC PERIOD IN CENTRAL AND SOUTH CHINA

The stylistic and technological variations in the material culture of different subregions offer the best evidence for regionalism during the Early Neolithic period. One of the best examples is the variation in style and method of house construction between the middle Yangzi region, where houses were typically constructed on the ground level or were semi-subterranean, and the lower Yangzi region, where *ganlan* became the main type of dwelling. These differences are explained by the different environments of the two subregions, but, like the differences in the styles of ceramic vessels discussed earlier, they also reflect the development of distinct local traditions. By the fourth millennium BCE it is possible to identify broad "cultural packages" that developed in each of the subregions. In the lower Yangzi region, this included typical local ceramics, *ganlan* structures, ritual platforms into which graves were dug, and the intensive production of ritual jade objects. In the middle Yangzi, the cultural package of the so-called Daixi culture included ceramics that were red on the outside and black on the inside and some vessels with painted decorations, houses built on the surface or semi-subterranean, and large sites enclosed by moats and walls.

The categorization of the two different cultural packages is somewhat misleading, however, because, on the one hand, each of the cultural spheres contained much internal diversity and, on the other, they were not mutually exclusive.

Research has not yet begun to explore this issue, and thus the currently evaluable data allow us only a limited glimpse at the cultural, economic, and social diversity that existed in this region during the Early Neolithic. For example, variation in economic adaptation existed not only between the broadly defined regions of China, but also within each of these regions. While much more research is needed to fully flesh out the patterns of this variation, some preliminary results already indicate that in the western part of Hubei province, for example, communities identified as belonging to the Chengbeixi culture led a much more mobile way of life based on hunting and gathering, while in other societies of the Yangzi River basin settlements and agriculture had already become a more central way of life. This economic variation is also reflected in local cultural attributes, such as the less evolved ceramic industry of the Chengbeixi culture (Yang 1991). An equally clear example of local variation is evident in south China, where we see the emergence of the marine-based economic adaptation by communities on the coast and islands, in contrast with the more agricultural economy that gradually developed in locations farther inland.

Cultural contact between the two subregions of the Yangzi River basin is, nevertheless, also apparent in the archaeological record. For example, ceramics in styles resembling the Lower Zaoshi styles of the middle Yangzi River were also found at Kuahuqiao in the lower Yangzi River valley (Jiao 2006). While I do not concur with Jiao's explanation that these similarities necessarily reflect the eastward migration of populations from the middle into the lower Yangzi River basin, they do, nonetheless, appear to reflect interregional contact and mutual influence. Jade ornaments such as *huang* pendants and *jue* earrings similar to those found at Lingjiatan have frequently been found at other sites throughout the Yangzi River basin (Zhang 2006), suggesting that Lingjiatan jades were traded to other communities and perhaps even imitated by local craftsmen. Either way, this is evidence for interaction and intercultural influences.

Long-Range Interactions

Long-range contact began by the Early Neolithic period, if not even earlier. As already noted, rice grains found at the Jiahu site, in Henan province, can be seen as evidence of contact between societies in the Yellow and Yangzi River basins. In much the same way, the introduction of domesticated rice during the fourth millennium BCE to communities such as Dingsishan in south China is attributed to contact with communities in the Yangzi River basin. Such contact might have been indirect, and the spread of domesticated animals and plants is perhaps more similar to a slow filtering process than to an exchange, but the final outcome is meaningful interregional contacts.

We should not assume that interactions and the spread of cultural traits stopped at the present-day borders of China. For example, Rispoli (2007) argues that by the sixth and fifth millennia BCE, societies in Vietnam were in contact with their counterparts in southern China. She bases this reconstruction on similarities in the cord-marked pottery and burial habits of the two regions.

The spread of populations from central and south China to the islands of the Pacific, the so-called expansion of the Austronesians, is a process that some scholars trace to the latter part of the Early Neolithic period. According to these models, by the fifth or fourth millennia BCE, populations in the lower Yangzi River region and on the eastern coast of south China had developed seafaring capabilities that allowed them not only to exploit marine resources, but also to travel to offshore islands such as Haitan Island, where the Keqiutou site is located, as well as to more remote locations such as the island of Taiwan. Evidence for contact with Taiwan during this period is found in the similarities between the material attributes of the Dapenkeng (大盆坑) culture of

Taiwan and its counterparts in eastern Fujian and Guangdong provinces (Jiao 2007: 91–4). Although there is as yet no evidence of agriculture at sites from the early part of the Dapenkeng, some scholars nonetheless see it as part of the route by which agriculture spread into the Pacific (Bellwood 2005: 134–41).

Interregional contact and the long-range interactions, suggested by the evidence presented in Chapters 4 and 5, were neither common nor intensive. However, they were an integral part of the socioeconomic development of communities in different parts of China. It would be wrong to think that only large-scale human migration or large volumes of trade can cause change. Sometimes even small quantities of domesticated grain from afar might catalyze economic change, and a few objects that filter through via hand-to-hand exchange can inspire the adoption of new technologies or the development of new social forms (though not necessarily related to the social forms in the society from which the objects originated). No less important, the patterns of interregional interaction observed during the Early Neolithic period are a prelude to the flourishing of these types of contact during the Late Neolithic period (Chapter 6) and the Bronze Age.

EXPLAINING THE ADVENT OF AGRICULTURE AND THE ORIGINS OF SOCIAL AND ECONOMIC CHANGE

Chapters 3 to 5 described the beginnings of and advancement of agriculture in different parts of China, as well as the incipient socioeconomic processes that took place among early agricultural societies. By way of concluding this part of the book, it is appropriate to revisit the big questions raised in these three chapters: What were the motivations and forces that brought about the transition to agriculture? What were the sources of social complexity and stratification during the Early Neolithic period? We consider the second question first: It would seem that the initial source of these developments was not agriculture but rather the transition to sedentism. The initial accumulation of property (artifacts), the need for social norms to regulate the community's life, and even the initial demographic changes are all related to people's ability and willingness to reside in permanent year-round settlements.

The different inputs that affected the socioeconomic developments during the Early Neolithic in China are, of course, not mutually exclusive. In fact, they are interrelated. For example, a demographic increase in the total number of people in a certain region and their concentration in a few sites is, from one perspective, a result of the transition to a sedentary way of life. It is also a catalyst for further economic development and the need to create social norms that regulate life in such densely populated communities. Agriculture and sedentism are also interrelated: when a community stays in one place for a prolonged period of time, its motivation to develop locally available resources increases. At the same time, the development of such resources, through cultivation and, finally, domestication, enabled more people to live in one place throughout the entire year. However, the currently available dates pertaining to cultivation and domestication suggest that both began to take place on a meaningful scale only after the transition to permanent settlement was well under way.

One possible reason for differences between the trajectories of north, central, and south China during Early Neolithic is to be found in the interrelations between sedentism and agriculture. In north China, where the two processes were closely interlinked from a very early stage – perhaps because full sedentism was possible in the north only when agricultural production supplemented the resources of the relatively poor environment – the rate of socioeconomic change was faster. In central China, where the environment provided far more plentiful wild resources that were available year round, sedentism was possible without agriculture, and the two processes became linked only at a later stage, when demographic expansion and cultivation reinforced one another.

In southern China, heavier rainfall and the rapid growth rate of wild plants may have posed an obstacle to cultivation. The fact that some rich resources, such as shellfish, are not suitable for cultivation and domestication may have been another such obstacle. Because of these natural obstacles, and perhaps also because of resistance to new cultural norms among local communities, sedentism (or semisedentism) existed in this region for a long period of time without being associated with cultivation and agriculture. This may also be one of the reasons for other major cultural differences between south China on the one hand, and central and north China on the other.

This discussion brings us back to the questions about the origins of agriculture raised in Chapter 3. Of the three main models discussed in the chapter – *push*, *pull*, and *social* – it would seem that the initial input is related to the *pull* group of models: the plentiful conditions that allowed for the permanent year-round settlement of hunter-gatherer communities were the trigger that started off the other processes. On the other hand, the evolution of agriculture from a secondary resource into the main economic source and its development into a complex "system of knowledge" may also be seen as the result of *push* and *social* factors. For example, the demographic processes launched by the transition to sedentism compelled local communities to intensify their agricultural production so as to be able to feed their larger populations in an environment that may have over time become depleted of natural resources. In much the same way, modes of social interaction in larger communities living together in the same place over a long time could have created social pressures to develop new agricultural resources. Such resources might be, for example, the prestigious foods needed for feasts held to mitigate social tensions or to reinforce the prestige of aspiring individuals.

Viewing agriculture as a process allows us to elaborate on such observations and correlate them with other processes observed in the archaeological record. Although agriculture continued to evolve in China during the Late Neolithic period and even beyond, in the following chapters we will shift our attention to the social, economic, and political processes that were initiated during the Early Neolithic, but reached maturity during the Late Neolithic and the Bronze Age.

CHAPTER 6

THE EMERGENCE AND DEVELOPMENT OF SOCIOPOLITICAL COMPLEXITY

The incipient beginnings of social complexity and stratification, which appeared during the Early Neolithic period, came to maturation during the Late Neolithic period. During this period agricultural production intensified substantially and polities that were larger in scale and more complex and stratified than their Early Neolithic predecessors emerged in different parts of China. According to many scholars this was also the period when the foundations of Chinese civilization were established, including the social patterns, technologies, and symbols that would become integral to Chinese societies during the Bronze Age and the imperial era.

The materials presented in this chapter provide us with an opportunity to address the topic of social complexity and stratification from a number of perspectives. To start, we have already noted that intersocietal contact intensified during this period, a process which, according to one of the most influential models – the Chinese interaction sphere model – was an important social catalyst responsible for the almost concurrent development of complex societies in different regions of China (Chang 1986: 234–94). Evidence of this contact is reviewed and analyzed in this chapter, though we also observe that the interaction sphere did not extend evenly across all of China, and that the evidence clearly points to a significant degree of regional variation. Another issue, touched upon

at the end of this chapter, is how developments during the Late Neolithic period affected the formation of a uniquely "Chinese" culture and how such ideas and cultural norms were transmitted through time and space.

THE MATERIAL CULTURE OF LATE NEOLITHIC SOCIETIES IN CHINA

Until the late 1970s, the Late Neolithic period was synonymous with the Longshan culture. When K. C. Chang published his influential Chinese interaction sphere model, he was writing about the "Longshanoid horizon" (Chang 1986: 234–42), implying a large degree of homogeneity among Late Neolithic societies. Subsequent research, however, has made it clear that these so-called Longshan societies displayed a great deal of regional variation (cf. Underhill 1997, 2002; Liu 2004). Moreover, discoveries in areas beyond the regions discussed by Chang have revealed an even larger degree of heterogeneity.

Settlement Patterns and Site Structure

The overall trend throughout most regions of north and central China is one of a substantial increase in population density during the third millennium BCE. The results of a systematic regional survey of the Rizhao (日照) area of

TABLE 4. *Late Neolithic archaeological cultures of north China*

Date BCE	Northwest (upper Yellow River)	Central North (Ordos region, Inner Mongolia, and northern Shanxi)	Wei River basin	Middle Yellow River	Lower Yellow River	Northeast
3500	Majiayao 马家窑 (3300–2500)		Late Yangshao 仰韶 (3500–3000)	Late Yangshao 仰韶 (3500–3000)	Dawenkou 大汶口 (4300–2600)	Hongshan 红山 (4500–3000)
3000		Laohushan 老虎山 (2800–2300 BC)	Longshan 龙山 (also known by other more localized names) (3000–1900)	Henan Longshan 河南龙山 (also known by other more localized names) (3000–1900)	Shandong Longshan 山东龙山 (2600–1900)	Xiaoheyan 小河沿 (3000–2200)
2500	Banshan 半山 (2500–2300) Machang 马厂 (2300–2000)					

southern Shandong demonstrate phenomenal growth, from 27 sites covering an area of 47.3 ha during the Late Dawenkou period to 463 sites covering an accumulated area of 2,005.4 ha during the Longshan period (Underhill et al. 2008: 6–8). Indications that this trend is similar to those in other regions in the lower Yellow River basin can be seen in the tripling of the number of sites

TABLE 5. *Late Neolithic archaeological cultures of central and south China*

Date BCE	Lower Yangzi	Middle Yangzi	Chengdu basin	South China (Lingnan)	Southeast coast
3500	Liangzhu 良渚 (3300–2100)	Qujialing 屈家岭 (3300–2600)		Dingsishan 顶蛳山 phase IV (4000–3000)	Xiantouling 咸头岭 (4000–3000)
3000				Shixia 石峡 (3000–2000)	Yangliang 涌浪 Lower Zhujiang (3000–2000) Tanshisan-Niubishan 昙石山-牛鼻山 (Fujian) (3000–2000)
2500		Shijiahe 石家河 (2600–1900)	Baodun 宝墩 (2700–1700)		

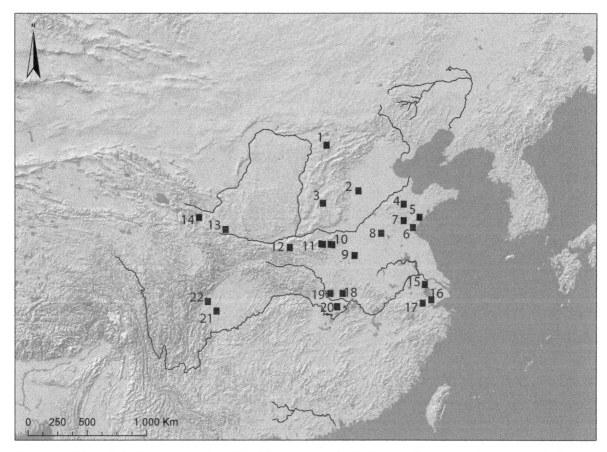

Figure 80. Map of all the sites mentioned in Chapter 6: 1. Laohushan; 2. Jiangou; 3. Taosi; 4. Xizhufeng; 5. Liangchengzhen; 6. Yaowangcheng; 7. Chengzi; 8. Gucheng; 9. Pingliangtai; 10. Guchengzhai; 11. Wangchenggang; 12. Kangjia; 13. Linjia; 14. Liuwan; 15. Sidun; 16. Mojiaoshan; 17. Fanshan; 18. Taojiahu; 19. Shijiahe; 20. Xiaojiawuji; 21. Baodun; 22. Mangcheng.

documented by the Culture Relics Bureau – from about 500 during the Dawenkou to around 1,500 during the Longshan (Guojia Wenwuju 2007).

The number of sites in the middle Yellow River basin reflects a similar increase from the late Yangshao period to the Longshan period (Guojia Wenwuju 2006). The results of a regional survey of the Yiluo area, in the heart of the middle Yellow River basin, suggest that population levels may have decreased during the Late Yangshao and the early Longshan periods, but that they recovered and proceeded to rise substantially during the middle and late Longshan periods (Liu et al. 2004: 88).

Population growth is also suggested, albeit more imprecisely, for other areas where systematic regional surveys have not been carried out. In many regions, not only are more sites known from this period in comparison with sites from the Early Neolithic, but the sites themselves, or at least some of them, are much larger than anything seen before. For example, on the Liyang (澧阳) plain in northwest Hunan province, the number and area of sites grew only slightly between the Daixi (ca. 4500–3300 BCE) and the Qujialing (3300–2600 BCE) periods. More impressive growth occurred in the transition from the Qujialing to the Shijiahe (2600–1900 BCE) periods, from 45 sites with an accumulated size of 91 ha during the former to 163 sites covering an accumulated area of 169 ha during the latter (Pei 2004). In the Chengdu plain, which was sparsely populated during the Early Neolithic, if at all, a relatively large number of Late Neolithic sites, some of them walled and quite large, suggest a rapid process of population growth (Chengdu 2010; Wang Yi 2003).

It is important to emphasize that not all regions of China share this trend of population growth during the Late Neolithic. Indeed, northeast China is an outstanding example of what would seem to be a decline in population levels during the third millennium BCE. The Xiaoheyan culture, which followed the Hongshan culture in this region, is not well defined, and our understanding of the local trajectory is therefore less than complete (Chifeng 2003). Nevertheless, results from the systematic Chifeng survey suggest that this region, which enjoyed population growth and a trend toward the clustering of sites during the Hongshan period, was sparsely populated during most of the third millennium BCE (Chifeng 2011).

In most regions, population growth during the Late Neolithic was coupled with the clustering of sites and the formation of site hierarchies. While in many regions most sites were not fortified, those that were stood at the apex of the settlement hierarchies. Until about twenty years ago, walled Neolithic sites were identified only in the Yellow River region and were thought to be a local phenomenon. The discovery of similar sites in many other regions, some quite large and elaborate, is one of the most exciting developments in recent Chinese archaeology.

The process of site clustering is exemplified in the Rizhao survey region, where no clustering of sites from the Dawenkou period is apparent. However, during the Longshan period, the settlement in this region clearly became clustered around two very large sites: Liangchengzhen (两城镇) (272.5 ha in size) in the northern part of

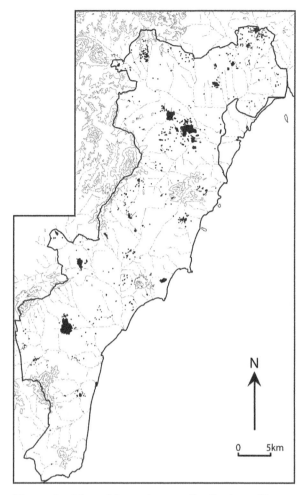

Figure 81. Map of the settlement distribution of Long-shan sites in the Rizhao area of southern Shandong.

the region and Yaowangcheng (尧王城) (367.5 ha) in the southern part (Underhill et al. 2008: 6–8) (Figure 81). Remains of walls have also been found at Liangchengzhen, though it is not clear what portion of the site they enclosed.

More than twenty walled sites dated to the Late Neolithic period have been found in the lower and middle Yellow River regions. Many of these fortified sites are distributed regularly at a distance of some 30 to 50 km from one another and seem to have served as the centers of polities (Guojia Wenwuju 2006, 2007; Liu 2004). Other evidence, such as the association of fortified sites with prestigious

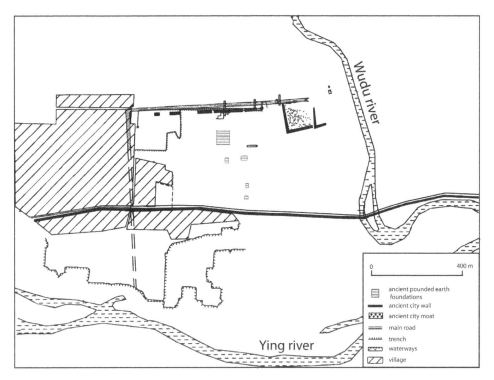

Figure 82. The walled Longshan site of Wangchenggang (after Beijing 2007: 26).

buildings and artifacts and with special productive activities, supports this hypothesis (Liu 2004: 104–5; Underhill et al. 2008).

In the lower and middle Yellow River regions, most fortified sites are around 50 ha in size, though some are much larger. A well-known smaller site is Wangchenggang (王城岗), where fortifications were made of several pounded earth wall enclosures (Figure 82). Two well-preserved small enclosures are located in the northeastern part of the site. The walls are built upon a foundation trench that is 4.4 m wide and 2.5 m deep and is filled with layers of pounded earth (Chang 1986: 273–6; Liu 2004: 104–5), but it is unclear what their above-ground height was. A much larger enclosure, of an area of more than 30 ha surrounded by walls and moats, was located to the west of the two smaller enclosures. Like the smaller enclosures, it is rectangular in shape and its pounded earth walls are up to 10 m wide (Beijing and Henan 2007). It remains unclear whether these enclosures

coexisted at the same time, or whether the larger enclosure replaced the two smaller ones.

A much larger walled site has been partially excavated at Taosi (陶寺) in Shanxi (Figure 83). The walls at this site are up to 10 m wide, and at the peak of the site's expansion they would have enclosed an area of some 280 ha. An internal pounded earth wall separated the residential and ceremonial quarters of the elite from the areas inhabited by commoners, thereby signifying the development of a stratified society (He 2013; Ren 1998; Zhongguo Shehui et al. 2005). A recent survey counted fifty-four Taosi period sites in this region in Shanxi; at least three of them, not including the Taosi site itself, are more than 100 ha in size, twenty-three are between 10 and 99 ha, and the rest are smaller (He 2013). The range in site sizes, the more or less even distribution of the largest sites, and the association between labor investment and the largest site (Taosi) all suggest the development of a regional settlement hierarchy and the

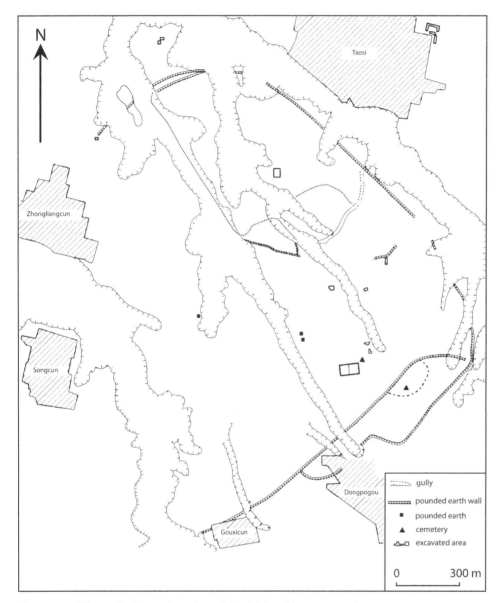

Figure 83. The walled Longshan site of Taosi (after Liu 2004: 109).

ability of the center(s) to recruit labor and accumulate resources.

An even larger fortified Neolithic site named Shimao (石峁) in Shenmu county, Shaanxi province has been preliminary reported. It is said to cover an area of 400 ha and to have been surrounded by a wall made of stones that encompassed three enclosures (Shaanxi et al. 2013). These measurements make the site the largest and most labor-

intensive of all late third millennium BCE sites found in China, but so far only very partial reports of the excavations have been published and crucial information, including the construction date of the stone wall, cannot be corroborated.

Fortified sites are not found all over China. For example, no walled sites have been reported in the Wei River Valley or in the lower Yangzi River region.[1] However, over the past thirty years

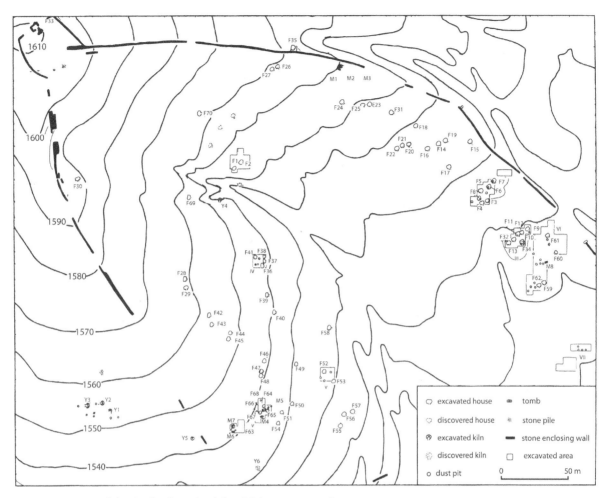

Figure 84. Map of the Laohushan site (after Neimenggu 2000).

it has become clear that the fortification of Late Neolithic communities was a much wider phenomenon than previously estimated. One of the more surprising discoveries is clusters of fortified sites in the Ordos region of Inner Mongolia and the northern part of Shanxi province, some of which are located in close proximity to one another. These sites, associated with the so-called Laohushan culture, are usually smaller than Longshan sites. The Laohushan site itself covers about 13 ha, and other sites are usually smaller (Figure 84). The construction technique of the Laohushan walls is unusual among Late Neolithic Chinese sites. While in other regions walls were built using the pounded earth (*hangtu*) or piled earth techniques, Laohushan walls were built from unhewed stones mixed with rubble and earth (Neimenggu 2000; Xu 2000: 19–23).

In the middle Yangzi River basin, the construction of site walls, which had begun during the latter part of the Early Neolithic, continued on a much grander scale during the Late Neolithic period. The walls of these sites are typically wide earthen piles. Earth dug up from the wide moats that surrounded each site was used not only for constructing the walls but also to elevate the ground inside the sites above the level of the flood plain.

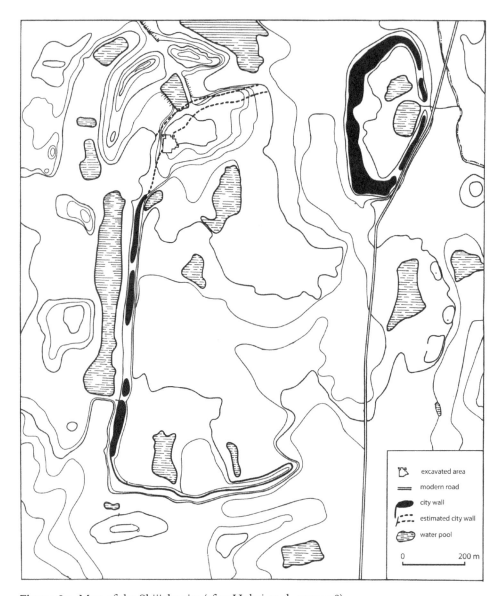

Figure 85. Map of the Shijiahe site (after Hubei et al. 2003: 18).

At least eight walled Shijiahe period sites are known. Of these, the Shijiahe site itself is the largest, with massive walls. Inside the walls, the site is more than 100 ha in size, far larger than most contemporary sites. One other site, Taojiahu (陶家湖), is estimated to be around 60 ha in size, but the rest are 20 ha or less. Well preserved sections of the Shijiahe walls are 50 m wide at the base, 4–5 m wide at the top, and more than 6 m

tall (Figure 85). Some studies estimate that about 700,000 m³ of earth were used in the construction of the Shijiahe wall. The Shijiahe walls were also surrounded by a huge moat, which at some points reaches a width of 100 m. Ceramic pipes excavated at Shijiahe suggest the development public facilities, such as drainage and sewage, which may have sustained the large population concentrated at this site (Hubei et al. 2003).

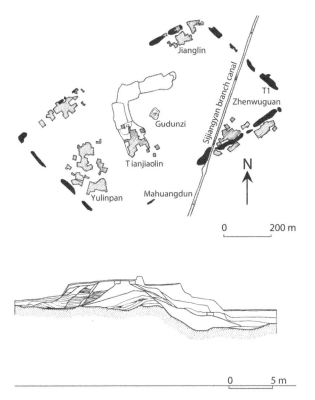

Figure 86. The piled earth and pounded earth walls of Baodun (after Wang Yi 2003: 112).

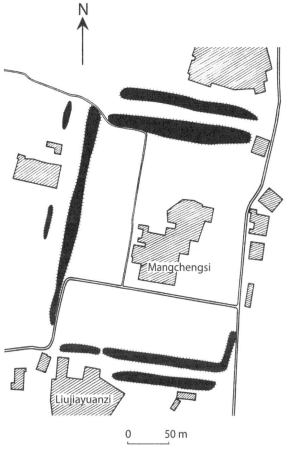

Figure 87. The piled earth and pounded earth walls of Mangcheng (after Wang Yi 2003: 119).

Walled Neolithic sites have also been found in the Chengdu plain of the upper Yangzi region (Sichuan). So far, at least six walled sites dated to the Baodun period have been found in this region, of which Baodun itself is the largest and best known (Figure 86). The Baodun enclosure is rectangular in shape and covers an area of more than 60 ha.[2] The walls at Baodun and other contemporaneous sites in the area are made of piled earth. While sections of this earth may have been pounded to make it more stable, the walls are not upright but sloping. The better preserved sections of the wall at Baodun are 3 to 5 m high, 30 m wide at the base, and about 8 m wide at the top (Wang Yi 2003). The contemporary site of Mangcheng (芒城) is much smaller, covering only about 10 ha, but is enclosed by two concentric sets of piled earth and pounded earth walls set 20 m apart (Figure 87). Each of the walls is enclosed by a

moat, thereby making it a formidable fortification (Wang Yi 2003: 118–20).

Domestic and Public Structures

The domestic structures of the Late Neolithic period continue the traditions established during the Early Neolithic. In the north, we are aware of both single- and multiroom structures. An example of the latter is found at the Kangjia (康家) site in Shaanxi, where at least seven rows of houses were found (Liu 2004: 49–53). Each row was divided into small rooms, each around 9 to 12 m², with separate entrances. The houses were built with pounded earthen foundations and brick

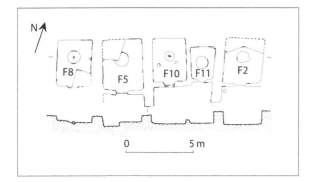

Figure 88. Multiroom house compound at Kangjia (after Zhongguo Shehui 2010b: 584).

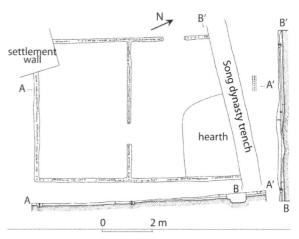

Figure 89. House F5 at Mangcheng (after Wang Yi 2003: 121).

adobe walls, and the floors were sometimes plastered with layers of lime. Each row of the houses at Kangjia was subdivided into smaller units of two to six rooms that were separated from one another by walls that created a common courtyard in front of the rooms (Figure 88). This division into nuclear units (nuclear families), larger cooperative groups (the extended family) that shared an outdoor activity area, and larger social units (multifamily corporative units) that shared the same multiroom building is quite suggestive with regard to the internal complexity of Late Neolithic society. In many other sites, such as Taosi, one-room houses continued to be the norm, though it is possible that several such structures clustered together functioned as an integrated unit.

Single-room houses appear to have been the norm in central China, but multiroom structures are also known. Multiroom row houses, very similar in shape to those at Kangjia, have been found in the middle Yangzi region at sites associated with the Qujialing culture (Pei 2004: 223). A different type of multiroom house was found in the Chengdu plain. While most of the houses that we know about from this region are quite small, with only a single room, some two-room houses are also known. The best example is house F5 at Mangcheng (Figure 89): It is a rectangular structure 50 m² in size, which is subdivided into two rooms connected by a door. The structure was

built on a bamboo framework using the wattle-and-daub method (Wang Yi 2003: 120–1).

In the lower Yangzi region, the continuation of the pole house (*ganlan*) method of construction is evident at some of the habitation sites associated with the Liangzhu culture. At other sites, surface-built rectangular houses have also been discovered. These houses are quite small, ranging from 5 to 20 m² in size, and were built using timber posts and the wattle-and-daub technique (Sun 1993: 5).

Larger and more elaborate structures, which are seen as representative of elite residences, or buildings used for public functions, have been found in most parts of north and central China. Placement on top of pounded earth platforms denotes many of these houses. Such foundations were found, for example, in the eastern of the two smaller enclosures of Wangchenggang. Complete and mutilated human skeletons found buried beneath these structures may represent foundation-laying sacrifices and the display of elite power (Liu 2004: 104–5).

A more complete large building was found at the walled site of Guchengzhai (古城寨) in Henan province. This "palatial compound" is enclosed by a wattle-and-daub wall and corridors. The main building within the compound wall was

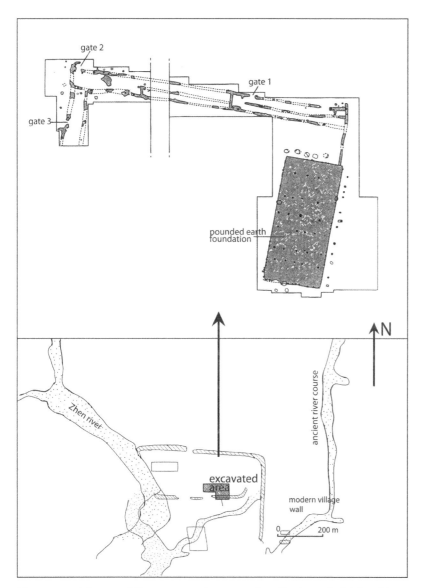

Figure 90. A large public compound excavated at Guchengzhai (after Liu 2004: 107).

constructed on pillars that rested on a pounded earth platform 28.4 m long and 13.5 m wide (Henan 2002; Liu 2004: 106–7) (Figure 90). Because this complex has been only partially excavated, its total size and complete layout are unknown. However, its overall size – including the open courtyard between the compound walls and the pounded earth platforms – must have been very large. While it was not necessarily a "palace," such a large structure and the bounded courtyard in front of it would seem to indicate a public space used for large gatherings, such as in political or religious activities. Indeed, it is quite similar in structure to public buildings known from the early second millennium BCE site of Erlitou (Chapter 7).

Remains of an even more complex and, thus far, poorly understood structure have recently been excavated inside the smaller walled enclosure at the southeastern side of the Taosi site (He 2013;

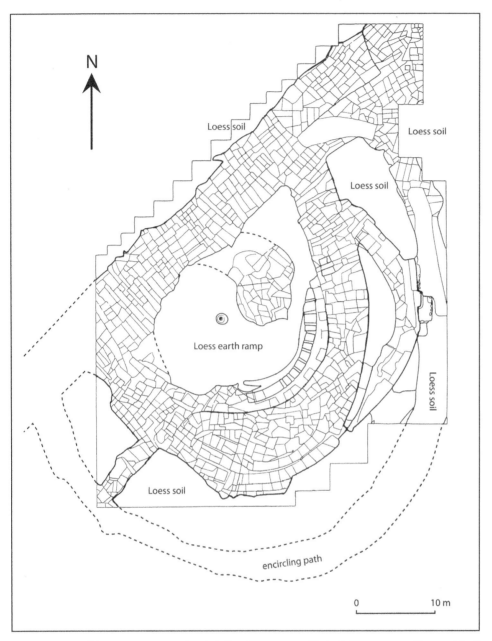

N

Loess soil

Loess soil

Loess soil

Loess earth ramp

Loess soil

Loess soil

Loess soil

encircling path

0   10 m

Figure 91. Building II FJT1 at Taosi (after Zhongguo Shehui Kexueyuan Kaogu Yanjiusuo Shanxidui et al. 2007: 5).

Zhongguo et al. 2007). A series of pounded earth foundations and retaining walls form a semicircular shape covering an area of about 1,400 m². A circular platform with pillar bases, also made of pounded earth, are arranged on top of the foundations (Figure 91). This uniquely shaped building, labeled II FJT1, was identified by the excavators as a ritual "astronomical observatory." While their hypothesis cannot be tested, the complexity of the structure, the amount of labor invested in it, and its unique shape all suggest that it was used for some sort of ritual or other public function.

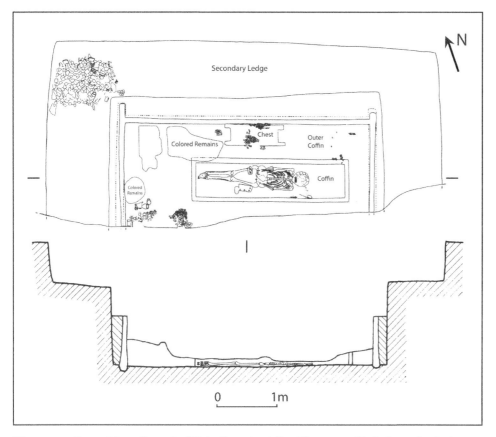

Figure 92. Grave M202 from the Xizhufeng site (after Zhongguo Shehui 2010b: 610).

Currently only a few remains of public buildings have been discovered in central China, most of them from the upper Yangzi region. The remains of one such structure were found at the center of the walled site of Gucheng (古城) in the Chengdu plain: An elongated rectangular foundation made of cobblestones and earth and measuring 50 m by 11 m. The foundations run parallel to the site walls. The building itself was supported by wooden poles, and it seems that it was a single, large, undivided room. Five piles of cobblestones set into shallow pits are regularly spaced inside the building and may have originally formed bamboo-supported platforms (Chengdu 2001; Wang Yi 203: 125–6). The building is seen as having served for community-wide rituals, perhaps even at the supra-community level.

Cemeteries, Burials, and Ritual Activity

Mortuary data are the most often cited source of information on Late Neolithic society, and although more domestic sites and contexts have been surveyed and excavated in recent years, most of the archaeological information about the Late Neolithic period in China still comes from graves.

Graves from the Late Neolithic period in the lower Yellow River region are famous for their elaborateness and for the expensive burial goods placed in them. This Shandong Longshan mortuary tradition is a direct continuation of the traditions of the Dawenkou period, though it is evident that during this period the disparity between poor and rich graves increased. In comparison with Dawenkou, fewer graves contain many items

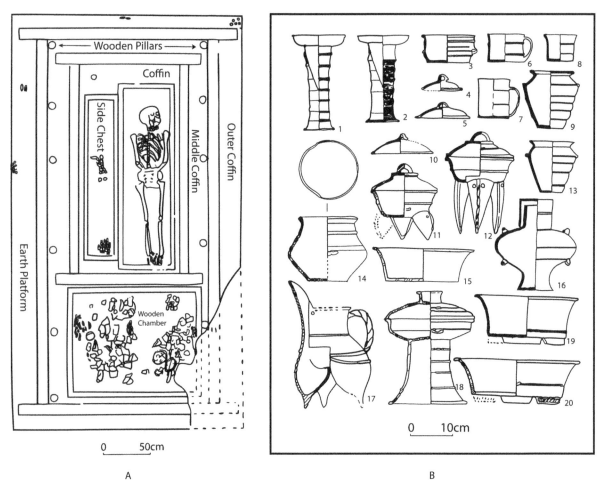

Figure 93. A. Grave M1 from the Xizhufeng site; B. Some of the ceramic artifacts found in grave M1 (after Zhang 2006: 93–4).

of pottery, but the few elite graves are exceptionally rich, not only in terms of the quantity of vessels placed in them, but more importantly, in the inclusion of highly labor-intensive ceramics (Underhill 2002: 147–98). The eighty-seven graves at the Chengzi (呈子) site range from 0.2 to 3.7 m² in size, and the number of artifacts found in them ranges from none to thirty-one; the larger the grave, the more goods were placed in it (Liu 2004: 143). Even larger and more elaborate graves were found at Xizhufeng (西朱封): The largest of the three elite graves excavated at the site, grave M202, is almost 7 m long and 3 m wide. It has a built ledge (*ercengtai*), upon which

some of the grave goods were placed, as well as inner and outer painted wooden coffins (Figure 92). Although the grave was partly destroyed, more than fifty burial goods were found in it, including jade artifacts, several eggshell ceramic cups, and a painted wooden box. At the same site, another grave, labeled M1, contains an even more elaborate structure of three nested wooden coffins and a special wooden chamber in which no fewer than fifty-four burial goods were placed (Zhang 2006; Zhongguo Shehui 2010b: 609–10) (Figures 93).

The cemetery at Taosi, in the middle Yellow River region, is one of the largest ever found in China. It covers 3 ha in size and contains thousands of graves, of which more than one thousand have been excavated. The results of these excavations have not yet been published in full detail, but archaeologists working at Taosi have assigned each grave one of three ranks according to its size and furnishings. Of the excavated graves, 87 percent were small pits, big enough to contain a corpse in the extended position, and contained few or no grave goods. Medium-size graves compose 12.7 percent of those excavated. They were larger, held a wooden structure (coffin), and contained several dozen artifacts – primarily pottery, but also a number of prestigious offerings, such as jade ornaments and pig mandibles. Of the graves excavated at Taosi, 1.3 percent were large tombs, some 3 m long and 2.5 m wide and up to 2 m deep, each containing a wooden coffin and hundreds of burial goods, including painted red pottery, jade artifacts, musical instruments, such as alligator and ceramic drums and large chime stones, painted wooden artifacts, complete pig skeletons, and more (Figure 94). Both men and women were buried in the small and medium graves, but the large graves contained only male skeletons (Chang 1986: 276–7; Liu 2004: 135–7; Zhongguo Shehui 2010b: 572–4). Drums made of wood and covered with alligator skin were probably the most prestigious items. They have been found only in the largest graves at Taosi and in graves of a comparable size in Shandong Longshan sites. It has been suggested that during this period the coastal area of Shandong was a natural habitat for alligators and that alligator skins were transported from there some 500 km inland to Taosi (Liu 2004: 122).

Unlike the very elaborate elite Longshan graves from the lower Yellow River region and from southern Shanxi (Taosi), contemporaneous graves in Wangchenggang and the Yiluo areas in Henan are relatively modest. Based on the currently available evidence, it appears that mortuary displays were less emphasized in these societies.

Late Neolithic societies in northwest China offer an interesting comparison to their contem-

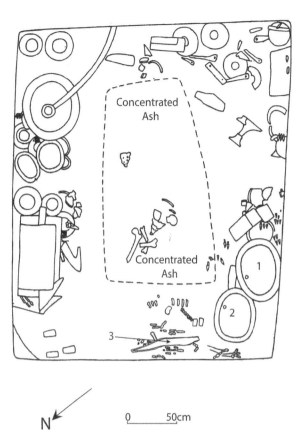

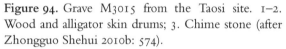

Figure 94. Grave M3015 from the Taosi site. 1–2. Wood and alligator skin drums; 3. Chime stone (after Zhongguo Shehui 2010b: 574).

poraneous societies to the east. Little is known about Late Neolithic settlement patterns in the Gansu-Qinghai region, but mortuary data from this region, on the other hand, are very rich. In the Liuwan (柳湾) cemetery alone, more than eleven hundred graves from the Late Neolithic period were excavated in area of some 11 ha (Qinghai and Zhongguo 1984; Chang 1986: 138–50). These graves are very different in shape and content from Longshan graves. Though single-person burials are most common, multiperson burials and secondary burials, not seen in the east, are by no means a rarity. The grave pits tend to be much deeper than regular graves in the east, and they do not contain a ledge. Larger graves have a passageway leading to the main burial chamber, with the two

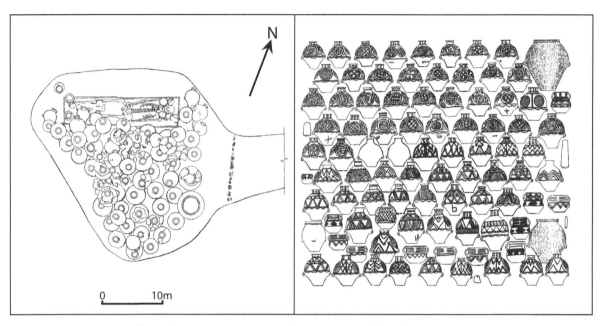

Figure 95. Grave M564 from the Liuwen cemetery and the grave goods found in it (after Zhongguo Shehui 2010b: 631).

parts of the grave sometimes separated from one another by a wooden frame (or fence). In larger graves, the burial chamber is of irregular shape, with the wooden coffin placed at one side while the rest of the chamber is filled with grave goods (Figure 95).

The burial offerings are also very different from those seen in the east. Most of the grave goods are large ceramic jars (hu 壶), with a very small number of jade artifacts or other prestigious objects. Although the jars are all very similar in size and shape, they are individually decorated.

There is evidence that throughout the Late Neolithic in northwest China, the disparity in terms of grave size and the quantity of decorated pottery placed in them increased. In the Liuwan cemetery, the 257 graves associated with the Banshan period range in size from ca. 0.5 m² to 6 m² and are usually quite shallow. On average, each grave contained only one ceramic vessel, and only a few had more than five. In contrast, the 872 graves dated to the Machang period are

much larger, some more than 10 m² in size and more than 3 m deep, with elaborate passageways and wooden fences. On average, each grave from this period contained some fifteen ceramic jars, but the disparity in numbers is great: while small graves contained only a few vessels, the richest grave, M564, held no fewer than ninety-five vessels (Allard 2001).

The jars placed in the Machang graves were painted on their upper parts, designed perhaps to be seen from above by participants at the funeral. These decorations include some of the oldest anthropomorphic figures found in China, which have been interpreted by some scholars as reflecting shamanic rituals (Chang 1986: 150). While the shamanic interpretation is no longer widely accepted, the decorations probably represent the development of local beliefs and rituals.

The lower Yangzi is one of the regions most famous for its Late Neolithic mortuary traditions. The Liangzhu culture is associated not only with very rich graves, but also with the construction

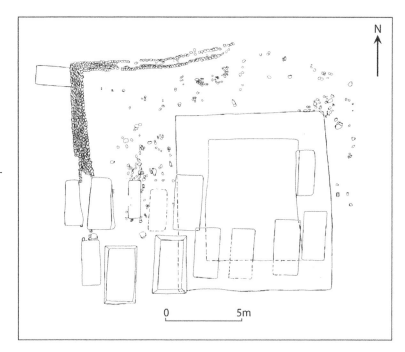

Figure 96. The burial mound at Fanshan (after Hubei et al. 2003: 690).

of large platforms (or mounds). These mortuary practices can be seen as a continuation of local traditions from the fourth millennium BCE (Chapter 5), though the scale and sophistication of jade production and of mortuary mounds construction reached its peak during the third millennium BCE.

Fanshan (反山) is a pounded earth mound about 2,700 m² in size and 4 m high (Figure 96). Eleven large pit graves were excavated from the top of this mound, containing some 1,200 grave goods, 90 percent of which were jades. Other items include fine pottery, stone tools, and small ivory objects. Some tombs contained lacquered wooden burial caskets (Zhejiang 2005). At Sidun (寺墩), another burial mound site in the lower Yangzi, the most lavishly furnished grave is that of a young adult male containing 127 grave goods: 49 ornamental jades, 24 jade rings and discs, 33 jade tubes (*cong*), and 3 ornamental jade axes, as well as 14 stone tools and 4 burnished ceramic vessels (Figure 97). The archaeologist who studied this grave suggested that 26 of the jades had been intentionally bro-

ken and/or exposed to fire during the burial ceremony (Huang 1992: 76–7). Extra human skulls and bones found at some of the more elaborate Liangzhu graves have been identified as the remains of human sacrifices (Chang 1986: 255). Because only a few lower status graves were placed in Liangzhu burial mounds, they are much less visible to archaeologists. The few that have been found are much smaller and contain no more than fifteen grave goods, most of which are utilitarian ceramics or stone artifacts (Zhang 1999).

Mojiaoshan (莫角山) is an example of a nonburial mound structure from the lower Yangzi River region. Dated to the Liangzhu period, this is a very large man-made (or at least partly anthropogenic) mound covering an area of 3 ha, and rising 7 m above its surroundings. The mound is made of pounded earth and unbaked clay layers, on top of which stand three smaller ramps, each some 3 m tall and ranging in size from 300 to 1,500 m². Other features located on the mound include two stone "sacrificial altars" and storage pits. Postholes, large column bases, and adobe bricks suggest

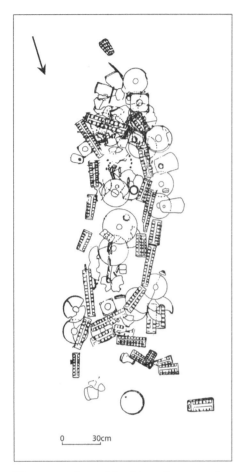

0   30cm

Figure 97. A wealthy Liangzhu grave from the Sidun site (after Nanjing Bowuguan 1984: 114).

that there was also a structure built on top of the mound, but its exact shape and dimensions are unclear (Zhang 1999).

Some regions, such as the middle Yangzi River and the Chengdu basin, are less known for rich elite graves, possibly because they have not yet been found, but maybe because differentiated mortuary practices were not emphasized by those societies. For example, known Qujialing burials are either poorly furnished rectangular shaft pits without coffins or simple urn burials (Zhang 2004: 175–81). Shijiahe period burials continue this tradition, with the coexistence of both pit and urn graves. Even the largest Shijiahe pit burials are not very big in comparison to contemporaneous

graves from other regions. The largest and richest Shijiahe grave discovered so far is M7 from the Xiaojiawuji (肖家屋脊) site. It is 3.2 m long and 1.8 m wide and has a ledge but no coffin. It contains 103 burial goods, mostly pottery (Figure 98). While jade offerings are sometimes found in Shijiahe graves, they are much less numerous compared to Liangzhu burials (Zhongguo Shehui 2010b: 669–72).

The Shijiahe period is better known for other types of ritual activity, in particular the large-scale production and consumption of small clay figurines representing animals and humans (Figure 99). In the northwestern section of the Shijiahe site (an area called Dengjiawan), thousands of such figurines were placed together inside pits, suggesting their use in a communal ritual. Indeed, large caches of artifacts seem to be a typical phenomenon in this region. A collection of some hundred thousand red pottery cups found at the Sanfangwan (三房湾) locale of the Shijiahe site has also been interpreted as a ritual deposit (Hubei et al. 2003; Yang Xiaoneng 2004: 2:98).

Craft Production and Technology

Evidence of increased technological sophistication and craft specialization is found for Late Neolithic societies in most of the regions discussed earlier. The fast pottery wheels became common in the production, not only of prestigious ceramic goods, but also of utilitarian ones (Underhill 2002). The Shandong Longshan culture is famous for its delicate eggshell cups and fine black burnished pottery, which have been found mostly in graves, but also in domestic contexts. While each artifact was individually produced and had unique decorations, the repetition of shapes and the consistency in size suggest the development of production standards (Figure 100). Only highly trained potters could have produced such artifacts: their firing would have required not only the ability to reach high kiln temperatures, but also absolute control over the

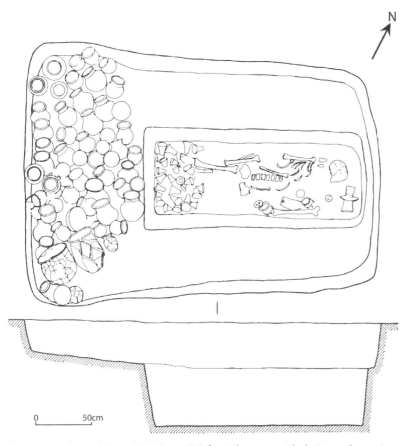

Figure 98. Grave M7 at Xiaojiawuji (after Zhongguo Shehui 2010b: 670).

firing process so as to achieve the desired effects and prevent the fragile artifacts from breaking when being fired and cooled. All this suggests a highly skilled labor force of specialists. The division of the production process into subspecializations (potters, kiln masters, etc.) points to a complex industry and the need for work coordination. Highly specialized ceramic production is also evidenced by findings in other regions, such as the central Yellow River and the lower and central Yangzi River regions.

In the northwest, large quantities of ceramic vessels, mostly identically sized jars with individually painted decorations (Figure 95), suggest a different, but no less complex, production system. It is reasonable to assume that the jars themselves were produced by large workshops in standard-ized "assembly lines," but that each was then decorated individually by an artist who might have been affiliated with the workshop or even worked in a separate location.

The jade industry of the lower Yangzi region is another striking example of technological sophistication and craft specialization. While there is plentiful evidence of the production of prestigious jade artifacts during earlier periods, such as in the Hongshan societies of northeast China (Chapter 4), Liangzhu jades are much more numerous, labor-intensive, and technically sophisticated. The carving of each jade object from its very hard raw material would have occupied highly specialized artisans for many hours and required the use of advanced technology. For example, drilling the shafts inside the famous Liangzhu jade tubes (*cong*)

Figure 99. Ceramic figurines from Shijiahe (photo by Gideon Shelach).

haps even some sort of centralized control over jade production. The raw jade stones were obtained from local resources (Jing and Wen 1996), but the acquisition of raw materials and their distribution to the workshops probably demanded a certain level of organization and coordination. Jade objects have been found in other regions of China as well, though not in such large quantities. Some might have been of Liangzhu origin, but others were undoubtedly produced by local artisans.

Bronze is a new technology that appeared during the Late Neolithic and would eventually become one of the most important industries in China, although its impact on Late Neolithic society was limited. The Late Neolithic societies of northwest China are credited with being the earliest metal producing cultures in China. A tin-alloyed bronze knife unearthed at Linjia (林家), in Gansu province, and dated to ca. 2900–2700 BCE is probably the earliest true bronze artifact to have been found in China, and more copper and bronze Late Neolithic artifacts are also known from this region (Sun and Han 1997). A number of bronze and copper artifacts have also been found at the Taosi site, in the middle Yellow River region, of which the most sophisticated is a small copper bell, probably made using piece-mold techniques (Zhongguo Shehui 2010b: 571). This bell and other metal objects were all found in relatively small graves, suggesting that bronze was not yet considered a prestigious material. Nevertheless, the production of these objects, even if small and relatively unsophisticated, required a certain level of technological knowledge.

The organization of craft production in Late Neolithic societies is an important issue. In particular, it is significant to know whether craft items were produced at the household level or in specialized workshops. Was craft production initiated and organized by the individual household, the local community, or its highest leaders? Unfortunately, we do not have much direct evidence with which to answer these questions. It has been

(Figure 101), some of which are up to 25 cm long, is a challenging task, even with modern technology. The range of Liangzhu artifacts is limited, and their decorations are quite repetitive (Figure 102), suggesting a high level of standardization and per-

Figure 100. Typical Shandong Longshan elite ceramic (photo by Gideon Shelach).

Figure 101. A Liangzhu jade *cong* (photo by Gideon Shelach).

suggested that the clustering of kilns around houses at Kangjia and the discovery of potters' tools in the same area indicate household specialization in ceramic production (Liu 2004: 101–2). Stone drills found inside one of the Liangzhu elite graves at Fuquanshan (福泉山) are interpreted as indicating the high status of jade carving in this society (Huang Xuanpei 2000). A number of Late Neolithic sites have been identified as centers of specialized production activities (cf. Liu 2004: 178), but the data available to fully address this issue are currently very limited.

REGIONAL VARIATION AND INTERREGIONAL INTERACTIONS DURING THE LATE NEOLITHIC PERIOD

Two seemingly contradictory processes took place during the third millennium BCE: on the one hand, local variation became much more pronounced than it was during previous periods, but on the other, contact and mutual influence between regions were also stronger than ever before. I would like to argue that these phenomena are actually two sides of the same coin: Not only did intensified regional and interregional interactions result in the creation of a shared cultural "language," but they also at the same time catalyzed the

need for the demonstration of local identities. We are quite familiar with such processes in the modern global era, and we will witness them at least once more over the period covered by this book (the Warring States period, Chapter 10). The two processes are examined separately.

Regional Variation

It is difficult to quantify the observation that interregional cultural variation became more pronounced during the Late Neolithic. However, when artifacts from different regions are compared with one another, the differences between regions are evident (compare, for example, Figures 95 and 100). The extent of such differences is even clearer when cultural attributes from each region are clustered together and compared to other regional clusters. This approach is, in fact, quite similar to comparing archaeological cultures in their descriptive sense, but here we are not assuming that each culture represented a distinct political system or a homogeneous group of people (or ethnos), but rather using it to inform us about the creation of intensive networks of interaction and exchange of ideas within each of the regions.

A comparison of three of the regions discussed earlier – the lower Yangzi River (Liangzhu culture), the central Yellow River region (the Taosi or Henan Longshan), and northwest China (the Machang culture) – will serve to illustrate the cultural diversity of the Late Neolithic period. Starting at the east, Liangzhu domestic sites seem to be relatively small with no known fortifications. In contrast, much effort was invested in the construction of ritual mounds (such as Mojiaoshan) and large burial platforms (such as Fanshan). The elaborate Liangzhu burials are not part of large-scale cemeteries, but rather are located exclusively on burial platforms and are better seen as forming part of a ritual monument. Prestigious Liangzhu ceramics were made on a fast wheel, black burnished, and relatively complex, but they

Figure 102. Typical Liangzhu jade artifacts (photo by Gary Lee Todd).

were not an important part of the burial inventory. The most important grave goods found inside elite Liangzhu graves are labor-intensive jade ornaments and ritual objects. Many of the jade forms and their decorations seem to have originated in the region, although some were later transmitted to other regions, where they were copied by local artisans.

The middle Yellow River region is typified by large fortified sites that are not found in the other two regions, as well as by labor-intensive public buildings. Their inhabitants lived in single- or multiroom houses, which may reflect the formation of large families and multifamily groups. Unlike the Liangzhu (but similar to Machang), large cemeteries with graves of different sizes and degrees of wealth are the norm. The most elaborate graves include wooden coffins and ledges upon which burial goods were placed. Prestigious ceramics are sometime similar to those of the Liangzhu, but also include painted pottery not seen there. Jade production and consumption is much less developed, but exotic materials such as crocodile skins and music instruments (drums and music stones) are highly valued.

We know little about the Late Neolithic domestic sites and structures in northwest China, but the mortuary and ceramic production traditions of Machang set it apart from the other two regions. Large and small graves are found together in large cemeteries. The shape and style of graves, with their deep and irregularly shaped pits, passageways, and wooden fences, are very different from the other two regions. The production of large closed vessels, and the emphasis on painted decorations, rather than on the sophistication of shapes and monochromic burnishing, also sets the Machang tradition apart from the other two regions.

More regions could be added to the comparison, and in many places where more intensive research has been carried out, such as the central Yellow River region, more nuanced differences between local societies could be identified.

It seems that this variation is the result of the long-term development of local traditions and, sometimes, as in the case of jade production, a locally based technology. It probably also reflects local values; for example, placing the elite's dead in either a communal cemetery or an exclusively elite monument is a reflection of such value differences. Another possibility is that, with the intensification of regional and interregional interactions, the culture of each region became more homogeneous, but that there was also a greater need to symbolize local identity in the face of nonlocal people. Such processes may have increased the visibility of the local "culture" (Shelach 2009).

Regional and Interregional Interactions

The three regional cultural complexes reviewed earlier, as well as the others discussed in the first part of this chapter, reflect intensive interactions between the communities that populated each region. Even if intraregional variation was greater than what we can currently observe, the scale of shared cultural attributes suggests that people from different communities were in close and frequent contact with each other. If we take symbols and artifacts to be the materialization of ideas and a form of communicating these ideas (cf. Wobst 1977), then the fact that identical symbols are found in substantial quantities throughout a given region means that people understood each other's symbolic language and used it in intercommunity communication. To take the Liangzhu culture as an example, we may not be able to decipher the meanings they attributed to the jade *cong* and its decorations, but the fact that a large number of virtually identical objects of this kind are distributed throughout the Lower Yangzi River region implies that it nonetheless had a shared meaning, and that this meaning was understood by the people living across this region.

The production sophistication and the uniformity of Liangzhu jades suggest centralized production and distribution among local elites. Similar patterns of production and distribution may also be true for elite Longshan ceramics such as the eggshell cups.

If each of the approximately evenly distributed walled sites in regions such as the middle Yellow River was a political center, then warfare between these small-scale polities was probably another type of intraregional interaction. Other types of interaction among these small-scale polities might have included the exchange of raw materials and finished artifacts, the exchange of marriage partners, and the like. Such contacts, whether peaceful or aggressive, would have contributed to mutual influences and greater cultural homogeneity.

Compared to regional-level interactions, long-range interregional interactions were carried out on a very different scale and had very different effects. A great deal of data pertaining to interregional contact became available during the early 1980s, after K. C. Chang established his Chinese interaction sphere model, and it has continued to accumulate ever since. Chang described these contacts as "Longshanoid horizon, which began in the north and the Yangtze Valley by the middle of the fourth millennium B.C. and continued along the eastern coast all the way to Taiwan and the Pearl River delta up to the middle of the third millennium B.C." (Chang 1986: 238). The clearest evidence for this shared "horizon" is the *dou* and *ding* ceramic vessels found throughout those regions (Figure 103). It is now clear that similar types of vessels are known from across an even larger region, including, for example, the middle Yangzi River and the Chengdu plain (Wang Yi 2003).

Chang's proposition that, while most of the vessels were probably produced locally, the close similarities in their shape and style cannot be accidental, is surely correct. These similarities clearly indicate contact between societies that populated distance regions. But what was the nature of these interactions? Although Chang's framework does

Figure 103. Ceramic *ding* and *dou* vessels from different parts of China (after Chang 1986: 240).

not point to any one society as having taken the lead, the fact that footed pottery vessels, such as *dou* and *ding*, first appeared in the Yellow River basin (or more exactly, in the lower Yellow River region), may suggest a spread of "culture" from there to other societies.

Pounded earth (*hangtu*) technology and the construction of large site walls, another component of Chang's definition, were identified by him only in Henan and Shandong provinces (Chang 1986: 287), strengthening the suggestion that these were the core regions of the system. However, during the past thirty years, Late Neolithic pounded earth and earthen and stone site walls have been found across a much larger region, including the lower and middle Yangzi River valley, the Sichuan basin, and the Ordos region. Some of these sites, such as Chengtoushan (Chapter 5), are as old as or even older than those found in the middle Yellow River region, while others, such as Shijiahe, are larger than most northern sites. This, therefore, appears to indicate contact between societies of equal strength and complexity, with cultural influences traveling in all directions.

Jade objects provide another famous example of interaction between Late Neolithic societies. Liangzhu jades were produced from locally available raw materials in the Lower Yangzi region. Significantly smaller quantities of Liangzhu-style jades, found at sites as far from the Lower Yangzi basin as northwest China, the Chengdu basin, and south China, are among the best evidence for longer range contact during this period. For example, a number of *cong*-like objects made of jade or stone have been found outside the area of the Liangzhu culture. To the north, these objects were found at Late Neolithic sites along the eastern coast, but they have also been found as far west as the Taosi site in Shanxi and sites of the Qijia and Majiayao cultures in Gansu (a distance of some 2,000 km from the core area of the Liangzhu culture). *Cong* have also been found upstream along the Yangzi River at sites all the way to the Chengdu plain in Sichuan, and to the south in sites of the Shixia culture of Guangdong (Huang 1992) (Figure 104).

Outside the lower Yangzi River region, *cong*, like other "Liangzhu" jade objects, are found singly or in small numbers, and usually inside wealthy local graves. They probably arrived at their final destination after passing through many hands and as a result of gift exchanges. Outside their local cultural context, the *cong* probably lost their specific ritual meaning, yet they retained their status as prestige objects, and maybe even saw it amplified owing to their extreme rarity. This may reflect the creation of an interregional elite network in which prestige items and exotic materials were exchanged by the elites of different societies and used locally to reinforce their status and, ultimately, their control over the local population. This reading of the data predicts not the creation of a homogeneous culture

covering a large territory, as Chang's model suggested, but rather the development of many local variants, each with its unique cultural norms and religious beliefs.

Moreover, it should not be assumed that there was one sphere or a single large network of interactions. Some regions probably interacted more intensively with certain others, depending on distance, ease of transportation, and maybe also their history of past interactions. For example, contact between the lower Yellow River and the middle Yellow River regions seems to have been quite extensive. High quality eggshell and fine burnished black ceramic serving vessels found at Wangchenggang, as well as alligator skins found at Taosi, are indicative of these interactions (Liu 2004: 156). Similarly intensive contact between the Chengdu plain and the middle Yangzi River region can also be inferred from the close similarities of their ceramics (Wang Yi 2003: 118). In light of this evidence of relatively intensive and direct interregional contacts, jade objects found a great distance from their places of origin, including the previously mentioned *cong*, are best viewed as evidence of sporadic and indirect interactions.

We have not yet discussed the societies of south China in this chapter. As we saw in Chapter 5, by the fourth millennium BCE, rice agriculture, which was probably introduced from central China, was well established in the region. During the third millennium BCE, agricultural communities thrived in inland locations, while the intensive exploitation of natural resources such as fish and shellfish continued along the southeastern coast. The kinds of population and social dynamics observed in regions to the north have not found in Lingnan and the southeastern coastal regions. South China seems to have been populated by small-scale and relatively autonomous communities during this period. On the other hand, the material cultures of these communities suggest that interactions with the developing polities to the north, especially these of east central China, were nonetheless quite intensive.

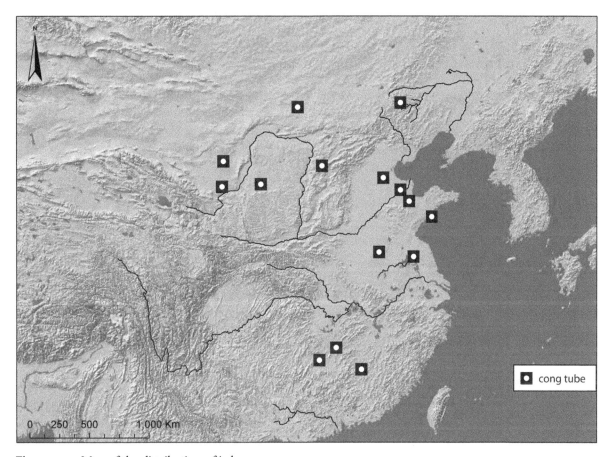

Figure 104. Map of the distribution of jade *cong*.

The jade artifacts found at the Shixia site in the Lingnan region illustrate this well. Some of the *cong* and *bi* artifacts from this site are identical to examples from the Liangzhu culture. *Cong* of lesser quality, also found at this site, illustrate a process whereby foreign objects, which may have reached this region via indirect down-the-line exchange, were imitated and incorporated into the local culture. Their original meaning, however, was probably lost during this transmission.

According to Allard (1997), data from the early phases of the Shixia culture point to an egalitarian society with a low level of craft specialization and no evidence of preexisting hierarchies. Rather than symbolizing the power that the elite already enjoyed, as was the case elsewhere, ownership of Liangzhu artifacts provided local strivers with the opportunity to distinguish themselves as

exceptional figures, maybe even thereby initiating their leadership. At sites of the Shixia period, the appearance of Liangzhu *cong* coincides with the beginning of differentiation in the size and richness of graves. The fact that these foreign objects are clearly associated with the largest, most elaborate, and richest graves suggests a connection between the two processes. However, because real Liangzhu objects were so rare, imitations made from inferior raw materials and with lesser craft skills were produced to supply the growing demands of the emergent elite. Because the local leadership was so dependent on external inputs, it quickly became unstable, perhaps when Liangzhu objects were no longer available, or because their symbolic power was diluted by the local imitations (Allard 1997).

Contact between communities on the Fujian coast and the island of Taiwan continued during this period, and, as noted, it is likely that agriculture was transmitted to the Pacific region through these interactions (Bellwood 2005; Jiao 2007). Similar patterns of a gradual diffusion of people and ideas are also associated with the spread of agriculture to northern Vietnam and northern Thailand during the third millennium BCE (Bellwood 2006: 108–9). At more or less the same time, agriculture was also transmitted westward from the Yellow and Yangzi River basins. Evidence of agriculture dated to the third millennium BCE – including domesticated grains such as rice and millet and bones of domesticated animals – has in recent years been discovered in regions of far western China, such as Yunnan and the Tibetan Plateau (Xiao 2001; Yao 2010). The diffusion of domesticated plants and animals, as well as of agricultural technologies of cultivation and harvesting, suggests contact, albeit at a low level of intensity, between communities in these regions and their counterparts in the more eastern parts of present-day China.

THE RISE OF ECONOMIC, SOCIAL, AND POLITICAL COMPLEXITY AND STRATIFICATION DURING THE LATE NEOLITHIC

The data presented in the first part of this chapter suggest that stratified and complex societies developed in different regions of north and central China during the third millennium BCE. Social complexity, as defined in Chapter 4, is clearly demonstrated by the evidence presented on craft specialization. This section focuses on the development of sociopolitical stratification by highlighting its concrete archaeological expressions. In particular, we ask the following questions: What level of stratification and complexity was attained by different societies? Are there variations in the ways in which stratification was structured and legitimized in different regions? What were the causes of increased sociopolitical stratification during the Late Neolithic period?

Levels and Forms of Sociopolitical Hierarchy during the Late Neolithic

Recent scholarship has proposed that Late Neolithic polities in China had a three- or four-tier hierarchy (Liu 2004: 172–8, 240; Liu et al. 2004; Underhill et al. 2008). This observation is based on the definition of a state-level society as having a four-tiered settlement hierarchy – the villages and three levels of decision-making hierarchy (cf. Wright 1978). Complex pre-state societies (or chiefdoms), therefore, would have had three hierarchical levels and two levels of decision makers. Regardless of whether such models are able to accurately differentiate states from pre-state societies, the archaeological correlates most often used in China to identify these hierarchical levels are problematic because they are based on one variable only: site size. The number of political levels read into a given region is derived from the clustering of sites on the site-size histogram. Clearly, however, this method can be arbitrary, and the same histogram could be interpreted as having two, three, or four clusters with an equal level of confidence (Peterson and Drennan 2011). More important, the political function of a site cannot be determined by its size alone; the productivity of the site catchment area (a big site can simply be the result of a very productive environment) and direct evidence for the administrative and economic functions of the centers must be taken into account as well (cf. Steponaitis 1981).

It is possible, and even plausible, that in different areas and at different times during the Late Neolithic some societies reached a higher level of stratification than others. It makes intuitive sense that large sites, such as Taosi, were able to extract more resources and control a larger territory than much smaller centers such as Wangchenggang. Nonetheless, based on the currently available evidence, we can confidently say that Late Neolithic polities had *at least* two hierarchical levels: the local villages and the large centers in which evidence of labor-intensive structures is found. The clustering

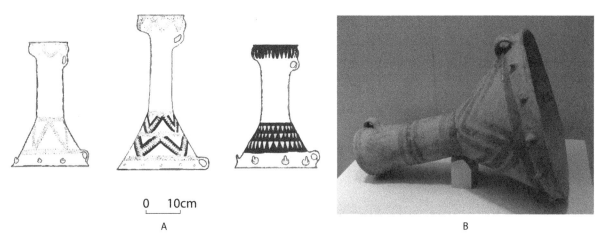

0   10cm

A   B

Figure 105. Ceramic drums found in Late Neolithic graves (A. after Zhongguo Shehui 2010b: 626; B. photo by Gideon Shelach).

of smaller sites around a large labor-intensive site indicates the formation of polities that transcended the individual community. Judging by the distances between large central sites, each such polity controlled an area that was roughly 50 km across.

The growing distinction between the centers and the villages that surrounded them is one of the most interesting phenomena of the period. The population of sites such as Taosi must have numbered at least several thousand, while population size remained fairly stable in the small sites. In the Liyang plain in northwest Hunan, for example, the accumulated site area almost doubled between the Qujialing and the Shijiahe periods, while the average site size decreased by half. Thus, we observe a process of polarization where many small sites cluster around one or a few much larger ones. Although no research on the carrying capacity of a site's catchment area has been conducted, it is plausible that the high concentration of people and resources needed to construct the large public structures found at sites such as Taosi or Shijiahe (large walls, moats, public buildings), indicate that the centers were able to extract labor and food surpluses from the dependent villages (Steponaitis 1981).

A growing disparity in the amount of labor invested in the building and furnishing of graves is

a more direct reflection of the mounting socioeconomic gaps between individuals. The widening gaps between the socioeconomic strata of Late Neolithic societies can be seen at cemeteries such as Taosi, where elite graves are more than ten times larger than the smaller graves. Moreover, they include structural features, such as ledges and coffins, not seen in other graves, and contain a hundred times more artifacts than the average commoner's grave. In term of labor investment, it is clear that elite graves were many times more expensive to build and furnish than those of low-ranking persons, once again suggesting that the elite were able to extract resources in the form of labor and goods from their societies' lower strata.

Unique artifacts found exclusively in elite graves, such as elaborate jades or eggshell ceramic cups, demonstrate the elite's monopoly over symbols of power and prestige. It is notable that musical instruments are among the elite symbols of power found in wealth graves in many parts of China (Figure 105). This suggests that performances and rituals played an important part in establishing, maintaining, and reproducing sociopolitical prestige and power across most regions.

Gender seems to have played a more important role in the construction of sociopolitical stratification during the Late Neolithic. As noted, in Taosi, the largest and most richly furnished graves contained only male skeletons, while in other cemeteries, such as the one at Chengzi, men's graves are on average larger and richer than those of women (Chang 1986: 276; Liu 2004: 144). The growing gap between the sexes may have been the result of a growing division of labor, or it may have had to do with an intensification of intersocietal conflicts and violence. Comparisons of early and Late Neolithic human skeletons do suggest an increase in physical stress (related perhaps to the intensification of agriculture) and dietary deficits. They also indicate greater differences both between men and women and between the elite and commoners in terms of the foodstuffs they consumed (Pechenkina et al. 2002; Pechenkina et al. 2005; Smith 2005).

Intrasocietal violence is indicated both by an increase in the number of mutilated skeletons found at Late Neolithic sites, as well as by evidence of human sacrifices. While human sacrifices are known to have taken place during the Early Neolithic, their number increased dramatically during the Late Neolithic, and there is evidence of these practices from almost all regions of China. At many sites, mutilated human skeletons are found inside postholes and house foundations (Liu 2004: 46–7), suggesting that they were used as sacrifices in foundation-laying ceremonies. In other locations, mutilated human skeletons accompany the deceased in elite graves, and may have been sacrificed in his or her honor or in order to keep the deceased company in the afterworld. Regardless of the specific ritual functions of these sacrifices, the fact that the elite could regularly enforce the killing of other people, presumably from the lower strata of society, directly evidences the very real power over life and death that the elite appear to have held.

Discoveries of larger concentrations of mutilated human bodies may indicate the execution or sacrifice of prisoners. Such evidence has been found at Jiangou (涧沟) in Hebei, for instance, where five layers of human skeletons were found buried inside a well. Some of the bodies display signs of violence, while others may have been buried alive (Chang 1986: 270–1). The construction of large site walls may be interpreted as evidence of wars between neighboring polities. However, these walls could have served other purposes as well and, in fact, they most probably did: In the south, it has been suggested that the function of site walls was to protect against floods (Wang Hongxing 2003). Large walls, especially in flat areas, were visible from afar and thus were probably also symbols of power. Nonetheless, the scale of work needed to construct such walls suggests that their main function was fortification. A fortified gate found at the Pingliangtai (平粮台) site in Henan (Chang 1986: 265–6) supports this view. The large quantities of stone arrowheads found at Late Neolithic sites is also seen as evidence of endemic warfare during this period (Liu 2004: 64).

The Road to Stratification: Models for the Development of Stratification during the Late Neolithic

Research carried out during the 1960s and 1970s on the origins of stratified society and the state, and on the functions of leaders, has shifted in more recent years to focus on the strategies adopted by aspiring leaders. The implicit assumption is that there will always be people who crave power and prestige, thus raising the question of what strategies they deploy in order to gain and maintain them. In recent years, a useful contrast has been developed in distinguishing between two types of sociopolitical and economic strategies: "corporate" and "network" (Blanton et al. 1996). In the corporate strategy, leadership is linked to the management and exploitation of the subsistent economy, while the network strategy is related to the production and manipulation of nonutilitarian prestige artifacts. Corporate strategies are thus expressed in the direct involvement of the leaders with the day-to-day activities of the people, the management and control of the production and distribution of resources, and the organization of communal projects. In network strategies, by contrast, the would-be elite gain their power through the manipulation of prestige objects and exotic materials, which are produced locally under the supervision of the elite and exchanged through elite networks with their counterparts in other regions.

These two strategies are not mutually exclusive, and it is to be expected that all leaders will utilize different combinations of both. A relatively more corporate leadership can be expected to place less of an emphasis on the individual personality of the leader and more of an emphasis on his or her communal functions. An archaeological expression of this might be the presence of labor-intensive public structures (such as city walls). Likewise, one would expect relatively little interpersonal variation in mortuary treatment under a more corporate leadership, and when it does exist, it is likely to be associated with the quantity rather than the quality of goods. In the case of a relatively more network-oriented leadership, on the other hand, the personality and unique qualities of the leader are emphasized. Rather than being associated with the day-to-day activities of the populace, a distance is created between the leader and his or her people. This distance is usually expressed through symbols and rituals and can be seen, for instance, in mortuary treatments that not only are more expensive, but are qualitatively different from those of commoners. Rituals are important for legitimizing and naturalizing both leadership strategies, but while in a corporate-oriented system we may expect evidence of rituals that are public and open to all segments of the society, in a more network-oriented system we should expect exclusive rituals in which exotic artifacts and materials are used.

The network model can be related to K. C. Chang's aforementioned Chinese interaction sphere. Although it is more a set of observations than an explanation, this model associates the rise of stratification in different parts of China

with intraelite emulation and competition. Proponents of the network strategy model are more explicit with regard to the role of regional and interregional exchange networks. The exchange of prestigious artifacts, materials, and even new ideas is used locally by leaders to boost their personal prestige. According to Earle, for example, "network strategies create broad systems of ideological and material exchanges binding leaders, would-be leaders, and followers together in networks of mutual support and competition" (Earle 2002: 17).

It would indeed seem that many leaders of Late Neolithic societies in China adopted a more network-oriented strategy. Liangzhu jades were probably imbued with elite ideology and distributed in the lower Yangzi River through a network of intensive elite interactions and interdependency. The same is probably true for the finest eggshell Longshan ceramics. The dissemination of Liangzhu jade to a much wider region was also part of elite network, albeit one in which contacts were much less frequent. The specific local meaning of each jade artifact was probably lost in the process of the long-range exchange, but their value as prestigious elite emblems may have even been amplified by their rarity and their foreign qualities. The same can be said for other exotic products that were exchanged over large distances, such as crocodile skins.

Elite Longshan and Liangzhu graves filled with prestige goods, and burial ceremonies that probably included music and feasting, are also typical of the network strategy. Elite Liangzhu graves in particular are spatially separated from the graves of commoners, and they are integrated into ritual structures – earthen mounds or platforms – that were symbolically visible and were probably used to restrict access to elite ceremonies.

Feasting during funerals and other ceremonial events may have been another strategy used by network-oriented elites to boost their prestige and gain power, something we are also familiar with from the ethnographic literature. Expanded feasting activities in the domestic community and during mortuary rituals, and especially the use of alcoholic beverages, were convenient arenas for gaining power and negotiating social relations. Such activities were responsible for an increasing demand for prestigious foods, beverages, vessels, ornaments, and ceremonial paraphernalia, thus encouraging craft specialization and the emergence of elite exchange networks (Underhill 2002). Elaborated drinking cups and wine vessels found in late Dawenkou and Longshan period graves and domestic contexts are seen as evidence of this. Chemical analysis of extracts from Late Neolithic pot shards (including fragments of drinking cups, and tripods and jars possibly used to serve alcohol) revealed that they contained fermented beverages made of rice, honey, and various fruits (McGovern et al. 2005).

Alcohol production and consumption were also probably controlled by the elite, and it is not improbable that alcoholic beverages, as well as the knowledge of how to produce them, were exchanged among the elites. In the Yiluo area, rice was found only at large sites, while the remains of millet were found at other sites (Lee et al. 2007). This can be seen as evidence that the elite had access to better or more prestigious food, perhaps also related to feasting. However, in light of an analysis by McGovern et al. (2005), which suggests that rice (but not millet) was used in the production alcoholic beverages during the Late Neolithic, the elites at the centers may have had control over both the resources for alcohol production and (presumably) its distribution during feasts.

Evidence of similar individualizing or network elite strategies is found in almost all Late Neolithic societies, though the stronger evidence has been found along the eastern coast. In more western regions, on the other hand, there is stronger evidence of corporate strategies being used. Individualized aspects of rituals are still notable, though

they are less emphasized among societies of the middle Yellow River region. Elite graves in this region are clearly distinguished from commoners' graves, not only in terms of size and richness, but also in terms of the ritual artifacts such as musical instruments contained in them, which were probably used during ceremonies, including at the funeral itself. However, elite graves are part of a larger cemetery, which includes smaller graves. Such inclusiveness in the afterlife may reflect the more mundane functions of the elite during their lifetime, for example organizing laborers to construct site walls, or perhaps serving as military leaders.

Judging by the graves, the leadership of societies in the middle Yangzi River and the Chengdu plain was even less individualized. In these regions, large public works, such as site walls and moats, and public facilities, such as the ceramic water pipes found at Shijiahe, are best associated with a corporate strategy. Ritual sites located within these walls, such as the structure at Gucheng, suggest less restricted access to public ceremonies than at the Liangzhu sites. The thousands of figurines and small ritual cups found concentrated in different parts of the Shijiahe site are also suggestive of inclusive rituals in which the site's large population, and perhaps the populations of the rural communities that surrounded it as well, all participated.

In northwest China, the Late Neolithic leadership may have been the least network-oriented and the most corporate in its strategy. Although large monumental works comparable to those found in other regions have not been found thus far, the local burial tradition is suggestive. As described earlier, the graves of the elite differ from those of the commoners more in quantity and size than in the quality of the artifacts and their ritual function. Allard (2001) has identified the large jars placed in Machang graves as grain containers. If proven correct, this would indicate a very strong association between the power of the elite and its functional ability to manage and control economic resources.

THE "ORIGINS OF CHINESE CIVILIZATION" AND THE TRANSMISSION OF CULTURAL ATTRIBUTES THROUGH TIME

We conclude this chapter with a brief examination of the place of the Late Neolithic period in the genesis of "Chinese civilization." This is a very popular research topic in China: a recent survey identified more than eight hundred publications on the origins of Chinese civilization by members of the Chinese Academy of Social Sciences alone (Chen 2009). As I have noted elsewhere (Shelach 2004: 20–3), the central theme of much of this research is the unbroken continuation of Chinese identity from the Neolithic all the way through to the late imperial period. In the context of the continuous development of what are identified as typical Chinese attributes – cultural traits, social norms, political institutions, written language, and so on – the Late Neolithic is seen as a crucial period during which a unique Chinese culture emerged. Some researchers even go so far as to associate this period with the legendary heroes of Chinese mythology and identify sites, mainly in the middle Yellow River region, as the "capital" cities where those legendary figures lived. Thus, for instance, despite a lack of any concrete evidence, Taosi and Wangchenggang have been identified with Yao (尧), Shun (舜), and Yu (禹) (cf. Cheng 2005; Fang and Xu 2006; Ma 2008).

The "Chinese" attributes thought to have emerged (or strongly intensified) during this period include sociopolitical hierarchies, walled cities and their association with political power, belief systems, including ancestor worship and the use of music in rituals, extended and internally stratified families, an incipient Chinese writing system, and traditional forms of artifacts, structures, and symbols (Dematte 1999; Keightley 1990; Zhongguo Shehui 2010b). Evidence for the emergence of some of these attributes, such as the development of a Chinese writing system, is problem-atic, while others, such as the evolution of sociopo-litical hierarchies, are not uniquely "Chinese." However the transmission of Neolithic forms and symbols is a phenomenon that merits our serious consideration.

Because transmission from earlier to later societies is seen by many as a natural, almost biological, phenomenon, scholars tend to project our knowledge of historic periods backward to prehistoric times. A relatively early example of such research is provided by K. C. Chang's paper, "An Essay on Cong." Following traditional Chinese antiquarian scholarship, Chang identified tubular jade artifacts found in graves from the Liangzhu culture with the ritual items called *cong* (琮) in the classical texts of the Eastern Zhou (771–221 BCE) and the Han (206 BCE–220 CE) period. He then uses this information to explain the meanings ascribed to those objects and the way they were ritually used during the prehistoric era. Chang's interpretation of the square exterior of the *cong* and their round interior shaft as symbolizing a cosmological perception of "round heaven and square earth" is particularly notable. Chang thus identified the Liangzhu *cong* as ritual instruments that served to unify heaven and earth (Chang 1989: 38).

This kind of backward projection assumes immense ideological stability during times of tremendous sociopolitical and economic change, as well as the direct and complete transmission of a symbolic representation over more than two millennia and across a very large region. Similar assumptions are implicit in much of the recent research on the meaning of jade artifacts and other Neolithic symbols (e.g., Allan 1991; Childs-Johnson 1995; Li 2004). Questions about the mechanisms of such transmission and how much real ideological continuity there was between Neolithic and post-Neolithic societies are rarely asked.

An alternative perspective sees the transmission of Neolithic attributes as indirect and punctuated.

According to this model, it is precisely because of their durability that jade objects provide some of the best examples of processes of transmission. Crucial evidence in support of this model is the temporal gap between the time of the production of the Neolithic jades and the reemergence of similarly shaped objects during the Shang period (ca. 1600–1050 BCE). A few original examples of Liangzhu *cong* and imitations of them have been found in Shang graves. The most notable examples are fourteen *cong* jades, some of authentic Liangzhu origin, found in the famous Fuhao (婦好) grave in Anyang (Zhongguo 1980: 115–16 and plates 81–83), but comparable examples are also known from other contexts (Falkenhausen 2003: 199–202). It is reasonable to assume that these artifacts were lost for many centuries until they rediscovered during the second half of the second millennium. Perhaps those ancient artifacts were venerated because of their antiquity, were given new meanings, and were copied by Shang artisans.

Interestingly, the *cong* shape fall into oblivion and was rediscovered a couple of times more during the history of China. *Cong* are rare in eastern Zhou (770–221 BCE) contexts and are almost nonexistent in sites and graves of the early imperial period (Hsia 1986: 221; Sun 1990: 365–71). Neolithic jades were rediscovered and occasionally reworked during the Han period, when they served new functions and embodied new imperial ideologies. The *cong* shape was rediscovered once again by collectors and antiquarians of the Song dynasty (960–1279), and was imitated during the late imperial era in different materials, such as porcelain and lacquer.

This "life history" trajectory is not unique to the *cong* shape, and similar trajectories can be traced for other shapes as well, such as the *bi* disc. The same type of "broken transmission" may also be true for jades of the Shijiahe period, which seem to have influenced the repertoire of jade carving in the Yellow River basin (Erlitou culture) and the Chengdu plain (Sanxingdui culture) during later periods (Falkenhausen 2003: 220). Although they leave behind no material traces, other types of transmission are also possible, such as oral traditions passed from generation to generation. However, even this kind of more direct transmission is actually mediated by many individuals, and so we should not expect any one meaning to remain stable over time. Intentional manipulations and unintentional transformations are to be expected.

In conclusion, societies that flourished in China during the Bronze Age and later periods were not as intimately connected to Neolithic societies as some researchers would have us believe, but neither were they completely removed from them. Over the long-term process of cultural transmission, much of the ideological content of symbols, and perhaps also of other social constructs, was lost or completely altered. However, connections to the past, including anachronistic projections of later ideas onto artifacts from earlier periods, were apparently important to many societies and individuals in China, even during the Bronze Age and the imperial periods. Indeed, similar connections made to the ancient past, much of it imagined or intentionally invented, are also very common in traditional Chinese texts from the first millennium BCE.

CHAPTER 7

STEPPING INTO HISTORY

Traditional textual accounts point to the Xia (夏) dynasty as China's entry point into the historical era, a transition centered in the Yellow River valley and dated by scholars to the beginning of the second millennium BCE. Not surprisingly, considering its importance to our understanding of the origins of the Chinese state and civilization, the period in question has attracted the attention of a great many historians and archaeologists interested in clarifying the chronology, geographical extent, and political organization of the Xia. However, these efforts have yet to resolve long-standing debates regarding the very historicity of the Xia, with many skeptical scholars pointing to the absence of writing at so-called Xia sites (e.g., Erlitou) and the absence of references to the Xia in Shang (oracle bone) inscriptions.

In archaeological terms, this chapter is about the period of transition from the Neolithic to the Bronze Age in China. We may thus term it the early or incipient Bronze Age. Such terms are archaeological conventions and should not be interpreted as a reflection of the importance of the bronze industry. In fact, bronze was not the most important industry of the time, and its economic, military, and ritual significance was overshadowed by other traditional crafts using such materials as ceramic, stones, and hard stones.

The chapter begins with a short discussion on the historical orientation of existing research and the utility of using the Xia as a framework for studying this period. For the most part, however, the chapter avoids historical discussions and, as with previous chapters, concentrates on surveying relevant archaeological discoveries and analyzing their social, economic, and political meanings. Understanding the evolution of the state is important for understanding Chinese history (the origins of "Chinese civilization"), as well as for comparisons with other regions in the world where states emerged independently. Based on theoretical considerations of what constitutes a state, and how it might be manifested in archaeology, we address issues related to the development of states in China.

Unlike the preceding Neolithic periods, most of the data from the early second millennium, and the data many think are most relevant for our understanding of the fundamental sociopolitical processes of this era, come from a single region – the central Yellow River region. A function of research priorities, our knowledge of some of the regions outside the central Yellow River area is limited at best, and comparisons between different regions have rarely been attempted. Nevertheless, in recent years more data have become available from regions in other parts of China, mainly in areas to the north and west of the Yellow River basin. To facilitate a comparison between these regions, the data are arranged not according to subject, as in Chapters 4 to 6, but rather according

TABLE 6. *Archaeological Periods by Region*

Area	Period	Dates BCE
Lower Yellow River	Yueshi 岳石	2000–1600
Middle Yellow River	Xinzhai 新砦	2000–1700
	Erlitou 二里头	1900–1550
	Xiaqiyuan 下七垣	1800–1500
Northwest	Qijia 齐家	2200–1600
	Siba 四坝	1900–1500
Ordos	Zhukaigou 朱开沟 phases I–IV	1900–1500
Northeast	Lower Xiajiadian 夏家店下层	2200–1600
Lower Yangzi	Maqiao 马桥	1800–1600
Middle Yangzi	"Post-Shijiahe" 石家河	1900–1500
Chengdu plain	Baodun 宝墩	2700–1700

to the different regions, so as to enable a coherent description of each.

STEPPING INTO HISTORY: ARE WE THERE YET (1)?

Many scholars believe that in the late third or early second millennium BCE China entered the historical era. Although no documents have survived from this period, descriptions of it appear in canonical Chinese texts written during the first millennium BCE. The information found in these and in other texts that have not survived was collated by the great Chinese historian Sima Qian (司馬遷 ca. 145–85 BCE) in the *Shiji* (史記). According to this by now canonical synthesis, Chinese history commences with the legendary Three August Ones (Sanhuang 三皇), followed by the Five Thearchs (wudi 五帝), the most famous of whom was the Yellow Emperor (Huangdi 黄帝). According to the *Shiji*, a great flood that occurred during the days of the last thearch, Shun (舜), was finally brought under control by Yu the Great (禹). Yu is credited with founding the first Chinese dynasty, the Xia, which boasted some thirty kings after Yu and ruled for more than four hundred years, until it was replaced by the Shang (商).

The reliability of this narrative is hotly disputed. While some historians accept it as the basic framework of early Chinese history, others point out not only that the *Shiji* was written a thousand years or more after the events, but also that the persons and events it describes are more mythical than historical. Many archaeologists currently working in China nonetheless tend to accept the history of the Xia as a reliable guide for archaeological research into the origins of Chinese civilization during the transition from the Neolithic to the Bronze Age (e.g., Zhongguo Shehui 2003: 21–3; for dissenting voices see Chen and Gong 2004).

Marrying archaeological data with the historical record is never easy. Even for periods for which we have a rich and varied historic record, the topics covered and the viewpoint from which the historical texts were written differ from those found in the archaeological record. Despite these difficulties, archaeologists should always welcome historical information that can enhance our research, provide additional outlooks, and help generate interesting research questions. When too much effort is directed at confirming or rejecting the historical record, however, we may lose sight of the interesting questions that archaeology is able to successfully address. In such cases, it is often

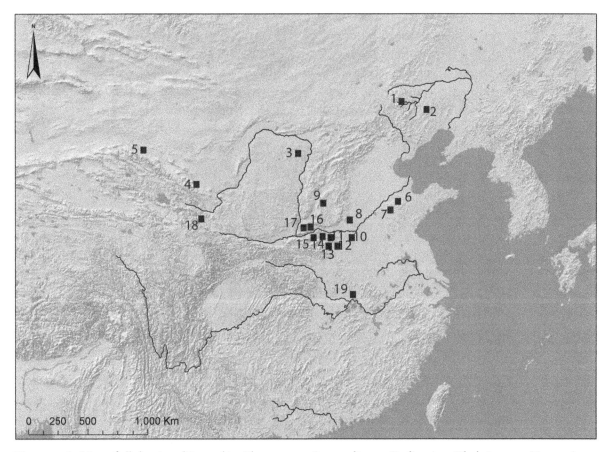

Figure 106. Map of all the sites discussed in Chapter 7: 1. Sanzuodian; 2. Dadianzi; 3. Zhukaigou; 4. Huangniang-niangtai; 5. Huoshaogou; 6. Chengziyai; 7. Jiaochangpu; 8. Mengzhuang; 9 Taosi; 10. Dashigu; 11. Shaochai; 12. Xinzhai; 13. Wangchenggang; 14. Erlitou; 15. Fucun; 16. Nanguan; 17. Dongxiafeng; 18. Liuwan; 19. Panlongcheng.

unclear whether the use of historic or semihistoric information is a blessing or a curse.

The archaeological search for the Xia is not new. Sparked by the success in identifying the remains of the Shang dynasty (Chapter 8), the quest began in earnest during the 1950s. Pioneering this work, Xu Xusheng (1959) used references in the classical texts to reconstruct the geographical extent of the Xia dynasty. Xu then surveyed the region he had defined in order to locate the sites that might have been capital cities of the Xia. One of his most important discoveries was the site of Erlitou (二里头), which, although identified by Xu with

the Shang, has since been the focal point of Xia archaeology.

Providing a historical framework for archaeological research in China became a top priority in the 1990s. To address this need, the government sponsored a five-year project in which the country's leading research institutes and some two hundred prominent scholars were divided into various research groups, which worked to provide a solid chronology for the preimperial "Three Dynasties" (Sandai 三代) – the Xia, Shang, and Zhou (周) – and to identify their archaeological correlates (Li 2002). Based on the available historic record, the Xia, Shang, Zhou Chronology Project team concluded that the Xia dynasty lasted from 2070 to 1600 BCE. The same project also radiocarbon-dated the Erlitou culture to ca. 1900–1600 BCE, even though it had been thought by many to represent the remains of the Xia. Moreover, recently published dates have pushed the beginning of Erlitou culture further forward into the eighteenth century BCE (Xia Shang Zhou 2000; Zhang et al. 2007). These discrepancies have compelled many, including the official chronology team, to identify the early part of the Xia with the archaeological remains of the late Longshan. This, as Chen and Gong (2004: 85) observed, contradicts one of the key arguments made since the 1970s in support of the identification of Erlitou with the Xia, namely, that the Erlitou archaeological culture is very different from the Longshan culture and should thus be identified with a new era in Chinese history.

Dating is not the only, or even the biggest, problem facing attempts to marry the historical and archaeological records. The main problem has to do with the nature of both data sources. On the one hand, the historical record of the Xia was written some thousand years or more after the fact, and even the most uncritical observer would have to admit that large parts of it must be read as legend. Much of Sima Qian's treatise on the Xia is devoted to the activities of Yu, for example his single-handed command of the flood. The rest contains very little concrete information that can be tested archaeologically.

Even if we were to accept the historical record regarding the Xia at face value after filtering out those parts that are clearly legendary or anachronistic, we would be left with nothing but genealogical information on the kings of the Xia. This information contributes nothing meaningful to our understanding of Xia society, its political organization, or even its culture. Furthermore, the very act of identifying an archaeological site with the Xia entails connotations that are unconsciously projected back to the data. Thus, for example,

public buildings found at "Xia" sites are labeled as "palaces" and interpreted as the dwellings of Xia kings. Because of such problems, in this chapter I treat the first half of the second millennium BCE as a prehistoric period, and analyze the archaeological data in much the same way as in previous chapters.

THE COLLAPSE (OR NOT?) OF LATE NEOLITHIC SOCIETY

In recent years, archaeologists have noted that around 2000 BCE, the complex Neolithic societies that had been evolving in different parts of China over several millennia experienced a decline in population density and level of complexity or disappeared altogether. Some attribute this process to natural environmental conditions, while others point to social factors and associate it with the subsequent rise of the state. Critically evaluating the evidence in support of this "collapse" is crucial for our understanding of both the Neolithic societies, which collapsed according to this model, as well as the newly ascendant Bronze Age societies.

Theories about the Late Neolithic collapse are based on observations, some systematically acquired and some more impressionistic, that at around 2000 BCE or a couple of centuries earlier, the size and number of sites declined and that evidence of socioeconomic complexity, such as large walls and public structures or specialized craft products, disappeared. Evidence of this process is most evident in areas along the eastern coastline. For example, most Liangzhu sites in the lower Yangzi River region disappeared around 2200 BCE, the construction of ritual mounds and the production of elaborate jade objects stopped, and the whole region seems to have been sparsely populated for several centuries until it recovered at around 1800 BCE (Stanley et al. 1999; Yu et al. 2000; Zhongguo Shehui 2010b: 692).

A systematic regional survey of the coastal area in the Yellow River region documented similar sociodemographic trends. In the Rizhao area of southern Shandong, for instance, the Neolithic population peaked during the middle Longshan, when the total site area reached about 1,700 ha, but dropped dramatically during the late Longshan to about 550 ha with a much lower density of ceramics than before. The evidence of hierarchical societies during the early and middle Longshan periods also disappears. The area continued to be sparsely populated for about a millennium, until the Western Zhou period (ca. 1050–771 BCE), when it was once again densely populated by hierarchical societies (Underhill et al. 2008). Other regions in the lower Yellow River basin appear to have gone through a similar process, though the rate of recovery may have been faster.

On the other hand, the collapse of the Neolithic is far less obvious in inland regions. Taosi, the largest walled Neolithic site in all of north China, seems to have undergone a process of decline. Sometime around 2000 BCE the large pounded earth enclosure was destroyed, and stone and bone debris found in the public buildings area suggest that it was converted into a workshop for craft production (Liu 2004: 110–11). However, Taosi was not abandoned altogether. Various evidence, including radiocarbon dates, suggests that it remained occupied until around 1700 BCE (Zhongguo Shehui 2003: 566, 838). Some even claim that the site's area was further expanded during this period (He 2013). In addition, the Wangchenggang site was at the peak of its development during the late Longshan, the same period when the Rizhao area experienced a sharp decline in population. Indeed, the largest walled enclosure at this site was built only around 2100 BCE. While it is unclear how long the wall was in use, it seems that the occupation of the site continued, perhaps on a smaller scale, throughout the first half of the second millennium BCE (Beijing and Henan 2007: 780–1).

Xinzhai (新砦), a site not far to the east of Wangchenggang, reached the peak of its

development during the early decades of the second millennium. Established during the late Longshan, it expanded during this time (the so-called Xinzhai culture) to about 100 ha and was surrounded by two concentric moats and pounded earth walls (Zhao 2009). The Yiluo area, to the northwest of Wangchenggang, also experienced a period of rapid population growth during the early years of the second millennium BCE. Indeed, it was at this time that the Erlitou site emerged as a paramount regional center. The population of the Yiluo survey region may have decreased somewhat during the transition from the late Longshan to the early Erlitou period, perhaps because some of its inhabitants moved to the Erlitou center, which was not included in the survey area, but it dramatically peaked during subsequent Erlitou phases (Liu et al. 2004).

In other regions of China the situation was also mixed. The population of the middle Yangzi region seems to have declined after the Shijiahe period (Liu 2007), but in the Chengdu plain, sites from the Baodun period, which flourished from the late third to the early second millennia, suggest continuity (Wang Yi 2003). In both regions systematic regional surveys and a better understanding of the chronology are needed in order to improve our understanding of the population and social dynamics.

North of the Yellow River, the picture is equally variegated. It has been suggested that society collapsed in the Ordos region after the Laohushan period, but this could be partly attributed to our poor understanding of the local ceramic assemblages dating to the beginning of the second millennium BCE (Indrisano and Linduff 2013). The Zhukaigou (朱开沟) site located south of the Laohushan cluster, on the other hand, represents a substantial concentration of people during the period of ca. 1900–1500 BCE (Linduff 1995). In the northwest, the Qijia and Siba are not much different from the previous Machang culture, and there is no evidence of the depopulation of the region or a decrease in social complexity. Finally, in northeast China, the late third and early second millennia BCE was a period of unprecedented growth in population density and social complexity. The Lower Xiajiadian was among the most populated periods in the Chifeng survey area, with total site area and shard density some twenty times higher than the highest levels of the Neolithic period (Chifeng 2011). High population levels were accompanied in this region by evidence of increased stratification.

It is generally believed that conditions at the beginning of the third millennium BCE were favorable: the mean annual temperature might have been slightly lower than during the fourth millennium, but it was about 2°C higher than the present. It was also wetter than today and sea levels were relatively low (Hong et al. 2001; Stanley et al. 1999). By the late third millennium, however, temperatures had decreased: some estimates suggest they were about 1 to 1.5°C lower than they are today. Also, precipitation is said to have increased during this period (Cao 1994). Other research suggests that the late third and early second millennia BCE were actually a relatively dry period (Li et al. 2003; Rosen 2008), though interregional variation could be a plausible explanation. Finally, a sharp rise in sea levels between 2600 and 2000 BCE caused a 50 to 100 km inland transgression by the sea along the eastern coast (Cao 1994; Stanley et al. 1999; Yu et al. 2000).

Associating the collapse of Neolithic societies in the coastal areas with dramatic fluctuations in sea levels is reasonable, especially in the lower Yangzi area, where changes in sea level were coupled with a 50 to 150 percent increase in the size of inland standing-water bodies. Thus, a combination of the inland advance of sea water by as much as 100 km and an increase in the size of lakes and marshes would have made the Yangzi delta region, which is where most Liangzhu culture sites had flourished, largely uninhabitable (Stanley et al. 1999; Yu et al. 2000; Zhang et al. 2005).

Similar reconstructions, albeit grounded in weaker data, suggest that flooding was also responsible for the collapse of societies in the middle and lower Yellow River regions (Han 2000; Xia and Yang 2003; S. W. Wang 2005). A lateral movement of the Yellow River, causing the flooding of large regions, is cited as one possible reason for social decline in this area (Liu 2004: 251). At the same time, Wu and Liu (2004) suggest that the anomalous monsoon patterns that caused flooding throughout central China around 2000 BCE created exceptionally dry conditions in north China. According to this model, the collapse (or devolution) of societies in north China was caused by a drought that diminished the carrying capacity of the local environment.

The problem with the drought-induced collapse theory is that it does not take into account the increased human occupation of areas that should have been most affected by it, especially in northeast China. Today, mean annual precipitation in the Chifeng area is about 60 percent of that of the central Yellow River basin, and there is no reason to believe that the situation was much different during the third and second millennia BCE. If in the middle Yellow River region societies collapsed because of severe droughts, then how can we explain the phenomenal increase in population in the Chifeng area during the Lower Xiajiadian period? More crucial to undermining the drought-induced collapse theory than these problems identified through empirical observations, though, is the idea that individuals and societies respond differently to ecological stress. That is, stress is no less likely to trigger hierarchical development than it is to cause the collapse of hierarchies. We should not assume one outcome over the other, but rather try to understand the social preconditions that lead to either response.

The collapse of Late Neolithic societies has also been attributed to human agency. For example, some blame the decline of the Liangzhu society on excessive expenditure by the elite on prestigious artifacts and the construction of ceremonial structures. Others have suggested that conflicts between societies, and even invasions, could have caused social collapse in different parts of China (Wu and Liu 2004: 156).

This brief survey of the changing ecologic conditions and cultural landscape during the late third and early second millennia BCE should make it clear that it is impossible to talk about a universal collapse or a single prime mover. We should, instead, aim for a more nuanced and regionally based understanding of these processes. While it is quite clear that societies in the coastal region were affected by environmental changes (and especially by the rise of sea levels), it is plausible that the more general variability is due to the cycle of rise and fall that appears to characterize all early complex societies. Without the institutionalized mechanism of the more advanced states, early complex societies (chiefdoms or early states) are much more dependent on the abilities of individual leaders to gain and maintain power, and, moreover, these same leaders' ability to transfer power from generation to generation is more limited. It is not surprising, perhaps, that societies in eastern China – where leadership strategies were more individualized and dependent on unstable elite networks of exchange (Chapter 6) – were more prone to fluctuation than inland societies – where leaders used corporate strategies to gain and maintain more direct control over crucial resources.

THE ARCHAEOLOGY OF THE EARLY SECOND MILLENNIUM BCE

The Central Yellow River Basin

The Xinzhai phase, about which we know very little, is seen by many to represent a transition period between the Henan Longshan and the Erlitou period. As discussed earlier, Xinzhai itself was a ca. 100 ha fortified site whose features resemble many of the better-known Longshan walled sites. The internal structure of the site is still currently being studied (Zhao 2009). Recent radiocarbon dates suggest that Xinzhai flourished well into the eighteenth century BCE (Zhang et al. 2007), thereby identifying it as contemporaneous with the rise of Erlitou rather than a transition phase leading into it.

THE ERLITOU SITE

Since its discovery in the 1950s, Erlitou (二里头) has been one of the most intensively studied sites in China, and although more than three hundred sites are ascribed to the so-called Erlitou culture, the type site is unique in terms of both its size and some of the features associated with it.

The Erlitou site is huge, covering an estimated 300 ha (Figure 107). Perhaps this is why our knowledge of it is still partial, despite more than fifty years of intensive excavations and surveys. Occupation of the site is dated from ca. 1900 (or 1850) to ca. 1550 BCE, and it is subdivided into four phases. It is estimated that the site was smaller and much less intensively occupied during phase I, reaching its maximum size and the zenith of its occupation and building activity during phases II and III, before declining during phase IV. Population estimates for the Erlitou site during the peak of its development (phase III) range between eighteen thousand and thirty thousand persons (Liu 2004: 229), but because the size of the residential area at Erlitou and the density of occupation have not yet been thoroughly studied, these estimates are inconclusive.

In contrast to large sites from the Longshan period, Erlitou was not fortified. The best studied part of the Erlitou site is a cluster of pounded earth foundations and the remains of public buildings situated more or less at the center of the site and known in the literature as the "palace city" or "palatial area" (*gongcheng* 宫城). This area was established during phase II, and the most impressive buildings in it were constructed in phase III. The palace city is about 11 ha in size, and it was

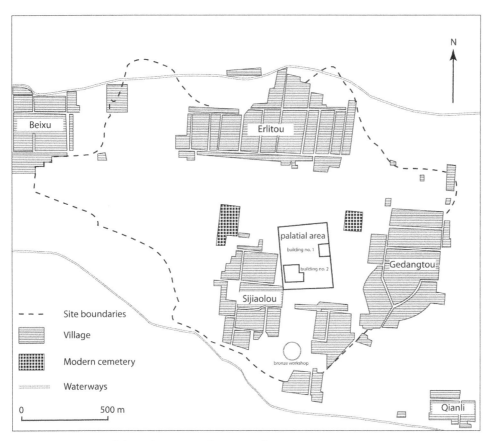

Figure 107. Map of the Erlitou site (after Du and Xu 2006: 479).

enclosed, during phase III, by pounded earth walls about 2 m in width and was surrounded by four large roads (Figure 108).

At least seven earthen platforms have been found inside this enclosure, ranging in size from about 300 m² to 9,600 m². The smaller platforms at the south and southwestern sides of the enclosure were gatehouses. Other platforms served as foundations for public structures and the courtyards in front of them. The two best preserved complexes inside the enclosure, dubbed "palace I" and "palace II," stand on top of pounded earth platforms that are 9,600 m² and 4,200 m² in size, respectively. Both are dated to phase III and share the same design elements (Figures 109); each complex more or less follows the cardinal directions. A large gated entrance in the south side opened into

a wide courtyard surrounded by walls and roofed galleries. The floor of the courtyard was pounded with ceramic sewage pipes laid beneath it. The main building, located at the northern side of the courtyard, stood on a second platform which elevated it above its surroundings. In palace I, this platform measures 36 m by 25 m, with a rectangular building 30 m by 11 m in size standing on top of it. The main hall of palace II is smaller, measuring some 22 m by 6 m, and better preserved, to the extent that we can see its internal division into three rooms (Liu and Xu 2007; Zhongguo Shehui 1999: 140–59; Zhongguo Shehui 2003: 65–8).

Other smaller structures built on pounded earth foundations located outside the palace city are thought to have been elite residences. These structures did not have adjacent courtyards or enclosing

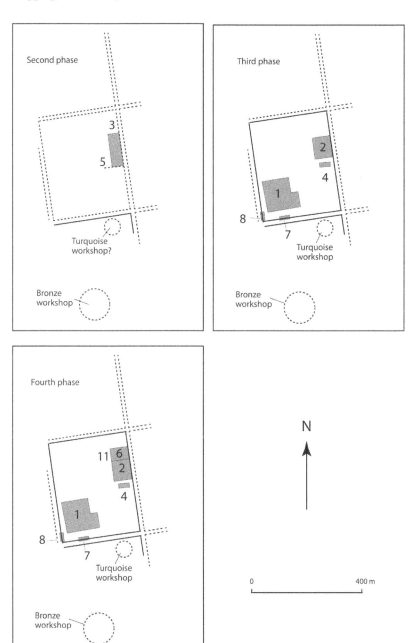

Figure 108. Map of the "palatial" area at Erlitou (after Xu Hong 2009: 68).

walls. Still other houses were built at the ground level. These were small and resemble Neolithic houses in the technique and quality of their construction (Thorp 1991; Zhongguo Shehui 1999: 159–65).

Craft Production. Evidence found at the Erlitou site points not only to highly specialized craft production, but also to the production of some types of artifacts in segregated workshops. The best evidence of this is offered by the remains

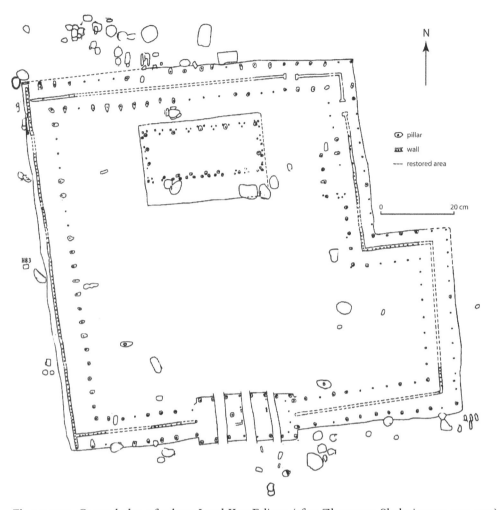

Figure 109. Ground plan of palaces I and II at Erlitou (after Zhongguo Shehui 1999: 139, 152).

of a bronze casting foundry located some 300 m south of the palace city and surrounded by its own pounded earth walls. The foundry's walls and the area's association with the center of elite activity both indicate that the elite had control over bronze production. Numerous remains of crucibles, casting molds, and slugs were found in this area (Liang and Sun 2004) (Figure 110).

Overall, more than a hundred metal items have been found at Erlitou, most of them made from copper mixed with a lead and tin alloy. While the proportions of tin and lead in different artifacts varied considerably (Zhongguo

Shehui 2003: 114–15), the craftsmen were clearly well versed in bronze production. The development of piece-mold techniques for casting complex bronze vessels was a major technological breakthrough, which is commonly attributed to the Erlitou period and which had a great impact on later societies in China. The mold parts and bronze vessels have helped date the beginning of this technique to phase III of the Erlitou site. A recent survey of bronzes found at Erlitou counted seventeen vessels, all but two of which were excavated from graves. The great majority of these vessels (fifteen of them) are small cups known as

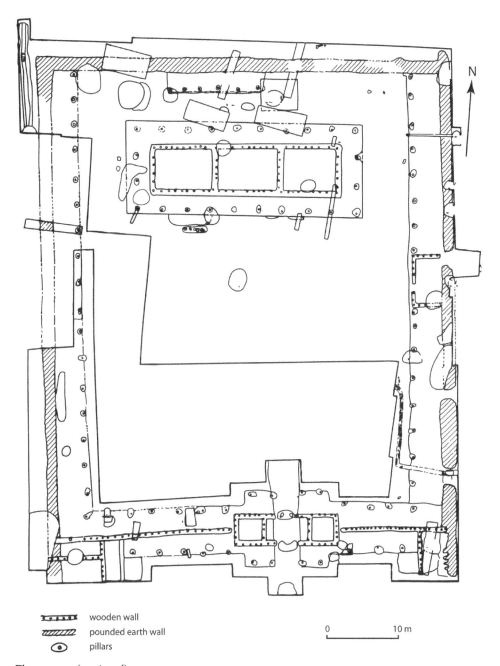

⚊∙⚊∙⚊	wooden wall
▨▨▨▨	pounded earth wall
◉	pillars

0 10 m

Figure 109 (*continued*)

jue (爵) and *jia* (斝). A *he* (盉) and a *ding* complete the collection. Of these seventeen vessels, six were dated to phase III (all *jue*), and nine to phase IV (Liang and Sun 2004) (Figure 111). Their shapes suggest continuity from the ceramic traditions of the Longshan period, and based on

correspondences with bronze vessels of the Shang and Zhou periods, they have been identified as ritual utensils.

Bronze vessels are considered the apex of Erlitou culture, but they are small and not very complex in comparison to vessels from later periods. Most

Figure 110. Remains of Erlitou casting molds and crucible (photo by Du Jinpeng).

are 20 cm or less in height, and only small amounts of bronze would have been needed to cast them. By phase IV, vessel types had become slightly more varied, but the overall casting capacity of Erlitou remained miniscule in comparison to later periods.

It seems that metal was not used to produce tools for agricultural use. Evidence for bronze production is found in a few other Erlitou period sites, but it would appear that they produced only simple artifacts and not sophisticated piece-mold vessels (Liu and Xu 2007). Indeed, other bronze artifacts found in Erlitou include knives, chisels, small bells, and other small artifacts such as awls and needles (Figure 112).

The production of turquoise artifacts at Erlitou may have been another elite-sponsored craft. The concentration of turquoise pieces and debris in an area outside the southern wall of the palace city suggests that a workshop was located there, and

Figure 111. Bronze vessels (*jue* and *he*) from Erlitou (photos by Gideon Shelach).

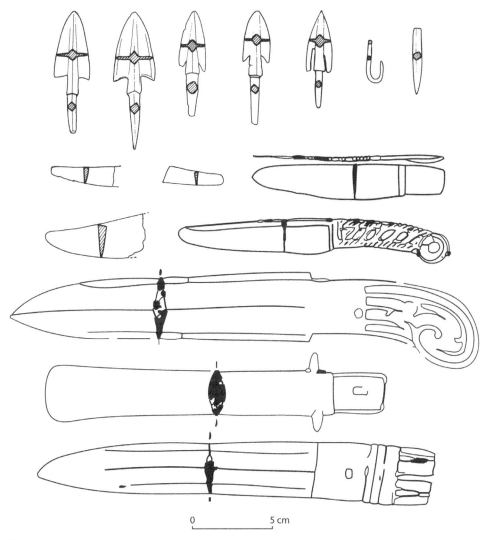

Figure 112. Bronze artifacts from Erlitou (after Zhongguo Shehui 1999: 269).

that it was directly associated with the elite center of the site (Liu and Xu 2007). Many of the turquoise artifacts found in elite contexts at Erlitou must have been produced by this or similar workshops. For example, an impressive dragon-shaped artifact made from about two thousand pieces of turquoise and jade was found in grave M3 (Figure 113). Some remarkable bronze plaques inlaid with turquoise were also found at Erlitou and serve as a good illustration of cooperation between the two elite-sponsored crafts. At

least three such plaques were found in Erlitou graves, each measuring about 15 cm and inlaid with numerous turquoise pieces carved into different shapes (Figure 114).

No direct evidence of other workshops has yet been located at Erlitou, but sophisticated jade artifacts such as long and fragile blades, the production of which was extremely time-consuming, suggest specialized craftsmanship, as does another unusual type of prestige artifact, namely white ceramic vessels made from kaolin clay.

Figure 113. A dragon-shaped artifact made of turquoise and jade pieces from grave M3 at Erlitou (phase II) (photo by Xu Hong).

Burials. Burial data from Erlitou are perhaps less impressive than one would expect given the size of the site and the impressive structures found in it. No obvious cemetery or segregated elite burial area has been located as of yet. The largest grave discovered so far, labeled VD2M1, is located behind the main hall in compound II. It is 5.2 m by 4.25 m in size and 6 m deep, with a secondary ledge around the perimeter and the remains of a lacquered wooden coffin. The grave was looted in antiquity, so it is difficult to tell how richly furnished it was (Zhongguo 1999: 157).

All other graves discovered at the site so far are much smaller, though some also contain a secondary ledge and a wooden coffin. The number of artifacts found in Erlitou graves ranges from none to about twenty. Ceramic vessels are the most common grave goods, but richer graves sometimes contain prestige artifacts such as bronze vessels and other bronze artifacts, turquoise, and jades. A layer of cinnabar is also distinctive to some of the more elaborate graves. Grave VI KM3 is an example of a relatively large grave dated to phase III. It is 2.3 m by 1.3 m in size and 1.7 m deep, with

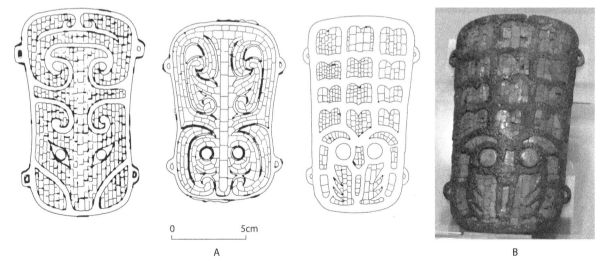

Figure 114. Bronze plaques inlaid with turquoise from Erlitou (A. after Du and Xu 2006: 108; B. photo by Gideon Shelach).

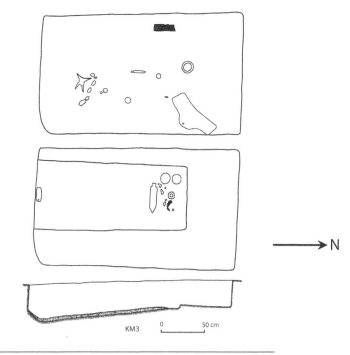

Figure 115. Erlitou graves VI KM3, IV M17, and VI M4 (after Zhongguo Shehui 1999: 242–5).

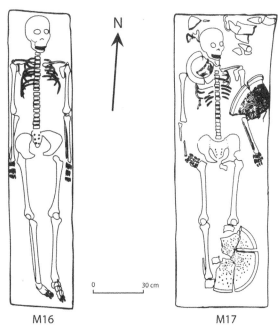

a ledge and probably a wooden coffin as well. A total of twenty-four artifacts were found in it, including a bronze *jue* vessel, two bronze weapons, ceramic vessels, a large jade blade, and a chime stone. Graves IV M17 and VI M4 are examples of smaller graves from the same period. The former is 1.75 m by 0.6 m and 0.7 m deep and contained five ceramic vessels, while the latter is 1.8 m by 0.4 m and contained no grave goods at all (Figure 115) (Zhongguo Shehui 1999: 241–2).

Northwest China and the Ordos Region

DOMESTIC SITES AND STRUCTURES

As in previous periods, most of our knowledge regarding the societies that inhabited northwest China during the second millennium BCE is derived from the excavation of graves, while much less is known about domestic sites and settlement patterns (Debaine-Francfort 1995; Linduff 1998; Zhongguo Shehui 2003: 535–62). Continuity from the third millennium is evidenced not only by the similarity of the ceramic traditions but also by the continued use of burial grounds such as Liuwan (柳湾) throughout the period. In contrast, a rupture between the Laohushan and Zhukaigou periods is suggested for the Ordos region, but it would appear that this is at least partly due to problems with classifying ceramics (Indrisano and Linduff 2013).

Qijia sites are much more numerous in northwest China than sites from previous periods, which probably represents an increase in the regional population density. Contrary to what some have argued (e.g., Shui 2001), these sites indicate a sedentary population. Domesticated pigs, which are indicative of a sedentary lifeway, make up 70 to 85 percent of the bone assemblages in Qijia sites, while herd animals, such as sheep and goats, compose less than 20 percent. The percentage of sheep and goat bones is higher in Zhukaigou, but here too pig bones are the most numerous (Shelach 2009: 50–1).

Qijia sites are relatively small; the largest known sites are no bigger than 20 ha, and the average Qijia site is 5 to 7 ha in size (Zhongguo Shehui 2003: 538–47). No fortifications or other public structures are known, though very few Qijia domestic sites have been excavated. Houses are mainly rectangular in shape, constructed of stone and mud bricks, and are relatively small, between 6 m² and 40 m².

Houses at Zhukaigou sites, in the Ordos region, are semi-subterranean or constructed on the surface and do not differ from houses of the Neolithic period. Small round and rectangular houses have also been found. On average, Zhukaigou houses are 11.5 m² in size, though some larger houses with two or three rooms are also known (Zhongguo Shehui 2003: 547, 577–8).

CRAFT PRODUCTION

Pottery associated with the Qijia period shows some unique attributes, such as flared openings and two large vertical handles, but, on the whole, it continues the traditions of earlier Neolithic periods in the northeast region (Debaine-Francfort 1995; Shui 2001: 195). Most ceramics were produced on potter's wheels, and their standardization suggests large-scale workshop production.

Bronze production in northwest China started early (Chapter 6), and the area remained an important center of bronze production during the early parts of the second millennium BCE. More than one hundred copper and bronze objects associated with the Qijia period and almost three hundred with the Siba period have been found. In the Huoshaogou (火烧沟) cemetery alone, more than two hundred metal objects were excavated, and approximately one-third of the graves in this site (106 out of 312) contained at least one bronze artifact (Li and Shui 2000; Mei 2003).

Common bronze artifacts include earrings, carved knives, daggers with leaf-shaped and pierced blades, spearheads, mace heads, socketed axes, and mirrors. Most artifacts were cast in simple two-part molds, but one of the artifacts found at the Huoshaogou cemetery – the "mace head with four sheep heads" – is more complex (Li 1993: 118; Li and Shui 2000: 39) (Figure 116).

Bronze slag and parts of furnaces for smelting bronze found at Qijia and Siba sites indicate local production. Scientific tests have proven that while some of the artifacts are made of copper, most are of a bronze alloy (Li 1993: 117). All of the evidence suggests a high level of craft specialization and production on quite a large scale. In contrast,

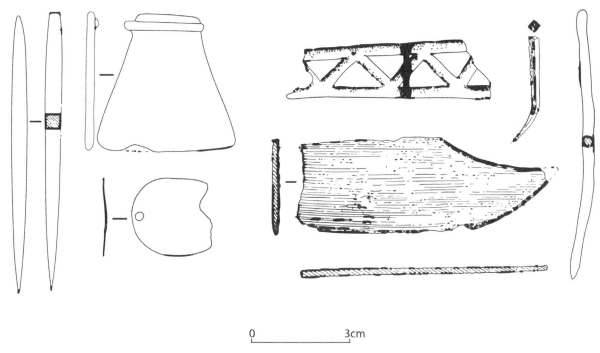

Figure 116. Typical metal artifacts from northwest China (after Mei 2003: 52).

the sophistication and scale of metal production in the Ordos region were probably lower during the first half of the second millennium BCE. Only forty-three small metal artifacts, such as needles, small chisels, arrowheads, and earrings, have been dated to the earlier phases of the Zhukaigou site (Li and Han 2000: 423).

Other evidence of craft specialization includes small silver and gold objects found in Qijia and Siba graves (Gansu 1990). More than three hundred jade artifacts found so far in Qijia graves suggest well-developed craftsmanship in hard stone carving as well. Although it has been suggested that some of these artifacts originated from outside the area, most were nonetheless probably produced by local specialists.

CEMETERIES AND GRAVES

Both the size of Qijia graves and the number of artifacts placed in them range widely. Large graves can be more than 4 m long and deeper than 2 m,

and many contain wooden coffins (not found in smaller graves). In some large graves, one skeleton is found inside a coffin, with other skeletons located outside it, suggesting that they might have been human sacrifices. Other graves contain two or three skeletons understood to be those of a husband and his wife (or wives) (Debaine-Francfort 1995: 130–5; Zhongguo Shehui 2003: 553–6).

Ceramic vessels are the most common burial offerings. Other grave goods include stone and bone tools, metal artifacts, and stone and jade ornaments and ritual objects. In the Huangniangniangtai (皇娘娘台) cemetery, the number of grave offerings found in a single grave ranges from one to ninety-four (Liu 2004: 149). The offering of animals is indicated by the pig and sheep bones found in large quantities in wealthy graves.

Zhukaigou burials also range considerably in size and content. Small graves measure approximately 1 m by 0.5 m and are 0.5 m deep, while the largest graves are 2.5 to 4 m long, 1.5 to 3 m wide, and up to 6 m deep. Fewer than 10 percent of the pit graves at the Zhukaigou cemetery contained an internal wooden structure. Most of the graves contained only a single human skeleton, though 14 percent (45 out 329) contained two, three, or even four skeletons. Most of these multiple burials were of a single male and a single female (Neimenggu 2000: 131–2). In contrast to these clear structural differences between Zhukaigou graves, the variation in terms of grave goods is much smaller. Only 36 percent of the graves at Zhukaigou contained offerings and even the richest graves contained no more than ten artifacts. Ceramic vessels are the most common type of artifact, and were sometimes placed in a niche dug into one of the walls of the grave. Other offerings include stone tools and ornaments, bronze tools, weapons and ornaments, and sacrificial animals. In addition to pit graves, urn burials are also known at Zhukaigou sites, mostly placed beneath the floor of a house or between houses in the residential area (Neimenggu 2000: 131–5).

Aside from burials, remains of oracle bones are the most common evidence of ritual practice in sites of the northwest and the Ordos regions. Circles of stone discovered at some Qijia sites have also been interpreted as the remains of ritual activity, though the nature of this activity is unclear (Shelach 2009: 39–41).

Northeast China

SITES AND DOMESTIC STRUCTURES

The late third and early second millennia BCE, the period known as the Lower Xiajiadian, was a time of considerable prosperity in northeast China. Although only a handful of sites and cemeteries from this period have been excavated, hundreds if not thousands of sites were identified in both systematic and opportunistic surveys. Within the roughly 1,200 km² area covered by the Chifeng regional survey, Lower Xiajiadian sites were found to cover a total area of 920 ha. The total

population of the survey area is estimated at 40,000 to 80,000 people, representing a density of 30 to 60 persons per km². The largest single community of this region is ca. 25 ha in size and had an estimated population of 2,500 to 5,000. Archaeologists have classified the regional population into about sixteen groups, which are identified as independent small-scale polities (Chifeng 2011).

One of the unique features of the Lower Xiajiadian period is the construction of permanent structures – built of stone, mud bricks, and earth – which were relatively labor-intensive. Most notable among these structures are the defense systems that surrounded some of the sites. These defense systems were made of large stone walls, some as wide as 10 m. In the recently excavated site of Sanzuodian (三座店), the walls now reach a height of 4 m and are estimated to have been at least 2 m higher. Some of the larger sites were surrounded by two large stone walls separated by a ditch, and sometimes reinforced with semicircular watch towers, as well as fortified gates (Figure 117). More than a hundred such sites were located in the Chifeng survey region and in the adjacent area that I surveyed in 1994–5, quite indicative of the prevalence of fortifications in this region (Shelach 1999; Shelach et al. 2011).

Features inside Lower Xiajiadian sites, such as paved walkways, water installations, terraces, and enclosures, were also solid constructions built of stone (Figure 118). Lower Xiajiadian period houses, in both fortified and unfortified sites, were built from stone or mud bricks. They were usually semi-subterranean, and either round or rectangular. In some instances a single house might have had two walls – an internal one and an external one – with the external wall located 1.5 m to 3 m from the internal wall (Figure 119). The area between the two walls may have been used for storage. Stone-walled open courtyards were found in front of some of the houses. These structures represent an impressive amount of labor investment in domestic structures, an investment also evident

Figure 117. Stone fortifications at the Sanzuodian site (photo by Gideon Shelach).

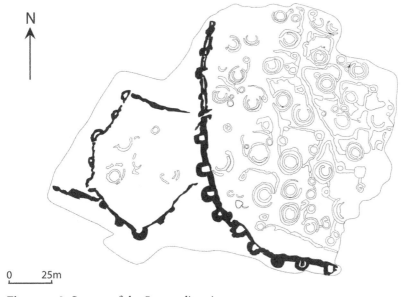

Figure 118. Layout of the Sanzuodian site.

Figure 119. House remains at Sanzuodian (photo by Gideon Shelach).

in the construction of storage pits, some of which were also lined with stones (Shelach 1999; Shelach et al. 2011).

CRAFT PRODUCTION

The ceramics of the Lower Xiajiadian period are of substantially higher quality and are much more standardized than in previous periods in the region, which may indicate a process of craft specialization. Ceramic items were usually made of a fine paste and fired at high temperatures, producing a homogeneous and very hard ceramic. Most vessels were produced on fast wheels, while special parts, such as legs, may have been produced in molds. A unique type of painted pottery was excavated from Lower Xiajiadian period graves, probably produced specifically for the purpose of serving as grave offerings. These vessels are painted in red, white, black, and vermilion, creating motifs that some have interpreted as animal masks, clouds, and dragons (Figure 120) (Zhongguo 1996: 101–55).

A handful of small metal objects were discovered in graves and domestic contexts in approximately ten Lower Xiajiadian period sites. These artifacts were probably cast in simple molds, and their chemical analysis indicates that some are made of a bronze alloy containing up to 10 percent tin, while others are made of copper (Beijing 1981: 298). An analysis of two small lead artifacts from Dadianzi (大甸子) shows they contain 80 to 90 percent lead and 5 to 10 percent tin (Zhongguo 1996: 334–6). All in all, this suggests a low level of production but a certain level of specialization and expertise.

Figure 120. Polychromic ceramics from Lower Xiajiadian graves at Dadianzi (photos by Gideon Shelach).

Possible workshops for the production of stone and bone artifacts have been reported from some Lower Xiajiadian sites, but otherwise we have little information on the organization of craft production.

CEMETERIES AND BURIALS

All of the known Lower Xiajiadian period burials are rectangular earthen pit graves. They are not marked above the surface, but their organization in cemeteries, some containing hundreds of graves, suggests that their location must have been known to the community. The best documented cemetery of this period, Dadianzi in the Aohan banner, is located in a defined area outside the walls of the primary settlement and contains some eight hundred graves (Zhongguo 1996). Most of the graves contain a single skeleton in the extended position and are usually 1.7 to 2.5 m long and less than 1 m wide. However, their depth is much more varied; while the mean depth of burials is 1.4 m, some are much shallower and others are more than 7 m deep. Approximately 25 percent of the graves contain an internal wooden structure (or "coffin"), and several contain structures made of mud bricks (Figure 121) (Zhongguo 1996: 39–58).

Ceramic vessels are the most common type of grave offering of this period. At the Dadianzi cemetery, 574 out of 716 well-preserved graves contained ceramic vessels, ranging in number from one to twelve vessels per grave. Other types of burial goods include stone and bone tools, spindle whorls, seashells, different kinds of stone and jade ornaments, small metal objects, oracle bones, and lacquered artifacts (Figures 122 and 123). Remnants of sacrificial animals are also commonly found, with most graves containing the remains of pigs or dogs. Some of the grave offerings were placed near the body of the deceased, but most were put in a niche (or niches) dug into the wall of the grave above the corpse's legs.

Although the range of grave offerings placed inside Lower Xiajiadian graves is not large,

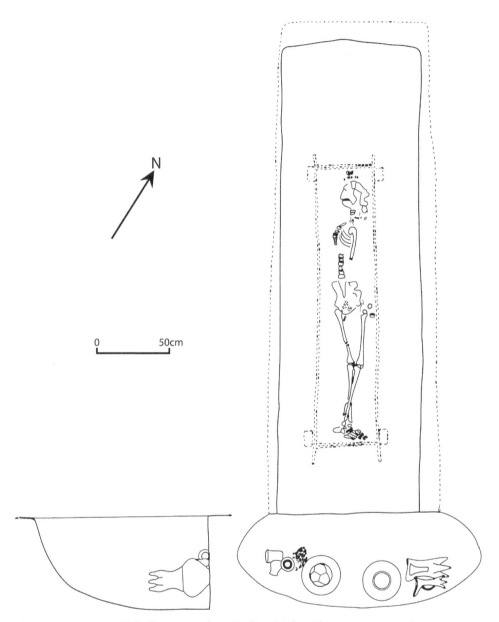

Figure 121. Lower Xiajiadian graves from Dadianzi (after Zhongguo 1996: 52).

statistical analysis of all well-preserved graves from the Dadianzi cemetery suggests a good degree of correlation among the size of the grave, the amount of labor invested in its construction, and the amount and quality of grave goods placed in it (Shelach 2001a). This correlation indicates a hierarchical society with clear sumptuary rules

associating sociopolitical status with postmortem treatment.

Oracle bones found in graves and in domestic contexts are the clearest evidence of ritual activity during the second millennium BCE. That these bones were polished and drilled before they were subjected to heat may reflect a ritual activity that

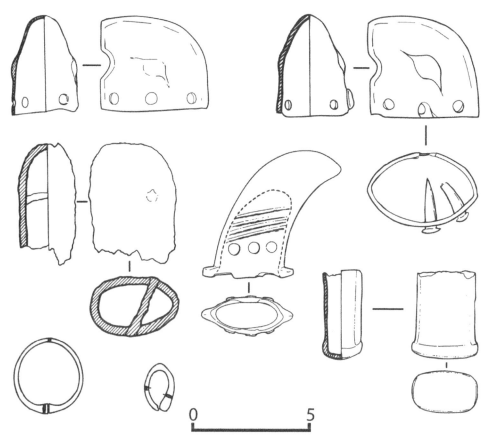

Figure 122. Metal artifacts from the Lower Xiajiadian period (after Zhongguo 1996: 190).

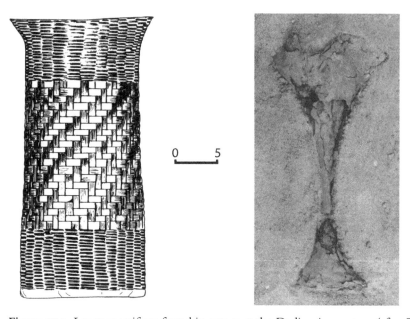

Figure 123. Lacquer artifacts found in graves at the Dadianzi cemetery (after Zhongguo 1996: 192 and plate 20).

was performed by individuals who specialized in this craft (Shelach 1999: 120–1). In addition, some scholars have suggested that several of the Lower Xiajiadian period sites, which were located on high mountains far from the river and containing stone structures, were dedicated specifically to ritual activities (Teng et al. 2003). However, direct evidence in support of this hypothesis has not yet been found.

Other Regions

Our archaeological knowledge of the first half of the second millennium BCE in other regions of China is quite limited. In some regions, such as the lower Yangzi River, this may be related to the "collapse" of Neolithic societies discussed earlier. In other regions, this is perhaps more of a consequence of the low resolution of the available chronological data or because of insufficient archaeological research. In the Chengdu plain, for example, sites from the Baodun period, some of them large and fortified, seem to have continued to flourish during this period, but the local chronology is not yet sharp enough to allow us to make more definitive statements.

In northern Henan and southern Hebei, the area bordering the Erlitou culture from the east, a so-called Xiaqiyuan (下七垣) period has been identified at more than eighty sites. Most of these sites are quite small, but at least one, Mengzhuang (孟庄), is fortified with pounded earth walls and covers more than 10 ha (Zhongguo Shehui 2003: 145–64). Human sacrifice and its association with stratification are suggested by three decapitated human skulls found inside a pounded earth structure at this site.

Farther to the east in the lower Yellow River region, the Yueshi (岳石) period has received more scholarly attention because it has been variously associated with such proto-historic entities as the Eastern Yi (东夷) or the proto-Shang (先商) people (Zhongguo Shehui 2003: 440–57). Sites of this period are distributed mainly in Shandong,

eastern Henan, and north Jiangsu, and are said to have evolved from the local Longshan culture. More than three hundred Yueshi sites have been identified in Shandong, but this number still represents a dramatic decrease when compared to the fifteen hundred Longshan sites that have been found in the same region (Guojia Wenwuju 2007).

The transition from the Longshan to the Yueshi is indicated by a change in the quality and style of ceramics. The fine elite pottery of the Longshan, such as the eggshell cups and highly burnished vessels, all but disappear; Yueshi ceramics are much less elaborate in shape and have much thicker walls. Elaborate burials and exquisite grave goods like jades, which were typical to the Longshan, are also unknown during this period. Other aspects of the Yueshi culture, however, suggest continuity between the two periods. In northern Shandong, pounded earth walls were preserved or built at a number of sites such as Chengziya (城子崖) and Jiaochangpu (教场铺). This suggests sociopolitical continuity from the late third millennium BCE. Single-, double-, and multiroom houses similarly represent continuity.

Alongside the decline in certain aspects of craft production, especially elite-related artifacts, other types of craft specializations flourished. For instance, the Yueshi metal industry is comparable to that of contemporaneous "cultures" in other parts of north China. A relatively large number of bronze and copper implements have been excavated at Yueshi sites, most of which are relatively small and utilitarian objects cast in simple molds, such as arrowheads, chisels, knives, awls, drills, and rings. Chemical tests of some such artifacts identify the use of leaded tin bronze as well as pure copper (Zhongguo Shehui 2003: 442).

THE EARLIEST STATE IN CHINESE HISTORY: ARE WE THERE YET (2)?

Disagreements over the identity of the first state in Chinese history have long been very heated and sometimes emotionally loaded. These debates are not unrelated to the authenticity of the earliest historical records in China discussed earlier since, as noted, the earliest states and the Xia are sometime used synonymously. Even when the identification of the earliest state is based on archaeological evidence alone, opinions range considerably: from early and Late Neolithic societies such as the Hongshan or Liangzhu (e.g., Shao 2000; Zhang 2000) to the Early Shang (e.g., Bagley 1999). The most common view, however, is that the first state-level society in China emerged in the central Yellow River region during the Erlitou period (cf. Liu 2004; Liu and Chen 2003; Zhongguo Shehui 2003).

Similarly to other places in the world, disagreements over the first state in China are in many cases semantic. The definition of a state and how one draws the line between states and their non-state predecessors determine the "discovery" of the earliest state. Although semantic definitions obviously can be manipulated in accordance to one's needs, they nonetheless also touch upon important theoretical issues related to our understanding of state and pre-state societies.

Models of the State and Their Archaeological Correlates

Early archaeological research on the world's first (or pristine) states produced lists of formal attributes that defined the necessary conditions that a polity would have to meet in order to qualify as a state. Such lists, which are commonly found even in more recent introductory texts, include the minimal size of the state's territory, the number of people living in this area and in the state's capital city, the construction of monuments, and more (Renfrew and Bahn 1996: 165–70). In Chinese research, the state and "civilization" are terms that are often used interchangeably, and the list is expanded to include traits such as writing systems and metallurgy.

Lists of traits were important in archaeological research on the state and its origins, but a formalistic reliance on such lists has been criticized for two related reasons. First, state attributes can manifest differently in different regions. For example, the capital cities of early states in the Levant are much smaller in size, and probably in population too, than many pre-state Neolithic sites in China. Second, and more important, a state should be defined according to its sociopolitical structure. The listed attributes may be archaeological manifestations of the state, but their analysis should not be based on static numerical figures (such as territory and population size). Instead, our analysis should adopt a dynamic approach that places these numbers in the context of the structure and functioning of the state system.

The dynamic approach lends itself to a basic theoretical question: how does the state function, and in what ways is this different from the functioning of pre-state polities? One approach, which focuses on the development of the political control system, suggests that state-level societies have a more hierarchical and specialized system of rule than pre-state polities. Pre-state entities (or chiefdoms) have a "generalist" system, in which the paramount leaders directly control the polity without a formal division of tasks and specialized institutions. A state system, by contrast, is one in which the functions of the ruling group are internally divided into specialized task-oriented subunits ("offices"), each of which is internally hierarchical and is regulated and controlled by a hierarchical chain of command up to the paramount leader (or king). This model of the state was influenced by cybernetic models of the regulation of information flows in a system. For example, control over the state's territory is conceptualized in terms of the flow of information to and from the center. The paramount center communicates with and through secondary regional centers under its control, which in turn do the same with the third-level centers that lie within their subterritories.

In archaeological terms, the state is often defined as a polity having a minimum of four tiers in its regional settlement hierarchy: three levels of political control above the ordinary villages (Flannery 1998; Wright 1978). One problem of such heavy reliance on the number of tiers in the settlement hierarchy as the primary criterion for defining statehood is that determining how many levels existed is often based on subjective evaluations of the site-size histogram (see discussion in Chapter 6). In order to establish the existence of a state regulatory system archaeologically, we should look for more concrete evidence, such as artifacts related to state administration (for example, official seals or status symbols) and structures related to its control (administrative centers and warehouses for tax collection).

A related issue (and unfortunately one that is often neglected in archaeological discussions) is that there is a fundamental difference between the paramount leaders of states (kings) and those of the pre-state polities (chiefs) in their ability to delegate power. The leadership strategy of these two types of leaders is fundamentally different: A chief relies on his personal charisma and can only secure the stability of his polity and his own position by maintaining personal control of the entire territory. On the other hand, a king's strategy for maintaining control and stability is to delegate responsibilities to his subordinates, but divide them among as many "ministers" as possible, so that no one of them wields enough power to challenge him. This system of delegation means that the king can control a much larger area and extract more resources. While a chief can effectively control only those areas that are within a day's travel from the center, no such limitations impede the king.

The most important archaeological implication of this perspective is that the trajectory from pre-state entity to state cannot be gradual. When observing the long-term regional trajectory, we should expect to find the rapid coevolution of multiple aspects related to the sociopolitical and economic functioning of the state during the period it begins to emerge (Shelach and Jaffe 2013). This is not to say that the state does not continue to undergo a gradual process of evolution, such as the institutionalization of the state apparatus, after it comes into being (Chapters 8–11).

The Erlitou State Reexamined

According to the accepted paradigm, the earliest Chinese state dates to the Erlitou period, and more specifically to Erlitou's phase III, where we find all of the crucial elements associated with the state. According the most advanced analysis by Liu and Chen (2003), these elements include the ascendancy of the Erlitou site as it became a large, densely populated central node (or capital) of the Erlitou polity, the formation of a four-tiered hierarchical system in the Yiluo basin, the construction of a walled "palace city" within which several "palace" complexes were constructed, the development of a large-scale and highly specialized state-sponsored bronze industry and other similar types of industry, and the development of state-level rituals using bronze vessels. According to their analysis, the state rapidly expanded to exert its control over areas as far as 500 km from the center. This military expansion was an essential part of the state formation process because it ensured the supply of resources that the state system needed and were not available locally – for example, the copper and tin needed for the bronze industry, timber for the construction of palaces, charcoal for fuel in casting bronzes, and salt for preserving food (Liu 2004: 232–4).

Liu and Chen are quite careful in explicitly laying out the evidence in support of their theory, but even they are not always able to escape a problem shared by most descriptions of the Erlitou state: the mixing of evidence and explanation, and the influence of implicit assumptions. For example, naming the public structures found in Erlitou "palaces" presumes that they were the residences of kings and the hub of the state administration. In what follows, some of these assumptions are rendered more explicit and their validity – and that of the entire state model – is tested.

CAPITAL CITY AND ITS PALACES

The identification of Erlitou as a state capital is based first and foremost on its exceptional size. It should be remembered, however, that Late Neolithic sites such as Taosi and Shijiahe are hardly any smaller. Moreover, no evidence for what may be seen as state-level monumental construction has been found at Erlitou. The best evidence supporting Erlitou having been the state capital is the construction of the so-called palaces in phase II, and particularly during phase III, including the demarcation of a "palace city" with enclosing walls and the more intensive construction of palaces I and II inside this area.

A palace is usually understood as a multifunctional building serving as the king's residence, as well as the central hub of the state administration. In this respect, comparisons of the Erlitou "palaces" with palaces of "archaic states" in other parts of the world (Liu 2004: 230) are unjustified. The examples to which Erlitou "palaces" are compared are all complex multiroomed structures that are reasonably interpreted as multifunctional palaces (Flannery 1998: 22–36). However, compounds I and II at Erlitou have only one roofed building each, measuring 330 m² and 132 m², respectively (Figure 109). These structures are, in fact, quite small as residences of a king and his household, and it is hard to see how they could have also housed the administrative center of the state. The courtyards in front of these buildings are impressive in size, and it has been estimated that each could have accommodated hundreds if not thousands of people. However, they are not partitioned into subareas, which might hint at multifunctioning. As Thorp (1991) has observed, these courtyards are better explained as places for public gatherings, rituals perhaps, when a large audience is convened. A political or religious leader could have addressed this audience from the elevated platform at the northern side of the courtyard and performed rituals inside the roofed building located on the platform. Such a reconstruction does not imply that the buildings were not associated with political authority, but it does suggest that the authority could have been that of a chief, and not a king.

At least one example of a building very similar to compounds I and II at Erlitou is known from the Late Neolithic site of Guchengzhai (Figure 90). It is therefore reasonable that these "palaces" represent continuity in style and function with previews periods rather than new types of buildings and a new form of authority.

LABOR INVESTMENT AND SUMPTUARY BEHAVIOR

Evidence for sumptuary consumption is suspiciously scarce at Erlitou. Sumptuary consumption is seen by many both as evidence for a king's ability to extract resources and labor from the population and as an expression of his legitimating propaganda (Flannery 1998; Trigger 2003). Although the one large grave at Erlitou was looted, other funerary evidence found so far at the site is not quantitatively different from that of Late Neolithic societies, nor does it differ much from burials of the early second millennium BCE found in other regions of China. In fact, some of the graves found at the Taosi site and at sites of the Shandong Longshan were more richly furnished and required a greater labor investment than those found so far in Erlitou.

Evidence of the labor investment in public structures at Erlitou is similarly not very impressive when compared with previous and contemporaneous sites. The main evidence of labor investment is, again, the "palace city." The enclosing walls of this compound are 2 m wide, and their total estimated length is 1,321 m. Assuming that the walls originally stood 4 m tall, the amount of pounded earth required to construct them would have been 10,568 m³. The two compounds are located atop pounded earth platforms measuring 9,600 m² and 4,200 m². These platforms were not very high above the ground, but their foundations varied from 3 m to 1 m in depth. Taking 2 m as the average depth, the accumulated volume of the pounded earth in the platforms would have been 27,600 m³. Altogether then, some 38,168 m³ of pounded earth would have been needed to build these structures. If we were to add to this figure the area of other smaller platforms and the extra depth of the foundations of the buildings inside the compounds, the accumulated volume was probably ca. 40,000 m³.

According to the Han mathematical manual, *Jiuzhang suanshu* (九章算術, Nine Chapters on the Mathematical Art), a single conscript worker was expected to excavate, transport, and construct 7.55 m³ of pounded earth wall in a month. Modern experimental work has come up with very similar estimates (Shelach et al. 2011; Shen et al. 1999: 258–9). Based on these estimates then, the construction of the entire palace city at Erlitou would have required 5,298 person-months of work. This may sound like a lot, but in fact it indicates that a relatively small proportion of the city's inhabitants could have built it in a reasonably short time, without the leaders needing to extract extra labor from neighboring communities. If the Erlitou population during phase III was eighteen to thirty thousand, then between one-third and one-fifth of the population could have constructed the entire palace city within a month, and about 10 percent to 16 percent of the population could have completed the work in two months.

In comparison, the investment in the contemporaneous Lower Xiajiadian fortified sites in northeast China seems much more extensive. For example, at the 2 ha site of Sanzuodian, whose population is estimated to have been between 183 and 308, the total labor investment in the construction of the enclosing stone wall is estimated at between 592 and 745 person-months (Shelach et al. 2011). In other words, the per-person investment of labor at Sanzuodian was between 58 and 122 days, while at Erlitou it was between 5 and 9 days. At larger Lower Xiajiadian sites, which had two concentric walls and a ditch, the amount of labor invested may have been even greater.

At large Late Neolithic sites such as Taosi, even more labor was invested in public works. Taking into account only the main enclosure walls at this site, which are about 9 to 10 m wide and have an accumulated length of about 7,300 m (Zhongguo Shehui 2010b: 568), and assuming that these walls were also 4 m high (like the much narrower walls at Erlitou), the amount of pounded earth needed for their construction would have been 292,000 m³. According to the estimates and calculations used above, the construction of this wall would have required 39,673 person-months, or seven times more effort than the work carried out at Erlitou.

BRONZE INDUSTRY AND STATE-LEVEL CEREMONIES

The bronze production at Erlitou clearly surpasses anything seen elsewhere in China before or during this period in regard to sophistication and quantity. The size and number of bronze tools excavated at the site, and especially the size and sophistication of the bronze vessels, suggest production at a considerable scale and degree of sophistication. This conclusion is supported by the amounts of production debris found at the bronze workshop. Nevertheless, it appears that the scale of this production is sometimes exaggerated. During fifty years of excavations at the site, only 117 bronze artifacts dated from all four phases have been found (Liang and Sun 2004). Even the largest artifacts, the bronze vessels, are relatively small (no taller than 20 cm) and other objects are even smaller. It would not be an exaggeration to estimate that all the bronze artifacts recovered from three hundred years of inhabitation at Erlitou weigh less than a single Early Shang (Erligang) bronze vessel (Chapter 8).

The functions of Erlitou bronze vessels are inferred by comparing them with the known ritual functions of Shang and Zhou period vessels, and such comparisons are offered as evidence for the development of state-level ceremonies (Lee 2004: 176). However, this is an anachronistic interpretation that projects back on to this period a state of affairs that we know only from the texts and inscriptions of later periods. In reality, the inventory of bronze paraphernalia from the beginning of the Shang was much more varied than that of Erlitou. Moreover, bronze vessels were much more numerous overall, and found in many more sites in comparison to Erlitou. If anything, the resemblance of Erlitou bronze vessels to Late Neolithic ceramic vessels in shape suggests the continuation of Late Neolithic rituals rather than the emergence of new state-level traditions.

SETTLEMENT HIERARCHY AND THE TERRITORIAL EXPANSE OF ERLITOU CONTROL

As discussed previously, a histogram of site sizes cannot by itself prove the formation of a four-tier settlement hierarchy in the Erlitou culture. Sites outside Erlitou that have been identified as second- and third-level centers have revealed no clear evidence for any of the functions associated with such status. It has been argued that Shaochai (稍柴) and Fucun (富村) (60 ha and 40 ha in size, respectively) were secondary administrative centers in the Yiluo basin (Liu 2004: 226). Shards of white kaolin pottery were found at Shaochai, as well as at some of the so-called third level centers (Liu et al. 2004), indicating a possible association with elites. However, no other data links it or other presumed "centers" with any administrative functions.

One of the assumptions made by the four-tier settlement hierarchy model is that resources were extracted from the lower levels of the system and used to support the nonproductive sectors at the higher levels, including the royal household and administration. However, no evidence for the management and storage of the large amounts of food such a hierarchy would require has been found. Such evidence might include large centralized granaries similar to those found in other parts of the world, and possibly even in at least one Late Neolithic site in China (He 2013). However, no such structures have been identified either at the Erlitou site or at the sites considered to be regional administrative centers.

Even more problematic is the evidence for the supposedly military expansion of the Erlitou polity. One of the crucial problems with this reconstruction is the assumption that the extensive distribution of Erlitou cultural materials is coterminous with the political boundaries of the Erlitou state. Similar assumptions are not made, for example, for the Shandong Longshan materials or other Late Neolithic regional cultures. Apart from similar cultural materials, what evidence is there that large regions were conquered and colonies up to 500 km away from Erlitou were established specifically for the purpose of extracting resources (Liu 2004: 232–4; Liu and Chen 2003)?

Looking at the spatial distribution of sites contemporaneous with Erlitou phase III, the fortified Mengzhuang site is thought to have belonged to a non-Erlitou polity, and the border between these two polities is said to have been the Qin River to the north and east of Erlitou (Liu 2004: 237). On the Erlitou side of this border, the walled Dashigu (大师姑) site, some 70 km east of the Erlitou main site, is identified as a secondary center. This identification of Dashigu as an Erlitou border fortress, however, is not supported by any clear evidence.

The expansion of Erlitou northwestward and its control over resources at the Hedong (河东) Salt Lake is one of the main components of the expansion theory. Two sites some 100 to 150 km away from Erlitou – Dongxiafeng (东下冯) and

Nanguan (南关) – are considered to have been secondary Erlitou administrative centers in this region (Liu 2004: 272). Once again, however, it is unclear why these sites are identified as parts of the Erlitou polity rather than as centers of neighboring polities. In fact, the classification of sites in southern Shanxi as belonging to the Dongxiafeng cultural variant (Zhongguo Shehui 2003: 89–94) suggests stylistic differences in the ceramic assemblages of the two regions that could lend support to an affiliation with two or more distinct polities. But even without such stylistic differences, much stronger evidence is needed before the expansion model can be confirmed.

Toward the south, small quantities of diagnostic Erlitou ceramics have been found at a very small number of sites in southern Henan province. This, and the fact that some of the ceramics can be stylistically dated to Erlitou phases I and II (Xu Yan 2009), is indicative of the gradual development of peaceful interactions rather than of the military expansion of the Erlitou polity. The idea that the Erlitou polity could have marched across this area and continued 500 km farther south to establish a military outpost at Panlongcheng (盘龙城) (Liu 2004: 233) is unrealistic.

Weapons found at Erlitou are also cited as evidence in support of the military expansion model. The number of weapons, mostly arrowheads, increased dramatically during phase III and reached its peak during phase IV (Guo 2009). It has been argued that this increase can be associated with the military expansion of the Erlitou polity during phase III (Liu 2004: 233), but in fact, the overall number of weapons found from this phase, although greater than in phases I and II, is not large. If anything, the fact that the quantity of weapons increased further during phase IV may indicate a war against the neighboring fortified site of Yanshi rather than expansion into distant territories.

Because elite-sponsored craft production did not occur on a large scale at Erlitou, control over resources, which, according to the model, motivated military expansion, may not have been such an urgent necessity. Even metal production, for which we have the most evidence, if carried out over a period of some two hundred years (phases II–IV), could have been sustained by resources acquired through peaceful exchange with neighboring polities.

A STATE OR NOT A STATE?

This discussion does not preclude the possibility that a state-level society did emerge in the Yiluo basin during Erlitou phase III. It suggests, however, that there is currently no clear evidence in support of this hypothesis. Based on currently available data, the local trajectory appears to represent a gradual shift rather than the step-like change predicted by the theoretical model. Erlitou was the largest and most centralized polity of its time in China. However, it was comparable in scale to large Late Neolithic polities, such as those centered around the Taosi and the Shijiahe sites. What is more, we have no real evidence for the development of a specialized ruling system.

My observations suggest that if we are looking for a qualitative step-like change in the sociopolitical trajectory of north China, then it is to be found during the next period: the Erligang (Shelach and Jaffe 2013). There is also a chronological issue that needs to be resolved. Currently evaluable C-14 dates for Erlitou phase III – the suggested period of Erlitou state expansion – fall between 1610 and 1550 (or even 1530) BCE. It is unclear, however, whether the supposed expansion happened prior to the establishment of the better-known Erligang (or Early Shang) state, which is radiocarbon dated from about 1600 BCE (Zhang et al. 2007; Zhongguo Shehui 2003: 659–63). Clarifying the chronological relations between these two periods, which are currently based on a very small number of C-14 dates, is crucial for our understanding of the dynamics of state formation in China.

INTERREGIONAL INTERACTIONS DURING THE FIRST HALF OF THE SECOND MILLENNIUM BCE

Similarly to previous periods, nonlocal materials provide the most concrete evidence for interregional interactions during the early Bronze Age. Lacquer artifacts and lacquer coating are a good example. Lacquer is produced from the resin of the *Rhus verniciflua* (*Toxicodendron verniciflumm*), a tree that grows in the warm and humid climates of central and southern China, as well as Southeast Asia. Producing lacquer artifacts entails the use of a highly specialized technique with a long history of development in the Yangzi River basin (Chapter 5), and it is likely that lacquer artifacts found in north China were imported from the south. Though not well preserved, lacquer artifacts were found at the Erlitou site, for example (Bagley 1999: 158–9), and farther to the north, in the Chifeng area in northeast China, no fewer than thirty-eight graves in the Dadianzi cemetery contained fragments of lacquer artifacts (Zhongguo 1996: 191–4), some of which are well preserved (Figure 123).

Cowrie shells are another illustrative example of the movement of materials, sometimes over long distances and in relatively large volumes. At Dadianzi, 659 cowrie shells were found in forty-three graves (Zhongguo 1996: 183–7), and similar findings are also known from Erlitou (Liu 2004: 234) and northwest China (Li 2006: 2). The exact source of these shells is disputed, but because they naturally thrive in warm sea waters they must have been imported to the north from the south China coast, if not from the Indian Ocean (Li 2006: 3), at least 1,000 km away. More research, including scientific testing on the source of raw materials, is certain to reveal much more data relevant to the study of the interregional movement of materials and artifacts.

Similarities in the style of artifacts and their decorations can be seen, as in previous periods, as evidence of intra- and interregional interactions. Most of these similarities continue in the broad type of shared styles typical of the Chinese interaction sphere model (Chapter 6). However, in a few cases the correlations are much more concrete. Eleven *jue* pottery vessels excavated from graves at the Dadianzi cemetery (Zhongguo 1996: 82–4) are almost identical to contemporary vessels excavated at the Erlitou site (Zhongguo 1999: 136) (Figure 124). Clearly, the *jue* and the somewhat similar *gui* pitchers were much more at home in Erlitou, where they were found in larger quantities than in the northeast. The vessels may have been imported to Dadianzi from the south or, more probably, produced locally in imitation of the foreign vessels. Either way, they offer clear evidence of direct interregional contacts. Some scholars see an influence moving in the opposite direction – from Chifeng to the Yellow River basin – in the decorations of the Lower Xiajiadian polychrome ceramic vessels, which they argue influenced the decorations on Erlitou inlayed bronze plaques and eventually gave rise to the *Taotie*, a dominant decoration motif of Shang and early Zhou bronze vessels (Figure 125) (Liu and Xu 1981). Whether or not the *Taotie* motif was inspired by models from northeast China is debatable, but the reciprocal nature of the interactions between the northeast and the Yellow River regions seems plausible.

A new type of interaction is indicated by the relative rapid spread of technologies. An increase in the production of bronze artifacts throughout north China could be seen as evidence of such processes. The fact that several bronze artifacts from northwest China are made of arsenic bronze could suggest contact with southern Siberia, where that alloy was common (Chernykh 1992: 270; Legrand 2004; Li and Shui 2000; Mei 2003). An object made of arsenic bronze was also identified at Erlitou (Mei 2006), suggesting a continuous flow of knowledge and possibly raw materials between regions.

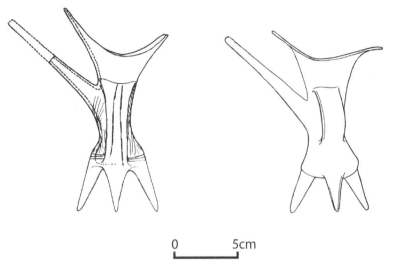

Figure 124. Ceramic *jue* vessels from Dadianzi (left) and from Erlitou (right) (after Zhongguo 1996: 84 and Zhongguo 1999: 136).

The rapid spread of oracle bone divination throughout north China is an even more striking example of the diffusion of knowledge. The earliest evidence of this practice was found in the Chifeng area and is dated to the fourth millennium BCE (Shelach 1999: 109). Several other early finds from Inner Mongolia and Gansu suggest that this practice might have originated in the north. By the early Bronze Age, extensive evidence of the practice of pyromancy, as it is called, is found in large quantities at sites of the Lower Xiajiadian period, Zhukaigou sites, Qijia and related cultures, Erlitou, and the Yueshi period (Figure 126) (Flad 2008). More advanced techniques of bone preparation, such as drilling in them before burning, also appear first in the northeast in sites of the Lower Xiajiadian period, and while there is considerable variation in the style of oracle bones and the raw materials used during the early Bronze Age, these preparations eventually became the norm, most

Figure 125. Comparison of the decorations on: A. Lower Xiajiadian polychrome ceramic vessels; B. Erlitou inlayed bronze plaque; and C. Taotie motif cast on a Shang bronze vessel (after Shelach 2011: 517).

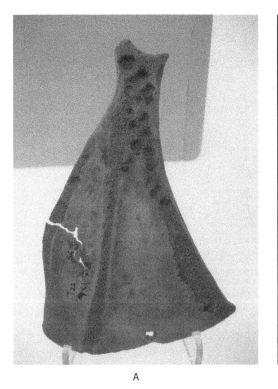
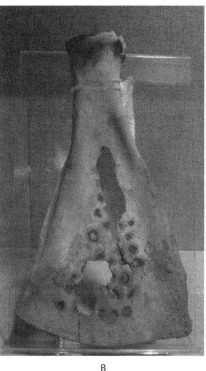

A   B

Figure 126. Oracle bones from early Bronze Age sites: A. From a Late Neolithic period site in northeast China; B. From the Erlitou site (photos by Gideon Shelach).

notably among the Shang (Chapter 8). This pattern suggests that interregional contact was continuous, and that techniques and practices, and perhaps the beliefs that underlined them as well, were transmitted between regions throughout the early Bronze Age.

The patterns of interregional interactions during the first half of the second millennium BCE illustrate an interesting process of change. On the one hand, trade in prestige objects, such as jades, so typical of the Late Neolithic, seems to have declined during this period. On the other hand, increased intersocietal contact is suggested by the wide spread of new technologies, such as bronze production and oracle bone divination. This can be interpreted as evidence of a shift from interactions that were mainly structured as part of elite exchange networks during the Late Neolithic, to more open and less controlled forms of interactions during the early Bronze Age. Although both bronze and oracle bone divination would come to be closely associated with the legitimation of the political hierarchy during the second half of the second millennium BCE, we have much less clear evidence of this kind of manipulation among societies of the first half of this millennium. Parallel to this process, we see the incipient development of interactions on a geographical scale that is much larger than before. The import of relatively large quantities of cowrie shells from as far away as the Indian Ocean represents a new phenomenon, one that anticipates the establishment of long-range exchange networks during the Shang and Zhou periods.

CHAPTER 8

THE SHANG DYNASTY: THE EMERGENCE OF THE STATE IN CHINA

Notwithstanding the debates regarding the historicity of the Xia, the Shang (or Yin 殷) dynasty stands as a significant watershed in Chinese history and archaeology.[1] Evidence of a sizeable, centralized, and highly stratified Shang state is provided by both the oracle bone inscriptions and the impressive archaeological record, which includes imposing city walls at such places as Zhengzhou, the size and contents of the royal graves at Xibeigang (西北冈), and an extensive and highly sophisticated bronze industry.

Following the astounding discovery of the oracle bone inscriptions in Yinxu (殷墟) at the turn of the twentieth century and the subsequent excavation of the site during the 1920s and 1930s, Shang archaeology became the most prestigious field of Chinese archaeology. The history of Shang archaeology in many ways parallels the overall history of Chinese archaeology with its different methodological and theoretical turns. Throughout this early period, the unique position of Shang archaeology was maintained by a constant flow of new discoveries and the ability of Chinese archaeology to correlate and integrate archaeological discoveries with written records. The unmistakably "Chinese" character of the Shang culture – evident in the extensive use of Chinese script, the forms of its ritual bronze vessels, and clear signs of ancestor worship, to mention just three examples – is

another reason for the fascination it has generated among Chinese scholars and the general public.

As in previous chapters, the first part of this chapter reviews the relevant major archaeological findings. While the internal chronology of the Shang period is taken into consideration, these findings are grouped according to their social and economic associations, as in the discussion of the Neolithic and Early Bronze Age. Special attention is also paid in this part to the oracle bone inscriptions and the information they provide about the Shang state.

The second part of this chapter considers how archaeological data and textual materials have been variously combined and used to uncover the workings of the Shang state, including its mechanisms for internal control and legitimation, the extent of its territory, the nature of its relationship with neighboring societies, and its systems of craft production. Finally, the chapter then considers the processes associated with the emergence, maintenance, and functions of the early state in China. While comparisons with early states in other parts of the world are beyond the scope of this book, I argue that the wealth of data available for the Shang period – both archaeological and epigraphic – are valuable as a model (perhaps one of many) for our understanding of human society in a global perspective. Such a perspective not only draws

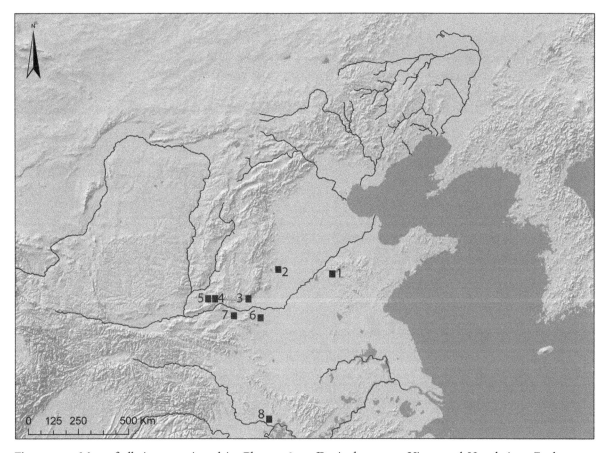

Figure 127. Map of all sites mentioned in Chapter 8: 1. Daxinzhuang; 2. Yinxu and Huanbei; 3. Fucheng; 4. Yuanqu; 5. Dongxiafeng; 6. Zhengzhou; 7. Yanshi; 8. Panlongcheng.

attention to the Shang's conspicuous cultural and material features but also strikes at the long-held assumption, rooted in beliefs about a shared human nature and held by many Western-trained archaeologists, of an underlying cross-cultural similarity in developmental trajectories.

Unlike previous chapters, this one is focused on a relatively small region of China – that which comprised the core territory of the Shang polity. This is a practical choice that should not be read as reflecting the relative importance of the Shang area vis-à-vis other polities and regions in China. Because so much information is available for this region, the development of contemporaneous societies in other parts of China is left

for discussion in Chapter 9, where we also compare their different regional trajectories and discuss interactions among them.

STEPPING INTO HISTORY: HISTORIC, EPIGRAPHIC, AND ARCHAEOLOGICAL SOURCES FOR THE STUDY OF THE SHANG

Many historians and archaeologists, Chinese and others, see the Shang period as a fully evolved historical era. Considering the problematic nature of the history of the Xia (Chapter 7), the Shang can be seen as embodying the dawn of Chinese history. This view, however, was not always universally accepted. In the early twentieth century, an influential intellectual movement, known as the "doubting antiquity school" (*yigu pai* 疑古派), challenged the authenticity and accuracy of the traditional texts, especially those pertaining to the pre-Zhou period. Using modern historiographical and philological techniques borrowed from the West, scholars such Gu Jiegang (顧頡剛) demonstrated the mythical nature of many of the supposedly historic texts about the ancient dynastic heroes and the Xia and the Shang. However, unlike the still ongoing debate about the Xia, disagreements over the Shang were concluded when the name "Shang," as well as the names of many of the Shang kings listed by Sima Qian in the *Shiji*, were identified in the oracle bone inscriptions (Figure 128).

Even the most skeptical scholars, such as Gu Jiegang, were convinced by this evidence that the Shang was a real historic entity (Bagley 1999: 126). This recognition, however, is not the same as the wholesale acceptance of traditional history about the Shang. Even though the information on the Shang dynasty found in the transmitted historical texts and summarized by Sima Qian is not much more detailed than that available for the Xia, historians and archaeologists constantly attempt to use this information as the foundation for studies of the period. For example, the important site at Zhengzhou (郑州) in Henan province was variously identified with the Shang capital cities of Ao (敖) or Bo (亳) (Chang 1980: 270–3). These debates are pointless, however, not only because it is impossible to prove or disprove any of the suggested identifications, but, more important, because even if we could conclusively associate a site with a historical name, it would not greatly advance our understanding of the history or the society of the Shang.

The difference between the Xia and the Shang lies not in our ability to better interpret the traditional texts, but rather in the combination of the discovered oracle bone inscriptions and the far more extensive archaeological record. After more than a century, the discovery of the oracle bones at Yinxu and the deciphering of the inscriptions incised on them remain one of the most dramatic achievements of modern Chinese archaeology and historiography. Unlike the traditional historical texts, which were written hundreds, if not thousands, of years after the events they describe and which underwent modifications and manipulations during their long transmission process, the oracle bone inscriptions have the advantage of having been written at the time of the events and buried soon after, meaning that they could not have been manipulated by later generations. Their other considerable advantage as a historical source is that they contain information not only about big historic events, such as wars and royal affairs, but also on issues not usually covered by historical documents, such as agriculture, economic resources, climate, diseases, and more.

The oracle bone inscriptions (*jiaguwen* 甲骨文) are not an ideal historical source: most texts offer a very concise description of one episode or one issue, and it is difficult to reconstruct a coherent narrative out of them. Moreover, as their name implies, the texts were written as part of divination or religious processes, and as such they are primarily occupied with ritual issues. Also, the fact that the inscriptions were produced within the framework of the royal court and under the supervision of the Shang kings suggests that they reflect the elite's perspective, and cannot be seen as objective sources. However, if we read the inscriptions critically, they provide invaluable information on numerous aspects of the Shang period.

Another significant difference between research on the "Xia" and the Shang is that, unlike the case of the "Xia," where the reconstruction of its culture depends on one site – Erlitou – the archaeology of the Shang covers a large area and is associated with many sites. Shang data also more completely cover crucial issues relevant to our

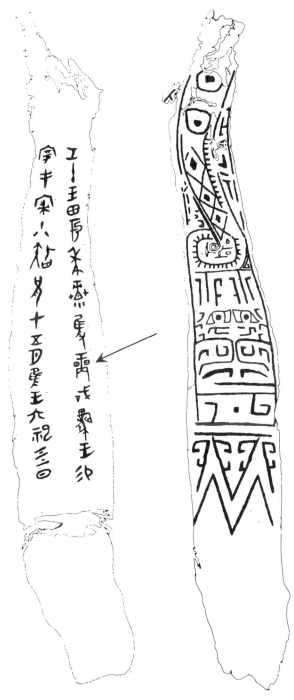

Figure 128. Oracle bone inscription with the character *Shang*.

understanding of the state system, some aspects of which are completely missing or only very partially known for the Erlitou period, including the layout of primary and secondary political centers, the location of craft production workshops, the identification of high-level cemeteries, and more.

In sum, the Shang period (ca. 1600–1050 BCE) can be seen as the gateway to history in China, not because we have one or several comprehensive historical narratives dated to this period, but because of our ability to combine the fragmented oracle bone inscriptions with other rich archaeological data. Such a "history" has the advantage of being more oriented toward the social and less preoccupied with big historic events. At the same time, we should keep in mind that it covers only a small portion of China, with very little written information pertaining to areas beyond the borders of the Shang polity.

THE ARCHAEOLOGY OF THE SHANG POLITY

Archaeological excavations at the Yinxu site began in 1928 (as opposed to plundering, which started earlier). This was the first large project undertaken by the newly founded National Research Institute of History and Philology. Headed by Li Ji (李濟), it operated for fifteen intensive field seasons until work was halted on the eve of the Japanese invasion in 1937. Excavations of Shang sites were resumed in the Yinxu area soon after the founding of the People's Republic of China, this time under the auspicious of the Institute of Archaeology, and have been ongoing ever since. While new locations were excavated and new sites, such as Huanbei (洹北), continued to be discovered in and around Yinxu, Shang sites were also identified and excavated in other parts of north and central China. Some of these sites, such as Zhengzhou, are comparable in size to Yinxu, and many smaller ones have also been intensively excavated. The amount of archaeological data generated from these sites is enormous and continues to grow. Only a small portion of these many sites are discussed later, and the data most relevant to our understanding of the Shang state and society are summarized.

Chronology of the Shang

Traditional accounts related to the dating of the Shang dynasty describe it as having had some thirty kings and lasting for anything between 496 and 600 years (Chang 1980: 18). The beginning of this period, even according to those who accept traditional history as accurate, is vague, but its end is ascribed to a specific event – the Muye (牧野) battle in which King Wuwang (武王) of the Zhou defeated the Shang. Traditional and modern scholars have variously dated this event to between 1130 and 1018 BCE. The Xia, Shang, Zhou Chronology Project team have fixed the date at 1046, suggesting that the Shang period in its entirety should be dated from 1600 to 1046 BCE (Xia Shang Zhou 2000). Here we take the general framework of 1600 to 1050 BCE to stand for the Shang period, and accept that during most of this time, if not all of it, a single polity, probably named Shang, dominated the central and lower parts of the Yellow River basin.

Dividing these 550 years into subperiods is crucial to our understanding of the development and decline of the Shang state. In this chapter, we adopt the tripartite division of the Shang archaeological record into Early (ca. 1600–1400 BCE), Middle (ca. 1400–1300), and Late (1300–1050). Early Shang is most typically identified with the sites of Zhengzhou, Yanshi (偃师), and Panlongcheng (盘龙城), and is sometimes known as the Erligang (二里岗) phase. The Middle Shang is a polity identified relatively recently with the remains of the Huanbei site, while the Late Shang is identified with the Yinxu site and the oracle bone inscriptions found there.

Settlement Patterns and Site Structure

The complete geographical extent of the Shang polity is unclear, though archaeologists have identified sites as being related to the Shang across a very large region, encompassing much of the lower and middle Yellow River basin and areas in the lower and middle Yangzi River basin. The chronology of Shang expansion to distant regions and the question of whether all of these sites were under the control of the Shang polity or only shared certain cultural elements with it are still debated. However, even according to minimalist views, the Shang controlled a much more extensive territory than any polity in China that preceded it.

The transition between the pre-Shang and Shang periods is most clearly observed in northern Henan province, around the modern cities of Zhengzhou and Luoyang. The construction of walled sites, not known for the Erlitou period, is the most outstanding marker of this transition. The construction of the two most prominent sites in this region, Zhengzhou and Yanshi, is contemporaneous with the Erlitou phase IV period, but the ceramics found in them are associated with a diagnostic Erligang style.

Erligang period settlement in the core area of northern Henan represents an unprecedented level of population concentration. The two major sites are very large — the area inside the walls of Yanshi is 200 ha, and the area inside the inner walls of Zhengzhou is some 300 ha, though the outer walls of the site may have incorporated an area as large as 1,500 ha — and the settlement around them is reportedly very dense, including relatively large secondary centers (Liu and Chen 2003: 87–101; Yuan and Zeng 2004). In the Yiluo survey area, the number of sites increased from thirty-one during the late Erlitou to forty-six during the Erligang period, but the total occupation area decreased from 130 to 98 ha (Liu et al. 2004: 92).

This decrease may be due to the fact that the survey area did not include the largest Erligang sites of the region, such as Yanshi. However, it also may be an indication that the center of political gravity shifted 70 km eastward to the area of Zhengzhou.

Aside from Zhengzhou and Yanshi, other contemporaneous fortified sites probably represent regional centers and Shang outposts. They include Fucheng (府城) in northernmost Henan province, Dongxiafeng (东下冯) and Yuanqu (垣曲 sometimes called Nanguan 南关), both in Shanxi and to the west of this core area, Daxinzhuang (大辛庄) to the east in Shandong province, and Panlongcheng in Hubei to the south. The scale of fortification at these other sites was small in comparison to Zhengzhou and Yanshi: the fortifications at Dongxiafeng and Yuanqu enclosed an area of about 13 ha each, and those of Panlongcheng and Fucheng 7.5 ha each (Thorp 2006: 64; Zhongguo Shehui 2003: 231–6).[2]

The relative small size of these sites and the similarities between the artifacts found in them and those from the core area are seen as evidence that they were in fact fortified outposts of the Erligang polity. The affiliation is most striking at Panlongcheng, which, although located some 500 km south of the core of the Erligang polity, exhibits cultural attributes that are almost identical to those found in the north. For example, the style and types of bronze vessels found here are identical to those found in Zhengzhou and Yanshi. Other similarities are found in the construction techniques of walls and house foundations, and in the layout of public buildings (Bagley 1999; Hubei 2001).

Obviously, many of the Early Shang sites, even some of the relatively large ones, were not fortified. That some of these unfortified sites nevertheless had elite residency and may have played a role in the Shang hierarchy is suggested by the discovery of pounded earth house foundations. Unfortunately, our knowledge of these sites is relatively limited (Thorp 2006: 76–8).

A dramatic shift in settlement patterns seems to have taken place around 1400 BCE, when Zhengzhou, Yanshi, and many of the smaller walled sites were abandoned. Almost no Middle and Late Shang sites are reported in the Yiluo survey area, a dramatic decrease from the forty-six sites dated to the Early Shang (Liu et al. 2004: 92). Not all of the fortified sites disappeared, however, and new sites were also established during this time. Huanbei in northern Henan province is the most important of these new sites. Its square enclosure covers an area of ca. 470 ha, larger than the inner enclosure of Zhengzhou, and it is thus taken by many to be the political center of the Middle Shang period. At the same time, the Shang's presence in the east became more widespread, perhaps representing a shift of the political center of the state from the south and west to the east.

The Huanbei site was abandoned at around 1300 BCE, but the center of the Shang polity remained in the same region with the establishment of the political/ritual center at Xiaotun (小屯), south of the Huan River, and the expansion of the extensive settlement known as the Yinxu. No city walls have been found at Yinxu, but it is, nonetheless, a very extensive and complex array of settlements covering an estimated area of some 30 km² (or 3,000 ha) (Zhongguo Shehui 2003: 295). Increased population density, a variety of activities indicated by archaeological discoveries, and information found in the oracle bone inscriptions, all indicate that this was the political center of the Late Shang state (Tang and Jing 2009).

Outside the core area, Late Shang materials are distributed across a very wide region, but the relationship between these materials and the direct political control of the Shang state is not always clear. To the east, the entire Shandong area, which was typified by the Yueshi (岳石) culture during the Erlitou and early Erligang periods, was gradually incorporated into the Shang's cultural sphere.

By the late Erligang, settlements with a typical Erligang assemblage appeared at Daxinzhuang in northern Shandong province. During the Middle Shang period, when the major sites at the Luoyang-Zhengzhou areas disappeared, Shang settlements in Shandong increased rapidly, at first around the Daxinzhuang site, and then in other areas as well. Markers of Yueshi culture, such as painted pottery, disappear and most of the material culture is similar to that of the Shang centers. This has been interpreted as the outcome of Shang colonization of the region (Liu and Chen 2003: 113–6).

In the middle Yangzi River region, Panlongcheng, which may have continued to exist during the Middle Shang period, had disappeared by the Late Shang period. Farther to the south, a new walled site was established at Wucheng (吳城), but it is unclear whether this was a Shang outpost or, more likely, the center of a non-Shang polity (Chapter 9).

City Organization and Public Structures

According to the currently available data, Shang urban planning is best divided into two phases: the Early and Middle Shang, when all the major sites were fortified, and the Late Shang, when the main city – Yinxu – was not fortified. The difference between the two phases may be related to practical issues, such as the economic and political power of the Shang kings, but it also may be associated with the symbolic manifestation of such powers and with changes in the concept of the city.

The walled enclosures of Early and Middle Shang cities vary considerably in size, but they nonetheless share many features. They are all more or less rectangular in shape and oriented to the cardinal directions (Figure 129). They are also all constructed using the pounded earth (*hangtu* 夯土) technique inherited from the Neolithic period, but improved upon during Shang. The walls were usually built on foundation trenches dug below the surface. The core of the wall was constructed in sections: thin layers of fine earth were laid between wooden frames and pounded with wooden sticks until they become solid; then another layer was laid on top of it. Sloping layers of pounded earth were then laid against the core on either side (Figures 130 and 131).

The core wall at Zhengzhou is about 10 m wide (with the sloping layers adding 5 m or more to each side at the base), and its maximum preserved height is 9 m. The walls at Yanshi are more or less similar in width, 17 to 25 m wide at the base, but they are not preserved to the same height as in Zhengzhou (Chang 1980: 273–6; Thorp 2006: 69). The areas within the site walls are not well preserved in most sites, nor have they been thoroughly excavated, but it seems that they were mostly devoted to elite and public structures. These structures are identified by their pounded earth platforms, which originally served as elevated house foundations. In Zhengzhou those foundations range in size from 100 m² to 2000 m², but their poor state of preservation makes it impossible to reconstruct their overall shape. A ditch excavated in this area, which is filled with animal bones, human skulls, and broken artifacts, is evidence of large-scale ritual activity (Henan 2001; Yuan and Zeng 2004).

The Yanshi enclosure is subdivided into two subareas by an inner wall: an inner city and an outer city (Figure 129). This subdivision is probably related to their function, with the inner city serving as a kind of elite citadel. Gates and the remains of pounded earth foundations are found in both sections, but those in the inner section are larger and thought to have been the "palatial area." This so-called palatial area is itself partitioned. Six large buildings in its southern part are identified as "palaces," while a large area (ca. 3,000 m²) in the center is identified as the location where rituals took place (Figure 132). The large quantities of plants, human bones, and bones of domesticated and wild animals found in this area are interpreted as the remains of sacrifices and rituals held

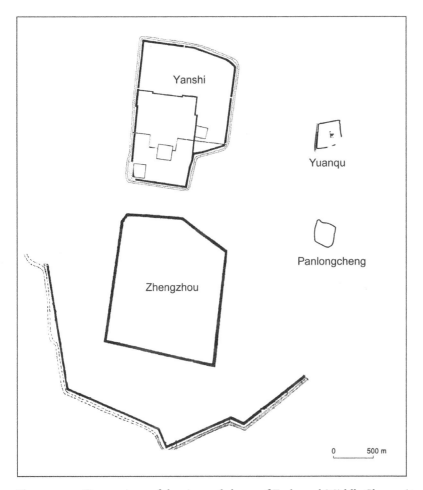

Figure 129. Comparison of the size and shape of Early and Middle Shang city walls.

there (Du 2006). Pounded earth foundations of large public buildings were also identified inside the walled enclosures of the Panlongcheng and Huanbei cities (Thorp 2006: 81–4).

Most evidence for other types of urban activity, including habitation and production areas, is located outside the pounded earth walls, or between the inner and the outer walls., Residential areas and storage facilities, a pottery workshop, and a bronze foundry were all found within the area of the outer city at Yanshi. Similar evidence on a much larger scale has also been found in Zhengzhou. Test excavations at the site have located segments of an outer wall and a moat south

Figure 130. Cross section of the wall at Zhengzhou (after Thorp 2006: 69).

Figure 131. A Ming period illustration of people constructing pounded earth walls (after Needham 1971: 39).

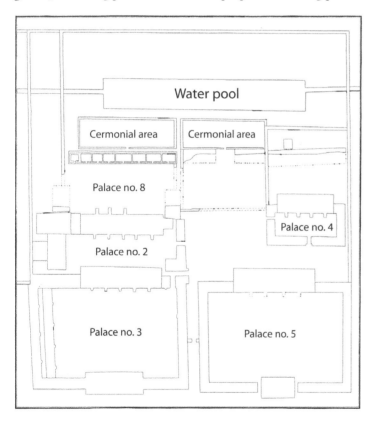

Figure 132. The "palatial area" at Yanshi (after Du 2006: 44).

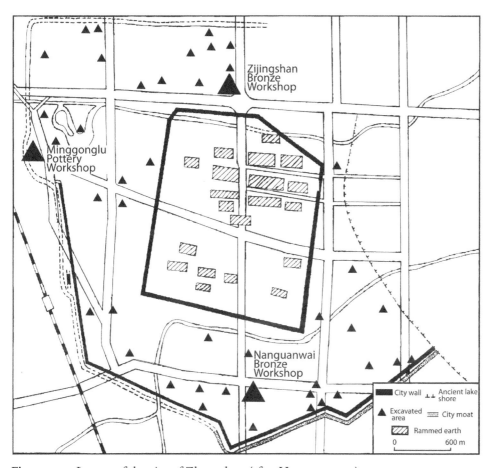

Figure 133. Layout of the city of Zhengzhou (after Henan 2001: 2).

and west of the inner wall (Figure 133). Thus far more than 3,000 m of this wall have been measured, but it is estimated that it enclosed an area of ca. 1,300 ha. Scattered excavations in the area between the two walls have revealed the remains of two bronze foundries, a ceramic production workshop, and a workshop for the production of bone tools. Also found here were house foundations, storage pits, burials, and other installations (Henan 2001; Yuan and Zeng 2004). Zhengzhou has thus been reconstructed as one of the largest walled cities of the ancient world. The political and ritual activities clustered inside the inner city were matched by a highly concentrated population and economic activity in the outer city, and probably outside the city walls as well.

The structure of Yinxu is different from that of earlier Shang centers, not only because it lacks a city wall but also because it is more diffuse (Figure 134). The political/ritual center of Yinxu was located at Xiaotun, a 70 ha area bounded by a bend in the Hui River from the north and the east, and by an artificial moat to the south and west. Fifty-three pounded earth foundations are concentrated in a complex in the western part of the area; some have been identified as royal residences, while others, associated with sacrificial pits containing human and animal bones, are identified as royal temples. A large concentration of oracle bones found in pits located to the south of the "palatial/temple" complex and close to the southern moat marks this as another area where

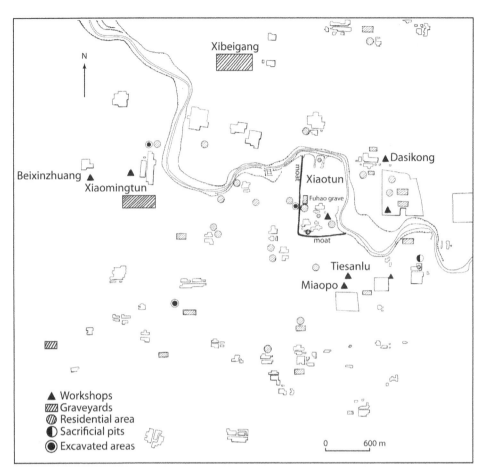

Figure 134. Map of the Yinxu site (after Chen Zhida 2006: 54).

important royal ceremonies would have been conducted. Elite burials, sacrificial pits, and craft workshops were also located within the Xiaotun area (Zhongguo Shehui 1994).

More than eighty years of archaeological research have not yet exhausted the potential of the wider Yinxu area. Although it is unclear whether all of it was occupied, the accumulation of discoveries suggests that it was densely populated. Among the more important discoveries thus far are the Xibeigang royal cemetery and sacrificial area, numerous other burials and sacrificial pits, residential areas for the elite and commoners, and no fewer than fifteen workshops for the production of bronze, pottery, stone, and bone artifacts (Li 2007; Zhongguo Shehui 1994).

Yinxu has long been recognized as a network of archaeological sites, each representing a functional node in the larger capital region (Chang 1980: 130). More recent research has suggested that Yinxu comprised clusters of small settlements (*yi* 邑), each with its own houses, storage pits, and other functional installations (Tang and Jing 2009). Based on the spatial segmentation of cemeteries and the distribution of characters inscribed on bronzes from these cemeteries, archaeologists have argued that Yinxu cemeteries, and by extension the nearby settlements, were lineage-based (Zheng 1995). This type of organization seems quite different from the much more nucleated and clearly structured cities of the Early and Middle Shang, such as Zhengzhou. However, in

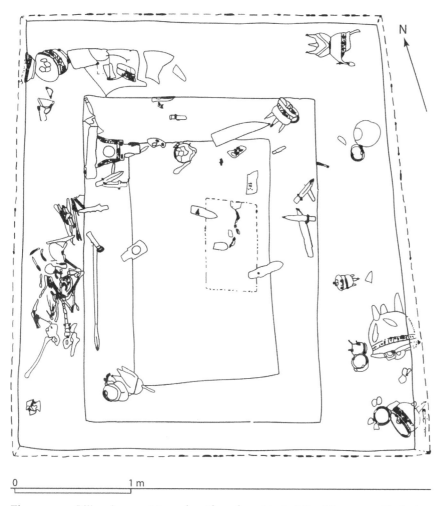

0   1 m

Figure 135. Lijiazui grave M2 and artifacts found in it (after Zhongguo Shehui 2003: 243, 244).

functional terms Yinxu is comparable to these earlier cities, and it may even represent a higher level of craft production, political and economic complexity, and population concentration.

Cemeteries, Burials, and Ritual Activity

In contrast to the limited evidence of large-scale elite graves dated to the Erlitou period, some Shang graves are royal both in their scale and in their furnishings. While no large-scale graves were found at Zhengzhou, graves dated to the Early Shang period at other sites hint at the size of the mortuary monuments at the political center of the Shang. At Panlongcheng, for example, grave M2 in the Lijiazui (李家嘴) locality is 3.75 by 3.4 m in size and has ledges on all four sides, a wooden chamber, a wooden coffin, and a waste pit dug under the body of the main occupant. The body of the main occupant is not well preserved, but there is also clear evidence of three accompanying human victims. The tomb contains twenty-three bronze ritual vessels, the largest of which is a 55 cm tall *ding*, forty bronze weapons, jade artifacts, and ceramic vessels (Figure 135). In contrast, most Erligang-phase graves are 2 m or less in length, with no ledges or wooden chambers. A few contain a wooden coffin and bronze vessels, while

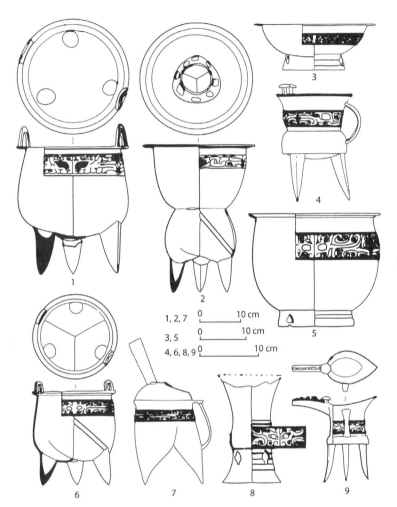

Figure 135 (*continued*)

1, 2, 7   0   10 cm

3, 5   0   10 cm

4, 6, 8, 9 0   10 cm

most are furnished only with ceramic vessels and stone artifacts (Zhongguo Shehui 2003: 242–6).

Evidence of the hierarchy of graves is even stronger for the Late Shang period. The Xibeigang area at Yinxu is identified as the royal cemetery: the eight largest tombs, identified as the graves of Shang kings, are cross-like in shape, with sliding ramps entering the burial chamber from the four cardinal directions. These graves are huge, ranging in size between 107 and 192 m², and are up to 12 m deep (Figure 136). Take grave M1001 for example: its main burial chamber is cross-shaped; it is 19 by 16 m in size and 10.5 m deep. Including the length of the four ramps, it is 66 m long from north to south and 44 m wide from east to west.

Remains of a huge wooden chamber built inside the main burial shaft are still visible on its floor and some of the walls (Figure 137). The walls of the wooden chamber, now mostly decayed, were painted and inlaid with shell, bone, and ivory. Sacrificial pits dug under the wooden floor contain remains of dog and human sacrifices. More remains of human and animal sacrifices were found in the fill of the ramps. Altogether, remains of some 150 human victims, twelve horses, and eleven dogs were found in the grave and its immediate vicinity (Chang 1980; Bagley 1999).

Beyond the eight largest tombs, additional smaller tombs were also found in the Xibeigang area, some with one or two ramps and some

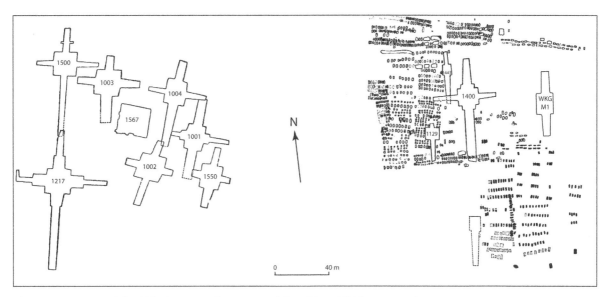

Figure 136. Map of the Xibeigang royal cemetery (after Chen Zhida 2006: 54).

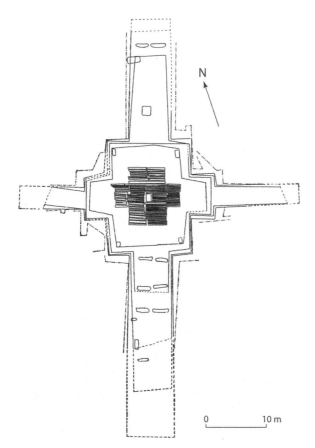

Figure 137. Grave 1001 from Xibeigang (after Chen Zhida 2006: 110–11).

without ramps. All of these tombs (large and medium) were looted in antiquity, and only occasional evidence of their furnishings remains. The largest intact grave in the Yinxu area (and the richest Shang grave known so far) is located at the Xiaotun area and, based upon the inscriptions on many of the bronze vessels found in it, has been identified as the burial site of Fuhao (婦好), a consort of the Shang king Wuding – whose name also appears in oracle bone inscriptions. The grave is 22 m² in size and 7.5 m deep, large in comparison to earlier graves, but only one-tenth of the size of the royal tombs (Figure 138). The measurements of the tomb and the identity of its main occupant indicate that, in terms of the Shang hierarchy, it was only of the third or fourth rank. The astounding quantity of grave goods found in it, therefore, offers a clue as to the even larger quantities of artifacts that must have originally furnished the highest ranking graves.

All told, some sixteen hundred burial goods, sixteen human victims, a sacrificed dog, and some seven thousand cowrie shells accompanied Fuhao to her grave. Of these, the bronze artifacts are the most impressive. They include 195 bronze ritual

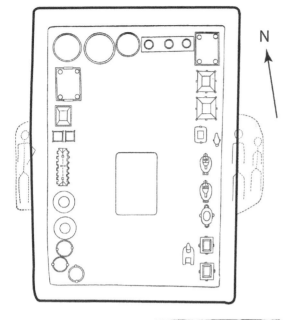

Figure 138. The grave of Fuhao at Yinxu (after Zhong-guo 1980: 8).

vessels and 271 bronze weapons, tools, and other small artifacts with a combined weight of 1,600 kg. In addition to the bronzes, the grave also contained 755 jade artifacts, 564 carved bone artifacts, some inlayed with turquoise, two ivory cups, and more (Bagley 1999: 194–202).

Hundreds of Late Shang graves have been located in Yinxu and other contemporaneous sites. As in previous periods, most graves are relatively small and simple, containing only a few inexpensive grave goods (Zhongguo Shehui 2003: 331–8). This gap between rich and poor graves clearly reflects a dramatic increase in sociopolitical and economic stratification. As of yet, we do not have evidence for the development of formal sumptuary roles that might have determined the size and type of the grave according to the status of its occupant. However, tomb features such as ramps, known not only from Yinxu, but from other sites as well, suggest a more direct status reference, at least among the paramount elite.

Evidence of Shang ritual activities, especially those related to the Shang kings and their courts, is plentiful. The best examples are of oracle bone divinations and the ritual activities referred to in the oracle bone inscriptions. The Xiaotun complex, where most of the oracle bones have been found, seems to have functioned as the ritual (or palatial-ritual) center of the Shang court during the Late Shang period.

Other dramatic indications of royal ritual include evidence of large-scale human sacrifices. Skeletons of human victims are found in both royal and elite graves, sometimes with one hundred or more victims in a single tomb, indicating that the large-scale sacrifice of humans (and animals) was a part of mortuary rituals. Large-scale human sacrifice dated to the Erligang period is also known from Zhengzhou, but the most striking evidence of human sacrifice is found in the eastern section of the Xibeigang cemetery, where more than a thousand small earthen pits are aligned in orderly rows, each pit containing up to twelve human skeletons. Many of the skeletons were decapitated, a method

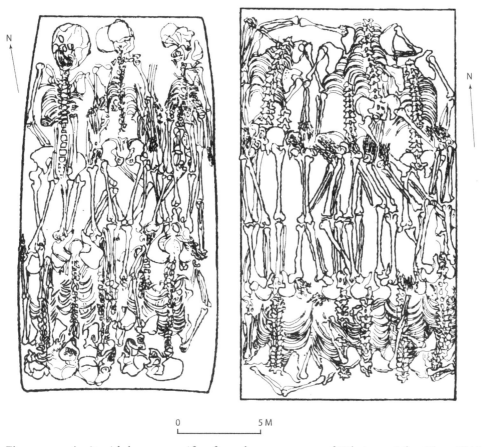

0   5 M

Figure 139. A pit with human sacrifice from the eastern part of Xibeigang (after Chen Zhida 2006: 121).

of sacrifice well known from the oracle bone inscriptions, and the skulls placed in separate pits (Figure 139). Apparently, while many of the human sacrificial victims found in graves and other contexts were to be retainers in the afterlife, the bodies placed in the pits were those of non-Shang captives who were sacrificed to the gods and ancestors (Shelach 1996).

Pits containing offerings or sacrifices seem to have played an important role in the royal and elite ceremonies of the Shang. In Zhengzhou, for instance, the richest concentrations of bronze vessels come from such pits (Thorp 2006: 85–91). Some special pits, found almost exclusively at Yinxu, contained a chariot with the two horses that drew it, its human drivers, and all of their equipment (Figure 140). A total of 25 "chariot pits" have been found in different localities in

Yinxu. This "extravagant" destruction of artifacts, animals, and humans must have been an impressive demonstration of the wealth and power of the Shang royal house.

Craft Production and Technology

Many lines of evidence point to a dramatic increase in the sophistication of craft production and the level of specialization during the Shang period. The most sophisticated products of this specialized craftsmanship were those used by the Shang elite, and the location of workshops in and around the political centers of the Shang suggests that the artisans working there were specialists directly sponsored and controlled by the Shang court. The sheer volume of production and the complexity of the production processes demonstrate a highly

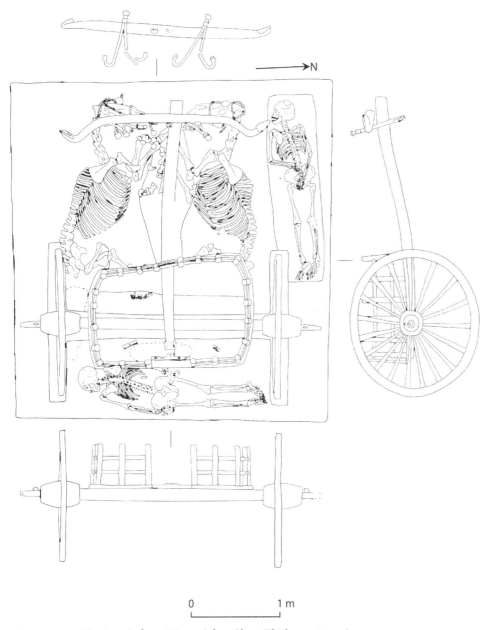

Figure 140. Chariot pit from Yinxu (after Chen Zhida 2006: 147).

developed Shang system for obtaining supplies of raw materials, overseeing the production process, and maintaining the specialists.

As noted, bronze is the craft for which the Shang dynasty is best known. The technology used to cast bronze vessels – the "piece-mold" or section-mold technique – was already developed by the Erlitou period, but it reach a much higher level of sophistication during this period. The first step of the piece-mold technique was the creation of a solid core made of clay that formed the desired inner volume and shape of the bronze vessel. An outer jacket made of several mold pieces was then built around this core. The outer mold pieces were

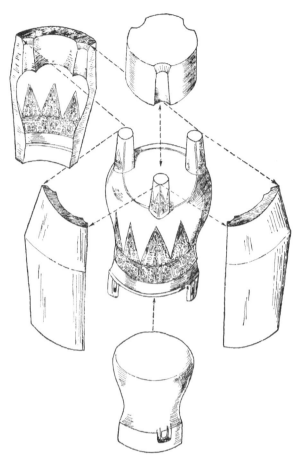

Figure 141. The "piece-mold" casting technique (after Zhongguo Shehui 1994: 259).

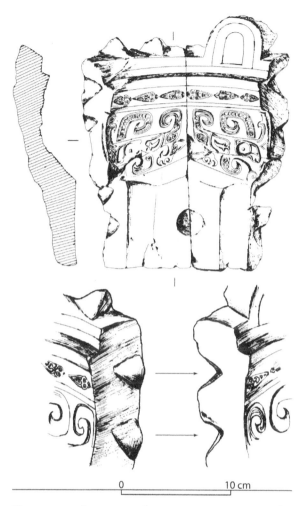

Figure 142. Grooves used to connect two parts of a casting mold found at the Xiaomingtun foundry, Yinxu (after Yinxu Xiaomintun 2007: 19).

also incised or stamped with the decorations to appear on the exterior of the vessel. The mold parts made of clay were fired, and then assembled so as to leave a thin gap between them and the core. Finally, the molten bronze was poured into this gap, and after the bronze solidified the mold was broken to release the vessel (Figure 141). More complex vessels with parts such as handles, legs, or spouts were often cast in more than one pour. The protruding parts were cast separately and then connected to the mold through preprepared holes so that, when the main body of the vessel was cast, they were welded to it.

The method for casting of bronze vessels required very high levels of accuracy. The mold pieces had to fit one another perfectly, so as to leave no gap into which the molten metal could leak and in order to form a perfect jacket of an even width around the core. The decorations, which were either incised or, more often, stamped into the inside of the mold pieces, were also expected to align perfectly and appear as a continuous curve on the finished vessel. To ensure this, nooks and bulges were added to the side of the mold pieces so as to secure them together (Figure 142). Spacers – small pieces of bronze – were wedged between the core and the outer jacket to prevent them from

Figure 143. Finished Shang bronze vessel showing traces of metal that filtered through the seam between the two parts of the casting mold (photo by Gary Lee Todd).

touching each other. Despite these efforts, as well as the retouching of the finished bronze vessels, lines of the metal that filtered through the seams between the parts of the casting mold can often be seen on both the outside and inside of Shang bronze vessels (Figure 143).

One of the difficulties involved in the piece-mold technique was preventing the mold from shrinking too much during firing and, in particular, preventing uneven shrinking that deformed the mold pieces and the decorations carved into them. Modern-day experiments have shown that Shang casters developed various techniques to minimize this shrinking and deformation, such as adding

plant ashes and crushed fired clay to the clay from which the molds were made (Li 2007).

Shang vessel shapes are much more varied than in previous periods and much more lavishly decorated (Figures 144 and 145). The complexity and sheer size of some of these vessels show their casting to have been a real technological achievement. For example, one square *ding* (*fangding* 方鼎) bronze dated to the Erligang period is 100 cm tall and weighs 86.4 kg, while three hoards of bronze objects discovered in the outer city of Zhengzhou contained twenty-eight bronzes with a total weight of greater than 500 kg (Thorp 2006: 86–91). By the Late Shang, the scale of bronze production reached unprecedented levels. For instance, a single bronze vessel discovered in Yinxu – the Si Mu Wu Fangding (司母戊方鼎) – weighs 875 kg, making it the largest bronze vessel cast anywhere in the ancient world (Figure 146). The extraordinary number of bronzes found at the Fuhao grave can only inspire us to imagine what the ten-times-larger graves of Shang kings may have contained. This overwhelming wealth of evidence brought one researcher to argue that China is the only place in the world where the term "Bronze Age" is deservedly used, because "the Bronze Age of China is set apart from all others by the enormous quantities of metal it has left us" (Bagley 1999: 137). The production of such large quantities of metal required a very substantial infrastructure to ensure the supply of copper and tin ores (obtained through organized mining or trade with mining societies), construct and maintain smelting and casting facilities, supply their fuel, and so on.

This production system was clearly not only very extensive but also highly complex. It demanded control over and coordination of different types of activity conducted at different localities, some of which, such as mining, were probably carried out far away from the Shang centers. According to one scholar, the successful casting of a bronze vessel required at least twelve different

Figure 144. Typical shapes of Shang bronzes (after Zhongguo Qingtong 1997: 2, 3, 5–8, 24, 29).

steps (not including the mining of ores and the initial casting of bronze ingots), each performed by a different specialist (Li 2007). In many respects, this kind of collaboration and interdependence among highly specialized artisans resembles the structure of far more modern industries.

The remains of slugs, crucibles, and casting molds located in and around Shang sites such as Zhengzhou, Panlongcheng, and Yinxu help identify the location of bronze foundries and workshops (Figure 147). Research on these workshops further illustrates the complexity and highly specialized nature of Shang bronze production. A study of mold parts found at the bronze workshops in Zhengzhou suggests that the Nanguanwai (南关外) workshop, for example, specialized in the production of ritual vessels (although it also produced tools and weapons), while another, Zijingshan (紫荆山), focused on weapons and small tools (Henan 2001: 307–83). Such workshop specialization, which can be seen in other crafts as well, may have to do not only with the artisans

Figure 145. Typical Shang bronzes and their decorations (photos by Gary Lee Todd).

working in each foundry, but also with the level of political control over and sponsorship of each of these workshops.

Some six bronze workshops have been found at Yinxu, with considerable variation in their size and production capabilities (Figure 134). Some were located inside the moated elite area of Xiaotun, suggesting a close association with the activities of the king's court, while others, outside of this area, may have been more independent. The largest area devoted to bronze production was found near Xiaomintun (孝民屯): this zone was subdivided into three separate workshops occupying a total area of more than 5 ha. Tens of thousands of mold and furnace fragments found here suggest production on a grand scale.

There is evidence of the production of ritual vessels and prestige artifacts, such as chariot gear,

at most of the workshops in Yinxu, but some seem to have been specifically dedicated to the production of particularly large and complex artifacts. At the Miaopu (苗圃) foundry, for example, mold fragments from the casting of a vessel very close in size to the Si Mu Wu Fangding were found. Identifiable mold fragments from the western foundry at Xiaomintun, on the other hand, suggest that weapons and tools were its main products, alongside less complex ritual vessels and chariot gear (Li 2007; Yinxu Xiaomintun 2007; Zhongguo Shehui 1994: 83–93).

Bronze production took place not only at the paramount center of the Shang polity, but in secondary centers as well. For example, the remains of crucibles and slag identified at five locations around the Panlongcheng site strongly indicate local production of bronze (Hubei 2001). It has

Figure 146. The Si Mu Wu Ding (四母戊方鼎) (photo by Gary Lee Todd).

been suggested that only the smelting of ores and perhaps the casting of simple bronze artifacts were performed locally, while the more complex bronze vessels found at Panlongcheng –identical in shape and decorations to those found at Zhengzhou – were brought from the north (Liu and Chen 2003:

116–17). However, regardless of whether bronze vessels were produced locally or imported to Panlongcheng from the Zhengzhou area, the fact that all of the bronze vessels found in areas far from the Shang center – not only in Panlongcheng, but in other places as well – are remarkably similar to vessels from the center of power suggests tight control over the production, distribution, and use of ritual bronze vessels.

Some of these attributes of bronze production are shared by other Shang crafts. A pottery workshop at found at the Minggonglu (铭功路) locality, west of the inner walls of Zhengzhou, yielded very limited variety of vessels, suggesting a high degree of workshop specialization (Henan 2001: 384–425). At Yinxu, the pottery workshop at Miaopubeidi (苗圃北地) seems to have specialized in the production of *dou* (豆) high-stem vessels. However, it is probable that ceramic vessels for everyday use were produced at the household or village levels, without the intervention of the state.

A great deal of evidence of bone production was found at Yinxu, which also suggests a combination of household-level and specialized workshop

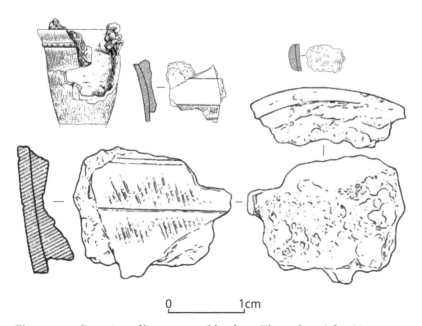

0   1cm

Figure 147. Remains of bronze crucibles from Zhengzhou (after Henan 2001: 350).

production. Much of the evidence of bone production, such as unfinished artifacts and production debris, is scattered within and across inhabited areas, but three large workshops, discovered at Beixinzhuang (北辛庄), Dasikong (大司空), and Tiesanlu (铁三路), appear to have specialized mainly in producing decorative pins (including hairpins), awls, and arrowheads (Campbell et al. 2011; Zhongguo Shehui 1994: 93–6). The scale of production is indicated by 34,000 kg of animal bones, most of them worked, which were excavated from a trench that composes only a small portion of the Tiesanlu workshop's total area. The remains at this workshop suggest a well-organized division of labor and a high level of specialization (Campbell et al. 2011). Almost five hundred decorated pins and hairpins found in the Fuhao grave (Zhongguo Shehui 1980: 208–13), as well as similar findings in other elite graves, suggest that they were prestige artifacts. However, findings of bone hairpins in nonelite contexts suggest that their distribution was not limited to the Shang elite. Other, more obviously prestigious bone and ivory objects are known from Shang graves, including the two ivory cups, one of them inlayed with turquoise pieces, from Fuhao's tomb (Figure 148) (Zhongguo Shehui 1980: 215–18). The workshops that produced such sophisticated artifacts, however, have yet to be found.

Other types of specialized craft known from Shang graves and domestic sites include jade carving, marble carving (in the production of architectural features, sculptures, and chime stones), and the production of lacquered artifacts and lacquer coating.

The Shang used many nonlocal raw materials for the production of prestige and elite-related artifacts, as well as for more general purposes. These nonlocal materials included the tin and copper used in the production of bronze, semiprecious stones such as jade, marble, and turquoise, the materials used to make lacquer, the cowrie shells found in graves, and the turtle shells used for div-

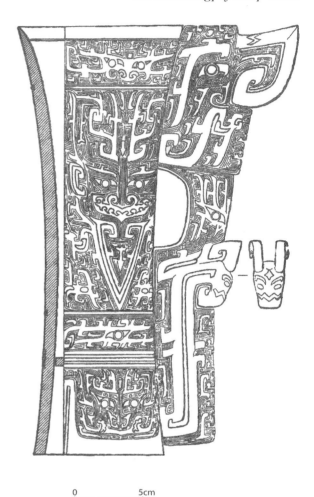

0   5cm

Figure 148. Ivory cup inlayed with turquoise pieces from the tomb of Fuhao (after Zhongguo 1980: 216).

ination. References in oracle bone inscriptions suggest that the Shang court was concerned with the supply of such materials, and that it probably played an active role in obtaining them.

THE ORACLE BONE INSCRIPTIONS

Since they were first identified in 1899, the search for and study of oracle bone inscriptions have been among the most powerful driving forces in Shang archaeology. During the 1910s, the source of the inscribed bones that appeared on the market was traced to the village of Xiaotun near Anyang, and during the 1920s and 1930s, the desire to obtain more inscriptions and study their contents led to the large-scale scientific excavations at Yinxu. These inscriptions not only provided definitive historical proof for the identification of the Shang with the archaeological remains at Yinxu and other sites, but also provided a framework for the analysis of much of the other archaeological data excavated from these sites. This section provides a short introduction to the format and functions of the oracle bones and the nature of their inscriptions. More detailed information on the inscriptions themselves is included in the following section, as part of the discussion of the structure of the Shang state and society.

Shang oracle bone divination represents the continuation of a tradition that was well established throughout north China during the Late Neolithic period, though by the Shang period it was practiced at much greater intensity, in a more standardized fashion, and under clear political control. Inscribing the process of divination onto the surface of a bone in writing – the earliest form of Chinese script known so far – is another Shang innovation. The inscriptions are dated from the reign of King Wuding (武丁, ca. 1200 BCE) through to the end of the Shang (Keightley 1999: 240–1; Keightley 2002: vii). So far, more than two hundred thousand Shang oracle bones (complete and fragments) have been discovered, the vast majority from Xiaotun. Many of these bones, though not all of them, carry inscriptions.[3]

The concentration of the oracle bones in caches inside the ritual center of the Late Shang polity suggests that divination was a state-level affair. The inscriptions themselves suggest that the rituals were performed by state officials and presided over by the Shang king, who was regarded as the highest divination authority. It appears that bones were used as a medium of communication with the ancestors and high spirits. The process was understood to not only predict the future but also influence it by communicating with and worshipping the deities. The various subjects that were divined upon according to the inscriptions include the ritual cycle and the ritual obligations of the king, military campaigns, the construction of settlements, royal hunts and excursions, the management of agriculture, climatic conditions, and the personal affairs of the king and his court, such as sickness, childbirth, and dreams.

The Shang were more selective in their use of raw materials for divination than previous cultures. Only certain types of bones – primarily turtle plastrons and cattle scapula – were used for divination, perhaps because of their supposed spiritual qualities, but more probably because these large, flat bones provided good surfaces for both the divination process and the inscriptions. In preparation for the ceremony the bones were cleaned and smoothed and two rows of hollows were drilled into them. During the divination process, an intensely hot object (perhaps a burning hardwood brand) was applied to the hollows, causing the bones to crack. The Chinese term "to divine" (*bu* 卜) is a graphic depiction of these cracks that were shaped by the predrilled hollows (Figure 149). The diviners and kings read (or divined) the ancestors' answers to their questions or statements in these cracks.

The process of oracle bone divination seems to have been very systematic and almost rational. Divination was never based on a single crack, but rather on a series of cracks. Each crack was numbered, and they appear to have been used in groups to counterbalance one another. The inscriptions show that, in many instances, the same statement/question was posed twice, once in the positive and once in the negative, and each was tested with several cracks, until a satisfactory conclusion was reached.

Because many uninscribed bones have also been found, it would appear that writing was not an essential part of divination, but it may have been understood as an improved form of communication with the ancestors that also enhanced the

Figure 149. Hollows on the reverse side of an oracle bone.

Shang court's monopoly over the ritual. All of the inscriptions follow a single formula: they begin with the day of the divination and the name of the diviner, and follow with the statement (known in the literatures as "charges") and the notation on the crack reading. For example, inscription HJ9735 reads, "Crack-making on jiawu day. Yan divined. The eastern land will receive harvest." On the reverse side of the bone is the same charge, repeated this time in the negative (" . . . the eastern land will not receive a good harvest"), and the crack notation, "auspicious," on the left hand side. In many cases, the king is named as the one making the cracks, pronouncing the charges, or interpreting the cracks, pointing to the personal participation of the king in the process of divination.

In a relatively small number of inscriptions, a verification section records what happened after the divination results were read and confirms their accuracy. Inscription HJ37380, for example, contains all the parts of the process, including the prognostication and verification. It reads, "On *renzi* (day 49) the king made cracks and divined. 'Hunting at *Zhi*, going and coming back there will be no harm.' The king read the cracks and said, 'prolonged auspiciousness.' Indeed (we) caught foxes, forty one; *mi*-deer, eight; rhinoceroses, one" (Keightley 1997: 41).[4]

Verification records that refer to events that happened after the divination suggest that the oracle bone inscriptions themselves were not (or not always) the primary records of the divination process; rather, it was first recorded on perishable materials and only later inscribed onto the bones. This reconstruction implies a much more comprehensive use of writing in Shang society, extending perhaps to the running of the Shang state and economy (Keightley 2006: 183–5). No less important, this complex process, in which the work of different state-attached specialists (bone preparers, diviners, scribes, and engravers) was coordinated over time and space, provides us with a valuable glimpse into the political system of the Shang.

SHAMAN OR TECHNOCRATS? THE RELIGIOUS FUNCTIONS AND LEADERSHIP STRATEGIES OF SHANG KINGS

In his book *Art, Myth, and Ritual: The Path to Political Authority in Ancient China*, the eminent Chinese archaeologist K. C. Chang proposed that the power and prestige of the Shang kings were related to their role as shamans. Shamans are religious specialists who communicate with the spirits thorough trance and rituals that often involve music, dance, and the use of animal costumes and animal parts. Shamans are commonly associated with curing illnesses, but also with resolving social tensions. Ethnographic studies first identified shamanism among the indigenous populations of Siberia, but it is (or was) common in many other parts of the world, including Mongolia and North America, for instance. Shamanic practices are well documented in Korea, as well as among Chinese-speaking populations, such as those in Taiwan and south China (cf. Shahar 1998).

Although shamanism is usually associated with tribal societies or folk beliefs, according to Chang, ancient states in China were founded on shamanistic principles. The charisma and legitimation of Shang kings was based on their role as mediators between the human world and that of the spirits, and their actions were guided by the results of this communication. Moreover, Chang identifies the decoration motifs on Shang and Zhou bronzes such as the *Taotie* (Figure 150) with shamanism. He argues that these motifs "are images of the

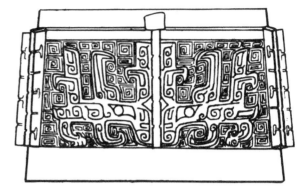

Figure 150. The Taotie motif on a Shang bronze vessel.

various animals that served as the helpers of shamans and shamanesses in the task of communication between heaven and earth, the spirits and the living" (Chang 1983: 65). According to Chang, the role of (real or mythical) animals as assistants to the shaman, serving as a kind of "cosmic vehicles," is ubiquitous in Chinese art of later periods as well. Chang and others believe that the crucial role played by shamanism in the formation and structure of early states in China set it apart from Western civilizations such as Mesopotamia and Egypt (Chang 1989; Liu 2004). Others strongly object to this proposition. Robert Bagley (1990), for example, argued that there is no evidence that connects Shang bronze decoration motifs with shamanism.

A close reading of the oracle inscriptions suggests a very formalistic and structured ritual rather than the energetic type of performance associated with shamanism (Keightley 1999: 262). Although the king communicated with the supernatural world, nowhere in the texts, or in later texts for that matter (cf. Falkenhausen 1993), do we have any hint that the king or any of his diviners was in a state of trance. On the contrary, the process seems to have been very "bureaucratic": the meticulous documentation of facts (place and time of divination, names, etc.), the repetition of the statements, the reading of cracking patterns, and even the post facto verification of the results are all much more suggestive of an administrative rather than an expressive shamanistic state of mind.

This is not so say that shamanism or shamanic-like practices did not exist in Chinese culture. In fact, texts from later periods, as well as ethnographic observations, do indeed document shamanistic practices, but they are usually associated with folk beliefs. People from higher levels of society, including emperors and the members of their households, might employ such practices in their private life, but usually not in affairs of state. This certainly seems to have been the case during the Shang and Zhou periods. State-level religion appears to have been highly ceremonial and performative. It required that the king or nobles follow strict roles and left very little room for deviations or personal expressions. While the charisma of the king (and of later emperors) was indeed related to his role as an intermediary between humans and the natural and supernatural world, this relationship was conceived of not in shamanistic terms, but rather in the terms that are familiar to formal state religions known in other parts of the world.

THE STRUCTURE AND EVOLUTION OF THE SHANG STATE

The territorial extent of the Shang state and the extent of its territorial integration are among the most hotly debated issues between Shang specialists. While some see the Shang as a relatively small-scale polity that controlled only a limited area in northern and central Henan province, others argue for a vast territorial expanse that includes the entire Yellow and Wei River basins, as well as areas to their north, and parts of the Yangzi River basin to the south (Chang 1986; Shaughnessy 1989). Others have suggested that the geographic extent of the Shang polity varied considerably throughout the Shang period. According to this proposition, the Shang period started with a rapid military expansion into a vast area that, in addition to the core area in Henan province, also included parts of Shaanxi (the lower Wei River)

and Shanxi (the middle Yellow River), western Shandong, and the middle Yangzi River region. A shift eastward and a gradual retreat from areas in the west occurred during the latter part of the Early Shang and the Middle Shang. During this period, the center of the Shang polity also shifted northward to the Anyang area. Finally, the territory under the control of the Shang state shrunk quite drastically during the Late Shang, when it lost control of territories in the middle Yangzi, and its control of some regions within the Yellow River basin was challenged as well (Liu and Chen 2003: 127–45).

This debate among the minimalist, maximalist, and dynamic models of the Shang's territorial extent creates a false impression of a territorial state with demarcated borders and a clear territorial definition. However, as many scholars have pointed out, one of the main attributes of the Shang state, and indeed of all early states in China, was its *lack of* clear concepts of borders and territorial integrity. Chang (1980: 210) describes the Shang state as a network of towns, while Keightley (1978–80) likens the Shang territory to Gruyere cheese, full of non-Shang holes. The important issue is, therefore, not so much the territorial extent of the Shang, but the way this territory was controlled.

The content of the oracle bones inscriptions suggests that during the Late Shang, the state (beyond perhaps the immediate area surrounding Yinxu) was conceived of not in territorial terms, but rather as a constantly negotiated coalition between the Shang and other groups. These coalitions were apparently quite fluid, and the Shang king was not certain that he would actually receive the support of the local leaders at any given time. For example, inscription Heji 6409 reads, "Crack-making on *dingyou*, *Que* divined: This season the king (wants to) raise 5,000 men to campaign against the *Tufang* (土方), he will receive assistance." The fact that this statement was divined upon makes it clear that the king did not control the five thousand men he wanted to enlist, and that he needed the support of the local chiefs.

Ideally, the Shang world can be described as a system of three concentric regions, each inside the other, but without clear borders that formally separated them from one another. At the center was the Shang capital and the territories adjacent to it, which were directly controlled by the Shang court. The second region was populated by Shang's allies or potential allies. This area was referred to in the oracle bone inscriptions as the Four Lands (*si tu* 四土), north, south, east, and west of the Shang center (Keightley 1999: 269). The king divined on matters such as the harvests of these regions, and so he must have had an interest in their well-being. However, it is clear that the Shang did not have a bureaucratic structure controlling these territories. Relations with them were highly dependent on the actions and persona of the king. According to some estimates, the Shang king spent about half his time traveling with his court through these territories and among the groups that lived there, hunting, performing rituals, demonstrating his powers, gaining legitimacy, and maintaining his alliance with the local leaders (Keightley 1978–80).

Beyond the sphere of the Four Lands were the lands of the Shang's enemies, known in the oracle bone inscriptions by the collective suffix *fang* (方). The adversarial nature of these groups is made clear by the fact that the Shang king never divined about the harvests reaped by those groups, as well as by the numerous mentions in the oracle bone inscriptions of war between the Shang and its allies and the *fang* groups (Keightley 2002: 66–8).

Some claim that the relatively weak Shang system as it is seen through the oracle bone inscriptions is a result of the demise of a much more centralized system that existed during the Early Shang period (Liu and Chen 2003: 127–45). I disagree with this trajectory reading, and believe that, given the current archaeological evidence, it is unlikely that the Late Shang system was weaker

or less centralized than that of the Early Shang. The oracle bone inscriptions aside, archaeological evidence relevant to the power of the Shang kings and their courts during the Late Shang period is much more impressive than that pertaining to the Early and Middle Shang. As discussed earlier, none of the graves from the Early and Middle Shang periods come close to the grandeur of the graves of Shang kings discovered at Xibeigang. While it is clear that the kings of the Early Shang were able to control resources and labor on a large scale, the currently available evidence suggests that these resources were used for more public projects, such as the walls of Zhengzhou, while during the Late Shang investments were more clearly associated with the persona of the king or with his courtiers. The scale and richness of the furnishings discovered inside Fuhao's grave are evidence of the quantity of resources (in terms of labor, expertise, and materials) that were expended on projects related to the personal prestige and well-being of high-status individuals.

The Shang system shows unmistakable signs of specialization and division of labor. Clear examples are the identification in the inscriptions of people in charge of specific tasks, such as preparing the bones and overseeing the divination process itself, keeping records, and so on (Keightley 1999: 236–7). Records of the Shang king ordering certain people to perform certain tasks – such as in inscription Heji 33209, "The king orders the Duo Yin (officers) to open up the fields in the west . . . " (trans. Keightley 2002: 62) – are also suggestive of the development of an incipient bureaucratic system. Control over craft production can be regarded as an archaeological correlate of such a system.

The overall impression, however, is that the Shang had a generalized administrative system. Seemingly official titles, such as "servitor" (*chen* 臣), appear to denote ad hoc appointments rather than permanent offices or administrative positions. Moreover, the king himself is often portrayed as personally ordering or inspecting even very mundane tasks, such as the opening of new fields (Keightley 1999: 278–88). The king seems to have been personally responsible for most aspects of the state's operation, including not only the functioning of the court in the capital, but also, in the course of his many tours, the inspection of public works, the maintenance of dominance over more remote territories, and relations with neighboring groups.

The State Economy of the Shang Polity

This contradiction in the Shang's bureaucratic system – between highly specialized segments and a very generalized overall structure – is also suggested for the economic system of the Shang. On the one hand, Shang craft reached very high levels of specialization and an almost unparalleled level of production. On the other, the state economy is usually portrayed as quite primitive: it lacked institutionalized mechanism of tax collection and was based on the king's direct control over agricultural land and animal herds, as well as on unsystematic tribute relations. For many scholars, this was an elite-based redistributive system (Chang 1980; Liu and Chen 2003; Underhill and Fang 2004). It may be true, as recent studies have argued (e.g., Campbell et al. 2011), that this interpretation is biased because most of the research has focused on the elite-oriented bronze industry and on the ritual oracle bone inscriptions. Nevertheless, I believe that the basic tenets of the commonly held view of the Shang state economy remain valid.

One of the most fundamental issues, and one that is extremely difficult to resolve, concerns the financing of the Shang state. On the one hand, it is clear that the maintenance of the Shang court and the large-scale projects it initiated, such as the constructions of city walls and royal tombs, required a substantial flow of resources (food supplies, manpower, materials). On the other hand, though, there is no evidence that the Shang had

any formal system for levying taxes. We know from the inscriptions that the Shang court received tributes from its neighbors, and sometimes from far away polities, but most of these tributes appear to have been materials related to Shang rituals, such as turtle shells and cattle required for divinations and other animals and human sacrificial victims needed for the royal rituals (Chang 1980; Underhill and Fang 2004). How the Shang obtained the more fundamental resources it needed is less clear.

According to one explanation, the king owned all the land under the control of the Shang (Chang 1980: 220–30). The fact that agricultural fields are sometimes referred to in the inscriptions as "my" or "our" fields (*wo tian* 我田) and the previously mentioned direct involvement of the king in activities such as ordering the opening of new fields or the inspection of agricultural production are used to support this claim. According to this model, farmers were organized in work groups called *zhongren* (眾人), which were managed by state officials and supplied with work tools produced en masse by the royal workshops. Batches of finished and unfinished stone tools found in the Xiaotun area, as well as the large-scale production of tools such as shovels in the bone workshops, are evidence in support of this model (Chang 1980; Keightley 1999: 277–80). While no large-scale facilities for storing and redistributing quantities of grain have been found at Yinxu, the shape of the character representing "granary" in the inscriptions suggests above-ground facilities that may have not been preserved in the archaeological record (Underhill and Fang 2004: 134).

While it is possible that the Shang court controlled the agricultural fields in the immediate area around Yinxu, it certainly had no stable control over, let alone ownership of, the land in the Four Lands regions, even those that were relatively close. The fact that the Shang king divined on the harvest and well-being of these areas suggests that it was in his best interests that they prosper, perhaps because that would help him gain their support, and maybe even extract manpower and food tributes from them. It does not imply that the king controlled these areas or that he could systematically levy taxes from them. The large number of domesticated animal sacrifices mentioned in the inscriptions and the enormous quantities of animal bones found in the debris of Shang workshops suggest a constant supply of animals whose meat was probably consumed by the Shang court, and whose other parts – bones, antlers, hide – were used by Shang artisans. The royal pastures (*mu* 牧) and the tending of herds mentioned in the inscriptions suggest that many of the animals were brought to the Shang capital from nearby regions directly controlled by the Shang king. Other animals, however, are mentioned in the inscriptions as tribute from more remote peoples (Campbell et al. 2011; Keightley 1999: 280–1).

Another state-level economic mechanism was the royal hunt, though it is not always recognized as such. The royal hunt is the most frequently divined upon subject in the oracle bone inscriptions, and it is clear that hunting was one of the most important activities of the Shang court (Chang 1980: 214–15). Hunting expeditions served not only for leisure but also to show off the powers of the Shang king, to forge alliances with neighboring groups, and perhaps even as a kind of military training. Moreover, the large numbers of animals caught during these expeditions suggests that they supplied a considerable amount of meat (for sacrifice and consumption), as well as other animal products. It is also possible that these hunts, together with the other royal tours, which occupied about half of the time of the king and his court, served as a kind of primitive taxing mechanism, whereby local groups had to provide provisions to sustain the large entourage passing through their territory (Keightley 1978–80).

Craft production, especially of elite products such as bronze vessels, was a state-run system in which attached specialists worked under elite supervision in large-scale workshops. Many of the finished artifacts were distributed among the court and to members of the local elite. The discovery of typical Shang bronzes in areas beyond the political control of the Shang suggests that some were also circulated within networks of gift exchange with the elites of neighboring or even more remote groups, or in exchange for resources from more remote areas (Underhill and Fang 2004; and see Chapter 9).

The bone industry of the Shang possibly exemplifies the intertwined nature of Shang's craft production. Detailed analysis of remains from the Tiesanlu workshop, located south of the Xiaotun center at Yinxu, suggests a mixing of elite and nonelite interests. The scale of production, evidence of a well-organized division of labor, and the fact that a large quantity of the raw materials was associated with royal ritual activities suggest elite control and management. However, while some of the products may have been redistributed among the elite, the scale of production and the nature of some of the artifacts suggest nonelite consumption. These nonelite artifacts, such as pins, awls, arrowheads, and shovels, could have been distributed in exchange for services or products, and they may have even circulated in a market system (Campbell et al. 2011).

In conclusion, the archaeological and written records suggest that the economic system of the Shang was composed of different levels and subsystems, and that different methods were employed to obtain the needed resources. At the subsistence level of the general population, it stands to reason that most communities were economically self-sufficient, while the court provided peasants with some agricultural tools, perhaps for large-scale works organized by the state. We know little about Shang period village life, but we do know that the technology for producing utilitarian artifacts, such as ceramic vessels and agriculture tools, as well as the construction of houses, remained unchanged from the Neolithic period, and so we have no reason to assume that the villagers could not have provided for their own needs.

Power, Institution, and Legitimation: A Model of the Shang State

The preceding discussion portrays the Shang system as the embodiment of what appear to be fundamental contradictions. These contradictions include the extensive sphere of the Shang's cultural influence on the one hand, and the relatively small region directly under the control of Shang kings on the other; the seeming weakness of the Shang king in his dealing with different peoples and local leaders inside his territory versus his considerable ability to control large labor forces in the core area; the generalized administrative system of the Shang on the one hand, and the highly specialized nature of some aspects of the Shang court (divination) and state-controlled industry (bronze) on the other; and finally a tribute-based redistributive economic system versus the ability to amass large quantities of basic resources.

The Shang kings were able to control the huge labor forces and resources needed to sustain the construction of large-scale projects and the production of prestige artifacts without the institutionalized and specialized administrative system that is usually associated with such activities. To give just one example, Zhengzhou was one of the largest walled cities anywhere in the ancient world, and its construction required a far greater investment than at Erlitou or anywhere else during the Late Neolithic period. Assuming that the walls were about 10 m high (they are currently preserved to a height of 9 m in some places), 20 m wide at the bottom and 10 m wide at the top, then about 200 m^3 of pounded earth would have been needed to construct just 1 m of wall (not taking into account the foundation trenches). The length of the inner wall at Zhengzhou is 6,960 m, meaning 1,392,000 m^3 of pounded earth would have been needed to construct the entire wall. Working with

the estimate – based on ancient sources and modern experiments – that a single conscript worker was expected to excavate, transport, and construct 7.55 m^3 of pounded earth wall in a month (Shelach et al. 2011), the construction of the inner wall at Zhengzhou would have required some 5,346,700 person/days of work. This is some five times more labor than the work required to construct the walls of Taosi, and some thirty-five times more than the work on the pounded earth platforms and enclosure at Erlitou. The exact length and dimensions of the outer walls at Zhengzhou are unknown, but the work required to construct them, and the moat that enclosed the city, must have been even greater.

It is difficult to comprehend how such a project could have been accomplished without a supporting bureaucratic system that kept records about the location of resources, potential workers, and the food to sustain them, and was able to mobilize and utilize them. However, this dichotomy between a highly powerful yet noninstitutionalized and generalist system, rather than being a reflection of the absence of crucial information or of misunderstanding, may actually be a key factor in understanding how Shang's sociopolitical, economic, and cultural dimensions were integrated. Such an understanding should take into consideration the issue of legitimation: the religious, ritual, and display mechanisms that ensured the submission of the population to the Shang king.

Large-scale human sacrifices and the ceremonial burial of expensive artifacts can be seen as one such mechanism. Oracle bone inscriptions describe large-scale sacrifices in which hundreds of people – probably captives – were slain in a single event; all told, thousands of such victims are mentioned (Shelach 1996). As mentioned, archaeological evidence of human sacrifice is found in many Shang-related contexts. According to the inscriptions, the Shang went to great lengths to obtain these victims, some of whom were captured in wars initiated by the Shang specifically as expeditions to seize captives, and some of whom were acquired through tribute relations with other groups (Keightley 1978–80). However, why would they waste in this manner a valuable resource that could have been used, for example, in Shang public works? I interpret the extravagant behavior of the Shang as a way of visually demonstrating the supreme powers of the king. The ceremonial killing of a large number of people is an especially potent act that vividly demonstrates the powers (real and divine) of the king over life and death. Precisely because the king's position was not institutionalized, but rather was dependent on his personal charisma, he had to frequently repeat such ceremonies in order to reaffirm this position. With the institutionalization of the king's office and the kingly systems during the subsequent Zhou period, the frequency and scale of human sacrifice rapidly declined (Shelach 1996). The visual effects of other Shang ceremonies and Shang monuments, the hierarchical nature of the Shang religion, and the monopoly of the Shang kings over communication with the ancestors are other examples of legitimating mechanisms that were an integral part of the Shang sociopolitical and economic system.

In a long series of seminal papers and books, K. C. Chang contrasts the early Chinese states founded on the control of communication through art, ritual, and extended family connections, with contemporaneous Western (Mesopotamian and European) civilizations, which were based on advances in food production, technology and trade, and the substitution of family ties with legal relations. Chang and others also thought that Chinese cities, which they described as political and religious nodes, were fundamentally different from Western cities that evolved as commercial and integrative centers (Chang 1983; Wheatley 1971). New discoveries and novel analyses suggest that these sharp distinctions between two supposedly divergent models of the early state are overly simplistic. Early Chinese states and their cities were not just about lineage relations and rituals – economic activities, and perhaps even an incipient market system, were no less important to the functioning of these polities (cf. Campbell et al. 2011) – and Western states may not have been so "rational" or devoid of kinship relations as the model suggests. More important, statehood should be seen not as a finite stage, but as a dynamic, variable, and continuous process. The example of the Shang, with its apparent internal contradictions and unique combination of economic, political, and legitimating mechanisms, is therefore an important case that should be included in any cross-cultural comparative attempt to understand the evolution of human society.

THE FORMATION OF CHINESE CULTURE DURING THE SHANG PERIOD

The remarkable similarity between aspects of Shang culture and attributes later seen as central to Chinese identity is one reason for the fascination it generates among both Chinese scholars and the general public. Unmistakably "Chinese" aspects of Shang culture include the extensive use of Chinese script, the forms of ritual bronze vessels, and clear evidence of ancestor worship, to give just a few examples. Unlike previous cultures with so-called Chinese attributes, such as the Longshan or Erlitou (Chapters 6 and 7), the association of Shang traits with later Chinese norms and identities is much more straightforward. Foremost among these Shang traits is the appearance of a writing system that is clearly ancestral to all later Chinese writings, not only in the shape of individual characters but also in the overall structure of the writing system. The Chinese writing of the oracle bone inscriptions is logographic – it uses graphs to record words rather than ideas, as in a ideographic system, or sounds as in alphabetic systems (Keightley 2006: 182). All Chinese scripts have evolved from this one, including scripts used today, and they all have the same basic characteristics.

The use of writing as a kind of cultural capital to legitimate the position of the Shang kings and to communicate with the spirits and goods (Keightley 2006) is also a clear attribute of the Chinese civilization that followed.

This use of the Chinese language and Chinese script, notions about the world of the gods, communication between the living and their ancestors (at least those of the elite), and the basic components of public worship are a convincing enough assembly of attributes to merit the identification of the Shang as the first clearly "Chinese" culture. Nevertheless, this is an observation that we are able to make only in hindsight. The Shang people and the other groups living in China during the second half of the second millennium BCE did not yet see themselves as belonging to a unified ethnos of any kind. There is no evidence of Shang self-identification that resembles anything like the all-inclusive notion of "Chinese" or "Xia" or "Huaxia" of the Eastern Zhou period (Chapter 10).

REGIONAL VARIATION AND INTERREGIONAL INTERACTIONS DURING THE BRONZE AGE: "CENTER AND PERIPHERY" OR "INTERACTION SPHERES"?

Over the past thirty years, the long-established focus on the archaeology of the Shang has given way to a broader geographical perspective. Research in such regions as the Sichuan basin, the middle Yangzi basin, and northeast China has highlighted the considerable regional variation between societies that were contemporaneous with the Shang. In this chapter, I return to one of the main themes of the book and address both the regional variation that existed during the so-called Shang period, and the different levels of intersocietal contact among Bronze Age societies.

The first part of this chapter reviews the archaeological data from these regions, placing particular emphasis on these societies' level of sociopolitical complexity and the ways in which these complexities were structured in each region. Addressing the interactions between the societies belonging to or affiliated with the Shang and those societies located on their periphery allows us to test different models concerning the type of interaction between societies at unequal levels of complexity and technological advancement. Can we describe such interactions as a core-periphery system? Did the more advanced societies of the core exploit the less complex peripheral societies? Or was it a symbiotic system, in which all participating societies became politically and economically dependent on one other? Can we discern the development of an elite network of exchange in prestige items and rare materials? The last section of this chapter addresses the increase in quite intensive, long-range interactions, which, for the first time in Chinese history, connected societies across thousands of kilometers.

THE ARCHAEOLOGY OF REGIONS OUTSIDE THE SHANG POLITICAL SPHERE

Chronological Issues

Comparing the archaeology of the Shang, discussed in Chapter 8, with that of contemporaneous societies in other parts of China is not always easy, not least because much more is known about the former than the latter. One of the main obstacles to such a comparison is the crude and incomplete nature of the chronology for many of these non-Shang societies (see Table 7). In the northeast, for example, the Lower Xiajiadian period ended at around 1500 or 1400 BCE, while the subsequent Upper Xiajiadian period is dated to between ca. 1200 and 600 BCE. The chronological gap between the two periods is attributed to the absence of good dating and not to an actual hiatus in the occupation (Shelach 2009: 37). In the Ordos region, the Zhukaigou culture ended at around 1200 BCE, while the dates for the subsequent Ordos Bronzes culture (鄂尔多斯式青铜器)

TABLE 7. *Archaeological Periods by Region*

Area	Period	Dates BCE
Northeast	Upper Xiajiadian 夏家店上层	1200–600
Ordos	Zhukaigou 朱开沟 (phase V)	1400–1200
Ordos	Xicha 西岔	Early first millennium
Northwest: Qinghai and parts of Gansu	Kayue 卡约	1600–600
Northwest (eastern Gansu and Shaanxi)	Siwa 寺洼	1300–600
Sichuan	Sanxingdui 三星堆	1700–1150
Sichuan	Shi'erqiao 十二橋	1200–800
Middle-Lower Yangzi	Wucheng吳城	1500–1100
Yunnan	Early Bronze	1000–500
Lingnan	Upper Layers of Shixia 石峡 and Yuanlongpo 元龍坡	1200–700

begin only around the eighth century BCE. Farther to the west, the Kayue culture of Gansu and Qinghai is dated from the mid-second millennium to the end of the first millennium BCE, or, more conservatively, from the mid-second to the mid-first millennium BCE (Gao 1993). This exceptionally long time frame renders it a difficult and confusing unit to work with and useless for many analytical purposes. In central and western China, chronological units also tend to be very long. In the Sichuan basin, the Sanxingdui period is dated to ca. 1700 to 1150 BCE and the periods that follow it are neither well known nor well dated. In Yunnan, the chronological sequence is even less secure, with so-called Neolithic cultures extending to the end of the second millennium BCE and Early Bronze culture dated to ca. 1000 to 500 BCE.

THE ARCHAEOLOGICAL RECORD

Northeast China

The second half of the second millennium and the early part of the first millennium BCE was a period of great transformation along China's northern frontiers. In the northeast, this transformation is archaeologically manifested in the transition from the Lower to the Upper Xiajiadian periods. This transformation, however, is not represented in the demographic record, which indicate continued high population densities. Within the roughly 1,200 km² area covered by the Chifeng regional survey, Upper Xiajiadian sites cover an accumulated area of 1,007 ha (compared to 920 ha during the Lower Xiajiadian). The total population of the survey area during the Upper Xiajiadian – calculated on the basis of occupation area, artifact density, and the duration of the period – is estimated at 60,000 to 120,000, some 50 percent higher than estimates for the Lower Xiajiadian population. Moreover, the nucleation of the population was also high (Chifeng 2011).

The changes between Lower and Upper Xiajiadian periods, which were once viewed as evidence of the transition from a sedentary agricultural to a pastoral nomadic society, are now viewed as a more complex political, economic, and cultural process (Shelach 2009). Unlike Lower Xiajiadian period sites, Upper Xiajiadian sites show no signs of massive defense systems or other types of public structures, and only a minimal amount of labor appears to have been invested in all their domestic structures. In fact, at the few excavations that have been carried out at Upper Xiajiadian sites, very few house remains were located and the most

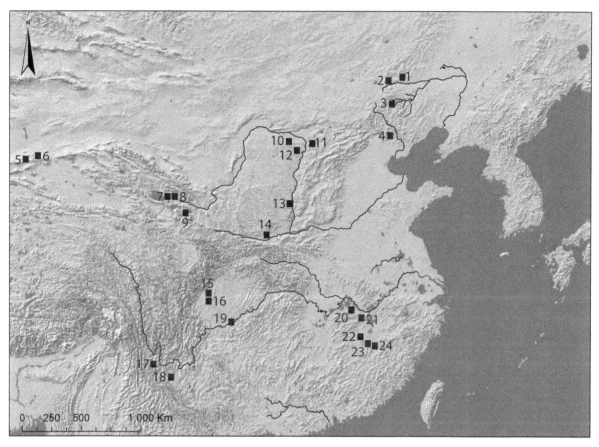

Figure 151. Map of all sites mentioned in Chapter 9: 1. Dajing; 2. Guandongche; 3. Dashanqian and Xiaoheishigou; 4. Chaodaogou; 5. Zahongluke; 6. Tiebanhe; 7. Dahuazhongzhuang; 8. Fengtai; 9. Xindian; 10. Ximaqing; 11. Xicha; 12. Zhukaigou; 13. Yantoucun; 14. Fengchu Qijiacun; 15. Sanxingdui; 16. Shierqiao Jinsha; 17. Haimenkou; 18. Wanjiaba; 19. Zhongba; 20. Tonglüshan; 21. Tongling in Jiangxi; 22. Wucheng; 23. Niucheng; 24. Dayangzhou (Xingan).

common features are pits – which may have been used for storage or refuse – that, in many cases, were dug into Lower Xiajiadian strata (Chifeng 2011).

No less dramatic a shift is evident in ritual practices, especially those associated with mortuary behavior. Upper Xiajiadian graves are found in clusters (or cemeteries), but, unlike Lower Xiajiadian cemeteries, they are not always associated with a specific domestic site and are sometimes located at a high elevation and far away from any settlements. Some of these clusters are relatively large, containing more than a hundred graves, but

others are much smaller (Shelach 1999: 149–50). Unlike graves from the Lower Xiajiadian period, most burials in the Upper Xiajiadian period were marked above the ground by a pile of earth and unhewed stones. Under this pile, large stone slabs were placed vertically in a pit, so as to form a narrow burial chamber or coffin. Most such coffins are approximately aligned along an east-west axis. Larger graves also contain evidence of a second wooden coffin, which was constructed inside the tomb's stone structure. A single individual in the extended supine position was placed in each of these tombs, and the stone coffin was

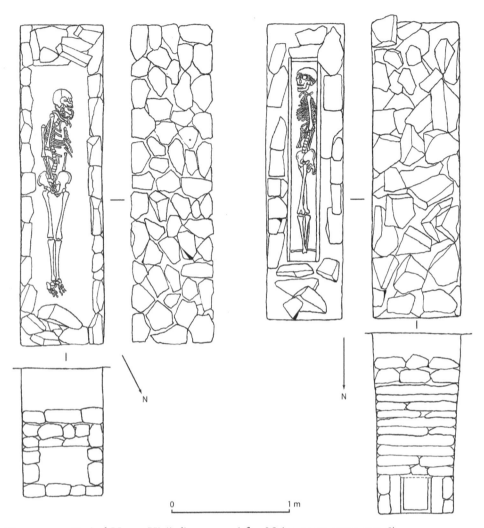

Figure 152. Typical Upper Xiajiadian graves (after Neimenggu 2009: 307–8)

then covered with a layer of horizontal stone slabs (Figure 152).

The artifacts placed in Upper Xiajiadian period graves also reflect a departure from the mortuary traditions of the Lower Xiajiadian period. Only few ceramic vessels have been found inside Upper Xiajiadian period graves, and the emphasis during this period seems to have shifted to placing personal ornaments, tools, and weapons, most of which were made of bronze, in the graves (Shelach 1999). The number of bronzes ranges from one or two in the small graves to more than two hundred pieces in the largest ones.

The development of craft specialization in northeast China is a more complicated issue, as it seems that the quality of some types of artifacts deteriorated in comparison to earlier periods, while other industries seem to have evolved. For example, the quality of ceramic production seems to have declined: the firing temperature of Upper Xiajiadian ceramics was probably lower than that of Lower Xiajiadian ones, producing soft and crumbly ceramics with inconsistent colors, a clear indication of poorer control over the firing process (Shelach 1999: 151–2). While many of the vessels were produced on a wheel, thick and

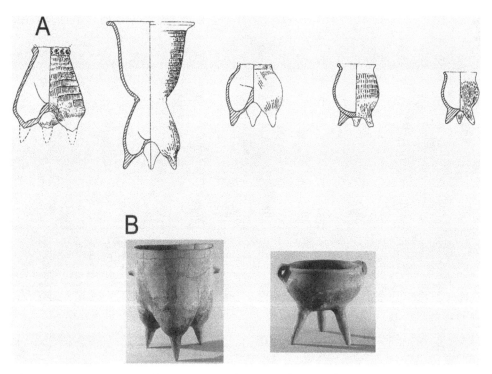

Figure 153. Comparison of Lower Xiajiadian period (A) and Upper Xiajiadian period (B) ceramics from the Chifeng region (after Shelach 2009: 22).

uneven vessel walls suggest an increasing level of hand production. Nevertheless, the shapes of these ceramic vessels reflect a clear continuity between the Lower and the Upper Xiajiadian periods (Figure 153).

In contrast, the production of metal artifacts seems to have grown both in quality and in quantity during the Upper Xiajiadian period. While only a handful of small bronze artifacts are known from the Lower Xiajiadian, thousands of bronze artifacts, some impressively large and complex, are dated to the late second and early first millennia BCE. The earliest evidence of the expansion of metallurgic production may be associated with the so-called Northern Bronzes Complex (*beifang qingtongqi* 北方青铜器) (Figure 154), but unfortunately many of the bronze artifacts that are associated with this group were found in isolated graves or as stray discoveries, detached from any archaeological context (Guo 1995b).

Thousands of Upper Xiajiadian period bronze artifacts, mostly excavated from graves, better illustrate the development of local metallurgy. Even a typical small Upper Xiajiadian grave usually contains from one to a few bronze artifacts. For example, all but two of the forty-five small intact graves excavated at the Xiaobaiyang (小白阳) cemetery in northern Hebei contained bronze artifacts. Indeed, a total of 20 knives, 10 daggers, 11 axes, 52 arrowheads, 911 plaques of varying sizes, and 1,013 smaller ornaments were found in those graves (Zhangjiakou 1987). Larger graves contain more complex bronze artifacts in even greater quantities. For example, a single large Upper Xiajiadian tomb from Xiaoheishigou (小黑石沟) contained 21 bronze vessels, 106 large bronze tools, artifacts, and weapons, more than 70 pieces of horse and chariot gear, and nearly 200 bronze and some 20 gold ornaments (Xiang and Li 1995) (Figures 155 and 156).

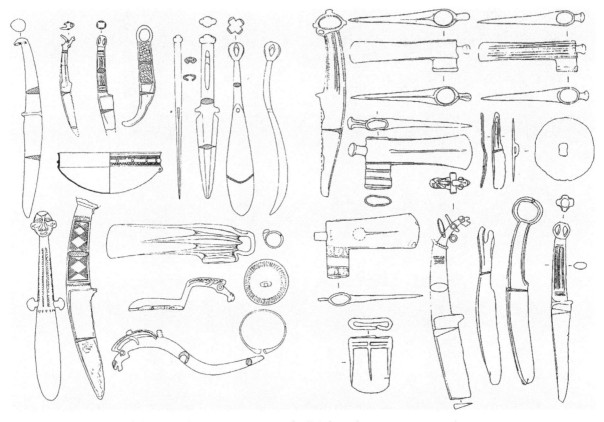

Figure 154. Artifacts of the "Northern Bronzes Complex" (after Zhongguo 1996: 190).

The extensive scale of local metal production in the Chifeng region during the late second and early first millennia BCE is attested to not only by the quantity of bronze artifacts found in graves, but also by the remains of a large copper ore mine found at the Dajing site (大井). This mine occupies an area of 2.5 km² and includes forty-seven mining trenches, some up to 100 m long and 8 m deep. There is also compelling evidence of local bronze casting, such as casting molds made of ceramic and stone (Figure 157).

North and Northwest China

THE ORDOS REGION

The history of human occupation in the Ordos region during the second millennium BCE is derived almost exclusively from one site – Zhukaigou.

Unfortunately, we know neither how representative it is of the entire region, nor what happened after the Zhukaigou site was abandoned. No systematic surveys have been carried out in this region, though indications are there was a dramatic decrease in the number of sites after ca. 1500 BCE. Approximately ten domestic sites are known from the early phase of the Zhukaigou period, thirty from the middle phase, and only three from the latter phase. By phase V, Zhukaigou seems to have been the only occupied site in the core area of the Ordos, although some sites have been identified further to the east (Tian and Han 2003).

Until recently, most researchers had suggested a hiatus in occupation, spanning a period between sometime in the late second millennium BCE and the eighth century BCE. However, recent discoveries of several sites dated to the Western Zhou

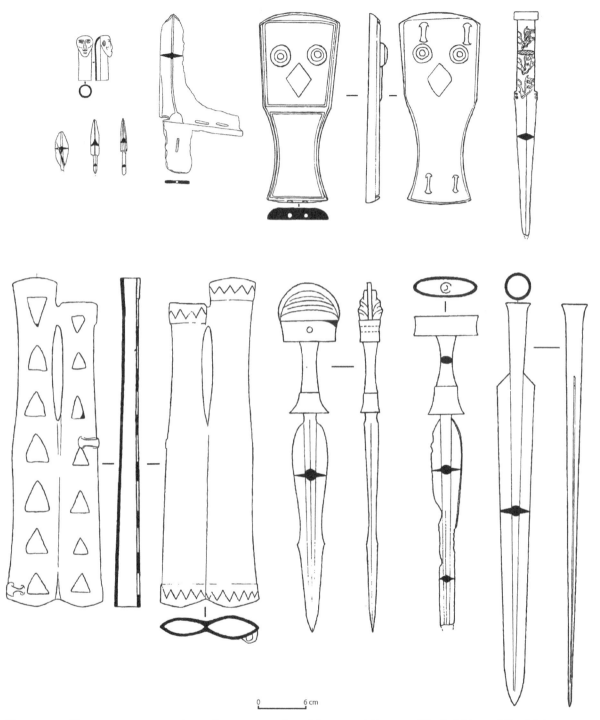

Figure 155. Bronze weapons, tools, and ornaments found in grave M8051 at Xiaoheishigou (after Neimenggu 2009: 7–275).

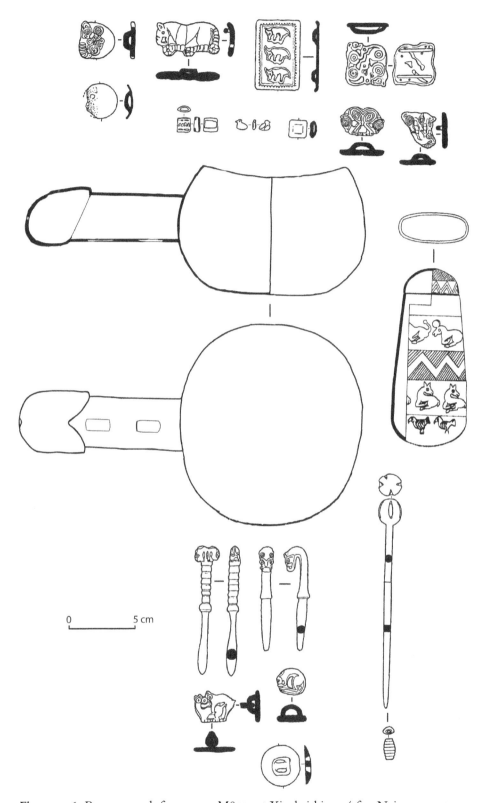

Figure 156. Bronze vessels from grave M8051 at Xiaoheishigou (after Neimenggu 2009: 274, 289).

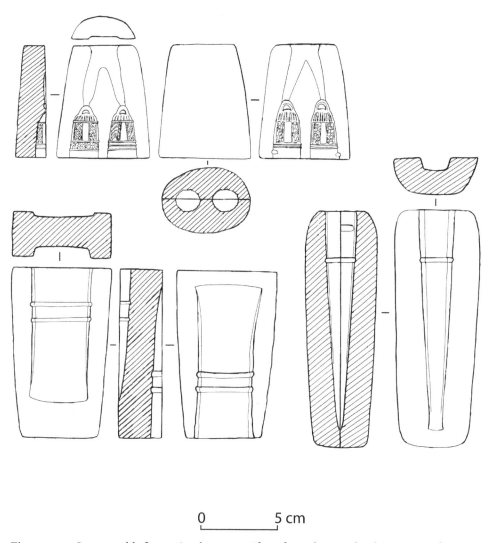

0   5 cm

Figure 157. Stone molds for casting bronze artifacts from the Xiaoheishigou site (after Neimenggu 2009: 405–6).

and the Spring and Autumn periods, collectively defined as the Xicha (西岔) culture (Neimenggu 2001), suggest that this gap in occupation is more ostensible than real. The Xicha site itself is located about 100 km east of Zhukaigou. It is ca. 120 ha in size and was occupied from the Neolithic period to the beginning of the first millennium BCE.

The majority of the eighty-three houses excavated at Zhukaigou are dated to phases II to IV (ca. 1900–1400 BCE), and only four are dated to phase V (ca. 1400–1200 BCE). House walls were built of mud, most houses were rectangular or square

in shape, and many contained holes for posts that supported an upper structure. In several houses, especially from phases IV and V of occupation, the floors were surfaced with white or yellow clay. Houses in the Zhukaigou site are relatively small, averaging only 11.5 m², and, moreover, their average size seems to have decreased over time (Neimenggu 2000: 21–40).

The number of storage pits – the second type of installation commonly found at the Zhukaigou site – does not follow the same pattern as that of the houses. While relatively few pits are associated

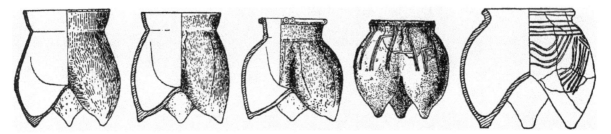

Figure 158. Evolution of the *li* ceramic vessel in the Ordos region (after Shelach 2009: 21).

with the first two phases of occupation (10 and 25 respectively), many more pits are associated with the final three phases (51, 57, and 61 respectively) (Neimenggu 2000: 321). This discrepancy is most strikingly evident in phase V, the phase with the fewest number of houses, but the greatest number of storage pits.

Excavations at the Zhukaigou site suggest a steady development in the production of characteristic utilitarian pottery and tools. Ceramics were mostly handmade, but over time a growing number of vessels, especially tripods, were made in molds, while some were produced on the wheel. Most vessels were decorated with cord or basket impressions, but no color decorations were found (Linduff 1995; Neimenggu 2000). *Li* (鬲) vessels with flower-shaped edges or *li* with a "snake" motif are regarded as the most typical expressions of the local culture. The production of such vessels in the Ordos region during the first millennium BCE is seen as evidence of local continuity and the indigenous development of the "Ordos Bronzes" culture (Figure 158) (Tian and Han 2003: 248–9).

In total, forty-three bronze artifacts were found at the Zhukaigou site: sixteen from phases III and IV, and twenty-seven from phase V. The artifacts from the earlier phases are all small objects, such as needles, small chisels, arrowheads, and earrings. Similar artifacts were also found in phase V strata, but larger artifacts were found as well, including knives, *ge* (戈, halberds), and three ritual vessels (Li and Han 2000: 423) (Figures 159 and 160). The shape and decoration of some of these artifacts,

such as the *ge* and the ritual *ding* and *jue* vessels, are very similar to those of artifacts from sites of the Shang period (Erligang phase) in the central plains. Some were probably imported to Zhukaigou from the east, but scientific tests of the weapons found at Zhukaigou suggest that they were all in fact produced locally – including those that are very similar to Shang weapons. These findings are further supported by the parts of a casting mold for an axe that were found in a stratum associated with phase V (Linduff 1995: 143; Han 1992).

Zhukaigou burials from phase V are similar to those of earlier phases, as described in Chapter 7.

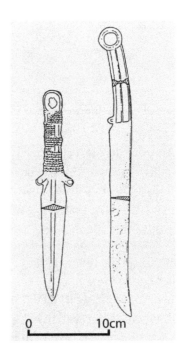

Figure 159. Bronze knives and daggers from the Zhukaigou site (after Neimenggu 2000: 234).

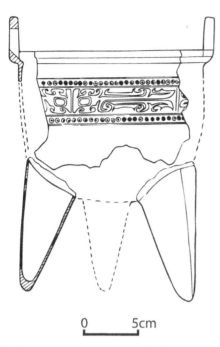

0   5cm

Figure 160. Fragments of a bronze *ding* vessel from Zhukaigou decorated with a band of *Taotie* motifs in the classical Erligang style (after Neimenggu 2000: 12).

They are modest in scale and degree of elaboration, and fewer than half contain any burial goods. Among the few graves attributed to the intermediate Xicha period are nineteen graves excavated at the Ximaqing (西麻青) cemetery. All these graves are earth pits containing a single human skeleton in the extended position, most of them oriented to the north. Ceramic vessels are the most common grave offering, but several bronze ornaments, such as bracelets, jade ornaments, and sheep bones, were found as well (Zhongguo Wenwuju 2003: 85). In addition, a bronze socketed axe and three bronze earrings were reported from graves at the Xicha site (Neimenggu 2001: 74).

NORTHWEST CHINA

Our knowledge of the archaeology of northwest China in the periods that followed the Qijia is likewise limited, and the chronology of the period is also quite fuzzy. Very few sites dated to the Kayue period have been located, and those we know of are quite small (between 30 and 300 m in diameter), though there is evidence of houses constructed of stone and mud brick (Gao 1993; Li 1993). It is unclear if this represents a period of sparse occupation or whether more fieldwork might bring more sites to light. An indication that the second scenario might be the correct one is provided by an unsystematic exploration of Guide county (贵德县), in eastern Qinghai, where remains of Kayue culture were found at 180 sites. In contrast, only 11 sites contained materials from the Qijia period. Some of the Kayue sites identified in this survey were quite large, with several estimated to be between 2 and 6 ha in size, four between 10 and 20 ha, and one 45 ha (Qinghai 1999). Cursory as they are, these results refute the idea of a hiatus in occupation some time during the late second millennium BCE, as suggested by several scholars (e.g., Lin 2003: 107–9).

Continuity of the Qijia ceramic tradition is found in all the later cultures of the Gansu region such as the Siwa and the Kayue (Figure 161). At the Xindian (辛店) site, for example, all the ceramics are handmade and most pots have flat bases, but footed *li* and *dou* vessels were also found. Many pots have two handles and resemble Qijia pots in their shape, but researchers have also identified influences from other Gansu cultures on these artifacts, as well as new local developments. The ceramic vessels associated with the Kayue culture are also all handmade of refined materials. This close correlation between the ceramic assembly at the Xindian site and those of the Kayue and Siwa traditions suggests long-term local developments and interactions between subregions in the northwest.

Continuity from the Qijia tradition is also reflected in the bronze industry of the Gansu region. For example, artifacts such as bronze knives, axes, spearheads, and arrowheads have been attributed to the Kayue culture. The most common bronze artifacts found, however, are small knives, mirrors, small bells, buttons, and beads. At the Dahuazhongzhuang (大华中庄) cemetery in northeastern Qinghai, 378 of the 438 bronze

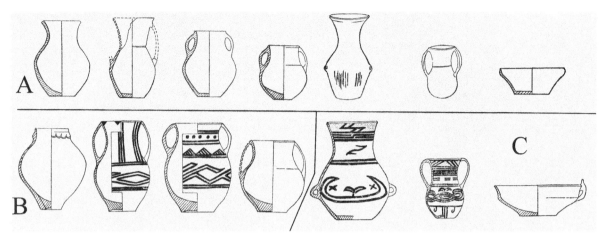

Figure 161. Continuation of the Qijia ceramic tradition (A) among the later cultures of the Gansu region: Kayue (B) and Xindian (C) (after Shelach 2009: 20).

artifacts excavated were small bells, buttons, and beads. Larger artifacts include six spearheads, three knives, and thirty-four bronze mirrors, as well as one artifact of a more complex nature – probably a pole top – on top of which are cast the small three-dimensional figures of a cow and a cub facing a barking dog (Figures 162 and 163). A relatively large number of gold artifacts are also

Figure 162. Bronze objects of the Kayue "culture" (after Shelach 2009: 25).

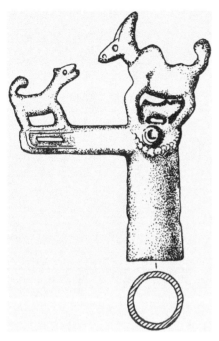

Figure 163. A bronze pole top from Dahuazhong-zhuang (after Qinghai 1985: 22).

associated with the Kayue tradition. For example, some forty gold artifacts, mostly small beads, earrings, and bracelets, were excavated from graves in the Shangsunjiazhai (上孙家寨) cemetery in northeastern Qinghai (Wang and Cui 2003).

The Qijia burial tradition seems to have been continued and elaborated upon in the Gansu area throughout the second millennium BCE. Graves from the Siwa period are classified according to their size and arrangement: some were relatively large and contain a secondary ledge and wooden coffins, while others did not. They also differ from each other in the richness of the offerings placed inside them: some graves contained only a few ceramic vessels, while others held up to seventy vessels together with bronze and stone implements and the bone remnants of sacrificial animals. Human sacrifices, probably more prevalent during this period than in earlier ones, were placed in special niches dug into the walls of the grave (Gansu 1990).

Graves associated with the Kayue culture exhibit some unique local attributes. At cemeteries such

as Dahuazhongzhuang, more than 90 percent of the skeletons found were of secondary burials (Qinghai 1985). The sizes of the graves in this cemetery also vary dramatically: the volume of earth removed from the graves ranges from less than 0.1 m³ to more than 30 m³. Larger graves from the Kayue period often contained an internal wooden structure (Figure 164), but they usually contained no more than one or two ceramic vessels, tools made of stone, bone, or bronze, and ornaments. For example, 104 of the 117 graves at the Dahuazhongzhuang cemetery contained offerings, but very few artifacts were found in each grave: only 74 ceramic vessels and 438 bronze artifacts, mostly small bells and beads, were recovered in total. Human sacrifices, in contrast, were quite frequent: more than 10 percent of the 244 graves excavated at the Panjialiang (潘家梁) cemetery, for instance, contained evidence of such sacrifices. Offerings of animals – such as sheep, dogs, pigs, horses, and cattle – were common, but instead of placing the entire animal in the grave it became common practice to bury only its hooves and skull (Gao 1993; Liu 2000). This custom, which may be associated with new rituals, continued in the region throughout the first millennium BCE.

The Lower and Central Yangzi River Basin

The area of the lower and central Yangzi River basin bordered the Shang polity to the south. During the Early Shang period, Panlongcheng may have been one of its outposts, controlling parts of the central Yangzi area, but it is likely that even then most of the region was not under the direct control of the Shang. Evidence of large-scale bronze production developing in this area by the Early or Middle Shang period and the unique local attributes of the artifacts that have been discovered suggest the development of local polities that were in close contact with the Shang, but which were independent from it.

Overall, data on settlement in this region are rudimentary at best, and even basic information

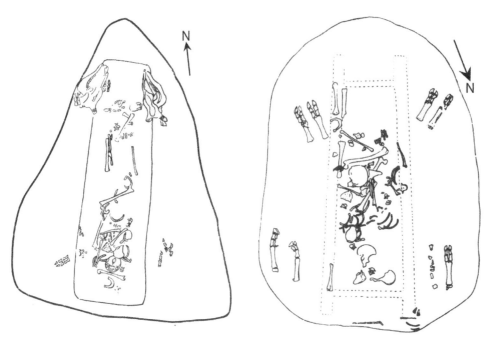

Figure 164. Graves M79 and M39 from the Dahuazhongzhuang cemetery (after Qinghai 1985: 159a).

on site size, house structures, and the like is scarce. The most extensive settlement data come from the Gan River (贛江) basin, south of the Yangzi in Jiangxi province. The local Bronze Age culture is sometimes called Wucheng after the largest and best known site in the region. The early strata at Wucheng are probably contemporaneous with the Early Shang. A pounded earth enclosure covering 61 ha was built here during the fifteenth century BCE. Its walls are more or less rectangular in shape, but unlike most other site walls in the Yellow River area, which were built on flat land, the Wucheng enclosure was constructed on hilly terrain (Figure 165). The walls are preserved to a height of more than 3 m, and they are 21 m wide at the bottom and 8 m wide at the top. Eleven openings in the wall have been identified as gates. Surveys around the enclosure suggest that it was the center of a much larger site (Jiangxi 2003; Peng 2005).

Both residential and public areas have been identified within the Wucheng enclosure. Evidence of public structures includes a red-soil plat-form – identified as ceremonial – and the remains of large buildings, including the foundations of houses and a large group of postholes. The excavators also identified the remains of a long large road and some fourteen kilns (Peng 2005). The overall configuration of the site, both within and outside of the walls, however, is still unclear.

In addition to Wucheng, several smaller sites are known from this region, most of them probably contemporaneous with the Late Shang. At least one other site – Niucheng (牛城) – is also walled. It covers about 50 ha, and its walls are approximately 15 m wide and preserved to the height of ca. 4 m (Zhu 2005). The location of Niucheng some 23 km east of Wucheng suggests that it was either a secondary center of the Wucheng polity or the center of another polity.

Evidence of craft production at Wucheng includes groups of kilns for making high-quality ceramics, including stamp-pattern hardware and proto-porcelain found in the northwest area of the site. Evidence of bronze production was identified

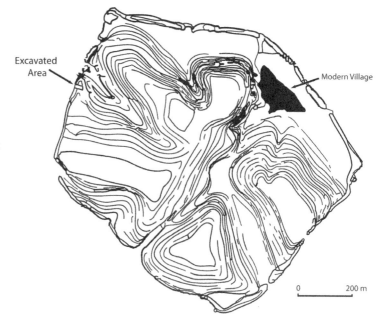

Figure 165. The walled enclosure at Wucheng (after Jiangxi 2003: figure 1).

in the northeastern part of the site: molds for making tools and weapons, but none for casting large composite vessels, were found here.

Artifacts found at Wucheng and other sites dated to the same period – for example, bronzes and high-quality ceramics – suggest an advanced level of craft specialization and production on a relatively large scale. An interesting local discovery were caches that include one or several bronze items, the most typical of which are bronze *nao* (鐃 bells) that can weigh up to 220 kg. While some similar bells have been found in the north of China, they are much smaller and rarer there, suggesting that the important tradition of bronze bell manufacturing was developed in the south. Bronze vessels from these caches are similarly local in style, and the most prevalent types found, *lei* (罍) and *zun* (尊), are not the most common ones in the Shang centers.

The most impressive collection of artifacts from this region was found in a single grave from Dayangzhou (大洋洲) in Xin'gan (新干) county, very close to the Niucheng site. The Xin'gan grave, as it is commonly referred to, has been dated,

based on the style of its artifacts, to the thirteenth century BCE (contemporary to the Huanbei or early Yinxu in the north). It contained about 1,900 burial goods, including pottery, 1,072 jade objects, and 480 bronze objects, not the least of which were 48 bronze vessels and four bronze bells (Jiangxi 1997). The basic shapes and decorations of the bronze vessels follow northern styles quite closely. However, the bronze animal and birds figurines that are attached to the handles of the vessels are of a distinct local style (Figure 166). Other smaller bronze objects, such as a human head pole top (Figure 167), are also cast in a unique local style, suggesting that the entire bronze inventory found in this grave was produced locally. Thus, the development of a local bronze industry was clearly modeled on the techniques and styles of the Shang, but it incorporated local elements and catered to local tastes and ritual needs.

The location of the Xin'gan grave, and of Wucheng sites in general, in an area known for its rich copper ores suggests that utilizing these resources for local consumption, as well as for trade, perhaps, could have been an important

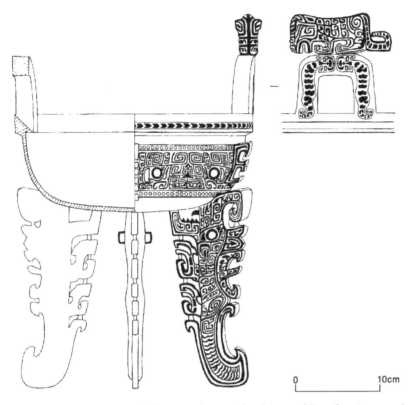

0   10cm

Figure 166. Bronze vessels from Xin'gan with a bronze feline figurine attached to the handle (after Jiangxi 1997: 23).

factor in the development of a local sociopolitical hierarchy. Evidence of an extensive exploitation of these ores, which dates back to the Erligang phase and continues through the Zhou period, has been found at the large mining site of Tongling (铜岭) in Jiangxi province. The size and organization of the Tongling site, as well as of the somewhat later Tonglüshan (铜绿山) site in Hubei, suggest a state-level operation. The mining shafts at Tonglüshan are well structured and cover an area of ca. 2 km², making it one of the largest ancient mining sites known in China.[1] The Tongling mines cover a smaller area of ca. 7 ha, but here too evidence such as mining tools and the wooden structures of the mine shafts suggests extensive and well-organized mining activities. The large amounts of slag found at these two sites suggest that copper was smelted on-site and then transported to production centers as metal ingots (Liu and Lu 1998).

The Sichuan Basin

Bronze Age discoveries in the Sichuan basin are among the most dramatic findings in Chinese archaeology of recent decades. They suggest that during the late second and early first millennia BCE, societies in this region were as complex and extensive as their counterparts in the middle and lower Yangzi River basin, and perhaps even comparable to Shang society in the Yellow River basin.

Of the Bronze Age sites in this region that date to the second half of the second millennium BCE, the most famous is Sanxingdui (三星堆). Additional sites from the period have been reported in the archaeological literature, but the overall number of sites and density of occupation in this region have not been yet documented. The Sanxingdui site is enclosed by a large pounded

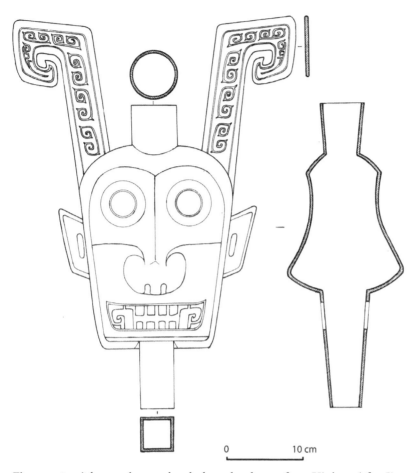

Figure 167. A bronze human head–shaped pole top from Xin'gan (after Jiangxi 1997: 132).

earth wall that is up to 40 m wide at the base and still stands 6 m tall at some places. This structure exemplifies a continuation of the local tradition from the Baodun period. Although the wall is not well preserved, local archaeologists estimate that it enclosed an area of 2.6 km², not much smaller than the area of the inner walls of the Shang city at Zhengzhou. Pounded earth foundations were found inside the walls, while evidence of habitation and industrial activity was found outside the walls in a 10 km² area. All this suggests to some that Sanxingdui was the center of a state-level polity (Falkenhausen 2003).

The most dramatic discoveries associated with Sanxingdui were found inside two pits excavated within the limits of the city walls and dated to the final centuries of the second millennium BCE. While not large – pits 1 and 2 measure 4.6 × 3.5 × 1.6 m and 5.3 × 2.3 × 1.6 m, respectively – they contained more than one thousand artifacts, including spectacular bronze statues, masks, and structures, the likes of which have not been found anywhere else in China. Some of these artifacts are among the largest ever produced in China, including a human figure measuring 2.6 m high (including the base) and a bronze tree, made from several parts that were cast separately but assembled together to form a structure 4.2 m in height (Figures 168 and 169). In addition to bronzes, the pits also contained gold objects, jade artifacts, elephant tusks and ivory objects, cowrie shells, and more (Falkenhausen 2002: 90–2).

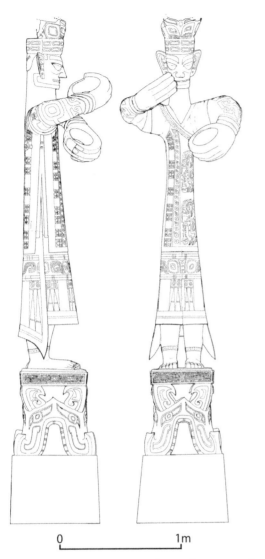

0   1m

Figure 168. Bronze statue of a standing person from pit 2 at Sanxingdui (Shelach 2011: 537).

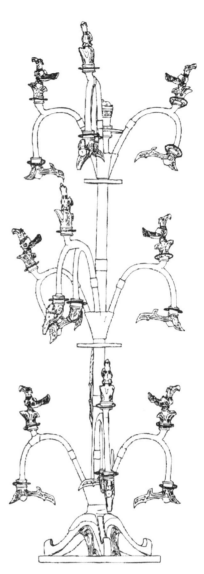

Figure 169. A composite bronze tree with birds from Sanxingdui pit 2 (after Shelach 2011: 537).

Much has been written about the affinity between the Sanxingdui bronzes and the bronze industry of the Shang. While the use of a similar technology of production (composite-mold technique) and correlations of some motifs found on the Sanxingdui bronzes with those of the Shang (Figure 170) support such a connection, the overall impression is that of a unique local tradition rather than a derivative one. While it is likely that some of the Sanxingdui bronzes, such as *zun* and *lei* vessels, were imported from the middle Yangzi region, there are no equivalents for the majority of objects in other parts of China. The unique features of the Sanxingdui bronze industry include an emphasis on statues rather than vessels; the distinctive nature of the images and their style; and a clear tendency not only of assembling different bronze parts (as in the bronze trees), but also of combining with other materials, such as gold and perishable materials (Figure 171).

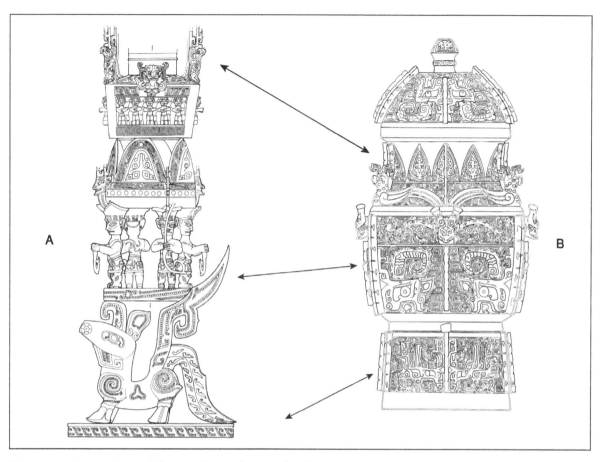

Figure 170. Comparison of the motifs on a bronze altar from Sanxingdui (A) and the motifs on a Shang bronze vessel from the Fuhao tomb (B).

Until recently, little was known about the Bronze Age societies that followed the end of Sanxingdui in this region. Shierqiao (十二橋), a typical site from this subsequent period, is best known for its remains of large wood-pile buildings, one of which was as large as 560 m². Elsewhere, other large-scale houses, as well as smaller ones, have been dated to this same period, possibly indicating a stratified society.

The discovery of the Jinsha (金沙) site during construction work in the suburbs of Chengdu has dramatically increased our knowledge of this period. The site yielded extensive evidence of occupation during the Shierqiao period, including the remains of some seventeen houses, pottery kilns, and a large number of ash pits. The most famous and most extensively reported part of this site, however, contains the sacrificial pits that seem to mark a ritual center.

While the pits at Jinsha seem to carry on local ritual traditions, not one of them is as rich as the Sanxingdui pits. At least sixty individual pits and deposits have been located, and more were probably destroyed during construction work. The artifacts found in these pits include a large number of elephant tusks, bronze objects (such as weapons, bells, and figurines, but no vessels), jade and stone artifacts, ceramic vessels, and animal bones. Most famous are more than two hundred gold objects found, mostly ornaments and golden foils

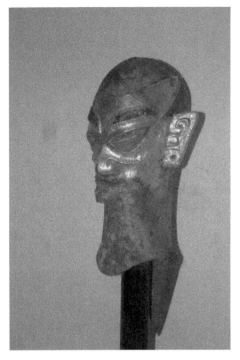

Figure 171. Bronze Statue from Sanxingdui pit 2. A. A human had with a gold "mask"; B. A "mask" with protruding eyes (photos by Gary Lee Todd).

(Figure 172). Some of the artifacts clearly reflect continuity with the style of Sanxingdui, though we currently lack evidence of bronze production continuing at the same scale as during the Sanxingdui period.

Areas to the West and South of the Yangzi River Basin

Societies in areas farther away from the centers of the Yellow and Yangzi River basins continued the slow evolution typical of the Neolithic period. An agricultural way of life, small-scale socioeconomic stratification, and even incipient bronze production were all part of this evolution, but there are no signs of the development of large-scale and complex societies comparable to those of the two large river basins, or even to societies from the northern frontier areas.

Bronze artifacts from the Wanjiaba (万家坝) site, in Yunnan province, dated to the beginning of

the first millennium BCE, are currently the earliest evidence of metallurgy in southwest China, but many believe that it had already begun during the second millennium (Yao 2010). Early bronze and copper artifacts such as knives, projectile points, axes, and adzes are similar in function to stone artifacts and, thus, cannot be seen to represent revolutionary change. Bivalve molds for casting axes have been discovered at a few sites. Analysis of fourteen artifacts from the Haimenkou (海门口) site, for example, indicates that four were made of pure copper, while the other ten contained less than 10 percent tin or lead (Li and Han 2006). This suggests an incipient level of local bronze production.

Little is known about domestic sites in Yunnan, but mortuary evidence suggests that the incipient production of bronze artifacts was not associated with distinct social change. More complex and hierarchical societies probably appeared in this region only after the eighth or seventh century

Figure 172. Gold ornaments form Jinsha (photo by Yuri Pines).

BCE, and culminated just before or simultaneously with the development of more frequent contact with the Chinese states to the east (Chapter 11).

The process in south China (including Lingnan and the southeast coastal area) is comparable to that in Yunnan. Bronze artifacts appeared there during the late second millennium BCE, but they are not associated with dramatic sociopolitical or economic change. Early bronze artifacts in this region are small, they are found in small quantities, and they do not seem to have played any significant social role. More significant evidence of technological development is found in hard ceramics impressed with geometric designs, as well as protoporcelain wares that seem to have served as status markers in graves (Jiao 2007: 69–80).

Evidence of social differentiation and stratification is very limited. Throughout the Late Neolithic and early Bronze Age, we see a recurrent process of the emergence of social complexity at various times and in different subregions, followed by periods of declining complexity and a return to more egalitarian social forms (Allard 1997). The Wusaoling (乌騷岭) cemetery in western Guangdong province, dated to ca. 2600–1900 BCE, is an example of the low degree of social differentiation. Of the 111 small pit graves excavated in the

cemetery, 26 contain no artifacts at all, and even the richest graves contained fewer than ten burial goods, mostly simple stone artifacts and ceramic vessels (Allard 1997: 44–5).

The slightly later cemetery at Yuanlongpo (元龍坡), in Guangxi province, might indicate intensified contact with the state-level societies of the Yangzi River basin as well as the evolution of local bronze production and social complexity. No fewer than 110 bronze artifacts were found inside the 350 graves excavated in this cemetery dated to the eleventh to eighth century BCE. Of these, two bronze vessels were probably imported from the north, but the rest are mostly tools and weapons of indigenous style that were probably cast by local artisans. Six complete bivalve casting molds and many more fragments of molds found at the cemetery, combined with similar finds from elsewhere in the region, constitute evidence for the development of a local bronze industry (Figure 173) (Ciarla 2007).

The graves at the Yuanlongpo cemetery show greater signs of stratification than those at Wusaoling. Beyond the 110 bronzes mentioned earlier, more than 1,000 artifacts have been excavated from the 350 graves, including more than 200 jades, 100 stone artifacts, and many ceramic vessels. Most of the graves are simple narrow pits, but twenty-one are larger, with evidence of a ledge or a side chamber. Fragments of lacquer, perhaps used to coat wooden coffins, were found in fifty-four of the graves. Although exotic foreign artifacts such as the two bronze vessels were also found in Yuanlongpo, the development of stratification seems to have depended more on local production.

REGIONAL VARIATION AND INTERREGIONAL INTERACTIONS

From a very broad perspective, we can divide the societies that were contemporaneous with the Shang into three groups: (1) societies on the northern frontiers of the Shang, which were nonstate complex societies with a relatively sophisticated bronze industry characterized by quite high levels of production, though not on a par with those of the Shang; (2) societies on the southern borders of the Shang in the Yangzi River area and the Sichuan basin, which may have been state-level societies with industry, including bronze production, comparable to that of the Shang; and (3) societies more remote from the Shang in Yunnan and south China, which were much less complex than societies in the other two regions. Bronze production, as well as stratification and social differentiation, were in their incipient stages.

Variation between these regions, as well as between societies within each of the regions, is expressed not only in terms of social complexity, but also through these societies' unique cultural attributes. For instance, the type and style of bronze artifacts produced by the societies from the northern frontiers are clear markers of differentiation from societies in other regions. While bronzes in the northern style are found in other regions, most notably in Shang graves, it is clear that they are foreign to this other context. Furthermore, within the larger grouping of "northern bronzes," each subregion has its unique style, suggesting the development of regional and subregional identities. Unique subregional styles of ceramic vessels – which in many cases continued earlier local traditions – and of other artifacts strengthen this observation (Shelach 2009). Even greater subregional differentiation is seen in the Yangzi-Sichuan zone. While bronzes produced in areas of the middle and lower Yangzi River are more similar to those in Shang traditions, albeit with added local flavor and preferences, bronzes of the Sanxingdui period in Sichuan are very different from the Shang model, with very little evidence to suggest direct contact between the regions.

Chinese archaeology has tended to invest a great deal of effort in correlating cultural variation in the archaeological record with ethnic identities. This tendency is particularly strong when it addresses the archaeology of "peripheral" areas during historical periods. Thus, for example, cultures in regions to the north of the Shang are identified with the *Rong* (戎) tribe, and those to the northwest with the *Qiang* (羌). Bronze Age societies in the Sichuan basin are identified with the *Ba* (巴) and the *Shu* (蜀), and in Lingnan with the *Yue* (越) people. All these different groups are mentioned in historical texts, but as argued in Chapter 1, such labels are both anachronistic and can contaminate our understanding of the archaeological record with later biases. Therefore, I avoid using these names here, and rely exclusively on an analysis of archaeological data.

Models of Interregional Interaction

Possible explanations for artifacts found outside of their original context, or for similarities between artifacts produced in areas far removed from one another, include diffusion, exchange, and trade. These mechanisms are significant in the case of the pre-state societies referred to in previous chapters and could be relevant for the interactions discussed here as well. With the rise of the state, however, we must also consider the possibility that interactions were shaped by differences in the sociopolitical, economic, and technological levels of the interacting partners.

Economic imbalance between regions is a key issue in evaluating models that suggest processes of exploitation and interdependency. Since the 1980s, one of the more popular versions of such models among archaeologists has been a simplified adaptation of Immanuel Wallerstein's "world system" model. Originally developed to explain the development of the present-day capitalist world, this model describes a multipolity interregional system in which underdeveloped peripheries are created for the benefit of the developed center. The center of this system is a technologically advanced society that is able, through unbalanced trade relations, to

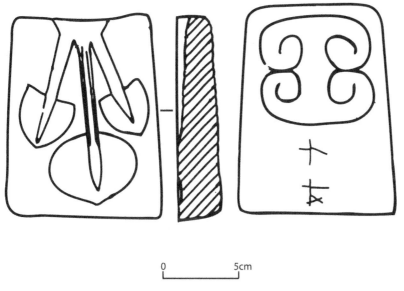

0   5cm

Figure 173. A bivalve casting mold from the Yuanlongpo cemetery, Wuming county, Guangxi (after Pigott and Ciarla 2007: 83).

economically exploit the less developed peripheral areas. The main premise of this exploitation mechanism is a global division of labor in which the periphery provides cheap labor and raw materials, while the center produces costly, technologically advanced objects and provides technological and economic expertise.

What makes the world system model attractive to many archaeologists is not so much the details of the model, which are not always applicable to precapitalist societies, but rather the more general notion of systemic but unequal interconnections between distant societies. Because the Shang polity is seen as a more advanced political and economic entity than its neighbors, models based on the concept of center and periphery are commonly used to explain the geopolitical and economic landscape of this period. For example, Liu and Chen (2003) have interpreted contact between what they see as the core and periphery during this period as evidence of a tributary system under the hegemony of the Shang territorial state. To test this model we should look for archaeological evidence that (1) the societies of the so-called center were

more advanced than those at the periphery in at least some aspects of their political, economic, or cultural makeup; and (2) interactions between the center and its periphery(s) reflect the center's dominance of the periphery and the benefits the center derives from such contacts.

According to some reconstructions, a unique type of "center-and-periphery" system evolved between pastoral and agricultural societies on the northern borders of the Shang. Because, as many have argued, people cannot support themselves solely on pastoral products, pastoral groups would have needed to supplement their diet with grains obtained from other societies (Cribb 1991: 13–14; Khazanov 1983). This paradigm leads to the assumption that the adoption of pastoralism as a way of life by societies on the northern frontiers of China led to their dependency on the agricultural products of Chinese societies to their south. However, for this model to be applicable to the second half of the second millennium and the beginning of the first millennium BCE, two related questions must be addressed: (1) Did societies on the northern frontiers of the Shang (and

Western Zhou) in fact make the transition to pastoralism? (2) Were these societies indeed unable to grow grain and produce the other agricultural products they needed on their own?

Economic Adaptation of Societies in Northeast and Northwest China

According to a commonly held view, a transition from sedentary agricultural societies to mobile pastoralism during the late second and early first millennia BCE shaped the socioeconomic landscape of the northern frontier region, forming the historic boundaries between the "steppe and the sown." This view has been shaped by much later descriptions of peoples living on the northern frontiers of China. An example of such a description can be found in the writings of the famous historian, Ban Gu (班固, 32–92 CE): "The people of the Yi and Di are greedy and seek profit.... Their food and drinks are not the same [as ours].... They follow their herds across the grasslands, and hunt for living."[2] This and other similar descriptions clearly made an impression on ancient and modern scholars, but we should try to avoid projecting the situation at the beginning of the first millennium CE back onto an earlier formative period. Instead, we need to analyze the archaeological record for concrete evidence about the economic adaptation of these societies.

Increased dependency on herding animals and a transition to a more nomadic way of life (though not necessarily full-scale pastoralism) seem to taken place earlier and more completely in the western part of the northern frontiers than in the central or eastern areas. The scarcity of domestic sites dated to the late second and early first millennia BCE in the western part of the northern frontiers is an *argumentum ex silentio* for a transition to a mobile way of life, which may have been associated with an emphasis on pastoralism.

Only a few grains of domesticated plants have been reported from sites of the Kayue period, but it is unclear whether that lack of data in fact reflects a nonagriculturalist society, as claimed by some (e.g., Shui 2001: 292). Excavations at the Kayue site of Fengtai (丰台) in the eastern part of Qinghai province recovered substantial amounts of domesticated grain from plants such as barley, wheat, and foxtail millet (Zhongguo 2004: 87–9). These findings illustrate the relatively advanced agricultural methods practiced by the people of the Fengtai community, but they also suggest that the deployment of advanced archaeological recovering techniques – such as the flotation method used by the excavators of this site – would probably result in comparable findings at other sites as well.

Animal bones found at sites ascribed to the Kayue culture seem to indicate an increased reliance on herding in comparison to previous periods. At the Dahuazhongzhuang cemetery in Qinghai, 64 percent of the 525 animal bones found in Kayue period graves come from sheep or goats, 15.2 percent are from cattle, and 20 percent are from horses. Only one pig skeleton and one dog bone, along with two bones from wild animals, were recovered (Qinghai 1985: 28–33). Such predominance of herding animals is suggestive.

In the central part of the northern frontier zone, in the Ordos region, the cultivation of grains is traditionally considered the main economic activity. Although grains have not been found in any site in this region, more than two hundred storage pits identified at Zhukaigou (Neimenggu 2000: 40) may possibly support this assumption.

It has been proposed that a transition to a more specialized pastoralist economy took place during phase V of the Zhukaigou site (Linduff 1998: 642), but this is not supported by the data. In fact, many of the storage pits at Zhukaigou are dated to the later phases of occupation. Moreover, very few animal bones have been recovered from graves and strata belonging to this phase, and the proportion of sheep or goat bones is lower than that of pig bones, not much different to earlier phases at the site (Huang Yunping 2000: 401–2). It would, thus, seem that the later phases of occupation at Zhukaigou represent a sedentary agricultural population. However, since no other contemporaneous sites and only a few later sites are known from this region, it is possible that other communities in the Ordos region had become much more mobile and relied on pastoralism for their livelihood.

The economic trajectory of societies in northeast China was quite different from those in the northwest. Agricultural production in this region seems to have continued on a relatively large scale during the Upper Xiajiadian period. Evidence of large-scale agricultural production includes storage pits excavated at many sites, which indicate the continuation of grain storage and consumption. Stone implements found at Upper Xiajiadian sites, for example, axes and hoes possibly used to clear agricultural fields, and pestles and mortars used to grind cereals, provide further evidence. Results from the flotation of earth samples from test excavations at two sites containing both Lower and Upper Xiajiadian strata in the Chifeng survey area suggest that millet production and consumption continued during the Upper Xiajiadian at more or less the same scale as during the Lower Xiajiadian (Chifeng 2011).

Sheep and goat bones are more commonly found in Upper Xiajiadian sites than in earlier sites in the Chifeng region, though still at much lower rates than in sites farther to the west. At Dashanqian (大山前), 59.9 percent of the 162 bone fragments attributed to the Upper Xiajiadian period are pig bones, 12.96 percent are dog bones, 12.96 percent are sheep or goat bones, and 11.73 percent are bones from cattle. Only two horse and two deer bones were found. Although these findings suggest continuity in economic patterns from the Lower Xiajiadian period at this site, the sample is rather small and may be contaminated with Lower Xiajiadian materials (Wang 2004). More reliable data were obtained in excavations of the Guandongche (关东车) site, to the north of the Chifeng region.

Here 32.2 percent of the 31 animals whose remains were identified were sheep or goats, 25 percent were pigs, 19.2 percent were cattle, and 16.2 percent were dogs. In addition, the bones of one horse and one wild animal were found at Guandongche (Zhu 2004: 433). This profile suggests a mixed agriculturalist-pastoralist economy.

Some of the bronze tools – found so ubiquitously in sites of the Upper Xiajiadian and in contemporaneous sites elsewhere in the northern frontiers zone – may be associated with pastoralist activity. Bronze knives might have been used for slaughtering animals and processing hides. Indeed, some scholars argue that the prevalence of animal motifs in the decorations of bronzes from the northeast (and the northwest) corresponds with the increased importance of animal herding to the economy of the societies that inhabited this region during the first millennium BCE (Wu 2002b: 437–8).

Taken together, though, the data suggest that rather than a swift or universal transition to a pastoral-nomadic way of life, the northern frontiers of the Shang were populated by a mosaic of societies characterized by different combinations of pastoral and agricultural economies. It is highly unlikely that, even in the western parts of this region, societies specialized in pastoralism to such an extent that they could not have produced their own grain or acquired them from a nearby society. This varied economic landscape, furthermore, precludes the possibility that these societies were economically dependent on the Shang or the early Zhou.

Economic Exchange and Interregional Interaction

Of all the industries of the Shang and early Zhou, metallurgy probably generated the highest demand for external resources. The scale of this industry exceeded anything seen before in China, and was at the time probably the largest industry in the world. If the accumulated weight of the bronze artifacts placed in a medium-sized grave like Fuhao's exceeded 1.5 metric tons, we can only imagine how much more was placed in the larger graves of the Shang elite and kings, or in the Shang's temples and ritual sites. Maintaining this industry would have required a constant supply of large quantities of copper, tin, and lead. Where these large quantities of metals were obtained and how they reached the centers of bronze production are crucial questions for researchers of the Shang and early Zhou. They are also extremely relevant to our understanding of other societies, such as Sanxingdui, which also produced large amounts of bronze artifacts.

Some of the copper used in the Bronze industry may have been mined locally, but the rest could have been imported into the Shang from the ore-rich areas of the middle and lower Yangzi River basin. As discussed earlier, two extensive copper mines – at Tongling and Tonglüshan – operated in this area during the Bronze Age. Excavations at these sites, as well as twenty other sites in the region, yielded extensive testimony to the smelting of copper ores, probably in the production of metal ingots that could have then been transported to production centers. The size and organization of the Tongling and Tonglüshan sites suggest a state-level operation. However, as noted earlier in this chapter, they were more likely to have been under the control of a local polity than the Shang. Production and exchange on such a large scale could have been one of the catalysts for the development of states in the middle and lower Yangzi region. These states, after all, were not only copper producers but also copper consumers on a large scale, as is exemplified by findings at the Xin'gan grave.

The sources of the tin and lead used in the bronze industry are more obscure than in the case of copper. Shang bronzes are remarkable for their high tin content. Of the ninety-five bronze vessels, tools, and weapons in the Fuhao tomb whose chemical composition was tested, most contained around 15 percent tin, with some containing 20

percent or more (Zhongguo 1980: 270–5). This implies that some 150 kg of tin would have had to be imported for every ton of bronze produced in the Yinxu site. Tin is a resource that is much scarcer than copper. Today it is found in the hills of south and southwest China, but it is possible that some tin resources existed closer to the Shang centers in the Yellow River basin and were depleted during ancient times (Underhill 2002: 231). Nonetheless, it is probable that at least some of the large demand for tin was met from other sources.

Studies of the lead content in Erligang and Yinxu period vessels have identified a rare radiogenic isotope that is common in vessels from sites in the north and the Yangzi River basin, including Sanxingdui (Jin 2003), thereby suggesting a common source of lead, and perhaps of tin across these regions. One possible source of tin and lead are the rich ores of northeastern Yunnan, where the same radiogenic isotope is also found. This possibility, however, in turn raises many fundamental questions: How were large quantities of metals transported over such great distances? What were the mechanisms of this trade, and who controlled it? The fact that bronze producing societies in the Sichuan basin, the middle and lower Yangzi River, and the Yellow River basins may have all used tin and lead from the same source might suggest that metals from west China were transported along the Yangzi River and from there, together with the local copper resources, to the Yellow River area. However, there is currently no concrete evidence of the large-scale mining of tin and lead ores in the Yunnan area during this period. The low socioeconomic level of local societies in Yunnan during this period seems to further, albeit indirectly, refute the possibility of large-scale mining during this period.

Many archaeologists believe that while the Shang and early Zhou polities did not manage the production of tin, they were at least able to control the network that transported it to their centers in the north. An important cornerstone of this hypothesis is the location of Panlongcheng deep in the middle Yangzi River area. As noted previously, some scholars interpret this as evidence of the Early Shang polity's direct political control over the middle Yangzi basin (Chang 1980: 303–9), while others believe that Panlongcheng was an outpost of the Shang (Underhill 2002: 230). That this outpost (or fort) was responsible for securing the inflow of materials, especially tin, to the Shang center, is a reasonable hypothesis, albeit one that has not yet been proved.

However, this center-oriented picture of Bronze Age exchange in metals and bronze production does not tell the entire story. While the Shang and early Zhou were undoubtedly centers of bronze production and consumption, they were not the only such centers. Contact between these multiple other centers – unmediated by the Shang – can be seen, for example in the features of the bronzes found in the two pits at Sanxingdui: these features suggest that influences from the Yellow River region filtered into the Sichuan basin over a long period of time, but were not very intensive during the heyday of the Sanxingdui culture. In fact, contact with the bronze producing cultures of the middle and lower Yangzi River seems to have been much more intensive than with the Shang polity. Of the twenty-two bronze vessels found in the two pits, twenty are "amphora-shaped" (*zun*, *lei*, and *hu*); while none are of the type favored in the Yellow River basin, these same types were also popular among societies in the middle Yangzi area and Han River valley. The fact that some of the Sanxingdui vessels were found filled with cowrie shells suggests the development of a ritual system that was markedly different from that of the Shang, but which was possibly shared with various polities located in the upper and middle Yangzi basin region (Falkenhausen 2003: 213–16).

Further evidence of interregional contact that was not controlled or mediated by the Shang can be found in the stylistic similarities between the bronze human head statue of the Xin'gan grave and bronze masks from Chenggu (城固), in Shaanxi (Figure 174). These similarities suggest contact between the polities of the Yangzi River basin and their counterparts in the Wei River basin (Bagley 1999: 179–80).

Other types of economic resources – salt is a good example – were probably exploited and distributed on a more limited regional scale. The salt consumed at the center of the Late Shang polity was probably sourced from the coastal area of Shandong. Indeed, evidence of salt production has been identified in many sites in the region (Shandong et al. 2010). The title "petty officer for salt" (*luxiaochen* 卤小臣) found in oracle bone inscriptions suggests that the acquisition and distribution of salt, and perhaps its production too, were a state enterprise. In the middle Yangzi River area, Zhongba (中壩) evolved as a specialized salt production site. Salt from Zhongba was probably distributed to the centers in the middle Yangzi River region and in the Sichuan basin, even if these centers did not control the production, which was carried out by the local Zhongba population (Flad 2011: 224–7).

In contrast with expectations based on the world system model, I do not see any evidence that the Shang, or other contemporaneous polities, economically exploited large regions. Some resources, such as metals, were certainly transported over large distances, but it is doubtful that the Shang had any direct control over the production of metal ingots or their transportation to the Shang center. Salt may represent an intermediate case whereby the Shang and other polities could control transportation but not production. The agricultural production required to support the political system and the large populations at the polities' centers was probably under more direct control. Nonetheless, each polity was able to control agricultural production and the distribution of agricultural products only in areas immediately surrounding its political centers.

The geopolitical situation during this period is best described as a mosaic of medium- and small-scale states, each in control of the basic economic system around its centers and interacting with other states to form political coalitions and in order to exchange materials and artifacts. Interactions within this elite network were more intensive than during previous periods, the volume of materials transported was sometimes quite large, and moreover the interactions included wars and coercion on a larger scale. However, as was the case during the third and early second millennia BCE, the elite gift exchange network remained a dynamic mode of interaction (Underhill and Fang 2004).

Other Types of Exchange and Interregional Interaction

Economic resources were not the only things imported to the Shang and other contemporaneous polities from the outside. Other goods that we know of are mostly prestigious goods and rare materials, such as cowrie shells, lacquer, jade, turquoise, and other semiprecious stones. These artifacts and materials, which were already part of the earlier interregional network, continued to play a part in the new elite-exchange system. For example, some of the jade artifacts found at the Fuhao grave resemble artifacts produced in northeast China, while others are more typical of the lower Yangzi area. The import of finished jade objects is mentioned specifically in several inscriptions, including one carved on a jade dagger-axe, which describes five similar objects that had been sent from a place named *Lu* (卢) (Zhongguo 1980: 135–9). Likewise, similarities in the form and quality of raw materials between some of the jade objects found at the Xin'gan grave and objects from Yinxu suggest that Shang jades were imported into the Yangzi River region.

The exchange of finished bronze artifacts must have followed the same patterns as those of jades. For example, Shang-style bronze vessels found in northeast China, on the one hand, and northern bronzes such as the typical bronze knives found in Shang graves at Yinxu, on the other, could have been exchanged within this elite network. The political and ritual system of the Shang generated a demand for new kinds of artifacts as well. For example, great quantities of turtle shells and cattle scapula were needed for the daily divination rituals performed by the Shang king. Research from the 1940s estimated that the vast amount of turtle shell fragments in the inscribed and uninscribed oracle bones excavated at Yinxu came from at least sixteen thousand complete turtle plastrons. Because the species of turtle used were not indigenous to the Yinxu region, they must have been imported from the south (Chang 1980: 155). Indeed, oracle bone inscriptions describe the presentation of large amounts of turtle shells, sometimes up to a thousand in one shipment, as tribute to the Shang court from neighboring polities (Keightley 1999: 281). Unfortunately, the inscriptions do not tell us what was given in return for those shells, or how the neighboring people were persuaded to send tribute to the Shang.

It is probably not coincidental that at the same time as the Shang were importing large quantities of turtle shells from their southern neighbors, oracle bone divination (or pyromancy) was becoming popular in the Yangzi River basin. By the late third and early second millennia BCE, pyromancy became widespread among societies of north China, but there is no evidence of the practice in the Yangzi River basin until the second half of the second millennium BCE. In this region, turtle plastrons were the most common material used for divination. Hundreds of such plastrons were found at the Zhongba site, for example, and others are known from the lower Yangzi region. In Sichuan too, at sites of the Sanxingdui culture,

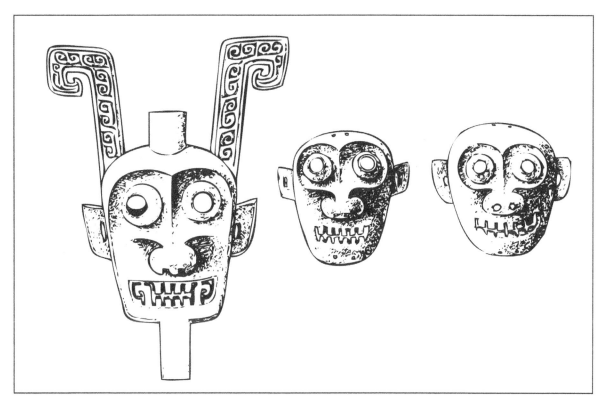

Figure 174. Bronze depictions of human heads from Xin'gan (left) and Chenggu (two on the right) (after Bagley 1999: 180).

turtle shells were the main medium for pyromancy (Flad 2008).

Livestock was another commodity Shang elite had to acquire from far away. Horses were probably obtained from regions to the northwest. In the Shang court, domesticated horses were probably valued for their size and bright colors and, together with chariots, they were used as display objects that symbolized the power and prestige of the Shang kings and higher echelons of the elite. Oracle bone inscriptions describe tributes of horses from neighboring polities – the horses' colors were sometimes mentioned – as well as horses that were captured in war (Keightley 1999: 280; Linduff 2003).

Among the more exotic animals that the oracle bone inscriptions mention being hunted are elephants and rhinoceroses. Because these beasts were never indigenous to north China, it has been suggested that they were brought from the southwest and kept in a "royal menagerie" (Keightley 2000: 111). Ivory, used by the Shang to produce exquisite goblets (Figure 148), may have been a by-product of this practice.

Another type of "livestock" that the Shang needed was victims for human sacrifices. As discussed earlier, the scale of human sacrifice – as mentioned in oracle bone inscriptions and found in sacrificial pits and other contexts – positions the Shang as one of the most excessive human-sacrificing polities in world history. The oracle bone inscriptions name most of the humans victims as "Qiang" (羌), most probably not the name of a specific tribe, but a general label for non-Shang people living to the northwest of the Shang centers (Shelach 1996). In some inscriptions the Qiang are mentioned as being given to the Shang court as gifts or tributes (Keightley 1999: 281), but in most cases it seems that military expeditions were organized in order to capture these victims in regions to the west and northwest of the Shang. This combination of oppressive power, political domination, and exchange – more dominant perhaps in the case of horses and turtle shells than in that of human victims – may be typical of the Shang's interregional network.

Effects of Interregional Interactions

The evidence suggests that by the second half of the second millennium BCE, the political landscape of China was composed of several states and pre-state societies. State-level polities interacted with the less complex societies in their vicinity and, to a degree, were able to dominate them. However, as seen in the oracle bone inscriptions, these smaller societies were not completely dependent on the Shang and could, in some cases at least, develop into distinct polities of their own. By the thirteenth century BCE, if not earlier, various state-level centers appear to have been interacting among themselves on a relatively equal basis, exchanging resources, information, and cultural attributes.

What were the effects of such networks of interaction? Clearly, they benefited the leaders of the state-level polities, who were able to obtain through these networks basic resources needed for their state-run industries, as well as various exotic materials and artifacts that bolstered their prestige and legitimated their dominant positions. On the other hand, such networks also provided individuals and groups of less complex societies with an opportunity to gain power and prestige. This may have been the case, for example, for societies in the middle Yangzi basin, where local leaders used their control of metallurgic resources – as

well as their control over exchange with the upper Yangzi basin, perhaps – to expand their power vis-à-vis the local population and their Shang counterparts.

On a broader cultural level, we can discern two parallel processes that are related to the intensification of interregional interactions: (1) the diffusion of cultural traits and the leveling of the cultural landscape across a large region and (2) the selective adaptation of external cultural traits into the local culture and the sharpening of unique local beliefs and rituals. An example of the first process can be found in the spread of oracle bone divination. Following a long period of slow diffusion among societies in north China, by Shang times, not only was pyromancy practiced among societies throughout China, but there was also a common movement toward the elaboration and standardization of the practice. Nonetheless, there remained much variation, especially at sites outside the realm of the Shang. In at least one known example – that of the oracle bones found at the Zhouyuan sites of Fengchu (鳳雛) and Qijiacun (齊家村), in Shaanxi – the spread of oracle bone divination was accompanied by the spread of the Shang writing system (Flad 2008), a phenomenon that may be seen as the beginning of the development of a unified Chinese script.

The selective adoption of external traits is exemplified in our discussion of Sanxingdui. Although a number of cultural traits, such as techniques (bronze casting), vessel shapes, and decoration motifs, can be traced to external origins, they are integrated into a coherent system that is uniquely local. This culture was probably formed through a long process that started during the Late Neolithic, when the functions of external elements were altered to suit local customs and needs. This was probably not a one-directional process; Shang and Zhou societies were also on the receiving end. For example, bronze bells, which first became important in the middle Yangzi River basin, were adopted by societies in the Yellow River basin and became one of the hallmarks of the Western Zhou civilization.

LONG-RANGE INTERACTIONS

In contrast to earlier periods, when interactions with distant regions were sporadic, we have much more evidence of long-range interactions during the second half of the second millennium and the beginning of the first millennium BCE. Some see this as one of the foremost factors influencing sociocultural developments in China. For example, the Russian archaeologist Elena Kuzmina has argued that the late second millennium BCE was an epoch of large-scale migratory movements in the Eurasian Steppes, which "were necessitated by demographic causes – population pressure – and intensified by climatic crisis" (Kuzmina 1998: 72). She also sees this as a period when intensive Western influences shaped Chinese civilization (Kuzmina 1998: 65).

While I do not agree with such "diffusionist" interpretations, the evidence is important enough to merit serious consideration. In some cases, the evidence of long-range interaction during the Bronze Age indicates the continuation of patterns already established during the Late Neolithic and incipient Bronze Age. Cowrie shells, for example, continued to be valued in areas far from their natural habitat in the warm ocean waters of south China and the Indian Ocean. The 6,820 cowrie shells found in the Fuhao grave (Zhongguo 1980: 15) suggest that they were now being transported in much greater quantities. Moreover, inscriptions on several Shang bronze vessels are interpreted as proof of trade in cowrie shells (Underhill and Fang 2004: 138). The consumption of cowrie shells was not unique to the Shang: more than 4,500 cowrie shells were found inside the two Sanxingdui pits, and they were also found in Neolithic and Bronze Age sites in Yunnan (Yao 2010), suggesting that this was one possible route through which they were transported from the Indian Ocean to the Yangzi

and Yellow River basins. The same route, from Yunnan and Sichuan through the middle Yangzi, could have also been used for the import of tin to the centers in the Yellow River basin.

A connection to the west is also indicated by the eighty intact elephant tusks found in the Sanxingdui pits. While it was suggested that wild elephants may have still roamed the Sichuan area during this period, the large number of tusks found there and at Jinsha suggest that at least some had been imported from tropical areas to the west and south of Sichuan.

More significant, perhaps, are the long-range interactions that brought new technologies and ideas to state centers in China. The introduction of chariots into China is the best known example of this kind of long-distant contact. Chariots, or any wheeled vehicle for that matter, are unknown in the Yellow River basin prior to their full-blown appearance in sacrificial pits at the Late Shang center of Yinxu, where they are dated to ca. 1250 BCE (Figure 175). Because much earlier chariots are known from Central Asia – the earliest dated so far are those of the Sintashta-Petrovka culture in modern-day Kazakhstan, dated to ca. 2000–1800 BCE – and because of the technological and stylistic similarities between the chariots of Central Asia and those found at Yinxu, it is generally agreed that the Yinxu chariots reflect the transmission of a new technology from the west into the Yellow River basin (Anthony and Vinogradov 1995).

The appearance of chariots represents the advent of a new very complex technology involving many challenging aspects (e.g., the construction of light but strong wheels, the harnessing of the horses so that the power is most effectively transmitted) and collaboration between different types of industry (carpentry, bronze casting, ornamentation). It also entails the mastery of new and diverse realms of knowledge, such as charioteering and horse grooming. How such a complex range of interrelated technologies and areas of expertise was transmitted over thousands of kilometers of

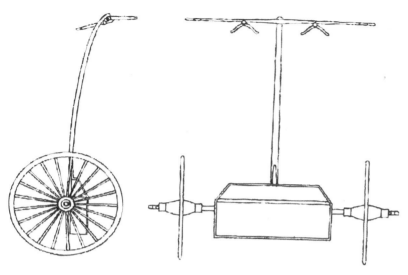

Figure 175. Reconstruction of a Shang chariot (after Guo 1998: 49).

very difficult terrain remains unclear. Nonetheless, this should be viewed not as an isolated case, but rather in the context of a much wider array of intensified contact between societies in present-day China and their counterparts in Mongolia and Central Asia, and all the way west to Eastern Europe (Shelach 2009). The most abundant evidence of such interactions is found in the bronze tools and weapons of a unique "northern" style found in northeast China (and to a lesser extent in the northwest) and in Shang elite contexts. These artifacts are closely related through their shape and style to artifacts found throughout the Eurasian Steppes.

One illustration of this is the distribution of one of the more diagnostic types of northern bronze artifacts – knives with animal heads, animal figures, or jingles attached to the top of their hilt (Figure 176) – the largest concentration of such artifacts in China is found in the northeast (the Chifeng region and Western Liaoning). Some were also found in northwest Hebei and northern Shaanxi, in sites such as Chaodaogou (抄道沟) Yantou-cun (燕头村). However, no such artifacts have been found in areas farther to the west, in Gansu or Qinghai. Very similar objects were also found

in graves from the Late Shang period, such as in the Fuhao tomb, but they seem to have been brought to the Yellow River region from the outside. Beyond the present-day borders of China, comparable knives are known from areas in northern Mongolia, the Karasuk culture of Minusinsk basin, and even west of the Ural Mountains in cemeteries of the Seima-Turbino complex.

In the Shang context, there is a clear association of such artifacts with chariots, suggesting that the two phenomena are linked. Sacrifice victims found inside the chariot pits were also often buried with bronze knives with animal heads, as well as with the "bow-shaped" bronze artifacts that may also have been of northern origin (Figure 177). This association suggests that non-Shang people from one of the regions to the north were present in the Shang center, perhaps providing workers such as chariot drivers, horse grooms, or even chariot builders.

It is interesting to note that the distribution of "northern style" artifacts links the Eurasian Steppes to northeast China through a northern route that passes along the borders between the steppe and the forest zones of Central Asia (Figure 178), suggesting therefore that chariots were

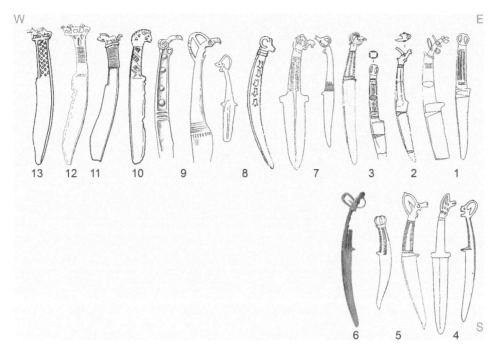

Figure 176. Knives with animal heads from different sites in the Northern Zone, north China, and the Eurasian Steppes. 1. Wenliu, Liaoning; 2. Chaoyang, Liaoning; 3. Chifeng, Inner Mongolia; 4. Anynag, Henan; 5. Chaodaogou, Hebei; 6. Yantoucun, Shaanxi; 7. Bayantala, Mongolia; 8. Transbikalia; 9. Karasuk; 10. Elunino, Russia; 11. Rostovka, Russia; 12. Turbino, Russia; 13. Seima, Russia (after Shelach 2009: 128).

introduced into China via the eastern part of the Northern Zone and not via its western part, as has commonly been assumed (Barbieri-Low 2000: 45–7). However, this does not preclude the existence of other more western routes of interaction, through the Gansu corridor, which connected societies in the Yellow and Wei River basins with their counterparts in Central Asia. Socketed weapons and other types of bronze artifacts associated with the Karasuk culture, for example, were also found in Xinjiang and in northwest China (Mei 2000: 28–9).

Contact with Central or even Western Asia during the Shang and early Zhou was not limited to the transfer of technologies (chariots) and the shapes of bronze objects. For instance, carnelian beads found in Bronze Age graves in China provide additional evidence of these interactions. In contrast to chariots and bronzes, which were locally produced using foreign styles and expertise, it is

clear that carnelian was imported from its natural sources in Western Asia. Early evidence of such imports is found in late second millennium BCE graves, but the majority of finds are from Western Zhou graves in the Wei River and Yellow River basins. It appears that at around this time some of the beads, such as the large biconical beads (about 3.5 cm in length), were imported as finished artifacts from Mesopotamia, where such artifacts are well documented (Rawson 2008).

What were the effects of such long-range interactions? Their immediate effect on the Shang and Zhou societies in the main river basins probably lay in the realm of display and prestige. As Shaughnessy (1988) has demonstrated, during the Shang, chariots were used for display and hunting rather than in warfare. In these contexts they were probably instrumental in elevating the prestige of the Shang kings and helped legitimize their position, though without contributing directly to their

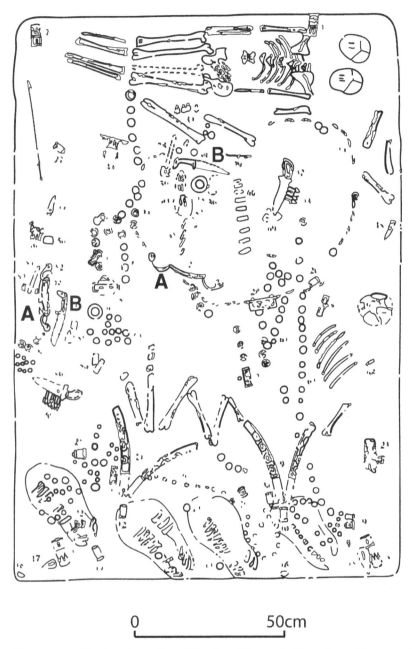

Figure 177. Chariot pit 20 from Xiaodun, Yinxu. A. Bow-shaped bronze objects; B. Knives with animal heads (after Guo 1998: 45).

military strength. It took hundreds of years, probably not until the second part of the Western Zhou, for the military potential of this innovation to be realized. By the Spring and Autumn period (770–453 BCE), however, chariots were considered the most important and advanced military technology of the Zhou states, so much so that the power of a state was expressed in the number of chariots it possessed and could deploy in battle. It is also reasonable to assume that other types of

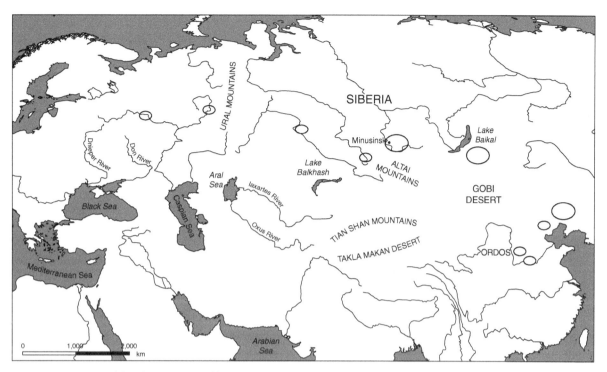

Figure 178. Map of the distribution of knives with animal heads.

vehicles, such as chariots and carts for transporting people and goods, were modeled after the Shang and Zhou chariots. It would therefore be more correct to view the introduction of chariots (and by extension, other foreign technologies) not as a one-directional and one-off event, but rather as an ongoing process of selection and modification by the receiving societies.

A different pattern of long-range interaction is embodied by finds in south China. Late Shang and Western Zhou bronzes were circulating in the Lingnan region, albeit in small numbers. The two vessels found at the Yuanlongpo cemetery and a few others known as stray finds from the Lingnan area (Ciarla 2007) may have arrived there, directly or indirectly, from the state-level centers of the Yangzi region, in exchange for prestigious Lingnan materials (for example, pearls and colorful birds feathers). Their consumption, however, was not associated with the position of chiefly leaders, as it was in northeast China. This is perhaps because

unlike in the northeast, where stratified society had emerged as early as in the Lower Xiajiadian period (ca. 2200–1600 BCE) if not earlier, comparable stratified societies are unknown in the Lingnan region. It is also possible that the interaction input in the Lingnan area was not powerful enough to spark significant sociopolitical change in the local societies. Indeed, during the subsequent period, when interactions with the Chu state intensified, the contact seems to have catalyzed the development of chiefly polities in Lingnan.

The long-term cultural and technological consequences may have been more substantial than the limited short-term effects. Evidence of the local production of small bronze implements, such as arrowheads, axes, and fishhooks, which are contemporaneous with the import into Lingnan of Shang and Zhou bronzes, suggests that the two phenomena are linked. Moreover, it is possible that Lingnan was the route through which bronze technology from the north filtered through to large regions in Southeast Asia, where it was adopted and developed to fit local needs and tastes (Ciarla 2007).

More significant than the exact route or routes of these interactions is the fact that what we see here is neither a world system model of interaction, nor a southward wave of diffusion with the wholesale adoption of the northern technocultural complex by local societies in the Lingnan and beyond. On the contrary, the archaeological data suggest the continuation of local cultures, and the adaptation of external technology in a way that was tailored to fit local needs. For instance, the composite mold technique – the hallmark of the northern bronze industry – was not adopted in Lingnan, where far simpler bivalve molds were used instead. The artifacts cast were also very different: not the ritual vessels used in the north to legitimate the state-level system, but rather small utilitarian artifacts used not very differently from similar artifacts made of stone. While the technology was certainly new, and its introduction into Lingnan and southeast Asia should be seen as an important development that affected the local social and economic structures of the region over the long run, this small-scale and utilitarian industry did not entail immediate changes, but rather allowed the foreign technology to be gradually integrated into the existing socioeconomic system.

Tarim Basin "Mummies" and East-West Contact during the Bronze Age

It is rare for the fame of an archaeological discovery to extend beyond narrow academic circles. However, the so-called mummies of the Tarim have done just that, with their photos appearing on the pages of popular magazines and on television news programs. Like that of "Ötzi the Iceman" from the Alps, this fame was triggered by the moving experience of a face-to-face encounter with perfectly preserved ancient corpses. The explorer Aurel Stein, one of the first to see well-preserved ancient corpses in the Tarim region, vividly described the experience: "It was not without a strange emotion that I looked down on a figure which, but for the parched skin and the deep-sunk eye cavities, seemed like that of a man asleep."[3]

The use of the term "mummies" in both popular and academic publications creates a slight misunderstanding. Unlike the ancient Egyptians, who intentionally mummified corpses so as to preserve them better, the ancient Tarim population did not treat their dead in this way. Rather, the corpses, along with their clothes and grave goods, have been perfectly preserved for thousands of years because of the dry conditions and extreme temperatures of the region. After their burial, the bodies of the deceased underwent a rapid drying process and lost 75 percent of their weight within two months, making them immune to bacteria. It is yet unclear why, in the very same cemetery, some of the corpses are well preserved while others decomposed. One theory suggests that corpses buried during the winter are better preserved, because exposure to the extremely cold conditions killed all the bacteria naturally found in the human body.

One such perfectly preserved corpse is that of a forty-five-year-old woman found at the Tiebanhe (铁板河) site and dated to around 1000 BCE. This woman's skin and facial features are extremely well preserved, as are her felt hat and the goat wool clothes in which she is covered. Even the lice that lived on her body are well preserved. An autopsy found large amounts of sand and charcoal dust in her lungs, attesting to the effects of fire smoke and sandstorms. Another well-preserved corpse is that of a three- to six-month-old baby from the Zahongluke (扎洪鲁克) cemetery (Figure 179). Nicknamed the "baby blue," it was wrapped in colorful wool and blue stones were laid on his eyes. A drinking horn was placed on one side of his body, and a sheep's skin bag, used perhaps as a baby bottle, on the other.

Well-preserved corpses have been found in the Tarim basin and reported by explorers such as

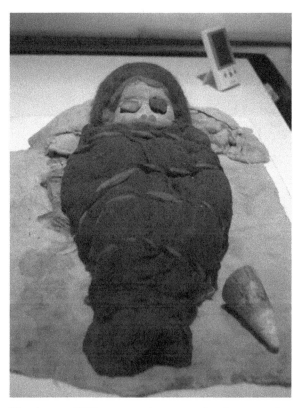

Figure 179. Well-preserved corpse of a three- to six-month-old baby from the Zahongluke cemetery (photo by Gideon Shelach).

Stein since the early years of the twentieth century, and Chinese archaeologists have been excavating them since the 1950s. They became truly world famous beginning in the 1990s, however, as a result of two factors: First, new research and advanced dating methods made it clear that some of the corpses were even older than previously suggested, contemporaneous with the formative period of Chinese states in the second millennium BCE. Second, the fact that many of these early corpses had light colored hair and Caucasoid facial features has prompted many researchers, especially in the West, to argue that the knowledge and technologies imported by these populations had a crucial impact on the formation of Chinese civilization. Furthermore, some researchers have argued that these were Indo-Iranian-speaking people, and more specifically the Tocharian people (Mallory and Mair 2000).

Much of the debate over the mummies, their ethnic and cultural identity, and their impact on the development of Chinese civilization is politically motivated. For example, the Uighurs, a Turkic ethnic group currently living in the Tarim region, claim the ancient corpses as their ancestors, while Chinese authorities have tried to downplay their non-Chinese traits. Even some of the more academic arguments are not very well founded. Judging from the artifacts found in graves dated to the second millennium BCE, the Tarim population did not possess any knowledge or technology not already present in the Yellow River region. For example, there is no evidence in the Tarim of the early use of metal or chariots. Moreover, while the Tarim basin is currently part of China, it is located some 2,000 km away from the centers of the Shang civilization. The Tocharian identification is equally problematic. The earliest documents in the Tocharian language found in this region date to the seventh to tenth centuries CE, more than two thousand years after the Tarim mummies lived and died.

Nevertheless, research on the Tarim corpses promises to generate interesting insights into population movements and long-range interactions. For example, studies of ancient DNA will undoubtedly shed new light on the origins of these populations. Moreover, not all well-preserved corpses in this region are dated to the Bronze Age. Studies of less ancient corpses are relevant to an understanding of the development of international contact and trade routes during the imperial era.

THE SOCIETIES AND CULTURES OF THE ZHOU PERIOD: PROCESSES OF GLOBALIZATION AND THE GENESIS OF LOCAL IDENTITIES

The Zhou period, which lasted from ca. 1050 BCE through to imperial unification in 221 BCE, is well documented in both transmitted texts and paleographic sources. The pertinent data are so rich and the changes that took place during these eight centuries so profound that even a whole book could not deal adequately with Zhou history and archaeology.[1] Here, more than in any other chapter of this book, I make no effort to summarize the range of available data or to address all of the key research issues. While some of the basic features of the archaeology of the Zhou are of course presented here, the chapter focuses on topics that continue the themes addressed in previous chapters, such as the continued development of social complexity and changes in the sociopolitical structure of society. We pay special attention to the increased "globalization" of the Zhou realm on the one hand, and the genesis of clearly distinct local cultures and identities on the other.

HISTORICAL BACKGROUND

The Zhou, or most precisely its early part, the so-called Western Zhou (ca. 1046–771 BCE), is traditionally regarded as the most illustrious dynasty in Chinese history and its golden age. During the Late Shang period, the Zhou were a powerful polity located in the Wei River basin, to the west of the core Shang area. According to tra-

ditional accounts, the ruling house in Zhou (the Ji 姬 clan) started out as an ally of the Shang, but their alliance came to an end because of the immoral and unjust conduct of the last Shang king, Zhouxin (紂辛). The semilegendary founder of the Zhou dynasty, King Wen (文王), was the first to challenge Zhouxin, but it was only under King Wen's son, King Wu (武王), that the pro-Zhou coalition dealt a decisive blow to the Shang armies and defeated them at a place called Muye (牧野), not far from the Shang capital, Yin. Zhouxin was killed and the Zhou quickly gained control over the Shang territories and beyond. The Zhou faced a grave crisis following the death of King Wu, when two of the late king's brothers revolted in coalition with Zhouxin's son. The rebellion, however, was broken by yet another of King Wu's brothers, the Duke of Zhou, and Zhou eventually became the longest reigning dynasty in Chinese history.

While the origins of the Zhou polity and many details of its early history are shrouded in myth, the basic framework of the narrative is largely confirmed by paleographic and archaeological sources. The Zhou polity is mentioned in the oracle bone inscriptions, first as an ally of the Shang and then as one of its adversaries (the so-called *fang* states) (Li 2008: 30), and its location in the central Wei River basin is also confirmed by archaeological findings. There is ongoing debate around the

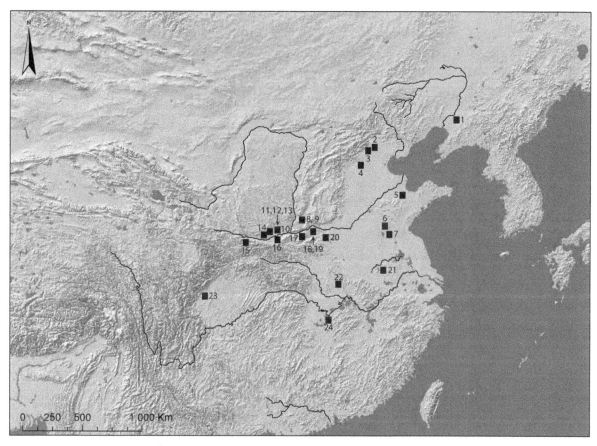

Figure 180. Location of all sites mentioned in Chapter 10: 1. Lianhuabao; 2. Liulihe; 3. Yan Xiadu; 4. Lingshou; 5. Linzi; 6. Qufu; 7. Capital city of Teng state; 8. Tianma-Qucun; 9. Xintian; 10. Xianyang; 11. Yunteng; 12. Zhougongmiao; 13. Nanzhihui; 14. Fengchu; 15. Dabuzi; 16. Yongcheng; 17. Shangcunling; 18. Chengzhou (Luoyi); 19. Wangcheng; 20. Xinzheng; 21. Qiujia Huayuan; 22. Leigudun; 23. Dujiangyan; 24. Yangjiashan.

precise dates of early events in Zhou history, that is, prior to 841 BCE, when Sima Qian began his chronological tables. The year 1046 BCE has more recently been accepted as the date of the Muye battle and the beginning of Zhou rule (Xia Shang Zhou 2000). Much of the progress in clarifying earlier stages of Zhou history was made thanks to the increasing volume of contemporaneous bronze inscriptions, which augment the sketchy data from textual sources. While the dating and reliability of historic sources remain controversial, it is widely accepted that at least some of the texts attributed to Zhou statesmen, such as the *Venerated Documents* (*Shang shu* 尚書) and *Book of Odes* (*Shijing* 詩

經), do indeed contain authentic materials about early Zhou history. Additional data are scattered throughout later texts, such as the *Zuo zhuan* (左傳) and Sima Qian's *Historical Records*.

The Zhou Administration and the Fall of the Western Zhou

The Zhou dominated a huge territory that encompassed the Wei and the middle to lower Yellow River basins, as well as parts of the Liao River basin to the northeast, and the Huai, Han, and northern reaches of the Yangzi River basins to the south. However, this territory was never directly controlled by the Zhou kings as a unified state. The kings of Zhou, who possessed the exclusive title "Sons of Heaven" (*tianzi* 天子), exercised direct control only over their royal domain, which stretched from the Wei River homeland, where their ritual center at the base of Mount Qi (岐山) and the political capital Hao (鎬) were located, to territory east of it in the middle reaches of the Yellow River, where a secondary capital, Chengzhou (成周, also known as Luoyi 洛邑), was established. This vast domain was the royal court's source of economic and military power. Areas farther to the east were ruled indirectly, through a series of fiefs granted to the king's relatives and allies, or through the royal recognition of preexisting polities and their absorption into the system of Zhou tributaries. One of the later texts claims that the Duke of Zhou granted seventy-one fiefs altogether, of which fifty-three were given to the members of the Ji clan; the eventual final number could be even higher (Figure 181). These "fiefs" were ruled by regional lords (*zhuhou* 諸侯), whose domains are sometimes described as "regional states" (Li 2008), "subordinate polities" (Falkenhausen 2006), or "colonies" (Shaughnessy 1999). The regional lords were ritually subordinate to the Zhou kings and were supposed to provide the Sons of Heaven with tribute and with military support in times of need. Royal supervisors were initially placed in some of the fiefs, but no integrated administrative system for the entire Zhou realm was ever established.

To describe the Zhou enfeoffment system, later Chinese texts often used the name *fengjian* (封建), a word that was eventually adopted as the Chinese translation of the Western term "feudalism," thereby causing much confusion (see Li 2003). Actually, the Zhou system of control outside the royal domain is better understood through the traditional term *zongfa* (宗法, "blood-relations system"). As noted, control of the regional lords was indirect and based on their familial and religious obligations toward the Sons of Heaven. In the early Western Zhou, these obligations were quite substantial: the kings could make rulers of subordinate polities relocate from one place to another, could intervene in issues of succession among regional lords, and required the lords to attend the Zhou court from time to time. The kings' exclusive access to the highest deity, Heaven, and to the deified ancestors of the Ji clan further bolstered their power.

As time passed, royal control over regional polities weakened, and they evolved into highly autonomous local polities, each with its particular administration and fixed territory (Li 2008: 235–70). As the Zhou kings suffered a series of military debacles, their prestige and actual ability to impose their will on distant subordinates weakened. More significantly, the very system of Zhou rule, in which allies and subordinates were rewarded with grants of territory and subordinate populations, could not be sustained after the initial period of territorial expansion. As the generations passed, kinship ties between the kings and some of the regional lords weakened as well, and the royal clan expanded beyond the limits within which the effective maintenance of internal solidarity was possible. Even in those polities where a Zhou elite was imposed upon the native population, the dominant process tended toward an increased "nativism" of elites and their growing identification with the local polity rather than with the Zhou center. While the Zhou kings continued to exercise religious authority, their most enduring asset, it could not compensate for the loss of actual military and economic power.

The decline of royal power was gradual and by no means unilinear. Recent archaeological studies suggest that the Zhou kings were still powerful enough during the tenth and ninth centuries BCE to initiate profound ritual reforms aimed at bolstering the sociopolitical order and strengthening the king's symbolic authority over their kin (Falkenhausen 2006: 29–73). This was not enough, though, to stop the dynasty's

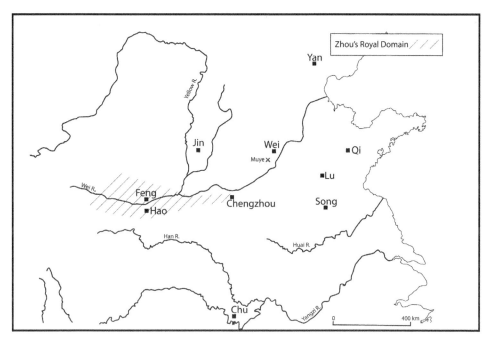

Figure 181. Map of the Western Zhou state, with area of the Royal Domain, location of the capital cities Hao (鎬), Feng (豐), and Chengzhou (成周), and the main "regional states."

gradual decline. A combination of increasing pressure from non-Zhou groups at the western, northern, and (to a lesser degree) eastern borders; conflicts between the kings and some of their regional lords; and, finally, a bitter succession struggle within the royal family together brought about the collapse of the Zhou dynasty. In 771 BCE an alliance of disgruntled regional lords and foreign invaders, the Quanrong (犬戎), overran the Zhou capital, killing the king and putting an end to Zhou rule in the Wei River basin. A new king was installed in the eastern capital of Chengzhou, inaugurating the period called the Eastern Zhou (770–221 BCE). The Zhou kings over the next five hundred years, though, never reattained their former power or glory.

The Eastern Zhou: A Multistate System

The Eastern Zhou is traditionally described as a period of moral decline and endless power struggles and wars. However, this was also the period when great Chinese thinkers (or philosophers) such as Confucius (Kongzi 孔子 ca. 551–479 BCE) and Mencius (Mengzi 孟子 ca. 379–304 BCE) set the foundations of Chinese ethical and intellectual traditions. It was also a period of great social, economic, and technological transformations, which shaped the history of China over the more than two thousand years that followed.

The Eastern Zhou is conventionally subdivided into two subperiods, the first of which is known as the Spring and Autumn period (*Chunqiu* 春秋) (770–453 BCE) and was the heyday of the multistate system. With the decline of royal authority, regional polities gained de facto independence. Their relations were marked by increased competition and warfare, but also by repeated efforts at achieving stability through diplomacy and through a common adherence to ritual norms. This age witnessed attempts to stabilize the interstate system, either through reliance on powerful "hegemons" who acted as surrogates of the Sons of Heaven and tried to impose common rules of behavior on minor polities, or through a system of alliances and periodic interstate covenants, and even two "disarmament conferences" in 546 and 541 BCE, which were aimed at achieving lasting "global peace" (Pines 2002: 105–35). Ultimately, though, these attempts were futile, and the Spring and Autumn period saw the accelerated subjugation and eventual annexation of minor polities by their powerful neighbors. As a result, the number of states in the Zhou system decreased from more than a hundred in the eighth century BCE to just about two dozen large and medium-sized polities by the mid-fifth century BCE.

The Spring and Autumn period was the golden age of the hereditary aristocracy in China. Within each state, a stratum of members of a few powerful lineages occupied all positions of importance, while the system of hereditary offices precluded outsiders from ever joining the top echelons of power holders. Economically, the aristocratic lineages relied on large hereditary allotments. The elevated position of the aristocrats was reinforced by the elaborate ritual system, the major goal of which was to maintain the hierarchy within the nobility and to preserve the nobles' supremacy over other social strata.

Competition among the aristocratic lineages, and between them and the lords (*zhuhou* 諸侯) who were the hereditary rulers of the states, precluded the formation of integrated territorial states. Rather, most of the political entities of the Spring and Autumn period were networks of autonomous settlements, with pockets between them that were inhabited at various times by non-Zhou populations. The political system remained dispersed, and state rulers were gradually losing power in much the same way as the Zhou kings centuries before. By the sixth century BCE the center of power in most polities had shifted from the regional lords to powerful aristocratic lineages.

Internal power struggles in the different states brought about one of the deepest systemic crises in China's long history. Over the Warring States

period (Zhanguo 戰國, 453–221 BCE) these loose aristocratic polities were replaced by well-integrated territorial and bureaucratic states ruled by powerful monarchs (Lewis 1999). The system of hereditary appointments and lifelong tenure in office was discontinued in favor of the flexible appointment of officials based on their merits. These officials were paid a salary in cash or grain, and were no longer granted hereditary allotments. Meanwhile, changes in agriculture (due to the widespread introduction of iron tools) and warfare (where aristocratic chariot-based armies were replaced with mass infantry armies staffed by peasant conscripts) reinvigorated the state apparatus and promoted unprecedented bureaucratic activism. The new "agro-managerial" states were able to fully utilize their economic and human resources, introducing a population census, imposing uniform laws, and, overall, exercising far tighter control over the lives of local communities than had been possible before. The activist states also mobilized their population for a variety of infrastructure projects aimed at boosting agricultural production and supporting the ever escalating military campaigns.

The bitter competition among the major states led to the progressive annihilation of weaker polities, leaving finally seven major powers to vie with each other for hegemony in the Zhou world. This world was expanding in all directions, most notably toward the southwest and the south, to encompass much of the Yangzi River basin as well as peripheral territories elsewhere (Figure 182). Ultimately, the ability to expand into the non-Zhou periphery most benefitted the states at the borders of the Zhou world, most notably Chu (楚) in the central Yangzi River basin and Qin (秦) in the Wei River basin. The latter state, Qin, emerged victorious at the end of centuries of bloody wars, conquering the other "hero-states" in 221 BCE and creating the first unified empire in Chinese history, which directly controlled all major regions of what we now call "China proper."

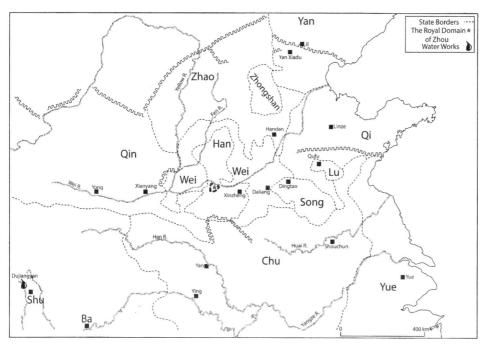

Figure 182. Map of China during the Warring States period, with the major states and the location of major "long walls."

THE ARCHAEOLOGY OF THE WESTERN AND EASTERN ZHOU

Settlements and the Development of Cities

The larger scale of political units during the Zhou period makes it difficult to design research projects, such as regional surveys, which can successfully address meaningful demographic trends. Moreover, because most of the archaeological research about this period shares the elite-oriented bias of the historical record and focuses on cemeteries of aristocratic lineages and other elite-related monuments, little is known about the lives and activities of the majority of the population, for example, their beliefs and or their distribution (Falkenhausen 2006). Nevertheless, the relevant historical records, probably based on the results of population censuses, and the existing archaeological data suggest the general trend of higher population levels in most areas and, especially dur-

ing the Eastern Zhou, the increased nucleation of the population inside large cities.

Textual analyses suggest that the cities of the Western Zhou were relatively small and served mainly as the centers of aristocratic activity. The population of these cities numbered from several hundred to several thousand families. During the Eastern Zhou, and especially by the Warring States period, cities evolved into hubs of political, economic, and cultural activity and their size increased dramatically, with the largest housing tens of thousands of families.

Unfortunately, we have little archaeological knowledge about the cities of the Western Zhou period. Excavations at the presumed locations of the capital Hao, near present-day Xian, and of the secondary capital Chengzhou, near Luoyang, did not uncover any city wall remains, and although a few pounded earth foundations were located, the structure of these buildings is unclear (Rawson 1999: 393–408; Zhongguo Shehui 2004: 54).

Evidence of city structures is equally outside of the Zhou royal domain. One of the only sites where remains of the city itself (as oppose to its cemeteries) has been found is Liulihe (琉璃河), located southwest of Beijing and identified as the capital city of the Yan state. The pounded earth city walls of Liulihe enclose a rectangular area measuring about 830 by 300 m. They are 3.5 m wide, narrower than most of the walls from previous periods, and are surrounded by a moat that was 25 m wide and 2.5 m deep. Pounded earth foundations discovered in the northern part of this enclosure were identified as belonging to "palaces," but their shape and structure are unclear. Other findings include pits, identified as the remains of the Yan nobility's ritual activities, but not much more is known about the organization of the city (Zhao and Guo 2004: 42–3).

In contrast to the paucity of domestic sites dating to the Western Zhou period, a large number of Eastern Zhou cities have been discovered. For instance, almost fifty city sites have been recorded in the area attributed to the Chu state alone (Zhongguo Shehui 2004: 227). Many of the cities we discuss later have their origins in the Spring and Autumn period, though they reached their peak of development and size during the Warring States period. Moreover, by this time, these cities were not just the capital cities of the major states, but also secondary cities and cities of minor polities. Eastern Zhou cities ranged considerably in size and in the amount of labor invested in the construction of walls, moats, and other public structures. This diversity is associated with the development of a city hierarchy related to the strength of the state to which they belong, as well as to their function and political position within the state.

As one might expect considering the complex political situation during the Eastern Zhou, the seat of the Zhou king – the "Royal City" (Wangcheng 王诚) near present-day Luoyang – was not the biggest or most glamorous city of the time. Although it boasted a rectangular enclosure covering some 9 km², with walls that were 5 to 15 m wide (Zhongguo Shehui 2004: 230–1), Wangcheng was small in comparison to many other cities from the Warring States period. One example of a much larger city is Linzi (臨淄), the capital of the state of Qi, located in northern Shandong province on the eastern bank of the Zi River (淄河). According to historic sources, the city's population during the Warring States period was somewhere between two hundred and five hundred thousand (Falkenhausen 2008). The walled area of Linzi covered some 20 km² in total, more than twice the size of Wangcheng, with pounded earth walls that were 17 to 43 m wide (Zhongguo Shehui 2004: 250). The Lower Capital of Yan (Yan Xiadu 燕下都, also known as Wuyang 武陽), in Central Hebei province, was even larger: pounded earth walls up to 60 m thick encircled an area of about 32 km² (Zhongguo Shehui 2004: 242–3). At the other end of the spectrum are relatively small cities, such as the capital of the small state of Teng (滕国古城), located in present-day southern Shandong. It covered an area of some 46 ha (or less than 0.5 km²), and its walls were between 5 and 8 m wide (Zhongguo Shehui 2004: 264).

Not only were many of the Eastern Zhou cities much larger than the ideal cited in classical Chinese texts, but they also did not adhere to the ideal of rectangular shape and very regular organization corresponding with the cardinal directions one finds in description of the model city (Wu 2001).[2] Apparently, in many cases the cities' layout was determined primarily by geographic constrains and by political and economic considerations. Many were located along major rivers and tributaries that both contributed to the city's defense and provided water. They also presented a means for garbage and sewage disposal, a crucial consideration in a city that might house upward of one hundred thousand people. A prime example of a city design that takes advantage of its environment is Xinzheng (新鄭), which first served

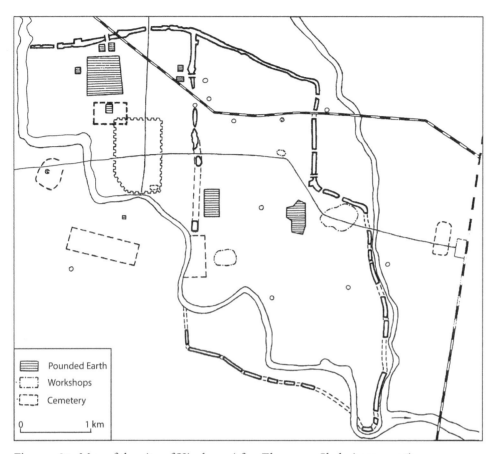

Figure 183. Map of the city of Xinzheng (after Zhongguo Shehui 2004: 236).

as the capital of Zheng and then, from the fourth century BCE, was the capital of the Han state. Located in Xinzheng county, Henan province, the city covered an area of some 15 km². The irregular shape of the city walls was largely determined by its location between the Huangshui (黄水河) and Shuangji (双洎河) Rivers (Figure 183). Other cities, including the previously mentioned Linzi (Figure 184), Yan Xiadu (Figure 185), and the main city of the Teng state (Figure 186), were more or less rectangular in shape, although, as can be seen, they were similarly located between rivers and tributaries.

As far as it can be reconstructed, the internal organization of those cities also varied quite considerably. The palaces and the altars of elite ceremonies were not usually located at the center of the city, according to the ideal model. Most large cities, moreover, were composed of several walled enclosures. This compartmental layout may represent growing gaps between different sociopolitical strata. Indeed, the fact that in many cases the so-called palace cities (*gongcheng* 宫城) were themselves fortified with walls and moats suggests that one of their functions was to defend the elite against possible riots by the commoners. Among the previously mentioned examples, Linzi best represents this new layout (Figure 184). The smaller enclosure at the southwestern corner of the city, identified as the palace city," was probably a late addition, most indicative of the city's layout during the heyday of the Warring States period (Falkenhausen 2008: 225): It covers an area of some 3 km² and had four gates that opened

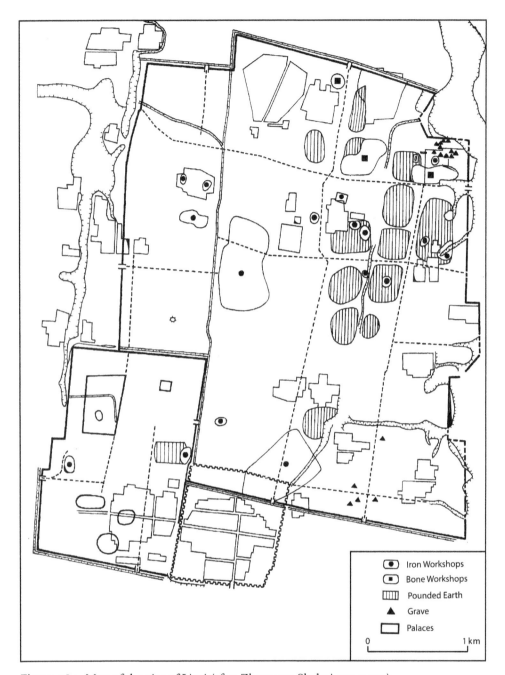

Figure 184. Map of the city of Linzi (after Zhongguo Shehui 2004: 249).

to the outside and two that connected it to other parts of the city. Outside its walls the palace city was further enclosed by a moat, suggesting that this was the best defended part of the city. A huge elliptical pounded earth platform inside the palace

city is thought to have been the site of the Qi king's palace. Likewise, the smaller, elongated rectangular enclosure at the northeastern side of Yan Xiadu (Figure 185) represents a very similar type of palace city. Other cities, such as Qufu (曲阜), the capital

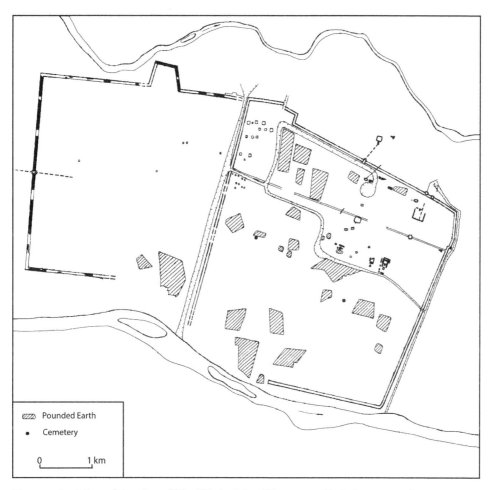

Figure 185. Map of the city of Yan Xiadu (after Zhongguo Shehui 2004: 243).

of Lu, had only one enclosure with no internal subdivisions.

Public Buildings

Palaces, the most conspicuous public buildings of the period – along with temples and altars that are discussed later – underwent a process of evolution that paralleled that of city structures and other aspects of elite culture. According to Wu Hung (1999: 665–75), there was a transition from the solemn "two-dimensional" and self-contained tradition of the Western Zhou to the "three-dimensional" monumental style of the Warring States period. The best example of a Western Zhou palace is found at Fengchu (凤雏). Located in the traditional homeland of the Zhou and its ritual center, in the so-called Zhouyuan (周原) area, this structure is dated to the late predynastic period or early years of the Western Zhou. The palace stands on a 1.3 m tall pounded earth platform and covers an area of about 1,500 m² (Zhongguo Shehui 2004: 57–9). The floor plan of this complex is remarkably similar to the layout of public buildings, such as temples, palaces, and even elite residences, from the imperial era. It was a walled compound, symmetrically arranged and oriented along the north-south axis, with an entrance from the south and

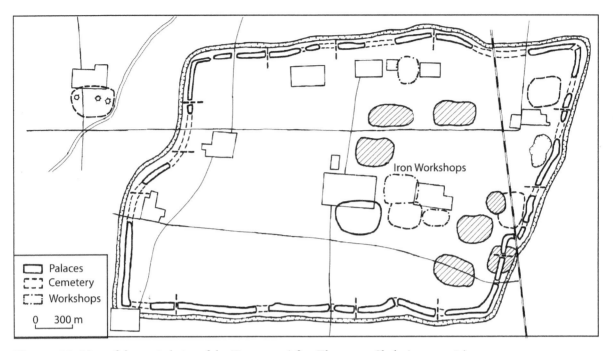

Figure 186. Map of the capital city of the Teng state (after Zhongguo Shehui 2004: 265).

alternating halls and open courtyards (Figure 187). While the size of the building and its placement on a raised platform would undoubtedly have been impressive, the architectural emphasis was on the inside of the complex, which was concealed from the outside view by the compound walls and a screen placed in front of its main entrance.

In comparison to the Western Zhou model, the most prominent feature of palaces and public structures from the sixth century BCE and onward was that they towered over their surroundings by virtue of being built on top of and around massive pounded earth platforms. As mentioned earlier, the platform at Linzi, named by the excavators "Duke Huan's platform" (Huangong Tai 桓公台), was some 90 by 150 m in size, and still stands 14 m high. Smaller platforms and architectural remains that surround this platform suggest that it was not merely a free-standing tower, but rather part of a larger palatial complex. An array of high platforms found at Yan Xiadu is also suggestive of a palatial complex with several buildings that towered high above the city skyline and were visible from far away.

While tall, palatial structures probably originated in the eastern states, their most impressive manifestations were at Xianyang (咸陽), the capital of Qin from 350 BCE, and its imperial capital after the unification of 221 BCE. It is here that we see the full development of "terrace pavilions" – monumental palaces built around tall pounded earth cores. While they were not strictly speaking real multistory monuments, the illusion of a huge conglomerate of buildings, piled one atop another, was created when viewed from the outside. For example, building 1, one of several palatial foundations found on the northern bank of the Wei River, was constructed around a core that was 6 m tall and extended 60 m from east to west and 45 m from north to south (Zhao and Gao 2002: 8). Archaeologists have reconstructed it as a three-tiered building that stood 17 m tall altogether (Wang and Liang 2001: 71) (Figure 188).

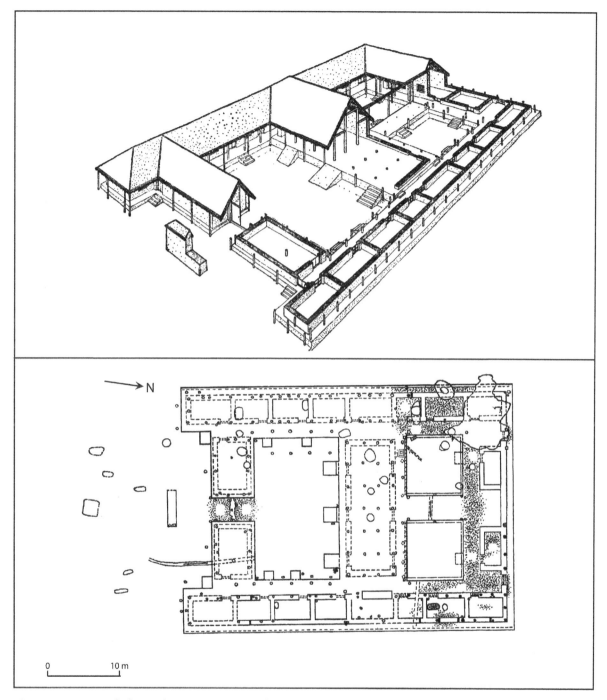

Figure 187. Ground plan and a reconstruction of the compound at Fengchu (after Zhongguo Shehui 2004: 58).

It is interesting to note that during the Warring States period, even smaller states or polities were constructing such buildings, though not on the scale of the complexes found at the capital cities of the larger states. For example, a pounded earth platform located in the northeast part of the

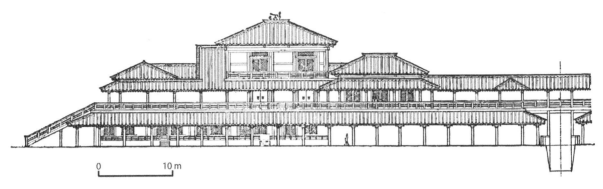

0   10 m

Figure 188. Reconstruction of palace 1 at Xianyang (after Steinhardt 1984: 67).

small Teng state's capital city is still standing at 7 m tall (Zhongguo Shehui 2004: 264). The platform, which covers an area of 2,400 m², is small in comparison to other Warring States period palaces, but still larger than the platform of the Western Zhou palace at Fengchu.

Long Walls

The construction of long walls (*changcheg* 长 城), sometimes hundreds of kilometers long and stretching over difficult terrain, is one of the hallmarks of the Warring States period. From a political perspective, these walls can be linked to the transition from the loosely organized network of settlements of the Spring and Autumn period to the highly centralized polities with fixed boundaries and a clear bureaucratic distinction between "us" and "others" that followed. The walls functioned not only to keep enemies out, but also to control the movements of subjects and keep them in. On a symbolic level, these walls served as enormous displays of the Warring States kings' power and of their ability not just to build such huge monuments, but also to transform the physical landscape of their states.

The construction of long walls is commonly associated with conflicts with nomadic populations on the northern frontiers, and the walls themselves are frequently seen as precursors to the famous "Great Wall" of China (Chapter 11). In fact, though, most of the more powerful polities of the Warring States period erected such walls, and many of the earlier walls were built between states in the interior of the "Chinese" realm (Figure 182). For example, one of the earliest long walls was built by the state of Qi as a defense against a coalition of the rival states Jin and Yue. According to the historical record, this wall was some 500 km long (Di Cosmo 2002: 138), and some of its remains were identified by an archaeological survey at Mulingguan (穆陵关), in Shandong province. In flat areas, the wall was made of earth, while in steep mountainous areas it was made of stone. It still stands 4 m tall in some places and is 8–10 m wide at the base (Zhongguo Shehui 2004: 272). Another example is the so-called Fangcheng (方城) wall, constructed by the state of Chu as a defense against the states of Qin, Wei, and Han. Remains of this wall have been identified in southern Henan province. It was mostly made of stone and in some places was up to 12 m wide at the base and preserved to a height of 2 to 3 m (Zhongguo Shehui 2004: 272).

Even more impressive are the walls built on the northern frontiers of the Chinese polities, serving to stake out new territories and ward off mounted pastoralist armies. The state of Qin built a wall that traversed the entire Ordos region, while the walls built by the states of Zhao and Yan spanned

Figure 189. Remains of the Qin wall near Guyuan in Ningxia province (photo by Gideon Shelach).

almost the entire length of the northern frontier of the "Chinese" sphere, from the great bend of the Yellow River in the west to the Liao River and beyond in the east. The length of the Qin wall alone, stretching from southern Gansu, thorough Ningxia, to northern Shanxi and Inner Mongolia, is estimated to be 1,775 km (Di Cosmo 2002: 145). In steep locations, the Qin wall was built of stone, sometimes mixed with soil, while in flat areas and on mildly rolling plains it was made of pounded earth. The walls are at least 6 m wide and stand up to 3 m tall. Remains of a moat have been identified outside some parts of the walls. Elevated platforms were built along the walls at a distance of about 250 m from one another (approximately 6,300 such mounds were found along the Qin wall) (Figure 189) and were probably used as watchtowers, but perhaps also as lodgings for soldiers. Remains of other facilities, such as forts,

watchtowers, and beacon towers, were identified along the route of the Qin wall on its inner side and up to 5 km away from it, and roads were opened along the walls and between the wall and the interior (Di Cosmo 2002: 145–7; Zhongguo Shehui 2004: 272–3).

Based on the information found in Chinese texts from the imperial period, and on ethnographic data and modern experimentation, I have estimated that between 68,900 and 94,900 persondays would have been required to construct one kilometer of such a wall (Shelach 2013). Thus, the investment in the construction of the Qin wall, not taking into account the added costs of constructing the watchtowers, forts, roads, and so on, amounts to somewhere between 122,297,000 and 168,447,000 person-days. This is a huge investment of manpower, even assuming that the construction took many years to complete, and thus exemplifies an exceptional capacity to mobilize manpower and resources on the part of the Warring States period states.

Ritual Structures and Paraphernalia

TEMPLES AND ALTARS

According to the canonical Chinese texts, ancestors' temples and "earth and grains" (*sheji* 社稷) altars were the most important loci of state religion during the Zhou period, so much so that in many texts the term "altars of the earth and grains" denotes "the state" (Pines 2002: 44). Identifying the remains of such structures is not always simple, however: the altars were probably pounded earth platforms, which are not clearly distinguishable in the archaeological record from other public structures. A complex composed of several pounded earth platforms that supported a structure of wooden pillars, excavated at Yunteng (云塘) in the Zhouyuan area, may have been a Western Zhou ritual complex, but it equally might have been a palace or some other type of public structure (Zhongguo Shehui 2004: 59–61).

The best preserved example of a ceremonial structure was excavated within the walled enclosure at Yongcheng (雍城), the capital city of Qin from 677 to 383 BCE, in Majiazhuang (馬家莊), Shaanxi province. Known as complex 1 and dated to the late Spring and Autumn period, it was identified as an ancestral worship center. It is a large walled enclosure measuring 30 by 34.5 m, with a symmetrical layout and a large gatehouse in the south. Inside this enclosure, three more or less identical buildings constructed of wood with tile-covered roofs were raised on low pounded earth platforms. They would have faced a central court in which 181 pits were aligned in rows (Figure 190). Bones found inside these pits are thought to be the remains of sacrifices to the ancestors. Most common are bones of cattle and sheep, but nine pits contained human victims and two contained chariots (Teng 2003: 66–72; Yongcheng et al.

1985). Although no other comparable ancestral temples from the Western Zhou or the Spring and Autumn periods have been found, the building techniques and the symmetrical arrangement of this complex with its southern entrance are clearly in line with the Zhou tradition.

No comparable ritual complexes are known from the Warring States period. While this could be the result of our partial knowledge, it may also reflect a real religious change. Inscriptions and archaeological data suggest that during the Warring States period, the ancestral spirits lost their prestige and the religious focus shifted to the afterlife and the well-being of the individual. This shift probably led to a greater emphasis on graves, not only as the focal point of individual and family worship, but also in the case of state worship at the graves of former kings.

RITUAL PARAPHERNALIA AND THE "LATE WESTERN ZHOU RITUAL REFORM"

Artifacts used in rituals and sacrifices have not been found in situ at any of the previously mentioned ritual centers. It is nevertheless widely accepted that bronze vessels and bells constituted the primary paraphernalia used at the ancestor halls and temples during the Western Zhou period. This understanding is based partly on information found in classical texts such as the *Book of Odes*, as well as on more than one hundred hoards discovered in the Zhouyuan area. Each of those hoards is an earth pit packed with bronze vessels and musical instruments, but with no other type of artifact or evidence of burial (Figure 191). It is commonly assumed that each hoard contained the ritual paraphernalia belonging to one of the many temples or ancestor halls of the Zhou royal clan and aristocratic lineages that were located in the Zhouyuan area. It has been suggested that the contents of each temple were hastily buried in these pits when the Zhou elite fled the Quanrong invasion in 771 BCE. The inscriptions on many of the vessels indicate that each hoard contained

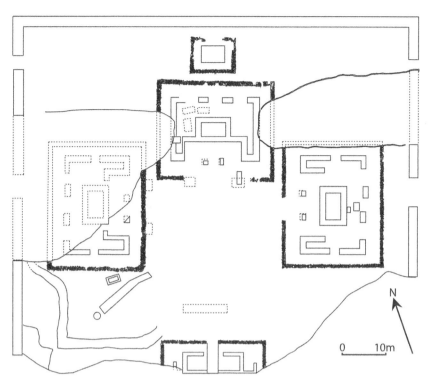

Figure 190. Ground plan of complex 1 at Majiazhuang (after Yongcheng et al. 1985: 14–15).

items that had been accumulated by a single lineage over many generations (Falkenhausen 2006: 36–8; Rawson 1999: 390).

Despite a number of differences between the assemblages of bronzes found in these hoards and those found in elite graves (Falkenhausen 2006: 38), most scholars assume that the graves of the Western Zhou aristocracy are mirror images of the ancestor halls that the same aristocrats had used during their lifetime. A study of bronzes from graves allows us to identify stylistic changes in their shapes and decor, and, more important perhaps, the changing composition of the ritual set. Based on such a study, Jessica Rawson identified a significant ritual reform that began sometime between the mid-tenth and the mid-ninth centuries BCE (Rawson 1999: 433–40). The so-called late Western Zhou ritual reform is associated with transformations in the decorative styles inherited from the Shang period (Falkenhausen 2006: 43–8) and with

changes in the composition of the ritual set, which reflect the transformation of religious, social, and political norms. Two notable changes are the disappearance of some Shang vessel types, most notably those identified as used for alcohol consumption, and the central role played in the new assemblages by vessels used for food consumption, especially *ding* (鼎, used for meat) and *gui* (簋, used for grain).

When compared with the heterogeneous nature of earlier bronze assemblages, from this period onward we find integrated sets, many of which seem to have been produced in tandem and were meant to be used together. Clear sumptuary rules related the composition of each set with the rank of the aristocrat for whom it was produced. According to this system, known as *lie ding* (列鼎), the number and types of bronze vessels to be buried with the deceased (and presumably those he had used in rituals during his lifetime) was strictly prescribed according to rank. Though scholars are still debating details of the composition of these ritual sets (cf. Hsu and Linduff 1988: 173–7; Li 1985: 460–3; Yin 2001: 185–7), it is clear that their main components were an odd number of *ding* and an even number of *gui*.

The actual numbers of vessels each social stratum was allowed may have changed by the beginning of the Spring and Autumn period (Yin 2001: 202–12), but the strict gradation remained intact. By the late Spring and Autumn period, however, the system started to disintegrate, and it completely disappeared during the Warring States period. This decline was part of the overall waning of the authority of the cult of the aristocratic ancestors and the emergence of new social and religious ideas focusing on the well-being of the family and the individual in life and after death (Poo 1998). One notable expression of this process was the replacement of bronze ritual vessels with cheap ceramic imitations. The use of such imitations, known as *mingqi* (明器), does not necessarily coincide with a lesser investment in graves – indeed some Warring States graves are among the richest in Chinese history – but rather is indicative of a different attitude toward the afterlife. Not only was less emphasis now placed on rituals, but new beliefs that the laws governing the world of the dead differ from those of our world seemed to emerge. Thus, in the world of the dead, those *mingqi* imitations, which in later periods include models of everything from food and artifacts of daily use to servants and houses (Chapter 11), would be transformed into the real things and be used by the dead.

Chime bells, which are very rarely found in Shang and early Zhou assemblages, became an integral part of the ritual set of the late Western Zhou and the Spring and Autumn period. The importance of music, played on bronze bells and other percussion instruments, in the ancestral rituals of the Zhou court and elite is described in classical texts from that period. In Ode 274 of the *Shijing*, for example, we find this passage that describes the ancestor worship ceremonies of the house of Zhou:

> Bells and drums sound magnificently; Musical stones and flutes chime in;
>
> [The former kings] send down blessings that are abundant; They send down blessings that are great. (Translated by Falkenhausen 1993: 26)

The Chinese classics abound with references to music (*Yue* 樂 in Chinese) as the supreme expression of esthetic value, as a profound ritual device, and as a means of transforming moral values and achieving harmony. The high reverence that Kongzi felt toward music is clearly reflected in the Analects. In one passage it is said, for example, that "the Master [Kongzi] while in Qi heard the Shao [ritual music], and for three months did not notice the taste of meat. He said, 'I never imagined that music had reached such heights.'" By Kongzi's time, however, ritual music was already on the decline. Its decline is associated not only with the previously mentioned religious changes but also with the introduction of new wind and string instruments that supplemented the traditional percussion instruments (bells, chime stones, and drums) and were used to produce a more exciting "new music," which was associated with entertainment and court life.

CEMETERIES AND BURIALS

Zhou archaeology, more than that of any other period in Chinese history, is dominated by the study of cemeteries and the excavation of graves. Many Zhou period cemeteries have been identified and mapped, and more than ten thousand graves have already been excavated. The mortuary information is so plentiful that any overview, let alone a short one such as that presented here, must necessarily do an injustice to the richness and diversity of the data.

It is commonly assumed that during the Western Zhou and the Spring and Autumn periods, members of the elite were buried in lineage cemeteries.

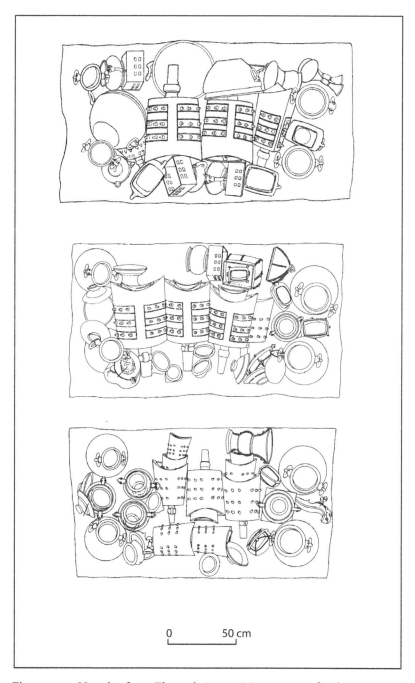

Figure 191. Hoard 1 from Zhuangbai containing seventy-five bronze vessels and twenty-eight bronze bells (after Zhongguo Shehui 2004: 63).

That is, each patrilineal kin group that owned an estate – be it one of the large states, a smaller estate within the royal domain, or one of the regional states – had its own designated burial ground. All those buried in lineage cemeteries were of aristocratic descent, but internally each lineage was also highly stratified in terms of the status and wealth of its members. Thus, it is to be expected that this stratification would be reflected in the scaling of graves – their size, structure, and furnishing – within each lineage cemetery. Notwithstanding these assumptions, Western Zhou cemeteries are, in fact, less structured than one would expect. They usually have no clear boundaries, and it is sometimes difficult to decipher the logic that governed the locations of different graves.

Preliminary reports claim the discovery of the Zhou royal cemetery in a place called Zhougong Miao (周公庙), located north of the sacred Mount Qi and west of the Zhouyuan area. The cemetery space may have been enclosed by a wall, a feature not found in other places, and it contains the largest known Western Zhou graves. However, because all the graves excavated there so far were looted, the identity of their occupants is unclear. Grave M18 has four descending ramps (*mudao* 墓道), a feature usually associated with the burials of kings. It is comparable to, but much smaller than, the graves attributed to the Shang kings found at Xibeigang (Chapter 8). Its southern ramp is 17.6 m long and 4.2 m wide, but the other ramps are so narrow (ranging from 1.3 to 0.9 m) that they may have been symbolic rather than functional. The main burial chamber is 6.8 by 6.4 m in size and is surrounded by a ledge 1 m wide (Xu 2006).

Outside the royal domain, the best known cemeteries are those belonging to the ruling lineage of the Jin State at Tianma-Qucun (天马-曲村), in Shanxi province, and to the ruling lineage of the Yan state in Liulihe, in Hebei province. More than 250 graves and chariot pits have been excavated at the Liulihe cemetery, located outside and to the east of the walls of the Yan capital. It is divided into two areas, labeled I and II (Figure 192), each of which, according to the excavators, was associated with a different population: Shang descendants and the local population were buried in the first section, and Yan lineage members of Zhou descent were buried in the second (Beijingshi 1995: 6). However, this clear-cut ethnic distinction, which is made based on evidence of

dog and human sacrifices (identified as a "Shang trait"), the style of bronze and ceramic vessels, and inscriptions cast in some of the bronze vessels, is not universally agreed upon (Falkenhausen 2006: 177–200). For example, Jaffe (2013) argues that mortuary practices at Liulihe were a stage for the negotiation of social status and identities by both the local population and the newcomer Zhou elites. Possible subclustering of graves within area II have been interpreted to reflect different kin subgroups within the larger lineage (Sun 2003), but the overall layout of the area is, nonetheless, in line with what we would expect from a lineage cemetery: it includes graves of different sizes, complexity, and richness; the larger graves are more or less clustered together in one area and are associated with most of the chariot pits; but there is also a great deal of mixing and spatial association between large, medium, and small graves.

All the graves at Liulihe are rectangular, and most contain wooden coffins (*guan* 棺) and a ledge upon which to place burial goods. Several of the wealthier graves have ramps leading down to the rectangular tombs, as well as a wooden chamber (*guo* 椁). The two largest graves excavated so far, both identified as the burial places of Yan dukes, are M202, which is 7.2 by 5.2 m and 7 m deep with a 15 m long ramp leading to it from the south and a 12 m long ramp with stairs leading to it from the north; and M1193, which has four shorter ramps leading to a burial pit that is 7.7 by 5.3 m and 10.3 m deep. Both graves contain a wooden chamber and a wooden coffin (Zhongguo Shehui 2004: 79–81). Thus far, none of the medium-size graves have been excavated, but smaller graves range between graves such as M254, which is 3.5 by 2 m in size and 4.4 m deep, and graves such as M208, which is 3.3 by 1.4 m and 1.8 m deep. As noted, the larger graves have been looted, but that is not the case for the smaller graves, where the number of grave goods varies between more than eighty and fewer than ten. A chariot pit associated with the

Figure 192. The Yan lineage cemetery at Liulihe: the layout of cluster II (after Beijing 1995: 8).

two large graves through its location contains the skeletons of forty-two horses and the chariots they pulled (Beijing 1995).

The cemetery of the ruling lineage of Jin at Tianma-Qucun is more clearly segregated. Nine pairs (in one case a triad) of large graves, identified as the tombs of Jin dukes and their wives, have been located in an area labeled Qucun locus III. As in Liulihe, these graves are associated with chariot pits, but unlike in Liulihe, no small-scale graves have been found in this section (Figure 193). The largest tombs, such as M63 and M93, have two ramps, similar to grave M202 from Liulihe, while others have only one. The total length of M93, including the two ramps, is 32.5 m, and the main chamber is 6.3 by 5.1 m and 7.8 m deep. Also unlike the graves in Liulihe, the interior burial

chamber is built of stone (Zhongguo Shehui 2004: 86–9).

The patterns of cemetery organization and the sociopolitical scaling of graves seem to have persisted through the Spring and Autumn period. The *Lie ding* system remained the ideal benchmark for mortuary sumptuary roles, although new elements were added to the grave furnishings. Nested wooden coffins coated with lacquer increasingly became an important status symbol, a feature that was further developed during the Warring States period (Falkenhausen 1999: 475). The cemetery of the ruling lineage in the small state of Guo (虢) at Shangcunling (上村岭), in Henan province, provides an example of the continuity in traditional arrangements of aristocratic cemeteries. More than two hundred graves excavated in this cemetery are

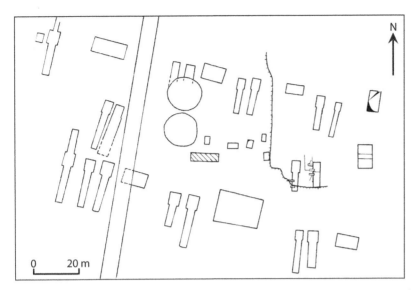

Figure 193. Graves of the Jin dukes and their wives at Qucun location III (after Zhongguo Shehui 2004: 87).

well organized, with smaller graves usually clustered around pairs of larger graves that may represent the founders or heads of an extended family and their principal wife. The largest and richest graves in this cemetery are clustered in a group and may have been the graves of the lineage's highest-ranking elite, but they are not segregated from the rest of the cemetery by a wall or clearly defined borders (Falkenhausen 1999: 471–4).

The state of Qin, in northwest China, may have been the first to develop real royal necropolises that depart from the aristocratic tradition of the Western Zhou period. The Nanzhihui (南指挥) necropolis, located southwest of Yongcheng, covers an area of more than 20 km² and contains thirteen clusters of tombs. Most of the clusters were walled and each contains several large and medium-sized tombs alongside sacrificial pits containing horses and chariots (Figure 194). Altogether, forty-two tombs have been identified, including eighteen with two tomb passages (called *zhong* 中 burials because of their similarity to the Chinese character), which were identified as the tombs of Qin rulers from the period of the capital's location at Yongcheng (677–383 BCE) (Teng 2003: 55–7).

The size of the Qin lords' (and later kings') tombs also anticipated the enormous size of the tombs of the kings and the upper elite during the Warring States period. As early as the eighth century BCE, the tomb of the Qin lord in Dabuzi (大堡子), in Gansu, was already larger than any other known contemporaneous tombs. This grave (M2) has two ramps entering it from the east and the west: the eastern ramp is 38 m long and 6 m wide, larger than in the supposed tombs of the Zhou kings at Zhougong Miao. The tomb chamber itself is approximately 12 m by 12 m at its mouth and 7 m by 5 m at the bottom, and is 15 m deep. The nearby grave M3 is even grander in scale and has two pits attached to it, each containing four highly decorated chariots and twelve horses (Figure 195a) (Dai 2000).

Of the larger graves identified at the Nanzhihui necropolis the only one that has been fully excavated so far is M1, identified as the burial of Lord Jing of Qin (秦景公, r. 576–537 BCE). As with other tombs of similar shape in Nanzhihui, the two sloping ramps lead to the bottom of the tomb from the east and the west. The eastern passage is 156 m long, the western one 85 m. The burial chamber itself is 60 m long (from east to west), 40 m

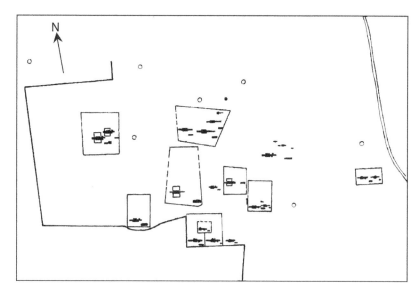

Figure 194. Layout of the Qin necropolis at Nanzhihui (after Zhongguo Shehui 2004: 324).

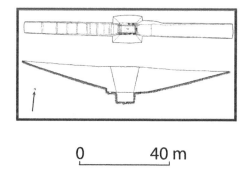

Figure 195. Graves of Qin lords: A. Grave M2 at Dabuzi; B. Grave M1 at Nanzhihui (after Wang and Liang 2000: 153; upper after Zhongguo Shehui 2004: 88).

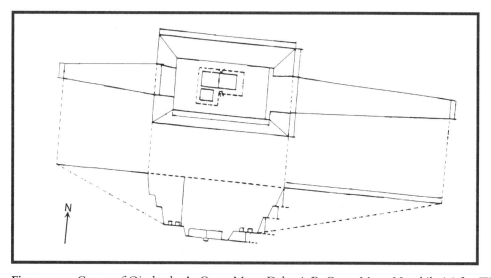

wide, and 24 m deep, a scale that far exceeds any-thing known from the Western Zhou and the Spring and Autumn periods (Figure 195b). The grave was looted in antiquity, so its ritual bronze vessels and other precious grave goods were not found. However, other findings, such as inscribed fragments of chime stones and 166 human sacri-ficial victims, each in his own coffin, as well as the massive wooden beams used to construct the burial chamber and evidence of a wooden struc-ture above ground (Teng 2003: 57), all suggest an extraordinarily rich burial.

The highly structured cemeteries of the Qin rulers and elite, and the size of the graves located in them, may have been extraordinary during the Spring and Autumn period. However, such fea-tures became the norm during the Warring States period, when clearly defined cemeteries were built outside the walls of most cities, and the rulers of even relatively small states disregarded Zhou stan-dards and the aristocratic sumptuary rules and con-structed extremely rich graves on a very large scale. The separation between cemeteries for the com-moners and the lower elite, on the one hand, and the necropolises of the kings and their wives and kin, on the other, was by now very clearly demar-cated, thereby reflecting the growing political and economic gaps between sociopolitical strata.

One of the best known examples of a Warring States period royal necropolis was found in Ling-shou (靈壽), the capital city of the Zhongshan (中山) state, in Pingshan county, Hebei. Although the rulers of Zhongshan were descendants of the Di (狄), a non-Zhou tribe, Zhongshan became one of the key players in northern China during this period, and they adopted many attributes from the Zhou cultural sphere. Two complexes of royal tombs were identified in Lingshou, one inside the area enclosed by the city walls and another outside of it. The better preserved burial complex is the one located outside the city walls and identified with King Cuo (d. 308 BCE). This area includes two large tombs: M1, identified as belonging to

the king, and M2, identified as that of his wife. The two graves are topped by huge pounded earth mounds, a feature not commonly seen during the Spring and Autumn period, but adopted univer-sally as an above-ground marking of kingly tombs during the Warring States period. The mound above M1 was more or less square, with each side measuring some 100 m at the bottom. Originally it stood some 20 m high, with a wooden build-ing on top of it. These two main graves were sur-rounded by six subsidiary tombs, two chariots pits, each containing twelve horses and four chariots, one long sacrificial pit, and a boat pit, contain-ing three boats, which may have been connected to the nearby river by a long underground canal (Figure 196). A large bronze plate – about 1 m long and 50 cm wide – discovered inside the stor-age pits of grave M1 and decorated with an inlayed gold design (Figure 197) is, based on the inlayed inscriptions, a blueprint of king Cuo's necropolis. Apparently the necropolis was planned to include five burial mounds enclosed by two concentric walls, but it was never completed (Wu 1999: 712–16).

Beneath the burial mound, grave M1 has two ramps descending from south to north with a total length of 97 m. The main burial pit is 30 by 30 m and contains a stone chamber constructed to hold four nested coffins. A unique feature of the Zhongshan tombs are storage chambers, which flank the main burial chamber but are not con-nected to it. Because these features were not com-mon, they were not discovered by looters and were found by archaeologists untouched.

The construction of burial mounds did not begin in Zhongshan. The earliest evidence so far comes from a late Spring and Autumn period necropolis near the late Jin capital of Xintian (新田), in present-day Houma, Shanxi province. Dur-ing the Warring States period, huge mounded burials were constructed, with some variations, in all the major states (Falkenhausen 2006: 336). These mounds, known as *ling* (陵) in Chinese

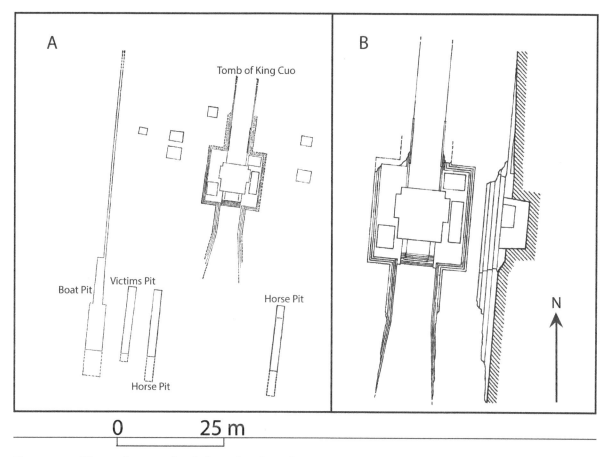

Figure 196. The royal necropolis of Zhongshan (partial map) and grave M1 (tomb of King Cuo) (after Falkenhausen 2006: 344 and Zhongguo Shehui 2004: 344).

Figure 197. Inlayed bronze plate with the design of the Zhongshan necropolis (photo by Yuri Pines).

texts, are part of the "monumentality trend" seen in other aspects of public architecture of the period, and continued to symbolize the greatness of the Chinese emperors during the imperial era.

Another important trend from the Warring States period is, as discussed earlier, a shift in ritual focus from the ancestral temples, which were the focal points of the highest rituals during the Western Zhou and the Spring and Autumn periods, to the graves. Both state- and family-level rituals were conducted in ritual structures built atop or beside the burial mounds and graves. At the same time, the very perception of the grave changed: if during the Western Zhou and the Spring and Autumn periods it mirrored the ancestors' temple with the ritual vessels placed in it, during the Warring States period the grave was viewed as a house – the eternal residence of the deceased (Falkenhausen 2006: 298–309; Wu 1999). This shift manifested itself in the shape of the graves: although most were still pit graves, which, unlike regular houses, are entered from above, the internal division of the wooden chamber now reflected the main parts of the house. The majority of burial goods were artifacts, or imitations of such artifacts, that were used by the grave owner in his daily activities rather than the ritual sets (or even their *Mingqi* imitations) associated with ancestor worship.

An early and very impressive example of such an "underground house" can be seen in grave M1 excavated at Leigudun (擂鼓墩) in Hubei province (Zhongguo Shehui 2004: 389–93). The main occupant of this tomb was the ruler of the small state of Zeng, known as Marquis Yi of Zeng (Zeng Hou Yi 曾侯乙), who died and was buried shortly after 433 BCE. The grave is 13 m deep and was submerged in underground water. As a result, the artifacts in it, including wood and lacquer items, are superbly preserved. The grave has no sloping ramps, and the burial pit measures 21 by 16.5 m, modest in comparison to the graves of kings and high nobility in the more powerful states.

The burial chamber was constructed with large wooden beams, creating four rooms. Based on their position and contents, the rooms are understood to stand for the four main components of the marquis's palace: the public reception and ceremonial hall, the ruler's private quarters, quarters for the ruler's wives, and the storage/arsenal rooms (Falkenhausen 2006: 306) (Figure 198). The tombs' four rooms were connected by miniature doors at the base of their wooden walls. Doors and windows were also painted on the marquis's enormous outer coffin (Figure 199a). Those features, found at other graves from the Warring States period as well, further signify the house-like idea of the grave. Smaller coffins containing the skeletons of thirteen sacrificed young women, presumably the marquis's wives, were found in the western chamber, and eight more victims accompanied the marquis in the eastern chamber. Human sacrifice on such a large-scale is quite unusual, since in many graves of the Warring States period human figurines had replaced real human sacrifices and stood for the wives, servants, soldiers, and others who accompanied the primary occupant of the grave in his death.

The grave of Marquis Yi of Zeng is the richest intact preimperial tomb ever excavated in China. It contained no fewer than 15,400 artifacts, including 117 bronze vessels, 4,700 weapons, gold, jade, and lacquer artifacts, textiles, bamboo documents, and more (Figure 199). The total weight of all the bronze artifacts in this tomb (including the massive bronze frame of the marquis's outer coffin) is more than ten metric tons. An investment of such scale is unknown even for the largest graves of the Shang, Western Zhou, or Spring and Autumn periods.

No fewer than 125 musical instruments were also found in the grave, the most famous being a set of 64 bronze bells, the largest set ever found in China (Figure 200). Other instruments include a set of chime stones hung from a bronze frame, seven zithers (string instruments), three drums, and an array of wind instruments, such as flutes

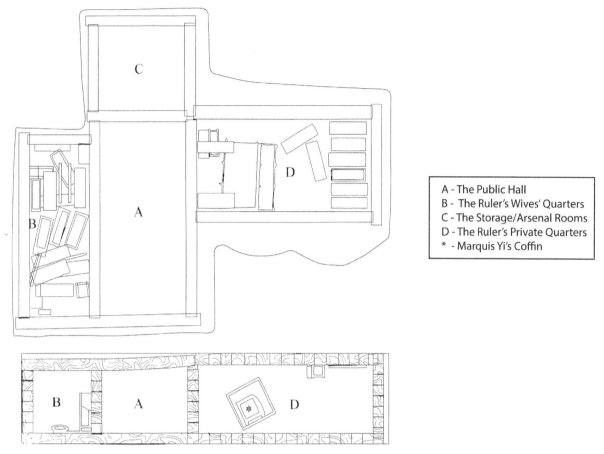

Figure 198. Tomb of Marquis Yi of Zeng from Leigudun, Hubei: A. The public hall; B. The ruler's wives' quarters; C. The storage/arsenal rooms; D. The ruler's private quarters; * Marquis Yi's coffin (after Tan 2001: 31).

and mouth organs. The placement of most of the musical instruments in the central chamber of the grave – which stood for the public space of the marquis's palace, where rituals took place and dignitaries were received – is indicative of the central role played by music in state affairs and religious rituals.

Unlike modern bells, Zhou-period bells did not have a clapper inside them; instead, they were hung from a rack with their mouths facing down, and played by striking them with wooden mallets (Figure 201a). Bells from the Zhou period typically have an almond-shaped cross section (Figure 201b). This feature does not appear in bells from later periods (or in other parts of the world), and

it is not mentioned or explained in the classical texts. Until the excavations at Marquis Yi of Zeng's grave, the significance of this shape was not understood. However, based on the inscriptions cast on some of the bells from the grave, it became clear that their unique shape enabled musicians to produce not one, but two, distinct tones from each bell: one by striking the central (wider) part of the bell and another by striking close to the bell's pointed sides (Falkenhausen 1993: 129–95). Despite the highly ideological reverence expressed by Chinese literati from the Warring States and the imperial periods for the ritual music of the Zhou, this musical technique and the accompanying technical expertise were probably forgotten

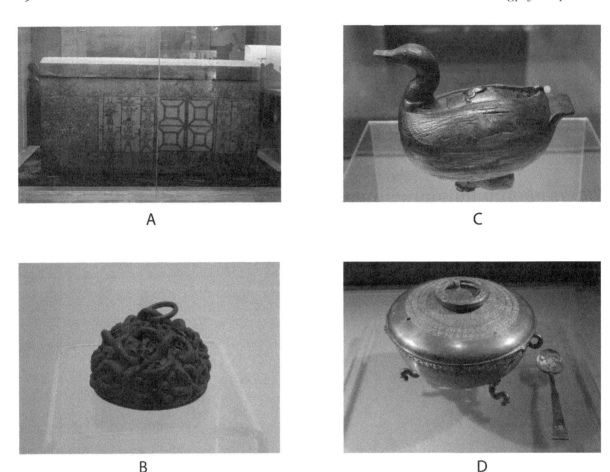

A

C

B

D

Figure 199. Artifacts from the tomb of Marquis Yi of Zeng: A. The outer coffin built with wooden planks on bronze frame and painted with lacquer colors; B. A bronze weight with intertwining dragons motif; C. Lacquer vessel in the shape of a duck; D. Cast gold vessel and a serving spoon (photos by Gary Lee Todd).

not long after the set from Marquis Yi's grave had been cast.

Although many of the large Warring States period graves were looted in antiquity, scattered findings, such as those made in the unlooted storage chambers of grave M1 in Zhongshan and in the tomb of Marquis Yi of Zeng, suggest that the quantity and quality of grave goods during this period were as impressive as the above- and below-ground structures of the graves. This, again, suggests a growing gap between the rulers of the states and their immediate kin and court on the one hand, and the rest of the population on the other. A related phenomenon is that many more smaller

and unfurnished graves from the Warring States period are known in comparison with the preceding Spring and Autumn period, perhaps because the cemeteries now also contained people who did not come from the nobility.

Craft Production and Technology

In many respects, the technologies and patterns of production that were established during the Shang period continued during the Western Zhou and the Spring and Autumn periods. These patterns changed dramatically during the late Spring and Autumn and the Warring States periods, however,

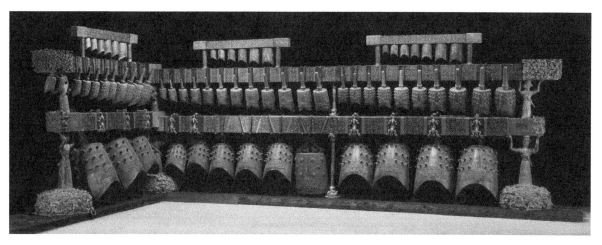

Figure 200. Set of sixty-four bronze bells mounted on a wooden frame and supported by human-shaped bronze pillars from the grave of Marquis Yi of Zeng (visual/corbis).

when new technologies were introduced and the scale of production accelerated rapidly. One of the most interesting archaeological phenomena is the location of large-scale production areas within the walls of the major Warring States period cities. For example, at Xinzheng, remains of bronze, iron, and bone workshops were located in the larger southeastern enclosure, alongside domestic remains (Figure 183). No fewer than fifteen sites of metal (bronze and iron) production have been identified at Linzi, as were the remains of several workshops for the production of bone artifacts (Figure 184). Some of these production zones are quite extensive, covering up to 40 ha. It is interesting to note that these production activities were located not only in the larger eastern enclosure, but also in the smaller enclosure, where the Qi palaces were located (Zhongguo Shehui 2004: 235–51). More traditional industries, such as ceramic production, have also been found within the walled areas of Warring States cities.

Some aspects of these craft industries, such as the casting of iron and bronze and the firing of ceramics, must have produced considerable pollution and inconveniences for the population at large: not only for commoners, but also for the elite who resided alongside them. Moreover, their loca-

tion would have made production more expensive, since the raw materials and fuel had to be brought to the cities, instead of locating the industries near the natural resources and then distributing the finished artifacts. The fact that these industries were nonetheless located inside the cities suggests that control over production provided the state with clear economic and political advantages.

THE IRON INDUSTRY

The emergence of the iron industry in China represents a major historic breakthrough, not only because of its new and highly advanced technology but, more important, because of its enormous effects on the economy, society, and political structures. A small number of iron artifacts dated to the ninth century BCE, such as iron blades that were combined with a bronze hilt to form short swords, are known, mainly from the western parts of China. These artifacts were produced using iron-smelting technology in small-scale furnaces (known as bloomeries). It is assumed that the smelting technology, which was at the time already well developed in Western Asia, was introduced into China by nomadic blacksmiths from Central Asia (Wagner 2008: 91–103). This new technology, however, had a very limited

Figure 201. A. Depiction of a ceremony cast on a bronze vessel from the Warring States period. Note the portrayal of musicians using mallets to strike bronze balls and chime stones (visual/corbis); B. Drawing of a typical bronze bell with an almond-shaped cross section.

effect, since it was conducted on a very small scale and used mostly to produce prestige items that were interchangeable with similar bronze artifacts.

More significant is the development of iron casting in China – a revolution in technology of global proportions – currently dated to the fifth century BCE. The advent of widespread iron casting is dated to the fourth century BCE, some eighteen hundred years earlier than anywhere else in the world. It seems that iron casting technology developed independently of the traditional iron

smelting methods. Although both make use of iron (*Fe*) ores, smelting and casting technologies are very different from one another. In smelting, the temperatures reached in the small furnaces are relatively low (800–1,000°C), such that the iron does not melt and the final product is a spongy mass of iron called a bloom. The final iron artifact is then consolidated and shaped by the blacksmith through repeated heating, hammering, and rapid cooling in water. Casting, in contrast, is based on the complete melting of iron, usually in combination with small amounts of carbon and silicon,

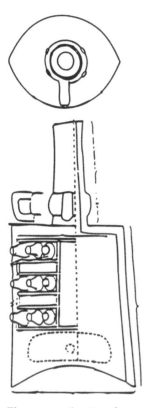

Figure 201 (*continued*)

in a large furnace that can sustain temperatures of around 1,150°C for a long time. The high-level skills required for furnace building evolved not from the small iron smelting hearths, but rather from constructing the much larger hearths used by the state-level bronze industries of the Shang and Zhou. It is interesting to note that this new iron technology probably did not evolve in the traditional centers of bronze production in the Yellow River basin, but rather in the Yangzi River basin, or even farther to the south in the states of Chu or Wu (Wagner 2008: 105–14). Nonetheless, iron artifacts are also common in north China.

Evidence of iron casting during the Warring States period – iron artifacts as well as workshops – has been found at some 350 sites distributed throughout the entire realm of the "Chinese" states. It is most abundant at the sites and graves of the Chu state: for example, no fewer than two

hundred Chu graves near Changsha (长沙) contained iron artifacts.

The earliest dated cast iron artifact is an iron *ding*, dated to the late Spring and Autumn period, excavated from grave M65 at Yangjiashan (杨家山), in Hunan province (Zhongguo Shehui 2004: 407–8). However, because the quality of cast iron was inferior to that of bronze, its main use was not for ritual vessels or prestige artifacts, but rather in the making of agricultural implements, such as hoe heads and plowshares, and other work tools. Excavations at a Warring States period granary near the Wangcheng site in Henan province yielded 126 iron tools and agricultural artifacts weighing more than 400 kg in total. Similarly, of the 80 iron artifacts excavated from the site of Lianhuabao (莲花堡) in Liaoning province, 85 percent were agricultural tools (Figure 202) (Zhongguo Shehui 2004: 409).

Iron weapons also became increasingly common, though they did not yet replace bronze weapons. A famous example is grave M44, excavated near Yan Xiadu. The grave, which contained the bones of twenty-two individuals, also held 120 artifacts and 1,360 coins. Of the artifacts, seventy-nine were made of cast iron, mostly weapons such as swords, spearheads, and halberd heads. One unique artifact is a helmet made of eighty-nine iron plates (Figure 203) (Hebei 1975). Similarly, most of the molds for casting iron artifacts discovered at various sites of the Warring States period were for the production of agricultural artifacts, tools, and weapons (Zhongguo Shehui 2004: 411–14).

OTHER INDUSTRIES AND TECHNOLOGIES

Bronze technology changed very little during the first part of the Zhou, and the gradual transformations in the style of bronze vessels suggests an evolutionary rather than a revolutionary process. The scale of bronze production, as indicated by the quantity of bronzes found in graves, probably increased during the Western Zhou and Spring

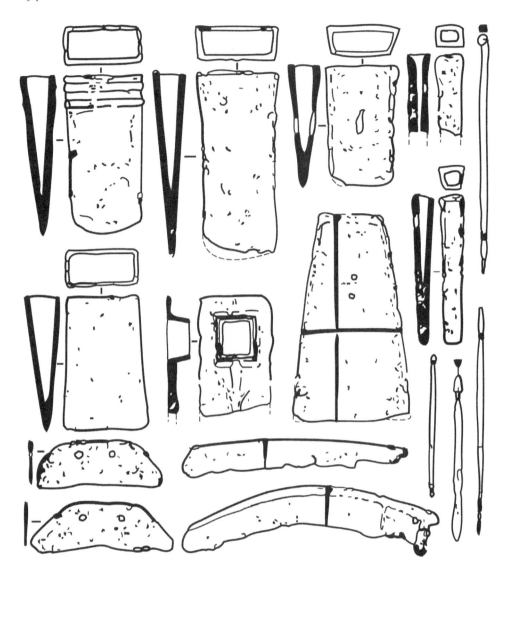

0   5 cm

Figure 202. Typical iron artifacts from Lianhuabao, Liaoning (after Wang 1964: 288).

and Autumn periods, but the major technological innovation occurred only around the beginning of the sixth century BCE, when the lost-wax method was introduced and gradually replaced the traditional "piece-mold" method (Wu 1999: 677). This new method, whether developed locally or introduced from the West – where it is known from much earlier periods – facilitated the casting of much more refined and intricate decorations. A *zun* vessel placed inside a matching basin in the grave of Marquis Yi of Zeng is an excellent example of the advancement of the lost-wax casting

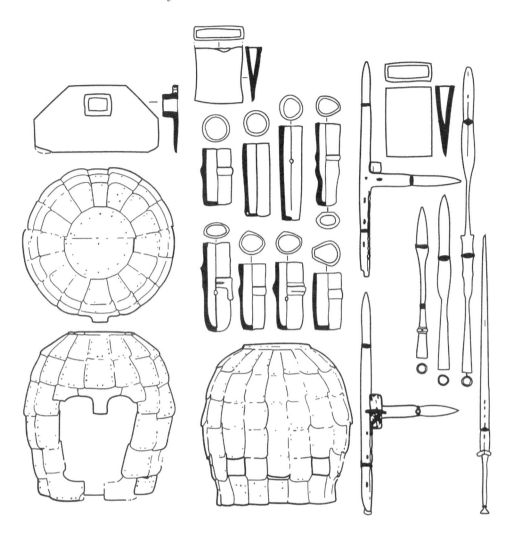

Figure 203. Cast iron weapons from grave M44 at Yan Xiadu, Hebei (after Hebei 1975: 231–3).

method in China. Even the best artisans working with traditional methods could not have produced the elaborate openwork decorations of this *zun* and other vessels found in the tomb. Such decorations were perhaps more suitable for the newly ascending socioeconomic strata than the much more subtle and serious traditional motifs.

Inlay is another new technique developed during this period, and also illustrates the development of a new elite taste. Inlay was used to create colorful decorations by filling depressed designs on the surface of a bronze vessel or artifact with different metals, such as copper, gold, and silver, or other materials such as turquoise or lacquer (Figure 204).

Figure 204. Inlayed bronze artifacts (photos by Gary Lee Todd).

More than half of the bronze vessels found in the grave of Marquis Yi were decorated in this way, testifying to the popularity of inlay decor among the highest elite of the Warring States period.

The supreme manifestation of the new elite tastes that developed during the Warring States period was probably not expressed in bronzes, but rather in lacquer objects. While the technique was not new – remains of lacquer artifacts are known from as early as the Neolithic period (Chapter 5) – the scale and diversity of lacquer production reached an unprecedented peak during the Warring States. Even small graves from this period, especially in the Yangzi River region, contain a certain number of lacquer objects, while larger graves, such as that of Marquis Yi, contained more

than two hundred, some of them quite large and elaborate. The production of lacquer artifacts was time-consuming and expensive, but the quantity of lacquer artifacts found in Warring States graves suggests that they were now being produced in a much larger workshops and could have become much more affordable, even to individuals of modest status (Wu 1999: 679–81). The bright colors of these vessels, which distinguished them from the heavy and dark demeanor of traditional bronzes, must have made them especially attractive to the new elite (Figure 205).

ECONOMIC CHANGES AND THEIR EFFECTS

The development of the iron industry, and especially the large-scale casting of iron artifacts from the fourth century BCE onward, had profound economic and social effects. The casting of iron weapons like swords and arrowheads had a clear and long-lasting impact on Chinese methods of warfare. Even more dramatic were the effects of the iron industry on agricultural production and the economy in general. After some six millennia during which stone artifacts were the basic agricultural tools, they were finally replaced by much more effective and widely available iron tools. Moreover, for the first time in Chinese history, the newfound ability to shape large and durable tools catalyzed the use of draft animals in agricultural work. The harnessing of animals such as oxen to a plow with an iron plowshare allowed the fields to be cultivated far more intensively (Hsu 1965: 130–3). Although it is not clear how prevalent the use of draft animals was during the Warring States period, it clearly paved the way for the almost universal use of this technology after imperial unification.

The use of iron tools in the hands of the large and well-organized working forces of the Warring States period enabled the construction of large-scale irrigation systems. A well-known example is the Dujiangyan (都江堰) project that the Qin

Figure 205. Lacquer artifacts from the Warring States period (photos by Gary Lee Todd).

state built in present-day Sichuan after conquering it in 316 BCE. This system, which is still functional today, includes large dams, canals, and earthworks, which prevented flooding by the Min River (岷江) and channeled its water to agricultural fields across a region covering more than 5,000 km², thereby transforming it into a highly productive area that served as one of Qin's strategic economic resources. Similar technology was used by other states, not only for irrigation but also to dry swampy areas. The combination of more agricultural land resources, intensive plowing, and better irrigation brought about a dramatic increase in the production of food, allowing for population growth, as well as the accumulation of food surpluses, which in turn financed the huge armies and large-scale projects of the different states.

Technological innovations were not the only driving force responsible for the economic changes that occurred during the Eastern Zhou period. The upward mobility of people from nonaristocratic origins in the administration and society during the Eastern Zhou period ushered in the formation of a new elite stratum with a new taste for prestige goods such as the lacquer discussed previously. The cities of the period, within which unprecedentedly large and heterogeneous populations were concentrated, were natural hubs for markets, where everything from everyday foods and commodities to prestige items were exchanged. As a result, the volume of trade by both private and state-sponsored merchants increased dramatically. This trade was also facilitated by the large-scale construction of roads and the development of water transportation along rivers and man-made canals.

Discussions of commercial activity are found in texts from the Eastern Zhou (Hsu 1965: 116–30), as well as in epigraphic records. A famous example was found at the Qiujia Huayuan site (邱家花园) in Shou county, Anhui province: A pair of bronze bamboo-shaped containers known

Figure 206. The E'jun tallies found at Qiujia Huayuan in Shou county, Anhui (photos by Gary Lee Todd).

as "the E'jun (鄂君) tallies" were inscribed with gold inlayed characters (Figure 206). These tallies, which were issued by the Chu state to Lord E'jun in 323 BCE, served as a kind of trading permit, with lists of quotas for transportation along pre-scribed land and water routes within the Chu state and specific exemptions from taxes. According to this document, E'jun was permitted to transport a considerable quantity of goods, as much as could be carried by 150 boats, 50 carts, 500 horses, and 1,000 men (Peters 1999: 111–12).

Trade connections also extended beyond the regions controlled by the "Chinese" states. For example, Chu-style bronzes found in the Lingnan region can be associated with the activities of Chu traders who brought back exotic products such as pearls and bird feathers from south China (Allard 2004; Peters 1999: 111–16).

The Evolution of Coins and a Monetary System

Like in other parts of the world, the rapid evolution of a system in which coins of different values were readily available transformed many crucial aspects of the economy: the ability to assign abstract value to commodities, to compare different values, and to calculate economic gains and losses; the ability to accumulate wealth and transfer value from one place to the other; and so on. The use of coins is based on abstract values because the value of each coin is not identical to the value of the metal from which it was made. A reliable political authority is a precondition for such a system, oth-erwise ordinary people would have no reason to trust the assigned value of coins. Needless to say, the political authority also profits from the distri-bution of the coins it mints and is able to better control the economy through the manipulation of currency values.

Bronze coins were first minted in China dur-ing sixth century BCE and became widespread and universally accepted during the Warring States period. Unlike coins in the Western part of Eura-sia, Chinese coins did not carry portraits of kings or other graphic symbols; they bore only charac-ters that identified their value and the place where they had been minted. Another difference from Western coins is the variety of coin shapes. Three shapes were typical during this period: a miniature spade shape, known as *bu bi* (布幣); a knife shape, or *dao bi* (刀幣); and a round shape, or *yuan qian* (圓錢) (Figure 207). *Bu bi* was probably the earli-est type of coin, minted during the sixth century BCE by the Zhou royal house and by the state of Jin. The earliest examples have a hollow "han-dle," imitating a real agricultural spade (Li 1985: 372–5). During the Warring States period, *bu bi* were common in north and central China, while *dao bi* were used mainly in northeast China; *yuan*

Figure 207. Different types of Warring States–period coins: A. *Bu bi*; B. *Dao bi*; C. *Yuan qian* (photos by Gary Lee Todd).

qian were mainly typical in states to the west and northwest. Because the value of each coin was very low, payments were made using strings of coins, a tradition that persisted in China through to the end of the imperial period. Holes in the coins (at the center of the *yuan qian* or in the "handle" of the *bu* and *dao bi*) were used to thread the coins together. Only in the state of Chu, in the southern part of the Warring States world, a different system, which included bronze tokens in the shape of cowrie shells and gold pieces, evolved (Li 1985: 398).

In principle, the minting of coins was a state-run monopoly. Much of the archaeological evidence of minting, including molds for casting coins, was found inside palace areas, a clear sign of close state supervision. It is worth noting, however, that according to historical texts, states sometimes granted powerful individuals or families the right to mint coins. Despite the fact that the individual states minted their own coins, and that different shapes of coin were used simultaneously, it appears

that most states used the same system of value and weights for their coins (Falkenhausen 2006: 413–15). This facilitated "international" trade relations between the states, and, indeed, nonlocal coins are commonly found in excavations of Warring States sites (Peng 2000: 189–206). The rise of affluent private merchants – some of them so rich that they accumulated substantial political power – is well known from the historical documents of the period and is probably related to the development of a market economy and the monetary system (Hsu 1965: 116–30).

The counterfeiting of coins is probably as old as the invention of money. Unique evidence of counterfeiting was found in Lingshou, the capital city of the Zhongshan state: eight molds for the casting of coins were found hidden inside three jars that were buried intentionally in antiquity in an area identified as the commercial district of Lingshou. Six of these molds were for spade-shape coins marked with the character "lin," which was typical of the currency of the Zhao state, and two were for the

Yan state's knife-shaped coins, with the character "yan." It is unclear if the forgery was carried out by profit-seeking merchants or whether it was sponsored by the Zhongshan government as a kind of economic warfare against rival neighboring states (Wu, in press).

REGIONAL IDENTITY AND CROSS-REGIONAL INTEGRATION

The Zhou is the first period in Chinese history when large parts of the territory we call China were integrated. It was also, however, a period for which particularistic local identities become more visible in the archaeological record. The tension between these two processes is evident in the interpretation of the material data by archaeologists and historians. A dominant tendency in the archaeology of the Eastern Zhou period is to define a separate "culture" for each of the different states (e.g., Jin culture, Qi culture, Qin culture, etc.). At the same time, it is also argued that these "state cultures" are modern constructs manufactured by crudely imposing historical definitions upon the diverse archaeological record, thereby masking the more salient process of the period, the increased cultural convergence of the different regions within the Zhou sphere (Falkenhausen 1999: 451).

Much of the evidence for the increased cultural homogeneity of the Zhou realm has already been discussed. Starting from the Western Zhou period, the common style of bronze vessels found in elite graves across the realm and, toward the late Western Zhou, the adaptation of the *lie ding* sumptuary roles almost simultaneously throughout the Zhou sphere offer early evidence of the "globalization" of the Zhou world. There is even more such evidence for the Eastern Zhou period, including clear broader trends, such as the similar patterns in city planning and the layout of city walls, in religious practices such as the spread of new burial types and the use of *mingqi* models, the distribution of

new artistic styles such as inlay decorations, and the diffusion of technologies such as the lost-wax technique and iron casting. Common to all these various cultural attributes is the rapid rate at which they were adopted in different parts of the Zhou sphere. For example, iron casting, which was most likely invented in south China during the sixth or fifth century BCE, was simultaneously adopted by the Yan state in northeast China, Chu in the south, and Qin in the west. This rapid spread of a complex technology indicates not only the intensity of intrastate interactions, including the movement of experts, but also a willingness (or even eagerness) for mutual learning. The replacement of real artifacts with *mingqi* imitations in burials is a tradition that began in the state of Qin but was rapidly adopted in other states (Falkenhausen 2006: 302), suggesting that not just new technologies but also cultural and religious innovations crossed political boundaries easily and became almost universally adopted throughout the Zhou world.

At the same time, manifestations of particularistic local cultures flourished, mainly in the border areas of the Zhou sphere, but in more central areas as well. The culture of the Chu state is probably the most celebrated example for this process. In archaeological terms, the characterization of Chu culture identifies elements of mixed cultural origins. In fact, up until the Warring States period it is almost impossible to identify a Chu culture that differs significantly from other Zhou states, and even during the heyday of the Warring States many elements of the Chu culture were inherited from the Zhou and shared by other states. Other elements of the archaeology of Chu have been attributed to cultural influences from the Sichuan area (Peters 1999: 108). Within this cultural mix, however, there is a stratum of artistic styles and techniques, religious beliefs, and habits that can be identified as reflecting an indigenous Chu culture. For example, although lacquerware pieces are found in other regions as well, their concentration in Chu graves and the variety of shapes

Figure 208. Chu lacquer statues of imaginary animals (Hubei Sheng 1982: 103–4).

and functions they served are specific attributes of Chu culture. Chu lacquers include elite vessels such as alcohol vases and drinking cups, as well as *mingqi* imitations of bronze ritual vessels. Unique to Chu in particular are three-dimensional lacquer artworks, such as statues of imaginary animals (sometimes identified as grave guardian figurines), sculptured screens, and stands for musical instruments (Figure 208). Preserved Chu textiles suggest that supernatural images that tend to intermix parts from different animals, as well as exquisite geometric designs, are also part of what we might term the "Chu artistic language," which is quite distinct from that of the northern states. As discussed earlier, Chu's monetary system was also different from that of the northern states. Therefore, although it is commonly argued that the Chu state was composed of many ethnic groups (Peters 1999: 108–9), it seems that by the Warring States period there was an effort to integrate all of those groups and distinguish them from the universal "Zhou" culture by promoting unique "Chu" cultural elements.

The state of Qin, Chu's main nemesis, is the other well-known example of a particular local identity that developed on the frontiers of the East-

ern Zhou world. Located in the west and expanding into areas that were occupied by non-Zhou groups, the otherness of the Qin was already highlighted in texts written during the Warring States period. For example, the *Zhanguo ce* (戰國策) contains the denunciations that Qin "has common customs with the Rong and Di ['barbarians']; a state with tiger's and wolf's heart; greedy, profit-seeking and untrustworthy, which knows nothing of ritual, propriety and virtuous behavior."[3] These statements, of course, are not unrelated to the fact the Qin posed the main threat to the other states, but it is interesting to note that even Qin's own statesmen seemingly accepted this definition (Shelach and Pines 2006).

From an archaeological perspective, and in stark contrast to the previous depiction, the Qin state appears to have been one of the most traditional states during the earlier years of the Eastern Zhou. Analysis of elite Qin graves suggests, for example, that it was one of the last societies to continue to adhere to the *lie ding* traditions of the Western Zhou. At some point during the fourth century BCE, however, new elements entered the Qin mortuary tradition, elements that seem to have derived from local habits and the belief system of the nonelite population. One such element was the appearance of the so-called catacomb burial (*dongshi mu* 洞室幕), where the deceased was placed in a horizontal chamber adjacent to a vertical shaft (Figure 209). Although catacomb burials are known in northwest China from earlier periods, early Qin graves were all pit (or vertical) grave types, similar to graves in the other Eastern Zhou states. Starting in the middle Warring States period, catacomb burials became common in Qin, and this tradition rapidly reached its zenith by the late Warring States period. The introduction of the catacomb burial tradition also coincided with other new elements in the burial tradition, such as the flex posture of human skeletons and new types of burial goods (Shelach and Pines 2006; Teng 2003).

Burial mounds are another example of how cultural elements, even those shared with other states, were used differently by the Qin. During the Warring States period all major states, including Qin, constructed huge burial mounds on top of the graves of kings and their close kin. These were usually built in the shape of stepped pyramids, with a wooden structure placed on each level to create the illusion of a multistory building. Only in Qin were the mortuary temples placed beside the mound rather than on top of it. This Qin tradition was continued with the construction of the first Qin emperor's burial complex (Chapter 11) and become the norm during the imperial period (Falkenhausen 2006: 336).

The Zhongshan state, located in present-day Hebei province, provides an example of local identity formation in the more central regions of the Zhou world. According to historical texts, the state was founded by a non-Zhou group, descendants of the Di tribes from the north. However, by the fifth century BCE it played an integral part in the interstate politics of the Warring States period, up until its final annihilation by Zhao in 296 BCE. Artifacts associated with the Zhongshan state suggest the development of a highly idiosyncratic culture

that combined features common to all states with those unique to the Zhongshan. This is seen, for instance, in the shape of the royal tombs, which combine the external appearance common to royal graves throughout the Warring States world with unique features in their internal organization, such as stone burial chambers and storage chambers that flank the grave without being connected to it. More to the point are the burial goods found inside the royal graves. The two intact storage chambers of tomb M1 in the royal necropolis at Lingshou provide a unique opportunity to examine a complete set of royal burial goods. Together they contained more than six hundred artifacts (made of bronze, jade, ceramic, and stone, as well as the badly decomposed remains of numerous lacquer artifacts). The western chamber contained standard Warring States ritual objects, including a set of bronze ritual vessels, musical instruments, and jade objects. While the shape of the bronze vessels conforms to the common style of the Warring States period, two of the vessels, a *ding* and a *hu*, were embellished with large inscriptions of more than four hundred characters each. Not only are such long inscriptions atypical for this period, but the placement of the inscription on the outside of the vessel rather than its inside, as was the Zhou norm, is sometimes associated with the non-Zhou origins of the Zhongshan kings. Nevertheless, the content of the inscriptions has been described as conveying values that are the most "Confucian" of all inscriptions known from this period (Mattos 1997: 104–11). Thus, even here we can identify the mixing of highly conservative "Zhou" values with novel local features.

In contrast to the content of the western storage chamber, the most important objects found in the eastern storage chamber were furnishings elaborately decorated in a distinct local style. According to one interpretation, the eastern chamber contained the personal effects of the Zhongshan king (Wu, in press). These furnishings included the bronze parts of a tent, a lamp, and animal-shaped

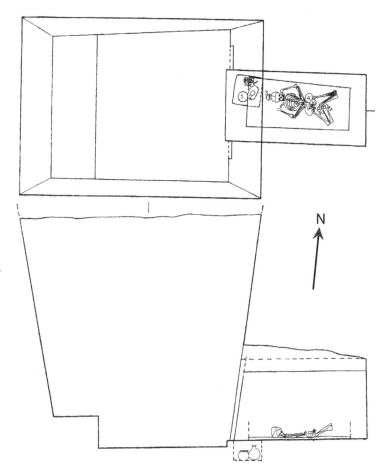

Figure 209. Typical Qin "catacomb" grave (after Xianyang 1998: 37).

decorative objects. Among the most famous artifacts from in the eastern chamber are bronze furniture and furniture parts: a square bronze table supported by four deer, four mythical animals, and four mythical birds and animal-like furniture legs. The animals are all decorated with gold and silver inlay designs (Figure 210).

In a recent analysis on these finding, Wu argues that "hybridity" is the most appropriate term for the culture of Zhongshan, and perhaps for other local cultures of the Warring States period as well. Hybridity is defined as the intentional combination of two or more distinct traditions, thereby

creating a new culture that has clear reference to the original cultures but that is also clearly differentiated from them (Wu, in press). This definition clearly fits the materials described earlier well, since it emphasizes that there was no intention to obliterate either the Zhou-originated pan–Warring States culture or the local features (traditional or invented) of each state, but rather to intentionally refer to and highlight both. This can perhaps be seen as an example of situational identity: the selection of an identity appropriate for the concrete context. The king of Zhongshan, for example, chose a common "Zhou" identity

Figure 210. Bronze furniture parts, shaped like mythical animals, from the eastern storage chamber of grave M1 at Lingshou, capital of the Zhongshan state (photos by Yuri Pines)

when performing rituals that were part of interstate diplomacy, but preferred a more local (or "Di") identity when conducting feasts with his kinsman, thus appealing to their "ethnic-like" solidarity.

The concept of hybridity can provide an initial explanatory framework for understanding the apparent dichotomy between the increased integration of the Zhou realm and its fragmentation into particularistic identities. However, we need first to return to the processes that underlay these two phenomena. Integration was not only the result of the political incorporation of different regions into the Western Zhou system, but, even more fundamentally, a long-term cultural process expressed in the emergence of a shared elite culture, the dissemination of elements of this culture to wider segments of the population, the increased movement of people (elite and nonelite) from

region to region, and more. Integration occurred not only horizontally (between different regions), but also vertically (between different social strata). During the eastern Zhou period, people from nonaristocratic origins were given more opportunities for upward mobility within the state bureaucracies and governments, as well as in the more open economic system. Nonelites brought with them cultural habits, religious beliefs, and ways of artistic expression, and these new elements were increasingly integrated into the culture of the aristocracy.

This second trend – of greater interaction and integration between social strata – can partly explain the process of hybridity and the creation of particularistic local identities. Nonelite cultural elements were, by definition, local in nature, and their integration with the high "Zhou" culture added a local flavor to the culture of the different states. In addition, political motivations no doubt also played a crucial role in this process. Under conditions of intensified interstate conflict, some of states found it advantageous to promote the "patriotic" feelings of the population and to portray other states as barbaric and hostile. This top-down process, in which the state adopted new legal definitions and actively promoted particularistic cultural elements, can be seen clearly in the state of Qin (Shelach and Pines 2006), but it was typical of other states as well.

The dualistic (or even contradictory) nature of social processes during the Zhou period is analogous to current processes of globalization and local resistance to them. The roots of globalization lie in the processes of political and military colonialism of the previous centuries (analogous to the expansion of the Western Zhou), but cur-rent developments are now driven by economic processes, including international trade, intensified interregional communication, and the migration of people from region to region and between states. On the one hand, resistance to the homogenizing effects of globalization is driven from below by people and communities whose culture and social norms are threatened, and at the same time it also comes from above by governments who see advantages in promoting local patriotic sentiments. Obviously, the conditions and processes of the modern world are quite different from those of the Zhou period in China, but using the concept of globalization to compare the Eastern Zhou (and other periods, such as the Roman and Byzantine Empires in the West) with the current world can generate interesting insights and help us better understand both periods.

CHAPTER 11

THE SON OF HEAVEN AND THE CREATION OF A BUREAUCRATIC EMPIRE

The issues addressed in this final chapter represent the culmination of the processes discussed throughout the book. At the same time, though, they also indicate the beginning of a new era in China that lasted for the next two millennia – that of the unified empire. The imperial unification that began with the Qin (秦, 221–207 BCE) and Han (漢, 206 BCE–220 CE) dynasties was founded on political institutions – some of which had been evolving in China since the Shang dynasty, if not before – and on a shared cultural legacy that may be traced to even earlier periods. The unification also stimulated the formation of new institutions on an unprecedented scale, as well as the adoption of new symbols of legitimacy and novel forms of artistic expression, all of which signify a departure from earlier periods. Cultural variation and intercultural interactions did not disappear during the early imperial era, though they did undergo substantial changes. The populations of areas that were integrated into the Chinese Empire were subjected to more intense political and cultural influence from the imperial center, while contact with regions beyond the imperial borders was often shaped by both imperial foreign policy and the counterpolicies of neighboring states and polities.

The period covered in this chapter is well documented in the historical sources, especially in Sima Qian's *Historical Records* (*Shiji* 史記), and Ban Gu's *History of the Former Han Dynasty* (*Han Shu* 漢書).

However, even for such fully historical periods, archaeological research can contribute much more than serving as mere illustrations of known historical "facts" by providing a wealth of data on many issues that were not commonly addressed by traditional historians. These data are relevant in addressing questions that have interested us throughout this book, and continue to form the focus of this, its final chapter. Indeed, this chapter reexamines some of the issues that run throughout the book and introduces some of the more dramatic archaeological discoveries related to the Qin and, to a much lesser extent, the Han periods. Because of these goals and the wealth of relevant archaeological data, this chapter is structured somewhat differently than previous ones. Specifically, the presentation of the data and the discussion of its significance are more closely intertwined than in previous chapters. Also, the emphasis here is intentionally on a few well-known highlights, such as the Qin and Han Great Wall, and the burial complex of the First Emperor of Qin.

HISTORICAL BACKGROUND

Qin Unification and Collapse

The year 221 BCE marks a major milestone in Chinese history.[1] After centuries of bitter competition and ever escalating warfare among the

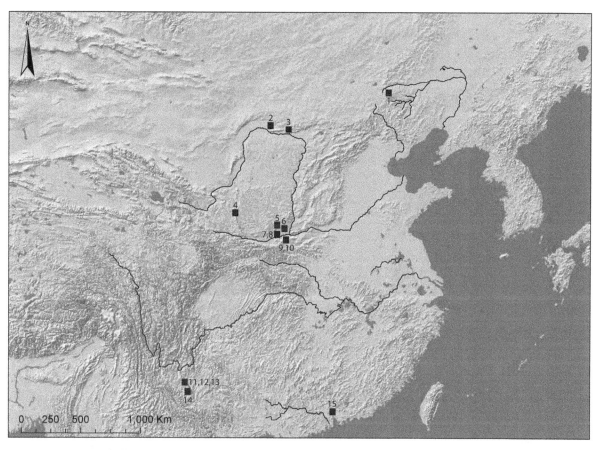

Figure 211. Map of all archaeological sites mentioned in Chapter 11: 1. Sanxingtala; 2. *Wulate* Front Banner; 3. Baotou; 4. Guyuan; 5. Xunyi; 6. Yangling; 7. Xianyang; 8. E'pang palace; 9. Lintong county; 10. Zhaojia Beihucun; 11. Dian; 12. Jincheng; 13. Shizhaishan; 14. Lijiashan; 15. Panyu.

major states, the Qin succeeded in conquering the other "hero states" and established the first unified empire in Chinese history (Figure 212). During the final campaign, which started in around 233 BCE, the Qin were reportedly able to deploy more than one million soldiers on different fronts, from the frozen Liaodong Peninsula to the subtropical areas south of the Yangzi basin. These campaigns were made possible by military, economic, and administrative reforms that had begun in the fourth century BCE and that had transformed the Qin into a highly efficient centralized state. Qin administrative documents discovered in recent decades offer ample testament to the extraordinary ability of the Qin bureaucracy in maintaining, controlling, and appropriating the human and material resources required by the ever expanding "state organized for war" (Lewis 2007; Pines et al. 2013; Yates 1995).

The two main historical figures associated with the ultimate ascendency of the Qin and the establishment of the Qin Empire are King Zheng (政王) of Qin, better known as the First Emperor of Qin (秦始皇帝 259–210 BCE, king 246–221, emperor 221–210), and his advisor and chief minister, Li Si (李斯 d. 208 BCE). Once they had completed military unification, the pair initiated a series of reforms aimed at solidifying the empire's political and cultural unity. These reforms imposed the Qin state's norms – its centralized administrative structure, its laws and ordinances, its weights, measures, and writing system, and more – on the entire unified realm. However, the Qin leaders were careful to present unification not as conquest by the Qin per se, but rather as the creation of a new unified entity. The ensuing novel political system was buttressed by King Zheng's adoption of a new, imperial title – *huangdi* (皇帝, literally "August Thearch," usually translated as "emperor") – instead of the erstwhile *wang* (王, "king"). It was further strengthened by imperial propaganda, which disseminated the ideology of the unified empire and its immense benefits to "all under Heaven" (Kern 2000; Sanft 2014).

Contrary to the emperor's claims that "[w]arfare will not arise again; disaster and harm are exterminated and erased; the black-haired people live in peace and stability; benefits and blessings are lasting and enduring,"[2] wars of expansion started soon after unification. The Qin moved northward into the territories of the pastoral-nomadic peoples, where it built the "Great Wall," and southward into present-day Guangdong and Guangxi provinces and the northern part of Vietnam. Additional state resources were spent on ambitious projects of road and canal construction, the building of palaces and shrines, and construction of the huge burial complex for the First Emperor (Shelach 2013).

Ultimately, the Qin Empire's overextension, and particularly its mobilization of the population, backfired and the Qin's collapse was even faster than its establishment as the single leader of all under Heaven. According to the historical record, the First Emperor died in 210 BCE, during an inspection tour of the conquered territories, and this succession was manipulated so as to catapult his inept son, Huhai, the "Second Emperor," to the throne. Huhai's reputation was severely besmirched in the historical records. However, even if we question their validity, we cannot ignore the extent of the crises that accompanied his reign: A minor rebellion that broke out

in 209 BCE soon engulfed most of the newly conquered territories of the eastern states. Within two years the once formidable Qin armies were decimated, the capital sacked by the rebels, and the empire shattered into pieces. This was a dramatic turn of events, memorialized thereafter in history books, literature, and art.

The anti-Qin wave of rebellion was not a single unified movement under a single leader. More precisely, it evolved into a series of opportunistic uprisings by numerous local gangs, some of which were led by men of humble origins, while others were headed by members of aristocratic families from the vanquished "hero states" of the east. The rebels' ranks were even swelled by a number of Qin officials and generals.

The Founding of the Han Dynasty and the Stabilization of the Imperial System

The unlikely victor who emerged out of the civil war that continued for five more years after the Qin's collapse was Liu Bang (劉邦, d. 195 BCE). Born to a peasant family, Liu Bang became the leader of one of the rebel groups and was fortunate enough to be the first to enter Xianyang, the capital of Qin. Though he was soon driven out by his former ally turned rival Xiang Yu (項羽, d. 202 BCE), Liu Bang was ambitious and determined enough to challenge Xiang Yu shortly thereafter. Xiang Yu made a major political mistake by abandoning the centralized political structure imposed by the Qin and replacing it with a loose confederation of polities over which he presided as "hegemon-king" (*bawang* 霸王). Soon enough, these polities became engulfed in deep turmoil, which allowed Liu Bang to launch a major counterattack from his small fiefdom in the remote Han River region (hence the name of his dynasty). Although Liu Bang was reportedly militarily weaker than Xiang Yu, he was skillful at political maneuvering: a coalition of the warlords under his aegis defeated Xiang Yu in 202 BCE,

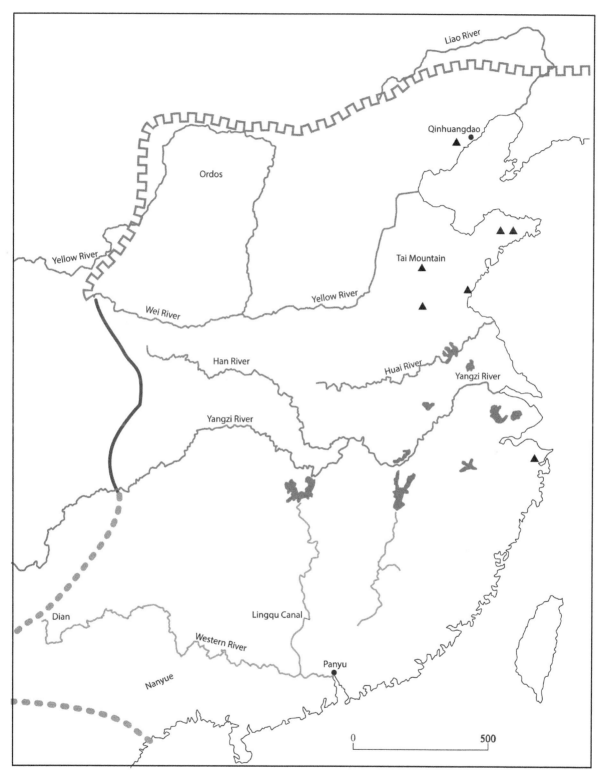

Figure 212. Map of the Qin Empire.

and Liu Bang was duly enthroned as the founding emperor of the Han dynasty (he was posthumously known as the Supreme Ancestor, Gaozu 高祖).

The Han period is commonly subdivided into the Western (or Former) Han dynasty (206 BCE–9 CE) and the Eastern (or Later) Han dynasty (25–220 CE), separated by the Xin dynasty interregnum (新 9–23 CE). The Han reign spanned a remarkably long period of 425 years, longer than any other imperial dynasty in China's history. This prolonged period was crucial for the evolution and solidification of the imperial system, as well as the idea of imperial unity, which would come to be seen as one of the most important aspects of Chinese identity. The importance of this period in the formation of a unified identity and culture is exemplified by the fact that the name Han (漢) is to this day used to identify the Chinese ethnicity, language, script, and so on. When the Han dynasty was first founded, however, it was far from clear that it would eventually be associated with one of the most glorious periods in Chinese history.

When Liu Bang ascended to the throne, the country had been devastated by seven years of civil war. The economic base was in ruin; much of the Qin administrative apparatus was shattered; and the emperor's ability to exert authority was minimal. In order to secure victory, Liu Bang had to placate some of his more powerful allies by granting them far-reaching autonomy in their newly established fiefdoms. To a certain extent, in its first years his empire resembled the Western Zhou state, in which the "Son of Heaven" controlled the western part of the country, while the eastern part was ruled by autonomous potentates. Yet Liu Bang and his successors were not content with this situation. Liu moved swiftly against his former allies, eliminating most of them and granting their territories to members of the Liu lineage. On other fronts however, Liu Bang and his immediate successors exercised restraint. Their goal was to restore the economy and power of the state by granting incentives to peasants and maintaining low tax rates, reinstating the bureaucratic system, and reinventing symbolic manifestations of imperial grandeur through the adoption of new rituals.

The first sixty years of the Western Han were, thus, a period of solidification. The dynasty barely survived various intrigues instigated by Liu Bang's widow, though after her death, when the pendulum shifted back in favor of the Liu lineage, the incumbent, Emperor Wen (文帝, r. 180–157 BCE), adopted a very lenient policy that accepted multiple loci of power in the empire's eastern precincts. This tolerance ended, however, under Emperor Wen's successor, Emperor Jing (景帝, r. 157–141 BCE). Having suppressed uprisings in seven major princedoms, Emperor Jing moved resolutely to curb the rights of regional princes and reassert centralized control over them. Meanwhile, economic and demographic recovery – the result of decades of peace – further contributed to the court's renewed assertiveness.

During its early decades, the Han dynasty also had to confront major difficulties at its margins, most notably in the north, where it was challenged by the Xiongnu (匈奴) Empire, the first unified empire of the steppe people. Beginning in the late second millennium BCE, the peoples living in the vast steppe belt, including on the northern and northwestern borders of China, became increasingly pastoral, and slightly later, with the use of horseback riding, they also became increasingly nomadic. Sometime around the sixth or fifth century BCE, they started taking advantage of their strengths as mounted warriors to raid the Chinese states. However, it was only in the late third century BCE, perhaps as a result of pressure from the expanding Qin state (Di Cosmo 2002), that the Xiongnu leader, Maodun (冒頓), broke out of the confines of the tribal system and formed a formidable confederacy that controlled a vast territory that spanned regions from present-day northeast China and Korea to Mongolia and the eastern parts of Russia.

In 201 BCE, when the Xiongnu became involved in the Chinese Civil War, Liu Bang tried to destroy them, but the results were disastrous: the Han troops were ambushed by Xiongnu forces near Pingcheng (平城), and the emperor just barely escaped capture. Humiliated, Liu Bang had to abandon his policy of military confrontation and resort to diplomatic means in order to maintain tolerable relations with the Xiongnu. This policy, known as the "harmony of relatives" (*heqin* 和親), included recognizing the Xiongnu as the Han's equals, demarcating boundaries between the two states, marrying Han princesses to Xiongnu leaders, who were also presented with lavish gifts of silk and other Chinese products, and the opening of border markets where agriculturalists and pastoralists could exchange their goods.

Centralization and Expansion during the Reign of Han Wudi

When the emperor known posthumously as Emperor Wu (Han Wudi 漢武帝, r. 141–86 BCE) ascended the throne, the sixty-year-old empire was already relatively stable and prosperous. For the emperor and his advisors this meant an opportunity to resume a level of military, administrative, and economic activism that had not been seen since the time of the Qin. The new policies were aimed at bolstering the prestige and authority of the emperor and the central government, as well as expanding the state's economic and military power. Emperor Wu completed the subjugation of autonomous princedoms to the throne and restored the centralized administrative system of the Qin – in practice, if not in name. He marked the start of a new era through a series of symbolic acts, such as reforms to the system of state ceremonies, the renaming of reign periods, and performing the *feng* and *shan* sacrifices on the summit of Mount Tai, as was done by the First Emperor of Qin.

Soon after becoming emperor, Emperor Wu put an end to the *heqin* policy and started a war against the Xiongnu that would last for several generations. Initially, Han troops inflicted major blows on the Xiongnu, expanding the Han Empire's territory northward and westward, toward the Ordos (a region that was lost to the Xiongnu after the Qin's collapse) and the Gansu corridor; and subsequent campaigns brought Chinese troops deep into the Tarim Basin (Figure 213). Further expansion, however, proved impossible, since the arid territories of the steppe belt could not be permanently controlled by the Han settlers, and the Xiongnu had time to readjust and regain some of the initiative. In the meantime, military expansion continued in other directions – to the southwest (present-day Yunnan province), the south (Guangdong, Guangxi, and northern Vietnam), and the northeast (present-day North Korea) – where the Han rarely faced effective military opposition. Here too, though, long-term control over tropical and mountainous areas and non-Chinese tribal populations proved to be difficult. Beyond the difficulties of directly incorporating the conquered territories into the empire, however, the Han's expansion catalyzed more intensive economic, military, and diplomatic interactions with remote areas and foreign cultures.

Activism typified Emperor Wu's other policies as well. He embarked upon a campaign to construct roads and canals, new cities and defensive walls, and extravagant places and shrines. These projects, combined with the resumed military campaigns and territorial expansion, placed a heavy financial burden on the state. In order to finance all these endeavors, the Han court sought to stimulate economic growth and increase its tax revenue, though without overburdening the peasants. Its preferred solution was to establish state monopolies over the minting of coins, the production and selling of iron implements and salt, and active intervention in commercial transactions in general. These policies served two purposes: to generate income for the state and, more generally, to strengthen the state's control over the economy and society.

The period after the death of Emperor Wu is beyond the scope of this book. Suffice it to say that the Han dynasty's overall power gradually declined over the course of the first century BCE, as did the emperors' ability to lead the realm in the face of bureaucratic opposition. The dynasty was overthrown by one of its leading ministers, Wang Mang (王莽), in 9 CE. Following Wang Mang's fall from power, however, the Han was restored, ruling for two more centuries as the Eastern Han or Later Han (侯漢 25–220 CE). While these events were accompanied by profound socioeconomic, administrative, and intellectual changes, the fundamental institutional, ideological, and cultural frameworks established during the Qin and early Han periods remained more or less intact for the next two millennia.

MONUMENTS OF UNIFICATION: THE ARCHAEOLOGY OF THE QIN UNIFICATION POLICIES

Archaeology is usually ill equipped to deal with periods as brief as the duration of the Qin dynasty. In this case, however, because of the unprecedented scale of public works undertaken by the Qin, we are able to pinpoint many findings to this time. In the sections that follow I discuss some of the more remarkable discoveries, many of which are associated with explicit attempts to unify the newly conquered empire and to establish the physical, ideological, and symbolic foundations for an enduring integration of diverse regions and populations.

Communication and Publicity

The First Emperor of Qin and his administration seem to have been well aware of the challenges they faced in controlling the huge empire

that they had conquered. According to the historical records, one of the first measures adopted by the Qin was to demolish the defensive walls built between the different states so as to practically and symbolically integrate the entire empire. They also embarked on the construction of a network of highways that connected the different parts of the empire and facilitated the movement of armies and administrators and the transportation of taxes. Based on place names mentioned in the historical texts, it is estimated that imperial highways stretching 6,800 km were constructed by the Qin (Bodde 1986: 61; Sanft 2014). These included the so-called "Straight Road" (Zhidao 直道), a very wide road extending north from the capital for some 800 km and described by Sima Qian as "cutting through mountains and filling in valleys" (Watson 1993: 3:209). While historians and archaeologists have debated the exact route of the Straight Road, most agree that its remains can be identified in at least a few places. For example, archaeologists have surveyed a 90 km section of what they say is part of the Straight Road near the road's supposed point of origin, in Xunyi (旬邑) county, Shaanxi province. The road is 20 to 30 m wide, is relatively straight, and has a relatively level gradient (of no more than a 10 percent). Auxiliary structures, such as forts, watchtowers, and fortified mountain passes, were built along the road (Guojia Wenwuju 2006). More or less the same characteristics are reported for remains excavated at the northern end of the Straight Road, near Baotou (包头) in Inner Mongolia, where in some places it was constructed on top of a roadbed raised 1 to 1.5 m above ground level (Sanft 2011).

The construction of such an extensive transportation system was not only very costly in terms of manpower and resources, but also quite visible to the population in different parts of the empire. In other words, like other large-scale projects discussed later, the process of constructing these roads not only served the direct purpose of providing fast and reliable transportation routes, but was also in

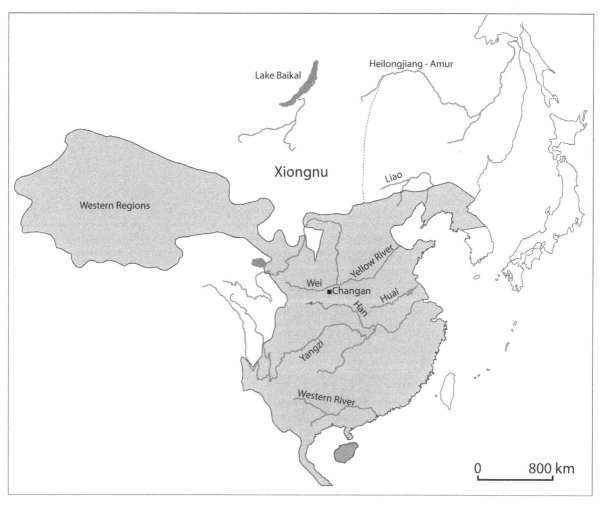

Figure 213. Map of the Han Empire during the reign of Han Wudi.

another sense a massive ideological campaign that communicated the idea of unification to almost the entire population – some of whom participated in the construction and others of whom witnessed it. While touring his empire, presumably on the newly constructed roads, the First Emperor of Qin erected steles on top of prominent and sacred mountains. The inscriptions carved into these steles – such as the one quoted earlier in this chapter – praise the achievements of the Qin and the First Emperor and laud the benefits bestowed upon the entire population (Kern 2000). The very process by which these steles were erected further illus-

trates the role of transportation routes in the Qin's unification propaganda (see Sanft 2014).

Another ambitious transportation project, known only from the historical records, was the Lingqu (靈渠), or "Magic Canal." According to modern scholars, the Lingqu connected the south-ward flowing Li River (灕江) and the north-ward flowing Xiang River (湘江) in present-day Guangxi province, thereby creating a transporta-tion route that connected the Yangzi River with the Xi River (西江) in the far South. While the canal itself was not very long, connecting two rivers flowing in opposite directions was an ingenious achievement, and cutting through the mountain ranges that separated the two rivers must have required monumental effort (Needham 1971: 299–306).

Measures of Standardization

The imposition of a universal set of standards on the entire empire is one of the most famous policies of the First Emperor and Li Si. Apart from its practical aspects, like the construction of roads, the extensive and all-encompassing campaign for standardization was also used to promulgate the idea (and ideology) of the unified empire. Indeed, one of their first acts after the Qin's military victory was to issue an edict decreeing the creation of a unified system of measures in all areas: for the first year of the unification (the twenty-sixth year of the King Zhao), Sima Qian reports that "[h]e [the First Emperor] unified the measurements of capacity, weight, and length. Chariots all had the same width between wheels, and writings all used the same characters" (Nienhauser 1994: I:137).

The units used as standards for the entire Qin Empire were, in most cases, based on those of the Qin state. For example, the varied forms of coins that existed during the Warring States period were all abolished, with the only coins permitted based on the form and values of the Qin's *yuan qian*. The most common coin minted by the Qin Empire was the *banliang* (半兩), which the state started to mint in 336 BCE. These coins have been discovered in large quantities throughout the regions controlled by the Qin Empire, suggesting that the reform was effective (Zhongguo Shehui 2010a: 163–7). Although the units of coins were changed during later periods, the circular shape with a central square hole remained the standard form throughout the imperial era.

The standardization of the Chinese script was another measure that was intended to facilitate the smooth running of the Qin's administrative system, but also had a long-lasting effect on Chinese

Figure 214. Square-shaped bronze vessel used for volume measurement inscribed with the name "Shan Yang," with an inscription of the First Emperor's edict added on its base.

culture. The standardization of measures of weight and volume was another famous reform designed to unify the system throughout the empire and facilitate tax collection and control over the economy. A clear indication that the units used in the First Emperor's reforms were based on those of the predynastic Qin state is provided by a square bronze vessel for measuring volume (*fang sheng* 方升) inscribed with the name of Shang Yang and dated to 344 BCE (Figure 214). An added inscription carved into the vessel's base and dated 221 BCE quotes the First Emperor's edict and proclaims the vessel a measure of standard volumes (Bodde 1986: 59–60).

Numerous Qin weights and volume measuring vessels have been found, many of them inscribed with quotations from the First Emperor's edict, or the renewal of the same edict by the Second Emperor of Qin. These artifacts are made from different materials – bronze, iron, and ceramic – suggesting an extensive and complex system of manufacturing. Their wide geographic distribution further indicates the successful universal imposition of the new system. For example, a total of more than 110 volume-measuring vessels have been found in a range of sites, some in regions as far as Inner Mongolia and in Jilin in the north, Shandong

Figure 215. Qin ceramic volume measurement vessel (*tao-liang*). The inscription reads, "In the twenty-sixth year [of his reign], the emperor unified the lords of the realm. The common people had great peace, and he established the title of emperor. Now he commands chancellors [Wei] Zhuang and [Wang] Wan: 'As for laws and units of measure that are disparate or doubtful, in all cases clarify and unify them'" (translated by Sanft, 2014).

in the east, and Jiangsu and Hubei in the south. They include bronze "scoop-shaped" vessels, similar to the one described earlier, but the most common are circular ceramic vessels known as *taoliang* (陶量), in various sizes reflecting the scale of Qin measurements. A quotation from the imperial edict was stamped onto the exterior of these ceramic vessels before they were fired (Figure 215), a technique indicative of bulk production and the replication of the text, something that resembles a mass communication campaign (Sanft 2014).

Qin weights were made from bronze or iron. Perhaps because they were made from more expensive materials that could have later been recast, fewer of them were found (Zhongguo Shehui 2010a: 160–3). An illustration of the way that the Qin system of weights and volumes most probably worked is provided by an iron weight excavated near the site of the E'pang palace. The weight was cast with an inscription containing the name of Gaonu (高奴), a place located more than 300

km away. It also had inscriptions quoting both the First and the Second Emperors, suggesting that after the Second Emperor ascended to the throne the weight was recalled to the capital to be inspected and marked with the Second Emperor's edict. It was not returned to Gaonu, though, perhaps because of the rapid collapse of the Qin thereafter (Sanft 2014).

The "Great Wall"

As noted in Chapter 10, the construction of long walls as border fortifications is one of the most dramatic features of the Warring States period. The Qin continued with this strategy, but dramatically expanded it and infused it with new meanings. The demolition of the walls that were built between the different states of the Warring States period and the construction of the so-called Great Wall along the northern borders of the empire can be seen as a symbolic act of internal unification and the delineation the borders of all under Heaven. Building the Great Wall necessitated the work of countless people, some of whom were transported to the north from remote parts of the empire. The very construction process itself can thus be seen as embodying unification.

Despite or perhaps because of the wall's status as one of the most famous monuments in Chinese history, the exact route of Qin's Great Wall and the amount of labor invested in it are passionately disputed among scholars. According to the *Historical Records*, General Meng Tian (蒙恬) was sent with 300,000 men to attack the tribes on the northern frontiers in 215 BCE. In an entry from the following year, Meng Tian's victories are described, followed by a statement that the Qin built a wall north of the Yellow River. The next year, more people were reportedly sent to work on the wall. Meng Tian's biography ascribes him explicit responsibility for constructing the wall, which is said to have been 10,000 *li* (萬里) in length (*Shiji* 88; Watson 1993: 3:207–13).

The measure 10,000 *li* (ca. 4,100 km) is clearly a symbolic figure that should not be taken to convey the actual length of the wall. Many scholars believe that the Qin made extensive use of walls constructed on the northern borders of the states of the Qin, Zhao, and Yan prior to the imperial unification and that Meng Tian and his workforce did not actually have that much to do (e.g., Waldron 1990: 16–29). Such minimalist views, however, are not supported by either the textual or archaeological records. Historical texts make it clear that the wall was built only after Meng Tian had defeated the northern tribes, and thus it is reasonable to assume that it was built in territories taken from Qin's enemies and not on the borders of the preunification states. Recent archaeological work has identified sections of this Qin wall, confirming that they are located north of the walls constructed by the states of the Warring States period (Xu 2002: 260–1). The total length of the Qin Great Wall comes to just longer than 2,800 km (Figure 216).

The wall's architects made use of the natural features of the terrain: in places that are naturally more difficult to cross, the artificial barrier was probably modest, while in flat areas, where armies were more likely to launch an invasion, they built more extensive fortifications, which may have included several lines of walls, as well as moats and other types of fortification. Stones were the main raw materials used in places where they could be easily collected, while in other regions only the outer and inner faces of the wall were made of stone and the inner core was made of earth and rubble. In yet other places the entire wall was made of pounded earth (Li 2001).

In one of the more comprehensive surveys of the remains of the Qin wall, archaeologist Li Yiyou (2001: 9) identified a wall section at Wulate Front Banner (烏拉特前旗) in Inner Mongolia as one of the best preserved sections, and possibly most representative of other locations as well. This section of the wall is 5 to 6 m high, some 6 m wide at the bottom, and 3 m wide at the top. Indeed, similar dimensions were reported at other well-preserved sites (Li 2001: 10, 13, 21). In other places, such as the visible remains of the wall near Guyuan (固原), in Ningxia province, semicircular towers attached at intervals to the outer face of the wall were also identified (Figure 189).[3]

If, as Li argues, the remains at Wulate Front Banner are typical, then 21.42 m³ of material would have been needed to construct one meter of wall– without taking into account the construction of the wall's foundations, attached towers, and other auxiliary installations. Elsewhere, I have calculated that the construction of this a wall over a distance of 2,800 km would have required an investment of 192,976,000 to 265,720,000 person-days. Assuming that a person worked 350 days per year, and that the project was completed in five years (214–209 BCE), it follows that between 110,272 and 151,840 people would have been needed to construct the entire Qin wall (Shelach 2013). This calculation does not take into account the construction of camps, beacon towers, and other installations that are known to have accompanied the line of the walls of the Warring States, the Qin, and the Han (Di Cosmo 2002: 144; Li 2001). Moreover, building walls in remote locations and in difficult terrains such as mountains and deserts would have required a great deal of resources beyond those directly invested in the construction of the wall itself, including routes for transporting supplies to the construction sites. This would have been especially true in sparsely populated areas, where there would have been no local food resources to draw upon. All in all, then, it does not seem an exaggeration to estimate that at least 300,000 men worked on the wall for five years, in addition to other direct and indirect expenses.

The Burial Complex of the First Emperor

In addition to the "Great Wall," the Qin dynasty period is known for the construction of

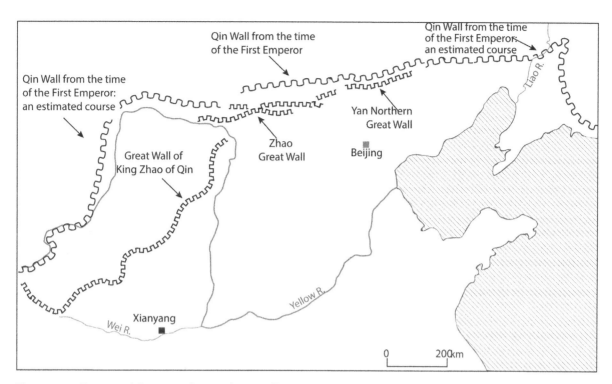

Figure 216. Routes of the preunification long walls and the great walls of the Qin and Han periods.

many other large-scale structures that would have required the recruitment of a massive workforce from the all over the empire. One well-known example is that of the 120,000 noble families from the six conquered states who were transferred to the Qin capital of Xianyang, where they were housed and taken care of by the state, including the construction of palaces that imitated those of the conquered regional lords (Nienhauser 1994: I:138). The ongoing construction in Xianyang itself is another example: according to the records, one particular structure in Xianyang – the so called E'pang Palace (阿房宫) – was so large that it was never completed (Sanft 2008). Recent excavations at the site identified with this palace have revealed a huge complex that included, among other buildings, a single pounded earth foundation platform sized 1,270 by 426 m, with some of it still preserved to the height of 12 m.

The largest of the Qin's projects in terms of scale and labor investment is the so-called mausoleum (but better described as a burial complex) of the First Emperor. In the past, the only evidence of this monument's existence was Sima Qian's brief description and the extant above-ground earth mound. Following the initial discovery in 1974 of the "Terracotta Army" pits in Lintong county (临潼), some 40 km east from Xianyang, intensive research was carried out in a wide area around the central earth mound and our understanding of the organization and contents of this burial complex have subsequently increased dramatically.

Continuing the tradition of the Warring States period, the grave itself was topped by huge earth mound. The mound, called Mount Li (郦) in the historical records, has a rectangular base of ca. 350 × 350 m and currently stands some 50 m tall; according to some estimates, it was originally more than 100 m tall (Zhongguo Shehui 2010a: 78–81). Sima Qian described the tomb under this mound as a cosmological world full of treasures and wonders:

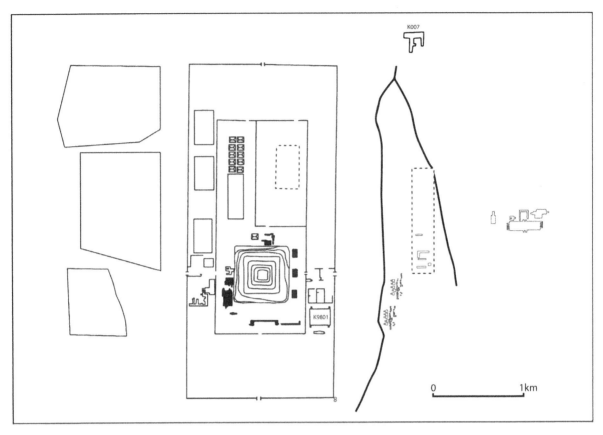

Figure 217. Map of the burial complex of the First Emperor of Qin.

More than 700,000 convict laborers from the world were sent there. They dug through three [strata of] springs, poured in liquid bronze, and secured the sarcophagus. Houses, officials, unusual and valuable things were moved in to fill it. He [the First Emperor] ordered artisans to make crossbows triggered by mechanisms. Anyone passing before them would be shot immediately. They used mercury to create rivers, the Jiang [Yangzi] and the He [Yellow River], and the great seas, wherein the mercury was circulated mechanically. On the ceiling were celestial bodies and on the ground geographic features. (Nienhauser 1994: I:155)

Unfortunately, the grave has yet to be excavated, and so Sima Qian's fantastic description cannot be verified. Nevertheless, during the past forty years of archaeological research in areas surrounding the burial mound, a number of impressive discoveries have been made. The mound was enclosed by two concentric walls: an inner one circling an area some 578 by 1,350 m in size, and an outer enclosure of 974 by 2,173 m. The entire area was packed with ritual buildings and pits filled with precious artifacts. Other groupings of monuments, including the famous Terracotta Army pits, are spread around this core in an area that is now estimated to cover between 35 and 60 km² (Ciarla 2005: 133; Duan 2011: 2; Zhao and Gao 2002: 16–17) (Figure 217). These estimates would mean that this is most probably the largest burial complex of a single ruler ever constructed anywhere in the world.

The above-ground structures of the First Emperor's burial complex were made of wood and

Figure 218. Panoramic view of pit 1 and the "Terracotta Army" in it (photo by Noga Feige).

are poorly preserved, but the below-ground pits and their content are remarkably well preserved. Most of these pits are not mere trenches excavated into the ground, but real underground buildings with paved floors, pounded earth walls, and wooden ceilings. The most famous are the three pits containing the Terracotta Army.[4] Located some 1.5 km east of the grave enclosures, these pits vary in size and content. The largest, pit 1, is 230 m long and 62 m wide, and was originally 4 to 6 m deep. Its floors were paved with as many as 250,000 ceramic tiles. It was internally divided into long corridors by 10 pounded earth walls that supported a roof made of large tree trunks. The tree trunks themselves were covered by layers of mats and fine earth and sealed with earth up to the original ground level. Originally, the life-size ceramic statues of warriors and horses stood in under-

ground corridors that were not filled with earth (Figure 218). However, sometime after the burial complex was completed – perhaps during the time of the revolt against the Qin – the wooden roofs were burned, causing them to collapse, thereby burying and breaking the statues. The wooden roof beams are better preserved in pit 2, where the pit construction techniques can be observed quite clearly (Figure 219). Pit 2 is smaller and R-shaped, measuring 98 m from north to south and 124 m in its widest east-west section. Pit 3 is smaller still, measuring 21 m from north to south and 17 m from east to west.

The pits were constructed to house a replica Qin army unit in fighting formation. Pit 1 contains the bulk of an infantry unit, with archers at the front and at the flanks, heavy infantry at the back, and field commanders riding chariots. Pit 2 contains

Figure 218 (*continued*)

foot soldiers and more fighting chariots, while pit 3 probably represents the headquarters of the unit commander, his chariot, and his guards. It is estimated that the three pits contain at least seven thousand ceramic human figures, six hundred ceramic horses, and one hundred wooden chariots, not all of which have been excavated and restored. They were equipped with real bronze weapons, horse and chariot gear, and other paraphernalia (Ciarla 2005: 187–217; Zhongguo Shehui 2010a: 99–103) (Figures 220 and 221). The army was not meant to be seen by anyone after being sealed inside the three pits. It was a gigantic *mingqi* (明器) – a model that was meant to become real in the netherworld and serve the First Emperor during his afterlife.

The manufacturing of all the human and horse statues that made up this huge replica army (and other similar statues, some of which are already known from other excavated pits, and many others that presumably have not yet been discovered) had to have been an industrial-scale operation. Each human figure weighs up to 200 kg, and the horse statues are heavier still. In order to overcome the technical difficulties involved in producing such huge ceramic statues, each was composed of several parts, produced separately and then assembled to form the complete figure. The body parts were shaped like hollowed tubes – hence the association with the bureau in charge of producing water pipes, roof tiles, and hollow bricks – and produced in a standardized fashion using unified measures and, in many cases, molds. Each mold could be used to produce multiple clay parts, in such a way that the entire army – which appears to be composed of unique individual figures – is in fact made

Figure 219. View of the wooden roof beams covering pit 2 (photos by Noga Feige and Netta Drucker).

up of different combinations of a limited number of basic component pieces. To enhance the individual appearance of the statues, artisans added or incised facial features, such as mustaches, eyes, eyebrows, hair, and the like.

The statues were fired in special large kilns, yet to be discovered, at temperatures of between 900 and 1,050°C. After being fired they were painted with bright lacquer coating colors (Ledderose 2000: 51–73). The preparation of those colors and their application to the surface of the statues must have been extremely labor-intensive, but they are not well preserved and can be seen in only a very few examples (Figure 222).

Characters stamped into the floor tiles suggest that they were produced by imperial workshops. Similar seal impressions were also found on differ-

ent parts of the human and horse statues, together with the names of palace artisans employed by the Qin bureau in charge of producing water pipes, roof tiles, and hollow bricks. Other statues carry incised inscriptions with the names of artisans (Figure 223) who normally worked in private workshops and who were probably conscripted for the task from areas as far away as 200 km from the site (Barbieri-Low 2007: 7–9). Although individuals are mentioned by name in these inscriptions, they were probably the foremen or chief artisans of teams. According to one reconstruction of the production process, one group of workers was in charge of producing one statue, up until it was assembled and ready to be fired, while the firing and painting were carried out by others (Ledderose 2000: 71). Simple and labor-intensive tasks such as

Figure 219 (*continued*)

preparing the clay and pressing it into the molds were performed by criminals or regular conscripts. Other tasks, such as designing and producing the molds, retouching the fine details on statues' faces, preparing the paints and painting the sculptures, and so on, were executed by professional artisans.

Despite their modern fame, the Terracotta Army pits were not actually one of the most important parts of the First Emperor's burial complex. Their position far outside the inner enclosures of the complex (Figure 217) suggests a relatively low status. Moreover, some of the pits closer to the center of the complex, while not as large, contained artifacts that would have been more difficult to produce and were made from expensive materials. One example is pit K9801, located inside the second enclosure around the

burial mound. This pit contained thousands of small limestone plaques that, according to one account, were attached to one another with bronze wires so as to make 150 suits of armor and 50 head armor pieces (or helmets) (Ciarla 2005: 178). One reconstructed suit consisted of more than six hundred plaques. Suits of armor and helmets made of stone are not practical, so like the Terracotta Army, they must have been ritual objects produced especially for the grave complex. Another example is pit K0007, located some 900 m northeast of the outer enclosing wall. This F-shaped pit is 60 m long and was originally filled with water and furnished with bronze statues of water birds – twenty swans, twenty geese, and three cranes – in imitation of a river scene (Selbitschka 2013) (Figure 224).

Figure 220. Examples of warriors and horses from the "Terracotta Army" pits (photos by Gary Lee Todd).

Other pits were found to contain not only statues and artifacts, but also bones of exotic animals (a zoo?) and horses (stables?), and additional pits

Figure 221. A bronze weapon from the "Terracotta Army" pits (photo by Gary Lee Todd).

are being discovered and excavated every year. Perhaps the most impressive discovery so far is a pit measuring 55 m in length, located inside the inner enclosure, only some 20 m from the burial mound, which contained bronze models of two chariots. Each chariot, measuring ca. 3 m long and 1 m high, is drawn by four bronze horses (Figure 225). These artifacts are each composed of seven thousand parts and weigh 2.4 tons, and are meticulous imitations, at a reduced size, of real Qin chariots. With their realistic details on the horses and charioteers and the inlaid decoration on the chariot parts, they also represent a remarkable level of artistic achievement that testifies to the craftsmanship of highly skilled artisans.

It is much more difficult to estimate the amount of work that was invested in the construction of

A   B

Figure 222. Fragments of the paint colors that covered the human and horse statues of the "Terracotta Army" (photos by Netta Drucker [A] and Gary Lee Todd [B]).

the First Emperor's burial complex than it is for the Great Wall. However, given its immense size and the wealth of findings in the small areas that have already been excavated, it appears that the tradi-

Figure 223. Stamped and incised inscriptions found on the human statues of the "Terracotta Army" (after Ledderose 2000: 69).

tional figures were not an exaggeration. According to Sima Qian, work on the grave started even before the unification of the empire, yet in an entry dated to 212 BCE he specifies that seven hundred thousand criminals were allocated to work on the project (Nienhauser 1994: I:155). This may refer to a dramatic increase in the scale or pace of the work, and, as noted, these conscripts probably performed unskilled manual labor. However, the more professional work would have required highly trained craftsmen. Thus, the actual number of people working on this monument over time was even greater.

The huge expenditure of resources in the construction of the Great Wall, the First Emperor's burial complex, and other Qin monuments, and the burden this would have placed on the common people in the form of taxes and conscription labor might have been partly responsible for the rapid collapse of the Qin after the death of the First Emperor. Other factors, though – including the Qin's very rigid sociopolitical system – may have been no less or even more significant (Shelach 2013).

A   B

Figure 224. A. Reconstruction of pit K0007 (after Selbitschka 2013: 152); B. Bronze bird statue from the pit (photo by Gary Lee Todd)

UNIFICATION, CULTURAL INTEGRATION, AND REGIONAL VARIATION

Cultural Integration under the Qin and Its Fate during the Han and Later Periods

Unification and integration – not only political but also economic, social, and cultural – are probably the greatest legacy of the Qin dynasty. The universal set of standards discussed previously, which continued to be used throughout the imperial era, is a clear example. The First Emperor's burial complex is another, demonstrating both continuity from the preimperial period and innovations that signify the beginning of a new era. The symbolic framework established in the First Emperor's burial complex borrowed from Eastern Zhou traditions (of the Qin and other states) many of its components, for instance, the use of a large earthen mound to mark the location of the ruler's grave and the placement of representations (*mingqi*) of humans and various artifacts inside the tomb and accompanying pits. However, in the First Emperor's burial complex, those elements were synthesized in a way that was both novel and unprecedented in scale. For example, while the statues of the so-called Terracotta Army are *mingqi*, their naturalistic style and life-size proportions have no precedent.

As can be seen in Yangling (陽陵), in the burial complex of Emperor Jing of the Han dynasty, the Qin traditions determining the layout and

Figure 225. One of the bronze chariots from the First Emperor's burial complex (photo by Gray Todd).

contents of the emperor's tomb were carried on to the early Han period (Yan et al. 2009). The scale of Yangling is quite impressive, although it is unlikely that it entailed anything like the amount of work invested in the First Emperor's burial complex.[5] Like the burial complex of the First Emperor, it is also concentrated around a massive burial mound surrounded by walls (Figure 226). Ritual pits with *mingqi* offerings, including ceramic statues of warriors, servants, animals, equipment, and more, this time mostly at a reduced scale, also take up large parts of the Yangling complex. The layout

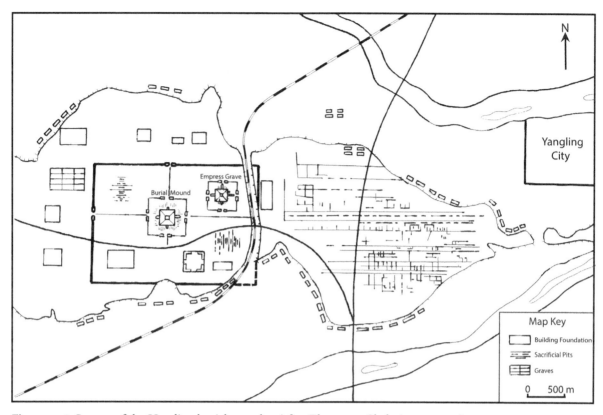

Figure 226. Layout of the Yangling burial complex (after Zhongguo Shehui 2010a: 313).

of emperors' burial complexes transformed during later periods, as seen, for instance, in the emergence of "Spirit Roads" (*shendao* 神道) that led to the imperial burial temple and burial mound (Paludan 1991). However, the basic organization and, more important, the symbolic meaning of these monuments show a marked degree of continuity throughout the imperial era.

The homogenization of religious beliefs and burial practices was not unique to the uppermost sociopolitical strata or to emperors. During the Qin and, even more so, in the Han period, many of the beliefs having to do with death and burial filtered down to the lower elites, and perhaps even to nonelite strata throughout the empire. The use of *mingqi* models became enormously popular, as can be seen in the scale as well as in the variety of such objects found in graves of the middle classes of the Han period (Erickson 2010: 65–77; Wu 2010: 87–126). In comparison with the *mingqi* artifacts

placed in emperors' graves – which were of high quality and produced by imperial workshops – those found in the graves of the lower strata were usually smaller and of lower quality. These artifacts, which were made of ceramic, wood, cloth, and other relatively inexpensive materials, vividly represented many aspects of life during the Han period: they included figurines of peasants and workers; models of their tools, livestock, fields, farms and houses, stoves, granaries, and watchtowers; statues of musicians and circus performers; and much more besides (Figure 227). The proliferation of this practice, together with the layout of graves, which increasingly came to imitate the layout of houses (Erickson 2010), suggest a process by which people throughout the vast empire adopted similar ideas of the netherworld as a mirror image of the world of the living. While local variation declined, it seems that political unification accelerated the process of cultural integration, which

had preceded it and continued to evolve throughout the imperial era.

Other aspects of material culture also reflect
the process of cultural and social homogenization
through the Qin and Han periods. For example,
a city-building project initiated during the Western Han period helped disseminate not only a city
structure that was similar throughout the empire,
but also, we can assume, concepts of city life and
of the function of cities as central nodes in the
empire's bureaucratic and economic framework
(Chen 2013). The production of iron tools at an
ever increasing scale, to the point that every peasant household now used them, combined with the
eventual monopolization of this industry by the
imperial authority, resulted in a homogenization
of artifact types and economic practices. Other
types of industry and art, such as lacquer production and stone carving, also reflect the diffusion of
techniques, styles, and artistic themes throughout
the empire.

The large-scale movement of populations also
contributed to the integration of the empire. We
have already mentioned the relocation of 120,000
noble families from the six conquered states to the
vicinity of the Qin capital. This policy, moreover,
was not limited to the upper strata of the population. Excavations at a kiln site located only 500 m
from the Terracotta Army pits yielded bones from
121 individuals who had not been formally buried.
An analysis of the bones suggests that they suffered from pathologies associated with hard manual
labor. It is, therefore, assumed that these individuals were part of the workforce brought in to construct the First Emperor's mortuary complex (Xu
et al. 2008: 1). Sequences of mitochondrial DNA
that the researchers were able to reconstruct for
nineteen individuals from this group show a great
deal of variation – indeed, more variation than can
be found among the thirty-two current population
groups of Han and non-Han people from different parts of China, with which they were compared (Xu et al. 2008: 5) – suggesting that workers
were brought to the construction site from differ-

ent regions across the newly conquered empire.
Epigraphic evidence further supports this observation. The nineteen epitaphs found on tombs of
the mausoleum's workers at the Zhaojia Beihucun
(趙家背戶村) cemetery, discovered in 1979, provide information on the origins of the workers, all
of whom came from the newly conquered eastern
territories (Yuan Zhongyi 2008: 31–2).

The large-scale relocation of workers, essential
for the execution of these grand Qin projects, led
to the intermingling of the empire's peasant populations, presumably helping lower traditional barri-
ers, "diluting" popular local cultures, and creating
a more homogeneous culture and society throughout the newly conquered empire. Policies such as
these continued during the Han period as well. For
example, emperor Wu of Han (r. 141–86 BCE) is
famous for moving enormous populations and set-
tling them in newly conquered territories in the
northern and western frontiers of his empire.

Regional Variation and Resistance to the Unified Culture

Thus far we have described all of the processes
during the Qin and the Han as leading to a cultural homogenization that went hand in hand with
political unification, but this is obviously a one-
sided picture. It is clear, for example, that areas at
the center of the empire were more rapidly and
more fully integrated into a unified "Chinese"
culture and society, while the process was much
more partial and took much longer in areas further from the center. Not only was political control over the periphery less stable, but indigenous
cultural affiliations in these areas – most of which
had only recently come into contact with "Chinese" culture – were stronger and more enduring.
Moreover, rapid political and cultural unification
must have caused local resistance. Throughout the
Han period we hear of uprisings, many of them
in faraway regions and some of them motivated
by, or at least legitimized in terms of, local identities. While political resistance was usually futile,

Figure 227. Examples of Han-period *mingqi* (photos by Yuri Pines and Gray Todd).

we can interpret the lingering presence of local styles, artifact types, habits, and so on as a form of cultural resistance.

An example of subtle regional variation is the practice in the Yangzi River region of producing wooden *mingqi* human figures dressed in miniature silk garments, a tradition inherited from the Chu state. In the Yellow River region, meanwhile, *mingqi* figurines were made of ceramic and painted after firing, in the tradition of the Qin and other northern states (Erickson 2010: 65–77). In the following sections I present two examples, from south and southwest China, which represent more dramatic cases of the persistence of local traditions even during periods of direct control by, and intensive interaction with, the Han Empire.

LINGNAN: INTEGRATION AND VARIATION

After unifying the central regions of the Yellow and Yangzi Rivers, the First Emperor of Qin embarked on an ambitious military expedition to the south. With an army of half a million soldiers he conquered the region of Lingnan, which was subsequently annexed to the empire. In order to facilitate control of this region and better integrate it with the north, the Qin constructed transportation routes, including the previously mentioned Lingqu Canal, and attempted to establish military command and administration centers. One of the generals dispatched to Lingnan, a man named Zhao Tuo (趙佗), took advantage of the internal chaos that followed the collapse of the Qin to establish an independent state, Nanyue (南越). Nanyue remained an independent state (though under the control of a ruling family from the north) for more than ninety years. In 112–111 BCE, however, Emperor Wu conquered all of southern China, including Hainan Island and areas that are currently parts of Vietnam, and annexed it to his empire, subdividing it into nine Han commanderies. Politically, the area remained calm for about 150 years. The local rebellions that broke out after 40 CE did not pose a real threat to the Han hegemony over Lingnan, which lasted until the final disintegration of the Han Empire during the second half of the second century CE, but they did bring to the surface suppressed ethnic tensions and highlighted the fact that the local population was not fully integrated into the shared Chinese culture (Yu 1986).

Not much is known about domestic sites in the Lingnan region. The best known examples come from the city of Panyu (番禺), the capital of the Nanyue state, located in present-day Guangzhou province. The most famous site at Panyu is the so-called Nanyue Palace: a large compound mostly composed of pools of different shapes and water canals, all of which seem to have been part of a royal garden. Large pounded earth palace foundations have also been partly excavated. Bricks and tiles found at the site are often stamped with Chinese characters representing the names of officials and other inscriptions in the Han fashion (Allard 2006; Yang 2004: 2:261–2).

A rich grave, identified as that of Zhao Mo (趙眜), the second king of the Nanyue state (r. 137–122 BCE), is one of the best examples of a combination of Han dominance with local cultural features. This was a complex vertical grave, dug into the hillside and lined with stone slabs. These characteristics, as well as the fact that the tomb imitates the structure of a house, are typical Western Han features. The body of Zhao Mo itself was encased in a jade suit, a privilege reserved for Han emperors and their close relatives. A seal with the title Emperor Wen (文帝) demonstrates not only the high aspirations of Zhao Mo, but also his cultural point of reference. The wall decorations of the tomb, in contrast, have been identified as deriving from Chu art. The grave's rich furnishings also reflect a mixture of Han-style artifacts (mainly jades) with artifacts in the Chu style and the local "Yue style," such as typical bronze *ding* vessels and bells, as well as artifacts derived from cultures further to the south, such as the Dongson of Vietnam (Allard 2006; Erickson et al. 2010).

The "Chinese" style of the grave is perhaps not surprising, considering the Zhao family came to the region from the north during the Qin conquest. However, more than two thousand smaller graves found in the Lingnan region suggest that northern influences were far more pervasive. Some of the graves belonged to Han officials and immigrants, but others must have belonged to the indigenous population. The layout and construction techniques of many of these tombs follow trends from the north: vertical pits with wooden coffins during the Western Han period, and horizontal brick tombs during the Eastern Han period. However, other elements, such as the common use of waste pits and pebble floors, are seen to

Figure 228. Ceramic *mingqi* artifact in the shape of a boat from the Lingnan region (photo by Gray Todd) and a typical southern house (photo by Yuri Pines).

represent the continuation of local traditions. The furnishing of graves also suggests a hybrid culture. From the middle of the Western Han period in particular, grave goods included typical Han artifacts, such as bronze mirrors, lacquer objects, and ceramic *mingqi* of different kinds. However, the *mingqi* objects themselves sometimes reflect the unique features of the local culture – such as the popularity of models of boats (reflecting the importance of water transportation in the region), and the depiction of houses in a typical local style (Allard 2006) (Figure 228).

THE DIAN OF YUNNAN: THE FLOURISHING
OF LOCAL CHARACTERISTICS AMID INTENSIVE
INTERACTIONS

Yunnan was never brought under the control of the Qin Empire, so direct Chinese involvement there was relatively late. During the Han, however, the history of this region was somewhat similar to that

of Lingnan. The area around Dian Lake, which is associated with the Dian (滇) polity, is geographically distant from the center of the Han dynasty, separated by tall mountains and rugged terrain. Expansion into this region commenced under Emperor Wu. In 122 BCE, the first Han envoy was dispatched to Yunnan, and thirteen years later, following the incorporation of the Nanyue kingdom in the south, it too was conquered by the Han Empire. Han control of the area was flexible and exercised in different ways: a formal Han commandery, named Yizhou (益州), was established, but a degree of authority was also delegated to the local elite; the chief of one of the local tribes was even honored with the title, King of Dian. Han control of Yunnan was far from stable: at least seven major rebellions between 105 BCE and 176 CE are reported in the historical texts, and although it remained part of the empire, control over the area seems to have been tenuous during the latter part

Figure 228 (*continued*)

of the Western Han and throughout the Eastern Han (Yu 1986: 457–460).

Chinese sources of the time describe Yunnan as a heterogeneous mix of ethnic tribes and cultural habits. Some of these tribes were agriculturalist and lived in sedentary communities, while others led a pastoral-nomadic way of life. The two groups discussed most extensively in the historical texts – the Yelang (夜郎) and the Dian – are described as having permanent settlements and even cities, a developed economy, and an evolved political hierarchy (Watson 1993: 2:253–8). This portrayal is at least partly supported by the archaeological record. Since at least the third millennium BCE, some societies in this region had been slowly developing agriculture and sedentism, eventually adopting

bronze technologies and developing sociopolitical hierarchies. Recent surveys suggest that large domestic sites existed in the Dian region by the second half of the first millennium BCE (Yao 2010: 226). It appears that the Han incursion into the region brought about changes in the local settlement patterns, which are not yet fully understood. Unlike earlier centers, which were usually located on the floodplain near Lake Dian, a large Han-style settlement, named Jincheng (晋城), was established in the foothills. The introduction of Han-style building techniques is evident in the ceramic roof titles (Yao and Jiang 2012).

In contrast with domestic arrangements, much more is known about mortuary practices in the Dian Lake region from excavations of cemeteries such as Shizhaishan (石寨山) and Lijiashan (李家山), and findings there have been used to define "Dian culture." Typical Chinese artifacts found in many of the Dian graves, such as lacquerware, bronze mirrors, and coins, reflect strong outside influence, which started before the actual conquest of the region but accelerated after it. It is tempting to see some of these artifacts as directly reflecting events described in the historical texts. A golden seal, found in grave 6 at Shizhaishan and inscribed with Chinese characters that read "Seal of the King of Dian" (滇王之印) (Figure 229), is a prominent example. A closer examination of Dian burial practices and the content of their graves, however, reveals a much more complex picture of sociocultural development on the fringes of the Han Empire.

Dian graves, some of which contained a wooden coffin, were for the most part rock-cut pits that do not resemble the common shapes of Han graves. Some graves were extremely rich, while others, especially those in more peripheral cemeteries, were quite poor, suggesting an evolved sociopolitical hierarchy independent of the Han system. According to one statistic, the two wealthiest graves in a sample of more than 200 Dian graves contained an average of 295 artifacts, mostly bronzes, while the 149 poorest graves had an average of only 2.41 artifacts (Lee 2001a).

Typical goods found in Dian graves include the various Chinese artifacts mentioned earlier and imitations of Chinese bronze weapons, but the majority of Dian grave goods and the most impressive were bronze artifacts unique to the Dian culture or artifacts that reflect cultural interaction with other non-Chinese groups. Among the most notable artifacts are bronze drums and bronze containers. The shape and decoration of the drums, some of which stand more than half a meter tall, are similar to those of artifacts found at Dongson sites in northern Vietnam, thereby pointing to an association. The boat motif decorations found on these drums and other artifacts

Figure 229. Gold seal from grave 6 at Shizhaishan inscribed with the characters "Seal of the King of Dian."

suggest intensive water-mediated contact between the two regions, probably through the many rivers that flow from the northwest to the southeast into the Gulf of Tonkin. Even more impressive are the containers topped by small bronze figurines of humans, animals, and structures, which form complex scenes (Figure 230). These scenes

Figure 230. Bronze container from the Shizhaishan cemetery topped with a scene of ritual activity, including the model of a shrine and drums (photos by Gary Lee Todd).

are unique to Dian culture and must have represented important events such as wars, rituals, feasts, tribute presentations, and so on. The very production of those bronze figurines, some of which are gilded, suggests a high level of craftsmanship.

The containers themselves were often filled with cowrie shells that were brought to Yunnan from the Indian Ocean.

Other types of objects typically found in Dian graves are small offering tables made of bronze,

Figure 231. Bronze offering table with long-horned bulls (photos by Gary Lee Todd).

which were often decorated with images of bulls with large horns. The graves also contained a large number of bronze plaques, some of which also depict large-horned bulls and other idiosyncratic local scenes (Figure 231), while others are more clearly associated with the bronze traditions of northern China, Mongolia, and Central Asia (Chapter 9). These plaques and many of the bronze weapons found in Dian graves indicate intensive contact with the non-Chinese groups to the north and west of the Han .Empire.

In contrast to the trajectory of Lingnan, where Qin and Han intrusions led to the adoption of Chinese habits and styles, albeit with local modifications and a certain degree of persistence of the local traditions, it seems that, in Yunnan, Han artifacts and influences were incorporated into local traditions alongside artifacts and styles that came from other directions. Even more interesting, it appears that increased contact with Chinese culture during the late preimperial era and the beginning of the imperial era was a catalyst for a tremendous flourishing of local culture. The large-scale production of ritual artifacts, some of which were large and complex, like the containers with the bronze figurine scenes, as well as of personal

bronze ornaments in the local style, was quite new. It is possible that internal competition among local elites and small-scale political units contributed to this cultural flowering (Yao 2010). This process is reminiscent of the one discussed in Chapter 10, where local cultures like the Chu state reached the pinnacle of their scale and creativity within the context of the increased "globalization" of the Chinese sphere. Perhaps in Yunnan, which was not as comprehensively integrated into the empire as Lingnan, the flourishing of local culture was a kind of resistance to Han influence.

Trade in exotic goods was one of the main motivations for the Qin's and Han's presence in Lingnan, and perhaps in Yunnan as well. Rarities such as rhinoceros horns, elephant tusks, turtles, pearls, cowrie shells, bird feathers, and exotic fruits are reported to have been brought to the court from Lingnan. Bird feathers and precious metals were probably procured from Yunnan (Erickson et al. 2010). A pillow filled with pearls found inside the grave of the second king of Nanyue might corroborate such reports. However, additional artifacts found in the same grave suggest that the Nanyue state was trading with other partners as well. Bronze artifacts in the Dongson style

Figure 232. A silver box from the grave of the king of Nanyue (Gary Lee Todd).

imply contact with areas further to the south – some have argued that contact reached as far as India and southeast Asia – while a silver box and a horn-shaped jade drinking cup are clearly of Iranian or Central Asian origin (Figure 232). A

wealth of archaeological evidence, such as the previously mentioned Dongson drums, cowrie shells, and northern style bronze plaques, all suggests that the Dian also established a network of long-range contacts.

Han artifacts similar to those found in Dian graves, such as lacquers, bronze mirrors, and coins, have also been found in areas beyond the borders of the Han Empire. The best examples are the Xiongnu graves in Mongolia and Russia (Brosseder 2011). Silk, which was probably one of the primary Chinese products to have been traded and is even mentioned in Roman texts, was found in the same Xiongnu graves and as far west as Palmira, although it is generally badly preserved in the archaeological record. These findings are often associated with limiting terms such as the "Silk Road," but what we actually see is the emergence of far more complex networks of commercial interactions and cultural exchange.

BY WAY OF A PERSONAL CONCLUSION: THE JADE DRAGON AS AN EMBLEM OF LOCAL AND NATIONAL IDENTITY

Although I am an archaeologist, my frequent visits to China confront me with current cultural trends that I cannot help but compare with the prehistoric processes described throughout this book. One such trend is the appropriation of archaeological artifacts found in excavations to be used as symbols of local and national identity.

The so-called jade dragon (*yu long* 玉龙), a C-shaped object 26 cm in height, is one such artifact (Figure 233). It was discovered outside of its archaeological context at Sanxingtala (三星塔拉)

Figure 233. The so-called jade dragon (photo by Gary Lee Todd).

village, in eastern Inner Mongolia and, based on stylistic analysis, is attributed to the Hongshan culture (ca. 4500–3000 BCE). This piece is one of the largest and most spectacular jades of the Chinese Neolithic, and while its cultural affiliation and symbolic meaning are contested, many consider it to be the earliest representation of the Chinese dragon.

Since its discovery in the 1980s, the jade dragon has been considered a national-level "cultural relic." However, I first noticed its use as a local and then national symbol around 2000. One of the first of such appropriations was the use of the jade dragon silhouette as the trademark of Chifeng Beer in the 1990s – the Chifeng region of eastern Inner Mongolia being one of the regions identified with the Hongshan culture. From there the use of the jade dragon symbol spread to other parts of northeast China, where it was deployed both as an emblem of local identity and for various commercial purposes (Figure 234). Most recently, however, the jade dragon can been seen in contexts that represent national identity, for example at the Beijing Airport, where it is one of a number of symbols that accompany the slogan "Welcome to China."

Why has the jade dragon become such an important symbol in contemporary China, and why was it chosen over other more elaborate or more beautiful discoveries? Its association with northeast China is evident, but even this region

Figure 234. Uses of the "jade dragon" symbol in different contexts: 1. Taxi in Fuxin city; 2. Shopping mall in Fuxin city; 3. Bottle of Ningcheng Old Wine; 4. Hua Xia Bank logo; 5. Beijing International Airport (photos by Gideon Shelach).

has produced far more spectacular finds. I believe that the jade dragon was chosen (consciously or otherwise) because it is safe: it is of local origins, but because it is identified with a well-recognized national symbol – the dragon – it does not evoke a separatist identity; instead, it is indicative of an identity as part of the Chinese sphere. It positions the northeast in competition for national primacy (as the place where the most ancient dragon was invented), while remaining within the framework of accepted Chinese identity.

Although many types of dragons exist in the mythology and art of premodern China, the celebrated "imperial dragon" is a mythic creature that combines different parts of real animals. It is described as having "nine resemblances": the body of a snake, the head of a camel (or ox), the eyes of a rabbit, the antlers of a deer, the ears of a cow, the scales of a fish, the belly of a frog, the claws of a hawk, and the paws of a tiger. This prompted the eminent Chinese scholar Wen Yiduo (聞一多, 1899–1946) to suggest that the dragon emerged as a combination of different tribal totems: each tribe originally had a real animal as its totem, but when those tribes were assimilated with one another – a process that gave birth to the Chinese people –

their totems were fused to form the combined symbol of the Chinese people and civilization.

Wen's hypothesis is by now considered anachronistic, because we now know that mythical creatures akin to the dragon existed in China long before the development of an inclusive "Chinese" identity (Shelach 2001b). Nonetheless, it is a pleasing allegory for some of the main processes described in this book. We have discussed many processes, some unique to one chapter or one period, while others, such as the development of economic adaptation, technological skills, and sociopolitical complexity, run through the entire book.

Another set of issues that has also been touched upon in almost every chapter relates to regional variation and interregional contact and interactions. To put it somewhat differently (and at the risk of being anachronistic myself), these issues can be looked at in terms of the existence and maintenance of local cultures and identities and the formation of an inclusive "Chinese" culture. As I have repeatedly demonstrated, these processes are not contradictory; on the contrary, they are often two sides of the same coin. Wen's description of the dragon is an ideal illustration of a process whereby local identities are preserved as parts of a universal identity. However, as we have seen, not all processes of integration were so harmonious. Sometimes, intensive contact and attempts to impose assimilation resulted in cultural resistance and the intensification (some would even say invention) of expressions of local identity.

Finally, although this book is about the archaeology of ancient China, I would suggest that it is not entirely irrelevant to our understanding of modern and contemporary China. It is not only that archaeologically derived artifacts such as the jade dragon are used both as national symbols and as symbols of more particularistic identities; also, and at a deeper level, the habits, beliefs, and cultural attributes that evolved during the period addressed here continue to resonate in China's contemporary culture. As a young scholar, I once wrote a paper in which I argued that one particular symbol had been replaced by another. A reviewer of the paper duly noted that in China nothing is ever completely replaced by something else; instead, symbols, attributes, ideas, and so on are accumulated and combined, thereby acquiring new (additional) meanings. This, I think, is a compelling insight with which to conclude this book.

NOTES

Introduction

1 For a more detailed discussion of the history of Chinese archaeology, see Chang (1986: 4–21) and Liu and Chen (2012: 1–21).

Chapter 1 The Geographic and Environmental Background

1 It is impossible to determine the exact area of the People's Republic of China because of unresolved border disputes with neighboring countries.
2 The Changjiang has different names in different sections. "Yangzi" is the name, in the local dialect, of the lower part of the river. For historic reasons, it was adopted in Western languages as the name for the entire river.

Chapter 2 Before Cultivation: Human Origins and the Incipient Development of Human Culture in China

1 Throughout this chapter I use the term "hominins" to refer specifically to humans (modern humans and our direct ancestors), and not hominids, which is a more general term that encompasses humans, chimpanzees, and gorillas (see Dennell 2009: 10).
2 One of the best summaries in Chinese is a book by Wang Youping (2005). Dennell's (2009) book provides a broad, extensive, and up-to-date summary of discoveries in Asia, including China and East Asia.
3 Tektites are spherical glassy objects that were created and lifted into the atmosphere by the impact of an asteroid that hit Southeast Asia some 800–780 ka ago. Tektites are distributed over a large region from India to Australia.

4 Because much of the initial research was done on mitochondrial DNA, which passed from mother to offspring without recombination with the father's DNA, this model is sometimes called the "Eve theory" – tracing back to the first mother who left Africa and spread the *Homo sapiens* genes to the rest of the world.

Chapter 3 The Transition to Food Production: Variability and Processes

1 Microliths are found in Bashidang (Hunan 2006: 276–85), suggesting possible cultural interactions between the middle Yangzi River region and regions to its north.
2 Most archaeologists do not make these claims explicitly, but nonetheless the Chinese usage of the term "Neolithic," translated literally from the term used by Western archaeologists as "Xin shiqi shidai" (新石器时代), the new stone tool age, carries with it the original connotation that equated the new type of stone tools, mainly polished stone axes and grinding stones, with the transition to agriculture. This term is misleading in the context of West Asia, but it is even more confusing in China and East Asia, where ceramics, which for historic reasons have become the defining criterion, appeared very early.
3 The dates of occupation at the Shangshan site are not yet secured, so some caution is needed when analyzing data from this site.

Chapter 4 The Development of Agriculture and Sedentary Life in North China

1 Because of the search for even earlier phases of sedentary agricultural societies, and because some equate the

term "Neolithic" with ceramic production, which, as discussed in Chapter 3, appeared in north and south China at an earlier period, many archaeologists refer to the period discussed here as the middle Neolithic.

2   A phytolith (lit. "plant stone") is a microscopic silica particle that occurs in many plants. Phytoliths are very rigid and preserve well over a long time. Because they vary in size and shape depending on the plant taxon, they are used by paleobotanists to identify plants that are otherwise not well preserved.

Chapter 6 The Emergence and Development of Sociopolitical Complexity

1   Although recent reports on the discovery of a wall at the Liangzhu site can change this picture.

2   Recent and as yet unverified reports note the discovery of a much larger outer wall, which was part of the late Neolithic occupation of Baodun (Flad and Chen 2013: 74).

Chapter 8 The Shang Dynasty: The Emergence of the State in China

1   Shang and Yin are interchangeable names of the dynasty in later texts, but in the oracle bone inscriptions only the name Shang is used, for both the dynasty and its capital (Keightley 1999: 232).

2   Recent reports suggest that an outer wall extended the area of Panlongcheng considerably.

3   A total of 41,956 inscriptions were reproduced in the Jiaguwen Heji (甲骨文合集) corpus, whose numerical system is used to refer to individual inscriptions. An additional 13,450 inscriptions were published in the Jiaguwen heji bubian (甲骨文合集補編) supplement, and several thousand more have been published in separate collections, including those of oracle bones held in museum collections outside China.

4   This phrase "zi yu" (兹御) serves in the oracle bones as the opening of the verification section. Keightley often translates it as "this was use," but its function is akin to something like "indeed . . ." or "following this prediction . . ." (Keightley 1978: 119).

Chapter 9 Regional Variation and Interregional Interactions during the Bronze Age: "Center and Periphery" or "Interaction Spheres"?

1   It is not clear how much of it actually dates to the Shang and early Zhou period. Findings dated to the Eastern Zhou period (770–221 BCE) suggest that the copper ores here were exploited over a long period.

2   Ban Gu, *Han Shu* 漢書, translated in Pines (2005: 80).

3   Quoted in Mallory and Mair (2000: 185).

Chapter 10 The Societies and Cultures of the Zhou Period: Processes of Globalization and the Genesis of Local Identities

1   For updated discussions on different aspects of Zhou history, see relevant chapters in Loewe and Shaughnessy (1999), Falkenhausen (2006), Li Feng (2006 and 2008), and Pines (2002).

2   The *locus classicus* of this model is the Kaogong ji (考工記) chapter in the *Zhouli* (周禮). The Kaogong ji is variously dated to anywhere between the fifth century BCE and the first century CE, but it is usually understood to reflect the situation during the Western Zhou and the early Spring and Autumn period.

3   He Jianzhang 何建章, *Zhanguo ce zhushi* 戰國策注釋 (Beijing: Zhonghua, 1991), "Wei ce 魏策 3" 24.8:907.

Chapter 11 The Son of Heaven and the Creation of a Bureaucratic Empire

1   For a comprehensive if sometimes outdated discussion of the history of the Qin and Han periods, see Twitchett and Loewe (1986). For a more recent synthesis, see Lewis (2007).

2   From the inscription on the stele on Mt. Yi (219 BCE), cited in Kern (2000: 14).

3   This section of the wall is attributed to the Qin state during the period of King Zhao before he unified the empire (Zhongguo Shehui 2010b: 300), but its structure is similar to that of walls built after the unification.

4   A fourth pit in this area was found empty.

5   Compare, for example, the total area of Yangling, which is estimated at 12 km² (Yan et al. 2009), to the ca. 54 km² of the First Emperor's burial complex.

REFERENCES

Aikens, M. C. 1992. Hunting, Fishing, and Gathering in Pacific Northeast Asia: Pleistocene Continuities and Holocene Developments, in M. C. Aikens & S. N. Rhee (eds.) *Pacific Northeast Asia in Prehistory*. Pullman, Washington State University Press: 99–104.

Allan, S. 1991. *The Shape of the Turtle: Myth, Art, and Cosmos in Early China*. Albany, State University of New York Press.

Allard, F. 1997. Growth and Stability among Complex Societies in Prehistoric Lingnan, Southeast China. *Papers from the Institute of Archaeology* 8: 37–58.

———— 2001. Mortuary Ceramics and Social Organization in the Dawenkou and Majiayao Cultures. *Journal of East Asian Archaeology* 3(3–4): 1–22.

———— 2004. Lingnan and Chu during the First Millennium B.C.: A Reassessment of the Core-Periphery Model, in S. Müller & T. O. Höllmann (eds.) *Guangdong: Archaeology and Early Texts*. Weisbaden, Harrassowitz Verlag: 1–21.

———— 2006. Frontiers and Boundaries: The Han Empire from Its Southern Periphery, in M. Stark (ed.) *Archaeology of Asia*. Malden, Blackwell: 233–54.

An, Zhisheng, et al. 2000. Asynchronous Holocene Optimum of the East Asian Monsoon. *Quaternary Science Reviews* 19: 743–62.

Anhuisheng Wenwu Kaogu Yanjiusuo. 2008. Anhui sheng Hanshan xian Lingjiatan yizhi diwuci fajue de xinfaxian [New Discoveries of the Fifth Excavation Season at the Lingjiatan Site, in Xinfa County, Anhui Province]. *Kaogu* 3: 7–17.

Anthony, D. W. 1990. Migration in Archaeology: The Baby and the Bathwater. *American Anthropologist* 92: 895–914.

Anthony, D. W. & N. B. Vinogradov. 1995. Birth of the Chariot. *Archaeology* 48(2): 36–41.

Ao, Hong, et al. 2010. Pleistocene Environmental Evolution in the Nihewan Basin and Implication for Early Human Colonization of North China. *Quaternary International* 223–4: 472–8.

Bagley, R. W. 1990. Meaning and Explanation, in Roderick Whitfield (ed.) *The Problem of Meaning in Early Chinese Ritual Bronzes: Colloquies on Art & Archaeology in Asia No. 15*. London, Percival David Foundation of Chinese Art, School of Oriental and African Studies, University of London: 34–55.

———— 1999. Shang Archaeology, in M. Loewe & E. L. Shaughnessy (eds.) *The Cambridge History of Ancient China*. Cambridge, Cambridge University Press: 124–231.

Baoding Diqu Wenwu Guanlisuo. 1991. Hubei Xushui xian Nanzhuangtou yizhi shijue jianbao [Preliminary Report of the Trail Excavation at the Nanzhuangtou Site, Xushui County, Hubei]. *Kaogu* 11: 961–70.

Barbieri-Low, A. J. 2000. Wheeled Vehicles in the Chinese Bronze Age (c. 2000–741 B.C.). *Sino-Platonic Papers* 99: 1–99.

———— 2007. *Artisans in Early Imperial China*. Seattle, University of Washington Press.

Barnes, G. L. & Guo Dashun. 1996. The Ritual Landscape of "Boar Mountain" Basin: The Niuheliang Site Complex of North-Eastern China. *World Archaeology* 28(2): 209–19.

Barton, L., et al. 2009. Agricultural Origins and the Isotopic Identity of Domestication in Northern China. *Proceedings of the National Academy of Sciences* 106(14): 5523–8.

Bar-Yosef, O. 2011. Climatic Fluctuations and Early Farming in West and East Asia. *Current Anthropology* 52(S4): S175–S193.

Bar-Yosef, O. & A. Belfer-Cohen. 1992. From Foraging to Farming in the Mediterranean Levant, in A. B. Gebauer & T. D. Price (eds.) *Transitions to Agriculture in Prehistory*. Madison, Prehistory Press: 21–48.

———— 2013. Following Pleistocene Road Signs of Human Dispersals across Eurasia. *Quaternary International* 285: 30–43.

Bar-Yosef, O., et al. 2012. Were Bamboo Tools Made in Prehistoric Southeast Asia? An Experimental View from South China. *Quaternary International* 269: 9–21.

Bar-Yosef, O. & Youping Wang. 2012. Paleolithic Archaeology in China. *Annual Review of Anthropology* 41: 319–35.

Beijing Daxue Kaogu Wenbo Xueyuan, et al. 2006. Beijingshi Mentougou qu Donghulin shiqian yizhi [The Prehistoric Site of Donghulin, Mentougou Distric, Beijing]. *Kaogu* 7: 3–8.

Beijing Daxue Kaogu Wenbo Xueyuan & Henan Sheng Wenwu Yanjiusuo. 2007. *Dengfeng Wangchenggang kaogu faxian yu yanjiu (2002–2005)* [Archaeological Discovery and Study of Wangchenggang in Dengfeng, between 2002 to 2005]. Zhengzhou, Daxiang Chubanshe.

Beijing Gangtie Xueyuan Yejin Shizu. 1981. Zhonggou zaoqi tongqi de chubu yanjiu [Preliminary Research on the Earliest Bronze Artifacts in China]. *Kaogu Xuebao* 3: 287–301.

Beijingshi Wenwu Yanjiusuo. 1995. *Liulihe Xizhou Yanguo mudi, 1973–1977* [Excavations at the Zhou Period, Yan State Cemetery, 1973–1977]. Beijing, Wenwu Chubanshe.

Bellwood, P. 2005. *First Farmers: The Origins of Agricultural Societies*. Malden, Blackwell.

———— 2006. Asian Farming Diasporas? Agriculture, Languages, and Genes in China and Southeast Asia, in M. T. Stark (ed.) *Archaeology of Asia*. Malden, Blackwell: 96–118.

Bettinger, R. L., et al. 2007. The Transition to Agriculture in Northwestern China, in D. B. Madsen, Chen Fa-Hu, & Xing Gao (eds.) *Late Quaternary Climate Change and Human Adaptation in Arid China*. Amsterdam, Elsevier: 83–101.

Bettinger, R. L., et al. 2010. The Transition to Agriculture at Dadiwan, People's Republic of China. *Current Anthropology* 51(5): 703–14.

Binford, L. R. & N. Stone. 1986. Zhoukoudian: A Closer Look. *Current Anthropology* 27: 453–75.

Blanton, R. E., et al. 1996. A Dual-Processual Theory for the Evolution of Mesoamerican Civilization. *Current Anthropology* 37(1): 1–14.

Blumler, M. A. & R. Byrne. 1991. The Ecological Genetics of Domestication and the Origins of Agriculture. *Current Anthropology* 32(1): 23–54.

Boaretto, E., et al. 2009. Radiocarbon Dating of Charcoal and Bone Collagen Associated with Early Pottery at Yuchanyan Cave, Hunan Province, China. *Proceedings of the National Academy of Sciences* 106(24): 9595–9600.

Boaz, N. T., et al. 2004. Mapping and Taphonomic Analysis of the Homo Erectus Loci at Locality 1 Zhoukoudian, China. *Journal of Human Evolution* 46(5): 519–49.

Bodde, D. 1986. The State and Empire of Ch'in, in D. Twitchett & M. Loewe (eds.) *The Cambridge History of China, Vol. 1: The Ch'in and Han Empires, 221 BCE-220 A.D.* Cambridge, Cambridge University Press: 20–102.

Boëda E. & Hou Xuemei. 2004. Jiushiqi shidai dongya xiya zhijian de gaunxi [Relationship between East and West Asia during the Palaeolithic Age]. *Disiji Yanjiu* 24(3): 255–64.

Brosseder, U. 2011. Belt Plaques as an Indicator of East-West Relations in the Eurasian Steppe at the Turn of the Millennia, in U. Brosseder & B. Miller (eds.) *Xiongnu Archaeology*. Bonn, Rheinische Friedrich-Wilhelms-Universitat: 350–424.

Byrd, F. B. 1994. Public and Private, Domestic and Corporate: The Emergence of the Southwest Asian Village. *American Antiquity* 59(4): 639–66.

Campbell, B. R., et al. 2011. Consumption, Exchange and Production at the Great Settlement Shang: Bone-Working at Tiesanlu, Anyang. *Antiquity* 85: 1279–97.

Cao, Bingwu. 1994. Henan Hu xian jiqi fujin diqu huanjing kaogu yanjiu [Environmental archaeological research at Hu district, Henan Province]. *Huaxia Kaogu* 3: 61–7.

Chang, K. C. 1980. *Shang Civilization*. New Haven, Yale University Press.

———— 1983. *Art, Myth, and Ritual: The Path to Political Authority in Ancient China*. Cambridge, MA, Harvard University Press.

———— 1986. *The Archaeology of Ancient China*. New Haven, Yale University Press.

———— 1989. An Essay on Cong. *Orientations* 20(6): 37–43.

Chen, Bo. 2013. *The Cities and City System of the Han Empire (206BCE–220CE): An Archaeological and Regional Perspective on the Establishment and Characteristics of the Great Unification in China*. Ph.D. dissertation. Jerusalem, Hebrew University.

Chen, Chun. 2007. Techno-Typological Comparison of Microblade Cores from East Asia and North America, in V. Y. Kuzmin, S. G. Keates, & Chen Shen (eds.) *Origin and Spread of Microblade Technology in Northern Asia and North America*. Burnaby, Archaeology Press: 7–38.

Chen, Chun & Gong Xin. 2004. Erlitou, Xia you Zhongguo zaoqi guojia yanjiu [Erlitou, Xia Dynasty and the Study of Early States in China]. *Fudan Xuebao* 4: 82–91.

Chen, Shengqian. 2006. Zhonggou beifang wangengxinshi renlei de shiying bianqian yu Fushe [The Spread of Human Populations and Changes in the Adaptation during the Late Pleistocene in North China]. *Disiji Yanjiu* 26(4): 522–33.

Chen, Yong. 2009. Yige cong "Li" tansuo Zhongguo wenming qiyuan de moshi [A Model for Exploring the Origins of Chinese Civilization from the Concept of "Li"]. *Wenwu* 2: 90–3.

Chen, Zhida. 2006. *Yinxu*. Beijing, Wenwu Chubanshe.

Cheng, Pingshan. 2005. Lun Taosi gucheng de fazhan jieduan xingzhi [Discussion on Development Stages and Characteristics of Taosi City]. *Jianghan Kaogu* 3: 48–53.

Chengde Diqu Wenwu Baoguansuo & Luanping Xian Bowuguan. 1994. Hebei Luanping Xian Houtaizi yizhi fajue jianbao [Preliminary Report on Excavations at Houtaizi, Luanping County, Hebei]. *Wenwu* 3: 53–74.

Chengdu Pingyuan Guoji Kaogu Diaochadui. 2010. Chengdu pingyuan quyu kaogu diaocha (2005–2007) [2005–2007 Archaeological Survey in the Chengdu Plain]. *Nanfang Minzu Kaogu* 6: 255–78.

Chengdu Shi Wenwu Kaogu Yanjiusuo & Pixian Bowuguan. 2001. Sichuan Sheng Pixian Gucheng Yizhi 1997 nian fajue jianbao [Brief Report on the 1997 Excavation of the Gucheng Site in Pixian County, Sichuan Province]. *Wenwu* 3: 52–68.

Chernykh, E. N. 1992. *Ancient Metallurgy in the USSR: The Early Metal Age*. Cambridge, Cambridge University Press.

Chifeng International Collaborative Archaeological Project (ed.) 2003. *Regional Archaeology in Eastern Inner Mongolia: A Methodological Exploration*. Beijing, Kexue Chubanshe.

——— 2011. *Settlement Patterns in the Chifeng Region*. Pittsburgh, Center for Comparative Archaeology.

Childs-Johnson, E. 1995. The Ghost Head Mask and Metamorphic Shang Imagery. *Early China* 20: 79–92.

Ciarla, R. 2005. *The Eternal Army: The Terracotta Army of the First Chinese Emperor*. Vercelli, White Star.

——— 2007. Rethinking Yuanlongpo: The Case for Technological Links between the Lingnan (PRC) and Central Thailand in the Bronze Age. *East and West* 57(1–4): 305–30.

Cohen, D. J. 1998. The Origins of Domesticated Cereals and the Pleistocene-Holocene Transition in East Asia. *Review of Archaeology* 19: 22–9.

Crawford, G. W. 2006. East Asian Plant Domestication, in M. T. Stark (ed.) *Archaeology of Asia*. Malden, Blackwell: 77–95.

Cribb, R. 1991. *Nomads in Archaeology*. Cambridge, Cambridge University Press.

Dai, Chunyang. 2000. Lixian Dabuzishan Qingong mudi ji youguan wenti [The Graves of the Qin Lords at Dabuzishan, Li County and a Few Related Questions]. *Wenwu* 5: 74–80.

Debaine-Francfort, C. 1995. *Du Neolithique a l'Age du Bronze en Chine du Nord-Ouest: la Culture de Qijia et ses Connexions*. Paris, Editions Recherche sur les Civilisations.

Dematte, P. 1999. The Role of Writing in the Process of State Formation in Late Neolithic China. *East and West* 49(1–4): 241–72.

Dennell, R. 2009. *The Palaeolithic Settlement of Asia*. Cambridge, Cambridge University Press.

Di Cosmo, N. 2002. *Ancient China and Its Enemies*. Cambridge, Cambridge University Press.

Ding, Lanlan. 2008. Luelun Zhengluo dixu Yangshao wenhua chengren wengguan ercizang [Discussion of the Yangshao Culture's Secondary Burial of Adults in Urns in the Zhengluo Region]. *Sichuan Wenwu* 3: 57–64.

Drennan, R. D. & C. E. Peterson. 2006. Patterned Variation in Prehistoric Chiefdoms. *Proceedings of the National Academy of Sciences* 103(11): 3960–7.

Du, Jinpeng. 2006. Yanshi Shangcheng di bahao gongdian jizhi chubu yanjiu [Preliminary Research of the Site of no. 8 Place at the Shang City of Yanshi]. *Kaogu* 2006(6): 43–52.

Du, Jinpeng & Xu Hong (eds.) 2006. *Erlitou Yizhi yu Erlitou Wenhua Yanjiu* [Research of the Erlitou Stie and Erlitou Culture]. Beijing, Kexue Chubanshe.

Duan, Qingbo. 2011. *Qin Shihuangdi lingyuan kaogu yanjiu* [Archaeological Research on the Burial Complex of Qin Shihuangdi]. Beijing, Beijing Daxue Chubanshe.

Earle, T. 2002. *Bronze Age Economics: The Beginnings of Political Economies*. Boulder, Westview Press.

Erickson, S. 2010. Han Dynasty Tomb Structures and Contents, in M. Nylan and M. Loewe (eds.) *China's Early Empires: A Re-appraisal*. Cambridge, Cambridge University Press: 13–82.

Erickson, S. & M. Nylan. 2010. The Archaeology of the Outlying Lands, in M. Nylan and M. Loewe (eds.) *China's Early Empires: A Re-appraisal*. Cambridge, Cambridge University Press: 135–68.

Eshed, V., A. Gopher, & I. Hershkovitz. 2006. Tooth Wear and Dental Pathology at the Advent of Agriculture: New Evidence from the Levant. *American Journal of Physical Anthropology* 130(2): 145–59.

Eshed, V., A. Gopher, R. Pinhasi, & I. Hershkovitz. 2010. Paleopathology and the Origin of Agriculture in the Levant. *American Journal of Physical Anthropology* 143(1): 121–33.

Falkenhausen, L. V. 1993. *Suspended Music: Chime-Bells in the Culture of Bronze Age China*. Berkeley, University of California Press.

——— 1995. The Regionalist Paradigm in Chinese Archaeology, in P. Kohl & C. Fawcett (eds.) *Nationalism, Politics, and the Practice of Archaeology*. Cambridge, Cambridge University Press: 198–217.

——— 1999. The Waning of the Bronze Age: Material Culture and Social Developments 770–481 BC, in M. Loewe & E. L. Shaughnessy (eds.) *The Cambridge History of Ancient China*. Cambridge, Cambridge University Press: 352–544.

———— 2002. Some Reflections on Sanxingdui, in *Regional Culture, Religion and Arts before the Seventh Century: Papers from the Third International Conference on Sinology*. Taipei, Institute of History and Philology, Academia Sinica: 59–97.

———— 2003. The External Connections of Sanxingdui. *Journal of East Asian Archaeology* 5: 191–245.

———— 2006. *Chinese Society in the Age of Confucius (1000–250 BC): The Archaeological Evidence*. Los Angeles, Cotsen Institute of Archaeology.

———— 2008. Stages in the Development of "Cities" in Pre-imperial China, in J. Marcus & J. A. Sablof (eds.) *Ancient City: New Perspectives on Urbanism in the Old and New World*. Santa Fe, School for Advanced Research: 209–28.

Fang, Yanmin & Xu Liu. 2006. Henan Dengfengshi Wangchenggang yizhi 2002, 2004 nian fajue jianbao [Preliminary Report on the 2002, 2004 Excavations at the Wangchenggang Site, Dengfeng City, Henan]. *Kaogu* 9: 3–9.

Fiskesjö, M. & Chen Xingchan. 2004. *China before China: Johan Gunnar Andersson, Ding Wenjiang, and the Discovery of China's Prehistory*. Stockholm, Museum of Far Eastern Antiquities Monographs no. 15.

Fitzgerald-Huber, L. 2003. The Qijia Culture: Paths East and West. *Bulletin of the Museum of Far Eastern Antiquities* 75: 55–78.

Flad, R. K. 2008. Divination and Power: A Multiregional View of the Development of Oracle Bone Divination in Early China. *Current Anthropology* 49(3): 403–37.

———— 2011. *Salt Production and Social Hierarchy in Ancient China: An Archaeological Investigation of Specialization in China's Three Gorges*. Cambridge, Cambridge University Press.

Flad, R. K. & Pochan Chen. 2013. *Ancient Central Asia: Centers and Peripheries along the Yangzi River*. Cambridge, Cambridge University Press.

Flad, R. K., et al. 2010. Early Wheat in China: Results from New Studies at Donghuishan in the Hexi Corridor. *Holocene* 20: 955–65.

Flad, R. K., Yuan Jing, & Li Shuicheng. 2007. Zooarchaeological Evidence of Animal Domestication in Northwest China, in D. B. Madsen, Chen Fa-Hu, & Xing Gao (eds.) *Late Quaternary Climate Change and Human Adaptation in Arid China*. Amsterdam, Elsevier: 167–203.

Flannery, K. V. 1969. Origins and Ecological Effects of Early Domestication in Iran and the Near East, in P. J. Ucko & G. W. Dimbleby (eds.) *The Domestication and Exploitation of Plants and Animals*. Chicago, Aldine: 73–100.

———— 1998. The Ground Plans of Archaic States, in G. M. Feinman & J. Marcus (eds.) *Archaic States*. Santa Fe, SAR Press: 15–57.

Frank, A. G. 1992. *The Centrality of Central Asia*. Amsterdam, VU University Press, Comparative Asian Studies 8.

Fu, Qiaomei, et al. 2013. DNA Analysis of an Early Modern Human from Tianyuan Cave, China. *Proceedings of the National Academy of Sciences* 110(6): 2223–7.

Fuller, D. Q., et al. 2009. The Domestication Process and Domestication Rate in Rice: Spikelet Bases from the Lower Yangtze. *Science* 323(5921): 1607–10.

Fuller, D. Q., E. Harvey, & Ling Qin. 2007. Presumed Domestication? Evidence for Wild Rice Cultivation and Domestication in the Fifth Millennium BC of the Lower Yangtze Region. *Antiquity* 81: 316–31.

Gansu Sheng Wenwu Kaogu Yanjiusuo. 1990. Gansu sheng wenwu kaogu gongzuo shi nian [Ten Years of Archaeological Work in Gansu Province], in *Wenwu kaogu gongzuo shi nian*. Beijing Wenwu Chubanshe: 316–26.

———— 2006. *Qin'an Dadiwan: Xinshiqi shidai yizhi fajue baogao* [Qin'an Dadiwan: Report on the Archaeological Excavations at a Neolithic Site]. Beijing, Wenwu Chubanshe.

Gao, Donglu, 1993. Luelun Kayue wenhua [Discussion of Kayue Culture], in Su Bingqi (ed.) *Kaoguxue wenhua lunji*. Beijing, Wenwu Chubanshe. 3: 153–65.

Gao, Guangren & Luan Fengshi. 2004. *Dawenkou wenhua* [Dawenkou Culture]. Beijing, Wenwu Chubanshe.

Gao, Qiang & Yun Kuen Lee. 1993. A Biological Perspective on Yangshao Kinship. *Journal of Anthropological Archaeology* 12(3): 266–98.

Gao, X. & C. Norton, 2002. A Critique of the Chinese "Middle Paleolithic." *Antiquity* 76: 397–412.

Goldberg, P., et al. 2001. Site Formation Processes at Zhoukoudian, China. *Journal of Human Evolution* 41: 483–530.

Gong, Qiming. 2002. *Yangshao wenhua* [Yangshao Culture]. Beijing, Wenwu Chubanshe.

Green R. E., et al. 2010. A Draft Sequence of the Neanderthal Genome. *Science* 328: 710–22.

Guo, Baojun. 1998. *Yinzhou cheqi yanjiu* [Research on Shang and Zhou Chariot Equipment]. Beijing, Wenwu Chubanshe.

Guo, Dashun. 1995a. Hongshan and Related Cultures, in S. M. Nelson (ed.) *The Archaeology of Northeast China*. London, Routledge: 21–64.

———— 1995b. "Northern Type" Bronze Artifacts Unearthed in the Liaoning Region, and Related Issues, in S. M. Nelson (ed.) *The Archaeology of Northeast China*. London, Routledge: 182–205.

Guo, Ruihai & Li Jun. 2002. The Nanzhuangtou and Hutouliang Sites: Exploring the Beginnings of Agriculture and Pottery in North China, in Y. Yasuda (ed.) *The Origins of Pottery and Agriculture*. New Delhi, Roli Books: 193–204.

Guo, Yanli. 2009. Erlitou yizhi chutu bingqi chutan [A Study of Weapons Recovered from the Erlitou Site]. *Jianghan Kaogu* 3: 66–75.

Guo, Zhizhong, et al. 1991. Linxi xian Baiyinchanghan yizhi fajue shuyao [Review of the Excavations at Baiyinchanghan, Linxi County], in Neimenggu Wenwu Kaogu Yanjiusuo (ed.) *Neimenggu dongbu qu kaoguxue wenhua yanjiu wenji*. Beijing, Haiyang Chubanshe: 15–23.

Guojia Wenwuju. 2006. *Zhongguo wenwu dituji Shanxi fence* [The Chinese Cultural Management Atlas, Shanxi Volume]. Beijing, Zhongguo Ditu Chubanshe.

———— 2007. *Zhongguo wenwu dituji Shandong fence* [The Chinese Cultural Management Atlas, Shandong Volume]. Beijing, Zhongguo Ditu Chubanshe.

Guojia Wenwuju Qin Zhidao Yanjiu Keti Zu & Xunyi Xian Bowuguan. 2006. Xunyi xian Qin Zhidao yizhi kaocha baogao [Report on the Examination of Remains from the Qin Direct Road in Xunyi County]. *Wenbao* 3: 75–8.

Han, Jiagu. 2000. Hebei pingyuan liangce xinshiqi wenhua guanxi bianhua he chuanshuo zhong de hongshui [Neolithic Cultures and Their Relationships with the Legendary Floods in the Margins of Hebei Plain]. *Kaogu* 5: 57–67.

Han, Rubin. 1992. The Study of Metallic Artifacts Unearthed from Zhukaigou, Inner Mongolia, paper presented in *The International Conference of Archaeological Cultures of the North Chinese Ancient Nation*. Huhehot, Inner Mongolia.

Hao, Shougang, et al. 2008. Donghulin sihao ren muzang zhong de guohe [Fruit Seeds Found at Grave no. 4, Donghulin]. *Renxue Xuebao* 3: 249–55.

Harlan, J. R. 1967. A Wild Wheat Harvest in Turkey. *Archaeology* 20: 197–201.

He, Nu. 2013. The Longshan Period Site of Taosi in Southern Shanxi Province, in A. P. Underhill (ed.) *A Companion to Chinese Archaeology*. Malden, Wiley-Blackwell: 255–77.

He, Y., et al. 2004. Asynchronous Holocene Climatic Change across China. *Quaternary Research* 61(1): 52–63.

Hebei Sheng Wenwu Guanlichu. 1975. Hebei Yi xian Yanxiadu 44 hao mu fajue baogao [Report on the Excavation of Grave no. 44 at Yanxiadu, Yi County, Hebei]. *Kaogu* 4: 228–43.

Hebei Sheng Wenwu Guanlichu & Handan Shi Wenwu Baoguansuo. 1981. Hebei Wuan Cishan yizhi [The Cishan Site, Wuan, Hebei]. *Kaogu Xuabao* 3: 303–38.

Hebei Sheng Wenwu Yanjiusuo, et al. 2010. 1997 nian Hebei Xushui Nanzhuangtou yizhi fajue baogao [Report on the 1997 Excavations at the Nanzhuangtou Site, Xushui County, Hebei Province]. *Kaogu Xuabao* 3: 361–92.

Henan Sheng Wenwu Kaogu Yanjiusuo. 1999. *Wuyang Jiahu* [Jiahu site, of Wuyang]. Beijing, Kexue Chubanshe.

———— 2001. *Zhengzhou Shangcheng* [The Shang City of Zhengzhou]. Zhengzhou, Zhongzhou Guji Chubanshe.

———— 2002. Henan Xinmishi Guchengzhai Longshan wenhua chengzhi fajue jianbao [Preliminary Report on the Excavation of the Longshan City Site at Guchengzhai, Xinmishi, Henan Province]. *Huaxia Kaogu* 2: 53–82.

Henan Sheng Wenwu Kaogu Yanjiusuo, et al. 2008. Henan Lingbaoshi Xipo yizhi mudi 2005 nian fajue jianbao [Preliminary Report on the 2005 Excavations at the Cemetery Site of Xipo, Lingbaoshi, Henan Province]. *Kaogu* 1: 3–13.

Hong, Y. T., et al. 2001. A 6000-Year Record of Changes in Drought and Precipitation in Northeastern China Based on a 13C Time Series from Peat Cellulose. *Earth and Planetary Science Letters* 185: 111–19.

Hou, Y. M., & L. X. Zhao. 2010. An Archeological View for the Presence of Early Humans in China. *Quaternary International* 223–4: 10–19.

Hsia, Nai. 1986. The Classification, Nomenclature, and Usage of Shang Dynasty Jades, in K. C. Chang (ed.) *Studies of Shang Archaeology*. New Haven, Yale University Press: 207–36.

Hsu, Cho-Yun. 1965. *Ancient China in Transition: An Analysis of Social Mobility, 722–222 B.C.* Stanford, Stanford University Press.

Hsu, Cho-Yun & K. M. Linduff. 1988. *Western Chou Civilization*. New Haven, Yale University Press.

Hu, Yaowu, et al. 2008. Stable Isotope Analysis of Humans from Xiaojingshan Site: Implications for Understanding the Origin of Millet Agriculture in China. *Journal of Archaeological Science* 35(11): 2960–5.

Huang, Tsui-Mei. 1992. Liangzhu – A Late Neolithic Jade-Yielding Culture in Southeastern Coastal China. *Antiquity* 66: 75–83.

Huang, Xuanpei. 2000. *Fuquanshan*. Beijing, Wenwu Chubanshe.

Huang, Yunping. 2000. Zhukaigou yizhi shougu de jianding yu yanjiu [Identification and Analysis of Animal Bones from the Zhukaigou site], in Neimenggu Zizhiqu Wenwu Kaogu Yanjiusuo, & E`erduosi Bowuguan (eds.) *Zhukaigou – Qingtong shidai zaoqi yizhi fajue baogoa* [Zhukaigou: A Report on the Excavation of an Early

Bronze Age Site]. Beijing, Wenwu Chubanshe: 400–421.

Hubei Sheng, Jingzhou Dichu Bowuguan. 1982. Jiangling Tianxingguan 1 hao Chumu [Chu Grave no. 1 from Jiangling, Tianxingguan]. *Kaogu Xuabao* 1982(1): 71–116.

Hubei Sheng Wenwu Kaogu Yanjiusuo. 2001. *Panlongcheng*. Beijing, Wenwu Chubanshe.

Hubei Sheng Wenwu Kaogu Yanjiusuo, et al. 2003. *Dengjiawan: Tianmen Shijiahe kaogu baogao zhi er* [Dengjiawan: 2nd Report on Archaeological Work at Shijiahe, Tianmen]. Beijing, Wenwu Chubanshe.

Hunan Sheng Wenwu Kaogu Yanjiusuo. 1993. Hunan Linli xian Hujiawuchang xinshiqi shidai yizhi [The Neolithic Site of Hujiawuchang at Linli County, Hunan]. *Kaogu Xuabao* 2: 171–206.

———— 2006. *Pengtoushan yu Bashidang* [Pengtoushan and Bashidang]. Beijing, Kexue Chubanshe.

———— 2007. *Lixian Chengtoushan: Xinshiqi shidai yizhi fajue baogao* [Chengtoushan, Li County: A Report on the Neolithic Site Excavations]. Beijing, Wenwu Chubanshe.

Indrisano, G. G. & K. M. Linduff. 2013. Imperial Expansion in the Late Warring States and Han Dynasty Periods: A Case Study from South Central Inner Mongolia, in G. E. Areshian (ed.) *Archaeological Histories and Anthropological Interpretations of Imperialism*. Los Angeles, Cotsen Institute of Archaeology: 204–42.

Jaffe, Y. 2013. Materializing Identity – A Statistical Analysis of the Western Zhou Liulihe Cemetery. *Asian Perspectives* 51(1): 47–67.

James, J. M. 1993. Is It Really a Dragon? Some Remarks on the Xishuipo Burial. *Archives of Asian Art* 46: 100–1.

Jia, Lanpo. 1985. China's Earliest Palaeolithic Assemblages, in Wu Rukang & J. W. Olsen (eds.) *Paleoanthropology and Paleolithic Archaeology in the People's Republic of China*. Walnut Creek, Left Coast Press: 135–45.

Jia, Lanpo & Huang Weiwen. 1985. The Late Palaeolithic of China, in Wu Rukang & J. W. Olsen (eds.) *Paleoanthropology and Paleolithic Archaeology in the People's Republic of China*. Walnut Creek, Left Coast Press: 211–24.

Jiang, Leping & Li Liu. 2006. New Evidence for the Origins of Sedentism and Rice Domestication in the Lower Yangzi River, China. *Antiquity* 80: 355–61.

Jiangxi Sheng Wenwu Kaogu Yanjiusuo. 2003. Jiangxi Zhangshu Wucheng Shangdai yizhi xicheng qiang jiepou de zhuyao shouhuo [Results of Excavations at the Western Part of the Site Wall of Wucheng, Zhangshu, Jiangxi]. *Nanfang Wenwu* 3: 1–14.

Jiangxi Sheng Wenwu Kaogu Yanjiusuo, et al. 1997. *Xingan Shangdai damu* [The Big Shang Dynasty Tomb at Xingan]. Beijing, Wenwu Chubanshe.

Jiao, Tianlong. 2006. Lun Kuahuqiao wenhua de laiyuan [Discussion on the Origins of the Kuahuqiao Culture], in Zhejiangsheng Wenwu Kaogu Yanjiusuo (ed.) *Zhejiang sheng Wenwu Kaogu Yanjiusuo Xuekan*. Beijing, Kexue Chubanshe: 372–9.

———— 2007. *The Neolithic of Southeast China*. Youngstown, Cambria Press.

Jin, Jiaguang & Xu Haosheng. 1994. Xinshiqi shidai zaoqi yicun Nanzhuagtou de faxian yu sikao [Reflections on the Discovery of Early Neolithic Remains at Nanzhuangtou]. *Wenwu Chunqiu* 1: 34–9.

Jin, Zhengyao. 2003. Qian tongweisu shizong fangfa yingyong yu kaogu yanjiu de jinzhan [The Application of Led Isotopes Study to Archaeological Research]. *Diqiu Xuebao* 6: 548–51.

Jing, Zhichun & Guang Wen. 1996. Mineralogical Inquiries into Chinese Neolithic Jade. *Chinese Journal of Jade*: 135–51.

Keates, S. G. 2010. Evidence for the Earliest Pleistocene Hominid Activity in the Nihewan Basin of Northern China. *Quaternary International* 223–4: 408–17.

Keightley, D. N. 1978. *Sources of Shang History: The Oracle-Bone Inscriptions of Bronze Age China*. Berkeley, University of California Press.

———— 1978–80. The Shang State as Seen in the Oracle-Bone Inscriptions. *Early China* 5: 25–34.

———— 1990. Early Civilization in China: Reflections on How It Became Chinese, in P. S. Ropp (ed.). *Heritage of China*. Berkeley, University of California Press: 15–54.

———— 1997. Shang Oracle-Bone Inscriptions, in E. L. Shaughnessy (ed.) *New Sources of Early Chinese History*. Berkeley, Society for the Study of Early China: 15–55.

———— 1999. The Shang: China's First Historical Dynasty, in M. Loewe & E. L. Shaughnessy (eds.) *The Cambridge History of Ancient China*. Cambridge, Cambridge University Press: 232–91.

———— 2000. *The Ancestral Landscape: Time, Space, and Community in Late Shang China (ca. 1200–1045 B.C.)*. Berkeley, Institute of East Asian Studies and Center for Chinese Studies.

———— 2002. *The Ancestral Landscape: Time, Space, and Community in Late Shang China (1200–1045 B.C.)*. Berkeley, Institute of East Asian Studies and Center for Chinese Studies.

———— 2006. Marks and Labels: Early Writing in Neolithic and Shang China, in M. Stark (ed.) *Archaeology of Asia*. Malden, Blackwell: 177–201.

Kern, M. 2000. *The Stele Inscriptions of Ch'in Shih-huang: Text and Ritual in Early Chinese Imperial Representation*. New Haven, American Oriental Society.

Khazanov, A. M. 1983. *Nomads and the Outside World*. Cambridge, Cambridge University Press.

Kim, Seung-Og. 1994. Burials, Pigs, and Political Prestige in Neolithic China. *Current Anthropology* 35: 119–41.

Kuzmin, V. Y. 2006. Chronology of the Earliest Pottery in East Asia: Progress and Pitfalls. *Antiquity* 80: 362–71.

———— 2007. Geoarchaeological Aspects of the Origin and Spread of Microblade Technology in Northern and Central Asia, in V. Y. Kuzmin, S. G. Keates, & Chen Shen (eds.). *Origin and Spread of Microblade Technology in Northern Asia and North America*. Burnaby, Archaeology Press: 115–24.

Kuzmina, E. E. 1998. Cultural Connections of the Tarim Basin People and Pastoralists of the Asian Steppes in the Bronze Age, in V. H. Mair (ed.) *The Bronze Age and Early Iron Age Peoples of Eastern Central Asian*. Philadelphia, University of Pennsylvania Museum Publications: 63–93.

Ledderose, L. 2000. *Ten Thousand Things: Module and Mass Production in Chinese Art*. Princeton, Princeton University Press.

Lee, Gyoung-Ah, et al. 2007. Plants and People from the Early Neolithic to Shang Periods in North China. *Proceedings of the National Academy of Sciences* 104(3): 1087–92.

Lee, R. B. 1968. What Hunters Do for a Living, or, How to Make Out on Scarce Resources, in R. B. Lee & I. DeVore (eds.) *Man the Hunter*. Chicago, Aldine: 30–48.

Lee, Yun Kuen. 2001a. Status, Symbol, and Meaning in the Dian Culture. *Journal of East Asian Archaeology* 3(1–2): 105–31.

———— 2001b. Yangshao, in P. N. Peregrine & M. Ember (eds.) *Encyclopedia of Prehistory. Vol. 3: East Asia and Oceania*. New York, Kluwer: 333–48.

———— 2004. Control Strategies and Polity Competition in the Lower Yiluo Valley, North China. *Journal of Anthropological Archaeology* 23: 172–95.

———— 2007. Centripetal Settlement and Segmentary Social Formation of the Banpo Tradition. *Journal of Anthropological Archaeology* 26(4): 630–75.

Legrand, S. 2004. Karasuk Metallurgy: Technological Development and Regional Influence, in K. M Linduff (ed.) *Metallurgy in Ancient Eastern Eurasia from the Urals to the Yellow River*. Lewiston, Edwin Mellen Press: 139–56.

Lewis, M. E. 1999. Warring States: Political History, in M. Loewe & E. L. Shaughnessy (eds.) *The Cambridge History of Ancient China*. Cambridge, Cambridge University Press: 588–650.

———— 2007. *The Early Chinese Empires: Qin and Han*. Cambridge, MA, Harvard University Press.

Li, Feng. 2006. *Landscape and Power in Early China: The Crisis and Fall of the Western Zhou 1045–771 BC*. Cambridge, Cambridge University Press.

———— 2008. *Bureaucracy and the State in Early China: Governing the Western Zhou 1045–771 BC*. Cambridge, Cambridge University Press.

Li, Shuicheng. 1993. Siba wenhua yanjiu [Research on the Siba Culture], in Su Bingqi (ed.) *Kaoguxue wenhua lunji*. Beijing, Wenwu Chubanshe: 3: 80–121.

———— 2002. The Interaction between Northwest China and Central Asia during the Second Millennium BC: An Archaeological Perspective, in K. Boyle, C. Renfrew, & M. Levine (eds.) *Ancient Interactions: East and West in Eurasia*. Cambridge, McDonald Institute: 171–82.

Li, Shuicheng & Shui Tao. 2000. Siba wenhua tongqi yanjiu [Research on Bronzes from the Siba Culture]. *Wenwu* 3: 36–44.

Li, Xiaoceng & Han Rubin. 2006. Yunnan Jianchuan xian Haimenkou yizhi chutu tongqi de jishu fenxi ji qi niandai [Analyses of the Metallurgical Techniques and Dating of Excavated Bronzes from the Haimenkou Site, Jianchuan County, Yunnan]. *Kaogu* 7: 80–95.

Li, Xinwei. 2004. Zhonggou sheqian yuqi fanying de yuzhouguan [Reflection on Ancient Cosmology from Chinese Prehistoric Jade]. *Dongnan Wenhua* 3: 66–72.

Li, Xiuhui & Han Rubin. 2000. Zhukaoigou yizhi chutu tongqi de jinxiangxue yanjiu [A Metallurgical Study of Bronze Artifacts from Zhukaigou], in Neimenggu Zizhiqu Wenwu Kaogu Yanjiusuo & E'erduosi Bowuguan (eds.) *Zhukaigou – Qingtong shidai zaoqi yizhi fajue baogoa* [Zhukaigou: A Report on the Excavation of an Early Bronze Age Site]. Beijing, Wenwu Chubanshe: 422–46.

Li, Xueqin. 1985. *Eastern Zhou and Qin Civilizations*. New Haven, Yale University Press.

Li, Yiyin, Cui Haiting, et al. 2003. Xiliao heliuyu udai wenming de shengtai beijing fenxi [Analysis for Ecological Background of Ancient Civilization in Xiliaohe River Basin]. *Disiji Yanjiu* 23(3): 291–8.

Li, Yiyou. 2001. Zhongguo beifang changcheng kaoshu [Discussion of the Great Wall of North China]. *Neimangu Wenwu Kaogu* 1: 1–51.

Li, Youmou. 2003. *Peiligang wenhua* [The Peiligang Culture]. Beijing, Wenwu Chubanshe.

Li, Yung-ti. 2006. On the Function of Cowries in Shang and Western Zhou China. *Journal of East Asian Archaeology* 5: 1–26.

———— 2007. Co-craft and Multicraft: Section-Mold Casting and the Organization of Craft Production at the Shang Capital of Anyang, in I. Shimada (ed.) *Craft Production in Complex Societies: Multicraft and Producer Perspectives*. Salt Lake City, University of Utah Press: 184–223.

Liang, Honggang & Sun Shuyun. 2004. Erlitou yizhi chutu tongqi yanjiu zongzhu [Research on Erlitou Bronze Vessels and Artifacts]. *Zhongyuan wenwu* 1: 29–39.

Liaoning Sheng Wenwu Kaogu Yanjiusuo. 1997. *Niuheliang Hongshan wenhua yizhi yu yuqi jingcui* [The Niuheliang Hongshan Culture Site and Its Wonderful Jades]. Beijing, Wenwu Chubanshe.

Lin, Yun. 2003. Zhongguo beifang changcheng didai youmu wenhua dai de xhingcheng guocheng [The Formation of the Northern Nomads Belt along the Great Wall Area of China]. *Yanjing Yuebao* 14: 95–145.

Linduff, K. M. 1995. Zhukaigou: Steppe Culture and the Rise of Chinese Civilization. *Antiquity* 69: 133–45.

———— 1998. The Emergence and Demise of Bronze-Producing Cultures outside the Central Plain of China, in V. H. Mair (ed.) *The Bronze Age and Early Iron Age Peoples of Eastern Central Asia*. Philadelphia, University of Pennsylvania Museum Publications: 619–43.

———— 2003. A Walk on the Wild Side: Late Shang Appropriation of Horses in China, in M. Levine, C. Renfrew, & K. Boyle (eds.) *Prehistoric Steppe Adaptation and the Horse*. Oxford, Oxbow: 139–62.

Liu, Guanming & Xu Guangji. 1981. Neimenggu dongbu diqu Qingtong shidai de liang zhong wenhua [Two Types of Bronze Age Cultures in the Eastern Part of Inner Mongolia]. *Neimenggu Wenwu Kaogu* 1: 5–14.

Liu, Jun. 2006. *Hemudu wenhua [Hemudu Culture]*. Beijing, Wenwu Chubanshe.

Liu, Li. 2004. *The Chinese Neolithic: Trajectories to Early States*. Cambridge, Cambridge University Press.

Liu, Li, S. Bestel, Shi Jinming, Song Yuanhua, & Chen Xingchan. 2013. Paleolithic Human Exploitation of Plant Foods during the Last Glacial Maximum in North China. *Proceedings of the National Academy of Sciences* 110(14): 5380–5.

Liu, Li & Chen Xingcan. 2003. *State Formation in Early China*. London, Duckworth.

———— 2012. *The Archaeology of China: From the Late Paleolithic to the Early Bronze Age*. Cambridge, Cambridge University Press.

Liu, Li, et al. 2004. Settlement Patterns and Development of Social Complexity in the Yiluo Region, North China. *Journal of Field Archaeology* 29(1–2): 75–100.

Liu, Li, et al. 2006. Zhongguo jiayang shuiniu de qiyuan [The Origins of Chinese Domestic Buffalo]. *Kaogu Xuabao* 2: 141–78.

Liu, Li, et al. 2010a. A Functional Analysis of Grinding Stones from an Early Holocene Site at Donghulin, North China. *Journal of Archaeological Science* 37(10): 2630–9.

Liu, Li, et al. 2010b. Quanxinshi zaoqi Zhongguo Changjiang xiayou diqu xiangzi he shuidao de kaifa liyong [The Exploitation of Acorn and Rice in Early Holocene Lower Yangzi River, China]. *Renleixue Xuebao* 29(3): 12–32.

Liu, Li, Judith Field, et al. 2010. What Did Grinding Stones Grind? New Light on Early Neolithic Subsistence Economy in the Middle Yellow River Valley, China. *Antiquity* 84: 816–33.

Liu, Li & Xu Hong. 2007. Rethinking Erlitou: Legend, History and Chinese Archaeology. *Antiquity* 81(314): 886–901.

Liu, Pigai. 2000. Kayue wenhua de xunzang [Human Sacrifice in Graves of the Kayue Culture]. *Qinghai Minzu Yanjiu* 11(1): 25–7.

Liu, Shizhong & Lu Benshan. 1998. Jiangxi Tongling tongkuang yizhi de fajue yu yanjiu [Excavation and Study of the Copper Mine Site at Tongling, Jiangxi]. *Kaogu Xuabao* 4: 465–96.

Liu, Shun. 2007. Hunan xinshiqi shidai de tese wenhua [Special Cultures of Neolithic Period Hunan]. *Huaihua Xueyuan Xuebao* 26(7): 9–11.

Liu, Y., Y. Hu & Q. Wei. 2012. Early to Late Pleistocene Human Settlements and the Evolution of Lithic Technology in the Nihewan Basin, North China: A Macroscopic Perspective. *Quaternary International* 295: 204–14.

Liu, Yi-Ping, et al. 2006. Multiple Maternal Origins of Chickens: Out of the Asian Jungles. *Molecular Phylogenetics and Evolution* 38(1): 12–9.

Loewe, M. & E. L. Shaughnessy (eds.) 1999. *The Cambridge History of Ancient China*. Cambridge, Cambridge University Press.

Lu, Houyuan, et al. 2009. Earliest Domestication of Common Millet (Panicum Miliaceum) in East Asia Extended to 10,000 Years Ago. *Proceedings of the National Academy of Sciences* 106: 7367–72.

Lu, Tracey L. -D. 1999. *The Transition from Foraging to Farming and the Origin of Agriculture in China*. Oxford, BAR International Series 774.

———— 2006. The Occurrence of Cereal Cultivation in China. *Asian Perspectives* 42(2): 129–58.

Ma, Shizhi. 2008. Dengfeng Wangchenggang chengyi yu Yu du Yincheng [On the Ancient City Site of Wangchenggang and the Yang City Founded by Yu]. *Zhongyuan Wenwu* 2: 22–6.

Ma, Xiaolin. 2005. *Emergent Social Complexity in the Yangshao Culture: Analyses of Settlement Patterns and Faunal Remains from Lingbao, Western Henan, China (c. 4900–3000 BC)*. Oxford, Archaeopress.

Ma, Xiaolin, et al. 2006. Lingbao Xipo Yangshao wenhua mudi chutu yuqi chubu yanjiu [Preliminary Study of Jades Unearthed at the Cemetery of the Xipo Site of the Yangshao Culture, Lingbao County]. *Zhongyuan Wenwu* 2: 69–73.

Madsen, D., et al. 1996. Settlement Patterns Reflected in Assemblages from the Pleistocene/Holocene Transition of North Central China. *Journal of Archaeological Science* 23(2): 217–31.

Mallory, J. P. & V. H. Mair. 2000. *The Tarim Mummies: Ancient China and the Mystery of the Earliest Peoples from the West*. New York, Thames and Hudson.

Mattos, G. L. 1997. Eastern Zhou Bronze Inscriptions, in E. L. Shaughnessy (ed.) *New Sources of Early Chinese History*. Berkeley, Society for the Study of Early China: 85–124.

McGovern, P. E., A. P. Underhill, Fang Hui, et al. 2005. Chemical Identification and Cultural Implications of a Mixed Fermented Beverage from Late Prehistoric China. *Asian Perspectives* 44(2): 249–75.

Mei, Jianjun. 2000. *Copper and Bronze Metallurgy in Late Prehistoric Xinjiang: Its Cultural Context and Relationship with Neighboring Regions*. Oxford, Archaeopress.

———— 2003. Qijia and Seima-Turbino: The Question of Early Contacts between Northwest China and the Eurasian Steppe. *Bulletin of the Museum of Far Eastern Antiquities* 75: 31–54.

———— 2006. Guanyu Zhongguo yejin qiyuan ji zaoqi tongqi yanjiu de jige wenti [A Few Questions about the Beginning of Metallurgy and the Earliest Bronze Artifacts in China], in Beijing Keji Daxue Yejin yu Cailiaoshi Yanjiusuo & Beijing Keji Daxue Kexue Jishu yu Wenming Yanjiu Zhongxin (eds.) *Zhongguo yejinshi lunwenji (4)*. Beijing, Kexue Chubanshe: 11–23.

Molina, J., et al. 2011. Molecular Evidence for a Single Evolutionary Origin of Domesticated Rice. *Proceedings of the National Academy of Sciences* 108: 8351–6.

Movius H. L., Jr. 1948. The Lower Palaeolithic Cultures of Southern and Eastern Asia. *Transactions of the American Philosophical Society* 38: 329–420.

Nanjing Bowuguan. 1984. 1982 nian Jiangsu Changzhou Wujin Sidun yizhi de fajue [1982 Excavation at the Sidun Site, of Changzhou, Wujin, Jiangsu Province]. *Kaogu* 1984(2): 109–29.

Needham, J. 1971. *Science and Civilisation in China: Vol. 4, Part 3, Civil Engineering and Nautics*. Cambridge, Cambridge University Press.

Neimenggu Wenwu Kaogu Yanjiusuo. 1997. Keshiketeng Qi Nantaizi yizhi [The Nantaizi Site in Keshiketeng Banner], in Wei Jian (ed.) *Neimenggu wenwu kaogu wenji*. Beijing, Zhongguo Dabaike Quanshu Chubanshe: 2: 53–78.

———— 2000. *Daihai kaogu (1): Laohushan wenhua yizhi fajue baogao* [Daihai Archeology, Vol. 1: Excavation Report on the Laohushan Culture Site]. Beijing, Kexue Chubanshe.

Neimenggu Wenwu Kaogu Yanjiusuo & Qingshuihe Xian Wenwu Guanlisuo. 2001. Qinshuihe xian Xicha yizhi fajue jianbao [Preliminary Report on Excavations at the Xicha Site, Qingshuihe County], in Neimenggu Zizhiqu Wenwu Kaogu Yanjiusuo (ed.) *Wanjiazhai shuili shuniu gongcheng kaogu baogao ji*. Huhehaote, Yuanfang Chubanshe: 60–78.

Neimenggu Zizhiqu Wenwu Kaogu Yanjiusuo. 2000. *Zhukaigou – Qingtong shidai zaoqi yizhi fajue baogoa* [Zhukaigou: Report on the Excavation of an Early Bronze Age Site]. Beijing, Wenwu Chubanshe.

———— 2004. *Baiyinchanghan – Xinshiqi shidai yizhi fajue baogao* [Baiyinchanghan: Report on the Excavation of the Neolithic Site]. Beijing, Kexue Chubanshe.

Neimenggu Zizhiqu Wenwu Kaogu Yanjiusuo & Ningchengxian Liao Zhongjing Bowuguan. 2009. *Xiaoheishigou*. Beijing, Kexue chubanshe.

Nelson, K. 2010. Environment, Cooking Strategies and Containers. *Journal of Anthropological Archaeology* 29(2): 238–47.

Nienhauser, W. 1994. *The Grand Scribe's Records*. Bloomington, Indiana University Press.

Norton, C. J. & Xing Gao. 2008. Zhoukoudian Upper Cave Revisited. *Current Anthropology* 49(4): 732–45.

Paludan, A. 1991. *The Chinese Spirit Road: The Classical Tradition of Stone Tomb Statuary*. New Haven, Yale University Press.

Pechenkina, E. A., R. A. Benfer, & Wang Zhijun. 2002. Diet and Health Changes at the End of the Chinese Neolithic: I Yangshao/Longshan Transition in Shaanxi Province. *American Journal of Physical Anthropology* 117: 15–36.

Pechenkina, E. A., et al. 2005. Reconstructing Northern Chinese Neolithic Subsistence Practices by Isotopic Analysis. *Journal of Archaeological Science* 32(8): 1176–89.

Pei, Anping. 2004. Liyang pingyuan shiqian juluo xingtai de yanjiu yu sikao [Analysis of Prehistoric Settlement Patterns on the Liyang Plain], in Jilin Daxue Bianjiang Kaogu Yanjiu Zhongxin (ed.) *Qingzhu Zhang Zhongpei Xiansheng Qishisui Lunwenji*. Beijing, Kexue Chubanshe: 192–242.

Peng, Bangben. 2002. In Search of the Shu Kingdom: Ancient Legends and New Archaeological Discoveries in Sichuan. *Journal of East Asian Archaeology* 4: 75–99.

Peng, Ke. 2000. *Coinage and Commercial Development in Eastern Zhou China*. Ph.D. dissertation. University of Chicago.

Peng, Minghan. 2005. Wucheng wenhua yanjiu sanshinian de huigu yu qianzhan [Reflections on 30 Years of Research on the Wucheng Culture]. *Yindu Xuekan* 4: 16–24.

Peters, A. H. 1999. Towns and Trade: Cultural Diversity and Chu Daily Life, in C. A. Cook (ed.) *Defining Chu: Image and Reality in Ancient China*. Honolulu, University of Hawaii Press: 99–117.

Peterson, C. E. & R. D. Drennan. 2011. Methods for Delineating Community Patterns, in Chifeng International Collaborative Archaeological Project (ed.) *Settlement Patterns in the Chifeng Region*. Pittsburgh, Center for Comparative Archaeology, University of Pittsburgh: 80–7.

Peterson, C. E., et al. 2010. Hongshan Chiefly Communities in Neolithic Northeastern China. *Proceedings of the National Academy of Sciences* 107(13): 5756–61.

Peterson, C. E. & G. Shelach. 2010. The Evolution of Yangshao Period Village Organization in the Middle Reaches of Northern China's Yellow River Valley, in M. Bandy & J. R. Fox (eds.) *Becoming Villagers*. Tucson, University of Arizona Press: 246–75.

_____ 2012. Jiangzhai: Social and Economic Organization of a Middle Neolithic Chinese Village. *Journal of Anthropological Archaeology* 31: 265–301.

Pigott, Vincent C. & Roberto Ciarla. 2007. On the Origins of Metallurgy in Prehistoric Southeast Asia: The View from Thailand, in S. La Niece, D. Hook, & E. P. Craddock (eds.) *Metals and Mines: Studies in Archaeometallurgy*. London, British Museum: 76–88.

Pines, Y. 2002. *Foundations of Confucian Thought*. Honolulu, University of Hawaii Press.

_____ 2005. Beasts or Humans: Pre-imperial Origins of the "Sino-Barbarian" Dichotomy, in R. Amitai & M. Biran (eds.) *Mongols, Turks and Others: Eurasian*. Leiden, Brill: 59–102.

Pines, Y., et al. (eds.) 2013. *The Birth of Empire: The State of Qin Revisited*. Berkeley, University of California Press.

Poo, Mu-chou. 1998. *In Search of Personal Welfare: A View of Ancient Chinese Religion*. Albany, State University of New York Press.

_____ 2005. *Enemies of Civilization: Attitudes toward Foreigners in Ancient Mesopotamia, Egypt, and China*. Albany, State University of New York Press.

Prendergast, M. E., Yuan Jianrong, & O. Bar-Yosef. 2009. Resource Intensification in the Late Upper Paleolithic: A View from Southern China. *Journal of Archaeological Science* 36: 1027–37.

Price, T. D. & A. B. Gebauer. 1995. New Perspectives on the Transition to Agriculture, in T. D. Price & A. B. Gebauer (eds.) *Last Hunters First Farmers: New Perspectives on the Prehistoric Transition to Agriculture*. Santa Fe, School of American Research Press: 3–19.

Puyang Xishuipo Yizhi Kaogudui. 1989. 1988 nian Henan Puyang Xishuipo yizhi fajue jianbao [Preliminary Report on the 1988 Excavations of the Xishuipo Site, Puyang, Henan]. *Kaogu* 12: 57–66.

Qiao, Yu. 2007. Development of Complex Societies in the Yiluo Region: A GIS Based Population and Agricultural Area Analysis. *Bulletin of the Indo-Pacific Prehistory Association* 27: 61–75.

Qinghai Sheng Huangyuan Xian Bowuguan, et al. 1985. Qinghai Huangyuan xian Dahuazhongzhuang Kayue wenhua mudi fajue jianbao [Preliminary Report on the Excavation of the Kayue Culture Cemetery of Dahuazhongzhuang, Huangyuan County, Qinghai]. *Kaogu yu Wenwu* 5: 11–34.

Qinghai Sheng Wenwu Guanlichu Kaogudui & Zhongguo Shehui Kexueyuan Kaogu Yanjiusuo. 1984. *Qinghai Liuwan* [The site of Liuwan in Qinghai]. Beijing, Wenwu Chubanshe.

Qinghai Sheng Wenwu Kaogu Yanjiusuo. 1999. Qinghai sheng Guide xian kaogu diaocha [Archaeological Survey at the Guide County, Qinghai]. *Koagu xue jikan* 12: 1–19.

Qiu, Zhonglang. 1985. The Middle Palaeolithic of China, in Wu Rukang & J. W. Olsen (eds.) *Paleoanthropology and Paleolithic Archaeology in the People's Republic of China*. Walnut Creek, Left Coast Press: 187–210.

Rautman, A. E. 2000. Population Aggregation, Community Organization, and Plaza-Oriented Peublos in the American Southwest. *Journal of Field Archaeology* 27(3): 271–83.

Rawson, J. 1999. Western Zhou Archaeology, in M. Loewe & E. L. Shaughnessy (eds.) *The Cambridge History of Ancient China*. Cambridge, Cambridge University Press: 352–449.

_____ 2008. Carnelian Beads, Animal Figures and Exotic Vessels: Traces of Contact between the Chinese States and Inner Asia, ca. 1000–650 BC. *Eurasia Antiqua* 1: 1–48.

Reich, D., et al. 2010. Genetic History of an Archaic Hominin Group from Denisova Cave in Siberia. *Nature* 468(7327): 1053–60.

Ren, Shinan. 1998. Zhongguo shiqian chengzhi kaocha [Survey of Prehistoric Walled Sites in China]. *Kaogu* 1: 1–16.

Renfrew, C. 1986. Introduction: Peer Polity Interaction and Socio-political Change, in C. Renfrew & J. F. Cherry (eds.) *Peer Polity Interaction and Socio-political Change*. Cambridge, Cambridge University Press: 1–18.

Renfrew, C. & P. Bahn. 1996. *Archaeology: Theories, Methods, and Practice*. London, Thames and Hudson.

Richerson, P. J., R. Boyd, & R. L. Bettinger. 2001. Was Agriculture Impossible during the Pleistocene but Mandatory during the Holocene? A Climate Change Hypothesis. *American Antiquity* 66(3): 387–411.

Rispoli, F. 2007. The Incised & Impressed Pottery Style of Mainland Southeast Asia: Following the Paths of Neolithization. *East and West* 57(1–4): 235–304.

Rosen, A. M. 2008. The Impact of Environmental Change and Human Land Use on Alluvial Valleys in the Loess Plateau of China during the Middle Holocene. *Geomorphology* 101: 298–307.

Sanft, C. 2008. The Construction and Deconstruction of Epanggong: Notes from the Crossroads of History and Poetry. *Oriens Extremus* 47: 160–76.

———— 2011. Debating the Route of the Qin Direct Road (Zhidao): Text and Excavation. *Frontiers of History in China* 6(3): 323–46.

———— 2014. *Communication and Cooperation in Early Imperial China*. Albany, State University of New York Press.

Sautman, B. 2001. Peking Man and the Politics of Paleoanthropological Nationalism in China. *Journal of Asian Studies* 60(1): 95–124.

Schortman, E. M. & P. A. Urban. 1992. The Place of Interaction Studies in Archaeological Thought, in E. M. Schortman & P. A. Urban (eds.) *Resources, Power, and Interaction*. New York, Plenum: 3–15.

Selbitschka, A. 2013. The Tomb Complex and Its Hidden Secrets, in M. Khayutina (ed.) *Qin: The Eternal Emperor and His Terracotta Warriors*. Zurich, Neue Zürcher Zeitung Publishing.

Shaanxi, Kaogu Yanjiusuo, et al. 2013. Shaanxi Shenmu Shimao yizhi [The Shimao Site of Shenmu, Shaanxi]. *Kaogu* 2013(7): 15–24.

Shahar, M. 1998. *Crazy Ji: Chinese Religion and Popular Literature*. Cambridge, MA, Harvard University Press.

Shandong Sheng Wenwu Kaogu Yanjiusuo, et al. 2010. Shandong Shouguang shi Shuangwangcheng yanye yizhi 2008 nian de fajue [2008 Excavation at the Shuangwangcheng Salt Production Site, Shouguang City, Shandong]. *Kaogu* 3: 18–36.

Shandong Sheng Wenwu Kaogu Yanjiusuo & Zhangqiu Shi Bowuguan. 2003. Dong Zhangqiu shi Xiaojingshan Houli wenhua huanhao juluo kantan baogao [Report on the Exploration of the Moat-Surrounded Settlement of Houli Culture at Xiaojingshan in Zhangqiu City, Shandong]. *Huaxia Kaogu* 3: 3–11.

Shang, Hong, et al. 2007. An Early Modern Human from Tianyuan Cave, Zhoukoudian, China. *Proceedings of the National Academy of Sciences* 104: 6573–8.

Shao, Wangping. 2000. The Longshan Period and Incipient Chinese Civilization. *Journal of East Asian Archaeology* 2(1–2): 195–226.

Shaughnessy, E. L. 1988. Historical Perspectives on the Introduction of the Chariot into China. *Harvard Journal of Asiatic Studies* 48(1): 189–237.

———— 1989. Historical Geography and the Extent of the Earliest Chinese Kingdoms. *Asia Major* 2(2): 1–22.

———— 1999. Western Zhou History, in M. Loewe & E. L. Shaughnessy (eds.) *The Cambridge History of Ancient China*. Cambridge, Cambridge University Press: 292–351.

Shelach, G. 1996. The Qiang and the Question of Human Sacrifice in the Late Shang Period. *Asian Perspectives* 35(1): 1–26.

———— 1999. *Leadership Strategies, Economic Activity, and Interregional Interaction: Social Complexity in Northeast China*. New York, Plenum.

———— 2000. The Earliest Neolithic Cultures of Northeast China: Recent Discoveries and New Perspectives on the Beginning of Agriculture. *Journal of World Prehistory* 14(4): 363–413.

———— 2001a. Apples and Oranges? A Cross-Cultural Comparison of Burial Data from Northeast China. *Journal of East Asian Archaeology* 3(3–4): 53–90.

———— 2001b. The Dragon Ascends to Heaven, the Dragon Dives into the Abyss: Creation of the Chinese Dragon Symbol. *Oriental Art* 47(3): 29–40.

———— 2004. Marxist and Post-Marxist Paradigms for the Neolithic, in K. M. Linduff & Yan Sun (eds.) *Gender and Chinese Archaeology*. Walnut Creek, Altamira: 11–27.

———— 2006. Economic Adaptation, Community Structure, and Sharing Strategies of Households at Early Sedentary Sites in Northeast China. *Journal of Anthropological Archaeology* 25(3): 318–45.

———— 2009. *Prehistoric Societies on the Northern Frontiers of China: Archaeological Perspectives on Identity Formation and Economic Change during the First Millennium BCE*. London, Equinox.

———— 2011. I processi di interazione interregionale tra la tarda Età Neolitica e l'inizio dell'Età del Bronzo in Cina, in La Cina [Interregional Interactions during the Late Neolithic and Early Bronze], in M. Scarpari (ed.) *The Chinese Civilization: From Its Origins to Contemporary Times; Vol. 1, Prehistory and the Roots of Civilization in China*. Turin, Giulio Einaudi Editore: 489–557.

———— 2012. On the Invention of Pottery. *Science* 336(6089): 1644–5.

———— 2013. Collapse or Transformation? Anthropological and Archaeological Perspectives on the Fall of Qin, in Y. Pines, G. Shelach, L. V. Falkenhausen, & R. D. S. Yates (eds.) *The Birth of Empire: The State of Qin Revisited*. Berkeley, University of California Press: 113–38.

Shelach, G. & Y. Jaffe. 2013. The Earliest States in China: A Long-Term Trajectory Approach. *Journal of Archaeological Research*.

Shelach, G., & Y. Pines. 2006. Secondary State Formation and the Development of Local Identity: Change and Continuity in the State of Qin (770–221 B.C.), in M. Stark (ed.) *Archaeology of Asia*. Malden, Blackwell: 202–30.

Shelach, G., K. Raphael, & Y. Jaffe. 2011. Sanzuodian: The Structure, Function and Social Significance of the Earliest Stone Fortified Sites in China. *Antiquity* 85: 11–26.

Shen, Kangshen, J. N. Crossley, & Anthony Lun (trans. & eds.) 1999. *The Nine Chapters on Mathematical Arts:*

Companion and Commentary. Oxford, Oxford University Press.

Sherratt, A. 1995. Reviving the Grand Narrative: Archaeology and Long-Term Change. *Journal of European Archaeology* 3(1): 1–32.

Shizitan Kaogudui. 2010. Shanxi Ji xian Shizitan yizhi di jiu dian faxian jianbao [Preliminary Report on Excavations at Locality 9 of the Shizitan site, Ji County, Shanxi]. *Kaogu* 10: 7–17.

Shui, Tao. 2001. Gansu diqu qingtong shidai wenhua jiegou he jingji xingtai yanjiu [Research on the Cultures and Economic Adaptation in Gansu during the Bronze Age], in T. Shui (ed.) *Zhongguo xibei diqu qingtong shidai kaogu lunji* [Collection of Papers on the Bronze Age of Northwest China]. Beijing, Kexue Chubanshe: 193–327.

Smith, B. D. 2001. Low-Level Food Production. *Journal of Archaeological Research* 9(1): 1–43.

Smith, B. L. 2005. *Diet, Health, and Lifestyle in Neolithic North China.* Ph.D. dissertation. Cambridge, MA, Harvard University.

Song, Minqiao. 2002. Zhongguo yuanshi nongye qiyuan zhi beijing fenxi [Analysis of the Background for the Development of Agriculture in China]. *Shangqiu Shifan Xueyuan Xuebao* 18(1): 52–5.

Stanley, D. J., Chen Zhongyuan, & Song Jian. 1999. Inundation, Sea-Level Rise and Transition from Neolithic to Bronze Age Cultures, Yangtze Delta, China. *Geoarchaeology* 14(1): 15–26.

Steinhardt, Nancy S. 1984. *Chinese Traditional Architecture.* New York, China Institute in America.

Steponaitis, V. P. 1981. Settlement Hierarchies and Political Complexity in Nonmarket Societies: The Formative Period of the Valley of Mexico. *American Anthropologist* 83: 320–63.

Stiner, M. C. 2001. Thirty Years on the "Broad Spectrum Revolution" and Paleolithic Demography. *Proceedings of the National Academy of Sciences* 98(13): 6993–6.

Sun, Ji. 1990. *Handai wuzhi wenhua ziliao tushuo* [Handbook of Han Dynasty Material Culture]. Beijing: Wenwu chubanshe.

Sun, Shuyun & Han Rubin. 1997. Gansu zaoqi tongqi de faxian yu yelian zhizao jishu de yanjiu [Discovery of Early Copper and Bronze Artifacts in Gansu and Studies of Their Smelting and Manufacturing Techniques]. *Wenwu* 7: 75–84.

Sun, Yan. 2003. Bronzes, Mortuary Practice and Political Strategies of the Yan during the Early Western Zhou Period. *Antiquity* 77: 761–70.

Sun, Zhixin. 1993. The Liangzhu Culture: Its Discovery and Its Jades. *Early China* 18: 1–40.

Suo, Xiufen. 2005. Xiaohexi wenhua chulun [Preliminary Discussion of the Xiaohexi Culture]. *Kaogu yu Wenwu* 1: 23–6.

Suo, Xiufen & Li Shaobing. 2008. Xiaohexi wenhua juluo xingtai [Settlement Patterns of the Xiaohexi Culture]. *Neimenggu Wenwu Kaogu* 1: 55–60.

Tan, Weisi. 2001. *Zheng Hou Yi mu* [The Grave of Zheng Hou Yi]. Beijing, Wenwu Chubanshe.

Tang, Jigen & Jing Zhichun. 2009. Anyang de "Shangyi" yu "dayi Shang" [The Terms "Shangyi" and "dayi Shang" of Anyang]. *Kaogu* 9: 70–80.

Teng, Mingyu. 2003. *Qin wenhua: cong fenggou dao diguo de kaoguxue guancha* [Qin Culture in Archaeological Perspective: From Feudal State to Empire]. Beijing, Xueyuan Chubanshe.

Teng, Mingyu, et al. 2003. Changing Patterns of Settlement Distribution in the Chifeng Region, in Chifeng International Collaborative Archaeological Project (ed.) *Regional Archaeology in Eastern Inner Mongolia: A Methodological Exploration.* Beijing, Kexue Chubanshe: 107–21.

Thorp, R. L. 1991. Erlitou and the Search for the Xia. *Early China* 16: 1–38.

—— 2006. *China in the Early Bronze Age: Shang Civilization.* Philadelphia, University of Pennsylvania Press.

Tian, Guangjin & Han Jianye. 2003. Zhukaigou wenhua yanjiu [Research on the Zhukaigou Culture], in Beijing Daxue Kaogu Wenbo Xueyuan (ed.) *Kaoguxue Yanjiu.* Beijing, Kexue Chubanshe: 5: 226–59.

Tong, Enzheng. 1995. Thirty Years of Chinese Archaeology (1949–1979), in L. Kohl & C. Fawcett (eds.) *Nationalism, Politics, and the Practice of Archaeology.* Cambridge, Cambridge University Press: 177–97.

Tong, Weihua. 1984. Cishan yizhi de yuanshi nongye yicun jiqi xiangguan de wenti [Agricultural Remains at the Cishan Site and Related Questions]. *Nongye Kaogu* 1: 194–207.

Trigger, B. G. 1989. *A History of Archaeological Thought.* Cambridge, Cambridge University Press.

—— 2003. *Understanding Early Civilizations.* Cambridge, Cambridge University Press.

Twitchett, D. & M. Loewe (eds.) 1986. *The Cambridge History of China, Vol. 1: The Ch'in and Han Empires, 221 BCE–220 A.D.* Cambridge, Cambridge University Press.

Underhill, A. P. 1997. Current Issues in Chinese Neolithic Archaeology. *Journal of World Prehistory* 11: 103–60.

—— 2002. *Craft Production and Social Change in Northern China.* New York, Kluwer.

Underhill, A. P. & J. Habu. 2006. Early Communities in East Asia: Economic and Sociopolitical Organization at the Local and Regional Levels, in M. T. Stark (ed.) *Archaeology of Asia.* Malden, Blackwell: 121–48.

Underhill, A. P. & Fang Hui. 2004. Early State Economic Systems in China, in G. Feinman & L. Nicholas (eds.) *Archaeological Perspectives on Political Economies.* Salt Lake City, University of Utah Press: 129–44.

Underhill, A. P., et al. 2008. Changes in Regional Settlement Patterns and the Development of Complex Societies in Southeastern Shandong, China. *Journal of Anthropological Archaeology* 27(1): 1–29.

Wagner, D. B. 2008. *Ferrous Metallurgy*. Cambridge, Cambridge University Press.

Waldron, A. 1990. *The Great Wall of China: From History to Myth*. Cambridge, Cambridge University Press.

Wang, Binghua (ed.) 1999. *Xinjiang gu shi* [The Ancient Corpses of Xinjiang]. Urumqi, Xinjiang Renmin Chubanshe.

Wang, Guodao & Cui Zhaonian. 2003. Qinghai Kayue wenhua chutu de jinqi [Golden Artifacts Excavated from Kayue Sites in Qinghai]. *Gugong Bowuguan Yuankan* 5: 43–8.

Wang, Hongxing. 2003. Cong Menbanwan chenghao juluo kan Changjiang chongyou diqu chenghaoquluo de qiyuan yu gongyong [Examining the Development and Function of Moats in the Middle Yangzi River Area through the Settlement Area of Menbawan]. *Kaogu* 9: 61–75.

Wang, Jian, et al. 1978. Xiachuan Wenhua: Shanxi Xiachuan yizhi diaocha baogao [The Xiachuan Culture: Report on Investigations of the Xiachuan Site in Shanxi Province]. *Kaogu Xuabao* 3: 259–88.

Wang, Jie. 1990a. Shilun Daixi wenhua de fazhang he shehui xingtai [A Discussion of the Development and Social Organization of the Daixi Culture]. *Huaxia Kaogu* 4: 57–67.

———— 1990b. Shilun Hunan Daixi wenhua [A Discussion of the Daixi Culture of Hunan]. *Kaogu* 3: 239–54.

Wang, Lixin. 2004. Liaoxi qu Xia zhi Zhanguo shiqi wenhua geju yu jingji xingtai de yanjin [The Evolution of Cultural Patterns and Economic Formation in the Western Liaoning Area from the Xia to the Warring States Period]. *Kaogu Xuebao* 3: 243–69.

Wang, S. W. 2005. Cultural Collapse and Abrupt Climate Change at 2200–2000 BC. *Advances in Natural Sciences* 15(9): 1094–9.

Wang, Xueli & Liang Yun. 2001. *Qin wenhua* [Qin Culture]. Beijing, Wenhua Chubanshe.

Wang, Yi. 2003. Prehistoric Walled Settlements in the Chengdu Plain. *Journal of East Asian Archaeology* 5: 109–48.

Wang, Youping. 2005. *Zhongguo yuangu renlen wenhua de yuanliu* [The Roots of Pleistocene Hominins and Cultures in China]. Beijing: Kexue Chubanshe.

Wang, Zengxing. 1964. Liaoning Fushunshi Lianhuabao yizhi fajue jianbao [Preliminary Report on the Excavations at Lianhuabao, Fushun City, Liaonong]. *Kaogu* 1964(6): 286–93.

Watson, B. (trans.) 1993. *Records of the Grand Historian*. Hong Kong, Chinese University of Hong Kong Press.

Weaver, T. D. & C. C. Roseman. 2008. New Developments in the Genetic Evidence for Modern Human Origins. *Evolutionary Anthropology* 17: 69–80.

Weiner, S., et al. 1998. Evidence for the Use of Fire at Zhoukoudian, China. *Science* 281: 251–3.

Wheatley, P. 1971. *The Pivot of the Four Quarters*. Edinburgh, Edinburgh University Press.

Wilkinson, E. 1998. *Chinese History: A Manual*. Cambridge, MA, Harvard University Asia Center.

Winkler, M. G. & P. K. Wang. 1993. The Late-Quaternary Vegetation and Climate of China, in H. E. Wright, J. E. Kutzbach, T. Webb III, W. F. Ruddiman, S.-P. F. Alayne, & P. J. Bartlein (eds.) *Global Climates since the Last Glacial Maximum*. Minneapolis, University of Minnesota Press: 221–64.

Winterhalder, B. & D. J. Kennett. 2009. Four Neglected Concepts with a Role to Play in Explaining the Origins of Agriculture. *Current Anthropology* 50(5): 645–8.

Wobst, M. H. 1977. Stylistic Behavior and Information Exchange, in C. Cleland (ed.) *For the Director: Research Essays in Honor of James B. Griffin*. Ann Arbor, University of Michigan Museum of Anthropology Anthropological Papers 61: 317–42.

Wright, H. T. 1978. Toward an Explanation of the Origin of the State, in R. L. Cohen & E. R. Service (eds.) *Origins of the State: The Anthropology of Political Evolution*. Philadelphia, Institute for the Study of Human Issues: 49–68.

Wu, En. 2002a. Lüelun Ouya caoyuan zaoqi youmu yishu zhong de juanqu dongwu xingxiang [On the Carved Animal Figure in the Art of Early Nomadic Tribes in the Eurasian Steppe]. *Kaogu* 11: 60–8.

———— 2002b. Ouya dalu caoyuan zaoqi youmu wenhua de jidian sikao [Some Thoughts on Early Nomadic Culture in the Eurasian Steppe]. *Kaogu Xuabao* 4: 437–70.

Wu, Hung. 1999. The Art and Architecture of the Warring States Period, in M. Loewe & E. L. Shaughnessy (eds.) *The Cambridge History of Ancient China*. Cambridge, Cambridge University Press: 651–744.

———— 2001. Rethinking Warring States Cities: An Historical and Methodological Proposal. *Journal of East Asian Archaeology* 1–2: 237–57.

———— 2010. *Art of the Yellow Spring: Rethinking Chinese Tombs*. Honolulu, University of Hawaii Press.

Wu, Wenxiang & Liu Tungsheng. 2004. Possible Role of the "Holocene Event 3" in the Collapse of Neolithic Cultures around the Central Plain of China. *Quaternary International* 117: 153–66.

Wu, Xiaohong, et al. 2012. Early Pottery at 20,000 Years Ago in Xianrendong Cave, China. *Science* 336(6089): 1696–1700.

Wu Xiaolong. in press. *Visualization of Political Power in Ancient China: The State of Zhongshan in Archaeology and Historical Memory*.

Wu, Xinzhi & Wu Maolin. 1985. Early Homo Sapiens in China, in Wu Rukang & J. W. Olsen (eds.) *Paleoanthropology and Paleolithic Archaeology in the People's Republic of China*. Walnut Creek, Left Coast Press: 91–106.

Xia Shang Zhou Duandai gongcheng Zhuanjiazu, 2000. *Xia Shang Zhou Duandai Gongcheng 1996–2000 Nian Jieduan Chengguo Baogao* [Report on the 1996–2000 Work of the Xia, Shang, Zhou Periodization Project]. Beijing, Shijie Tushu Chubanshe.

Xia, Zhengkai & Yang Xiaoyan. 2003. Woguo beifang 4 ka BP qianhou yichang hongshui shijian de chubo yanjiu [Preliminary Study on the Flood Events about 4 ka B. P. in North China]. *Disiji yanjiu* 23(6): 667–74.

Xian Banpo Bowuguan. 1988. *Jiangzhai: Xinshiqi Shidai Yizhi Fajue Baogao* [Jiangzhai: Report on the Excavations of a Neolithic Site]. Beijing, Wenwu Chubanshe.

Xiang, Chunsong & Li Yi. 1995. Ningcheng Xiaoheishigou shiguomu diaocha qingli baogao [Report on Research into the Stone Coffin Grave Found at Xiaoheishigou, Ningcheng]. *Wenwu* 1995(5): 4–22.

Xianyang Shi Wenwu Kaogu Yanjiusuo. 1998. *Taerpo Qin mu* [Qin Grave of Taerpo]. Xian, Sanqin chubanshe.

Xiao, Minghua. 2001. Yunnan kaogu shulue [A Brief Discussion of the Archaeology of Yunnan]. *Kaogu* 12: 3–15.

Xu, Hong. 2000. *Xian Qin chengshi kaoguxue* [The Archaeology of Pre-Qin Cities]. Beijing, Yanshan Chubanshe.

————— 2009. *Zuizao de Zhonggou* [The Earliest China]. Beijing, Kexue chubanshe.

Xu, Pingfang. 2002. The Archaeology of the Great Wall of the Qin and Han Dynasties. *Journal of East Asian Archaeology* 3(1–2): 259–81.

Xu, Tianjin. 2006. Zhougong miao yizhi de daogu suohuo suosi [Reflection on Discoveries from the Archaeological Excavations at the Zhougong Miao Site]. *Wenwu* 8: 55–62.

Xu, Xusheng. 1959. 1959 nianxia Yuxi diaocha "Xiaxu" de chubu baogao [Preliminary Report on the "Xiaxu" 1959 Summer Survey of Western Yu]. *Kaogu* 11: 592–600.

Xu, Yan. 2009. Yunan diqu Erlitou shiqi yicun de xiangguan wenti shixi [Preliminary Analysis of Questions Related to the Erlitou Period Remains in the Yunan Region]. *Huaxia Kaogu* 2: 80–92.

Xu, Zhi, et al. 2008. Mitochondrial DNA Evidence for a Diversified Origin of Workers Building Mausoleum for First Emperor of China. *PLOS ONE* 3(10): 1–7.

Yan, Wenming. 1999. Neolithic Settlements in China: Latest Finds and Research. *Journal of East Asian Archaeology* 1: 131–47.

Yan, Xinzhi, et al. 2009. Han Jingdi Yangling yanjiu huigu yu Zhanwang [Reflections on the Past and Future of Research at the Yangling Mausoleum of Emperor Jingdi of the Han]. *Wenbao* 1: 25–33.

Yang, Quanxi. 1991. Shilun Chengbeixi wenhua [A Discussion of Chengbeixi Culture]. *Dongnan Wenhua* 5: 206–12.

Yang, Xiaoneng (ed.) 2004. *New Perspectives on China's Past: Chinese Archaeology in the Twentieth Century*. New Haven, Yale University Press.

Yang, Xiaoyan, et al. 2009. Starch Grain Analysis Reveals Function of Grinding Stone Tools at Shangzhai Site, Beijing. *Science in China Series D: Earth Sciences* 52(8): 1164–71.

Yang, Xiaoyan, et al. 2012. Early Millet Use in Northern China. *Proceedings of the National Academy of Sciences* 109: 2630–9.

Yang, Xiaoyan & Jiang Leping. 2010. Starch Grain Analysis Reveals Ancient Diet at Kuahuqiao Site, Zhejiang Province. *Chinese Science Bulletin* 55(12): 1150–6.

Yang, Zhaoqing. 1997. Shilun Zhengzhou Xishan Yangshao wenhua wanqi guchengzhi de xingzhi [Discussing the Layout of Late Yangshao City Site of Xishan, Zhengzhou]. *Huaxia Kaogu* 1: 55–9, 92.

Yao, Alice. 2010. Recent Developments in the Archaeology of Southwestern China. *Journal of Archaeological Research* 18(3): 203–39.

Yao, Alice & Jiang Zhilong. 2012. Rediscovering the Settlement System of the "Dian" Kingdom in Bronze Age Southern China. *Antiquity*. 86: 353–67.

Yasuda, Y. 2002. Origins of Pottery and Agriculture in East Asia, in Y. Yasuda (ed.) *The Origins of Pottery and Agriculture*. New Delhi, Lustre Press and Roli Books: 119–42.

Yates, R. D. S. 1995. State Control of Bureaucrats under the Qin: Techniques and Procedures. *Early China* 20: 331–65.

Yi, Sangheon, et al. 2003. Holocene Environmental History Inferred from Pollen Assemblages in the Huanghe (Yellow River) Delta, China: Climatic Change and Human Impact. *Quaternary Science Reviews* 22(5–7): 609–28.

Yin, Qun. 2001. *Huanghe hongxiayou diqu de Dong Zhou muzhang zhidu* [The Burial System of the Lower Reaches of the Yellow River during the Eastern Zhou Period]. Beijing: Shehui Kexue Chubanshe.

Yinxu Xiaomintun Kaogudui. 2007. Henan Anyangshi Xiaomintun Shangdai zhutong yizhi 2003–2004 nian de fajue [Excavations during the Years 2003–2004 at the Shang bronze Production Site of Xiaomintun, Anyang City, Henan Province]. *Kaogu* 1: 14–25.

Yongcheng kaogudui, et al. 1985. Fengxiang Majiazhuang yiho jianzhuqun yizhi fajue jianbao [Preliminary Report on the Excavations of Complex no. 1 at Majiazhuang, Fengxiang]. *Wenwu* 2: 11–5.

Yu, Shiyong, et al. 2000. Role of Climate in the Rise and Fall of Neolithic Cultures on the Yangtze Delta. *Boreas* 29: 157–65.

Yu, Ying-shih. 1986. Han Foreign Relations, in D. Twitchett & M. Loewe (eds.) *The Cambridge History of China, Vol. 1, The Ch'in and Han Empires, 221 BCE–220 A.D.* Cambridge, Cambridge University Press: 377–462.

Yuan, Guangkuo & Zeng Xiaomin. 2004. Lun Zhengzhou Shangcheng neicheng he waicheng de guanxi [Discussing the Relations between the Inner and Outer Walls at the Shang City of Zhengzhou]. *Kaogu* 3: 59–67.

Yuan, Jing. 2008. The Origins and Development of Animal Domestication in China. *Chinese Archaeology* 8: 1–7.

Yuan, Jing & R. K. Flad. 2002. Pig Domestication in Ancient China. *Antiquity* 76(293): 724–32.

Yuan, Jing, R. Flad, & Luo Yunbing. 2008. Meat-Acquisition Patterns in the Neolithic Yangzi River Valley, China. *Antiquity* 82: 351–66.

Yuan, Zhongyi. 2008. Qin taowen zongshu [A Compendium of Qin's Ceramic Inscriptions]. *Qin Wenhua Luncong* 15: 1–36.

Zeder, A. M., et al. 2006. Documenting Domestication: Bringing Together Plants, Animals, Archaeology and Genetics, in A. M. Zeder, D. G. Bradley, E. Emshwiller, & B. D. Smith (eds.) *Documenting Domestication: New Genetic and Archaeological Paradigms.* Berkeley, University of California Press: 1–12.

Zhang, Chi. 2009. Mengcheng Yuchisi (di er bu): Xinshiqi shidai, Dawenkou wenhua wanqi huanhao juluo [Mengcheng Yuchisi, Part 2: A Neolithic Age Late Dawenkou Culture Moat-Surrounded Settlement). *Kaogu* 5: 87–96.

Zhang, Chi & Hung Hsiao-Chun. 2008. The Neolithic of Southern China: Origin, Development, and Dispersal. *Asian Perspectives: Journal of Archeology for Asia & the Pacific* 47(2): 299–329.

Zhang, Jia-Fu, et al. 2011. The Paleolithic Site of Longwangchan in the Middle Yellow River, China: Chronology, Paleoenvironment and Implications. *Journal of Archaeological Science* 38: 1537–50.

Zhang, Jingguo. 2006. *Lingjiatan.* Beijing, Wenwu Chubanshe.

Zhang, Q., et al. 2005. Environmental Change and Its Impacts on Human Settlement in the Yangtze Delta, P. R. China. *CATENA* 60(3): 267–77.

Zhang, Senshui. 1985. The Early Palaeolithic of China, in Wu Rukang & J. W. Olsen (eds.) *Paleoanthropology and Paleolithic Archaeology in the People's Republic of China.* Walnut Creek, Left Coast Press: 147–86.

Zhang, Wenxu & Pei Anping. 1997. Li xian Mengxi Bashidang chutu daogu de yanjiu [Research on the Ancient Rice from Bashidang, Mengxi in Li County]. *Wenwu* 11: 36–41.

Zhang, Xuehai. 1999. Lun Mojiaoshan guguo [On the Ancient City of Mojiaoshan]. *Liangzhu Wenhua Yanjiu* 18–22.

———— 2006. *Longshan wenhua* [The Longshan Culture]. Beijing, Wenwu Chubanshe.

Zhang, Xuelian, et al. 2007. Xinzhai – Erlitou – Erligang wenhua kaogu niandai xulie de jianli yu wanshan [Refining the Sequence and Chronology of the Xinzhai, Erlitou and Erligang Cultures]. *Kaogu* 2007(8): 74–89.

Zhang, Xuqiu. 2004. *Qujialing wenhua* [The Qujialing Culture]. Beijing, Wenwu Chubanshe.

Zhang, Zhongpei. 1985. The Social Structure Reflected in the Yuanjunmiao Cemetery. *Journal of Anthropological Archaeology* 4(1): 19–33.

———— 2000. Zhongguo gudai wenming xingcheng de kaoguxue yanjiu [Archaeological Research on the Formation of Chinese Ancient Civilization]. *Gugong Bowuyuan Yuankan* 2: 5–27.

Zhangjiakou Shi Wenwu Shiye Guanlisuo. 1987. Hebei Xuanhua xian Xiaobaiyang mudi fajue baogao [Report on the Excavations at the Xiaobaiyang Cemetery, Xuanhua County, Hebei]. *Wenwu* 5: 41–51.

Zhao, Chaohong, et al. 2003. A Study on an Early Neolithic Site in North China. *Documenta Praehistorica* 30: 169–73.

Zhao, Chunqing. 2009. Xinzhai juluo kaogu de shijian yu fangfa [Methods of Settlement Archaeology of Xinzhai]. *Kaogu* 2: 48–54.

Zhao, Congcang & Guo Yanli. 2004. *Liang Zhou kaogu* [Archaeology of the Two Zhou Periods]. Beijing, Wenwu Chubanshe.

Zhao, Huacheng & Gao Chongwen. 2002. *Qin Han kaogu* [Archaeology of the Qin and Han]. Beijing, Wenwu Chubanshe.

Zhao, Zhijun. 2004. Cong Xinglonggou yizhi fuxuan jieguo tan Zhongguo beifang zao zuo nongye qiyuan wenti [Addressing the Origins of Agriculture in North China Based on the Results of Flotation from the Xinglonggou Site]. *Dongya Guwu* 12: 188–99.

Zhao, Zhijun, et al. 2005. Guangxi Yongning xian Dingsishan yizhi chutu zhiwu guishi de fenxi yu yanjiu [Analysis of Plant Phytolith Found at the Dingsishan Site, Yongning County, Guangxi] *Kaogu* 11: 76–84.

Zhao, Zhijun & Zhang Juzhong. 2009. Jiahu yizhi 2001 niandu fuxuan jieguo fenxi baogao [Report on the Analysis of the Floatation of the 2001 Season at the Jiahu Site]. *Kaogu* 8: 84–93.

Zhejiang Sheng Bowuguan Ziranzu. 1978a. Hemudu yizhi dongzhiwu yicun de jianding yanjiu [Identification and Research of Animal and Plant Remains from the Hemudu Site]. *Kaogu Xuabao* 1: 95–107.

Zhejiang Sheng Wenwu Guanli Weiyuanhui & Zhejieang Sheng Bowuguan. 1978b. Hemudu yizhi diyi qi fajue baogao [Report on the First Excavation Season at the Hemudu Site]. *Kaogu Xuabao* 1: 39–94.

Zhejiang Sheng Wenwu Kaogu Yanjiusuo. 2005. *Fanshan*. Beijing, Wenwu Chubanshe.

Zhejiang Sheng Wenwu Kaogu Yanjiusuo & Xiaoshan Bowuguan. 2004. *Kuahuqiao*. Beijing, Wenwu chubanshe.

Zheng, Ruokui. 1995. Yinxu "Dayishang" zuyi buju chutan [Preliminary Discussion of the Distribution of Clan Settlements at Yinxu]. *Zhongyuan Wenwu* 3: 83–93.

Zheng, Yunfei, et al. 2009. Rice Fields and Modes of Rice Cultivation between 5000 and 2500 BC in East China. *Journal of Archaeological Science* 36(12): 2609–16.

Zhengzhou Shi Bowuguan. 1979. Zhengzhou Dahecun Yizhi Fajue Baogao [Report on the Excavations at the Dahecun Site, Zhengzhou]. *Kaogu Xuabao* 3: 301–75.

Zhengzhou Shi Wenwu Kaogu Yanjiusuo. 2001. *Zhengzhou Dahecun*. Beijing, Kexue Chubanshe.

Zhongguo Kexueyuan Kaogu Yanjiusuo Guangxi Gongzuodui, et al. 1998. Guangxi Yongningxian Dingsishan yizhi de fajue [Excavations at the Dingshishan Site at Yongning County, Guangxi]. *Kaogu* 11: 11–33.

Zhongguo Kexueyuan Kaogu Yanjiusuo Guangxi Gongzuodui, et al. 2003. Guangxi Nanning Baozitou beiqiu yizhi de fajue [Excavation of the Shell-Middens Site of Baozitou in Naning, Guangxi]. *Kaogu* 10: 22–34.

Zhongguo Qingtong Qi Quanji Bianji Weiyuan Huibian. 1997. *Zhongguo qingtongqi quanji* [Collection of Chinese Bronzes]. Vol. 2. Beijing, Wenwu Chubanshe.

Zhongguo Shehui Kexueyuan Kaogu Yanjiusuo. 1980. *Yinxu Fuhao mu* [The Fuhao Grave at Yinxu]. Beijing, Wenwu Chubanshe.

———— 1994. *Yinxu de faxian yu yanjiu* [Discoveries and Research about Yinxu]. Beijing, Kexue Chubanshe.

———— 1996. *Dadianzi: Xiajiadian xiaceng wenhua yizhi yu mudi fajue baogao* [Dadianzi: Excavations of a Domestic Site and Cemetery of the Lower Xiajiadian Period]. Beijing, Kexue Chubanshe.

———— 1997. *Zhaobaogou: xinshiqi shidai juluo* [Zhaobaogou: A Neolithic Settlement]. Beijing, Zhongguo Dabaike Quanshu Chubanshe.

———— 1999. *Yanshi Erlitou 1959 nian – 1978 nian kaogu fajue baogao* [Report on Excavations from 1959 to 1978 at the Erlitou Site]. Beijing, Zhongguo Dabaike Quanshu Qubanshe.

———— 2003. *Zhongguo Kaoguxue: Xia Shang Juan* [Chinese Archaeology: The Xia and Shang Volume]. Beijing, Zhongguo Shehui Kexue Chubanshe.

———— 2004. *Zhongguo Kaoguxue: Liang Zhou Juan* [Chinese Archaeology: The Zhou Volume]. Beijing, Zhongguo Shehui Kexue Chubanshe.

———— 2010a. *Zhongguo Kaoguxue: Qin Han Juan* [Chinese Archaeology: The Qin and Han Volume]. Beijing, Zhongguo Shehui Kexue Chubanshe.

———— 2010b. *Zhongguo Kaoguxue: Xinshiqi shidai Juan* [Chinese Archaeology: The Neolithic Volume]. Beijing, Zhongguo Shehui Kexue Chubanshe.

Zhongguo Shehui Kexueyuan Kaogu Yanjiusuo, et al. 2003. *Guilin Zengpiyan*. Beijing, Wenwu Chubanshe.

Zhongguo Shehui Kexueyuan Kaogu Yanjiusuo Henan Yidui, et al. 2007. Henan Lingbaoshi Xipo yizhi 2006 nian fajue xin de Yangshao wenhua zhongqi daxing muzang [New Yangshao Culture Graves Excavated in 2006 at the Xipo Site, Lingbao City, Henan]. *Kaogu* 2007(2): 3–6.

Zhongguo Shehui Kexueyuan Kaogu Yanjiusuo Neimenggu Gongzuodui. 1985. Neimenggu Aohan Qi Xinglongwa yizhi fajue jianbao [Preliminary Report on Excavations at the Xinglongwa Site, Aohan Banner, Inner Mongolia]. *Kaogu* 10: 865–73.

———— 1997. Aohan Qi Xinglongwa juluo yizhi 1992 nian fajue jianbao [Preliminary Report of the 1992 Excavations at the Xinglongwa Site, Aohan Banner, Inner Mongolia]. *Kaogu* 1997(1): 1–26.

Zhongguo Shehui Kexueyuan Kaogu Yanjiusuo & Qinghai Sheng Wenwu Kaogu Yanjiusuo. 2004. Qinghai Huzhu Fengtai Kayue wenhua yizhi fuxuan jieguo fenxi baogao [Report on the Analysis of Flotation Results from the Kayue Culture Site of Fengtai, Huzhu, Qinghai]. *Kaogu yu Wenwu* 2: 85–91.

Zhongguo Shehui Kexueyuan Kaogu Yanjiusuo & Shaanxi Sheng Kaogu Yanjiusuo. 2007. *Shaanxi Yichuan xian Longwangchan jiushiqi shidai yizhi* [The Paleolithic Site of Longwangchan, Yichuan County, Shaanxi]. *Kaogu* 2007(7): 3–8.

Zhongguo Shehui Kexueyuan Kaogu Yanjiusuo Shanxidui, et al. 2005. Shanxi Xiangfen Taosi chengzhi 2002 nian fajue baogao [Report of the 2002 Excavations of the Taosi City Site, Xiangfen, Shanxi]. *Kaogu Xuabao* 3: 307–46.

———— 2007. Shanxi Xiangfen xian Taosi zhongqi chengzhi daxing jianzhu II FJT1 jizhi 2004–2005 nian fajue jianbao [The 2004–2005 Excavation of Large Building Foundation II FJT1 at the City-Site from the Middle Taosi Period in Xiangfen County, Shanxi]. *Kaogu* 4: 3–25.

Zhongguo Shihui, Kexueyuan Kaogusuo Yanjiu Guangxi Gongzuo Dui, Guangxi Zhuangzu Zizhiqu Wenwu Gogzuo Dui, et al. 1998. Guangxi Yongning xian Dingsishan yizhi de fajue [Excavations at the Dingsishan site, Yongning county, Guangxi]. *Kaogu* 1998(11): 11–33.

Zhongguo Wenwuju (ed.) 2003. *Zhongguo wenwu ditu ji: Neimenggu zizhiqu fence* [Cultural Relics Map of China: the Inner Mongolia Autonomous Region Volume]. Xian, Xian Ditu Chubanshe.

Zhou, Benxiong. 1981. Hebei Wu'an Cishan yizhi de dongwu guhai [Animal Remains from the Cishan Site, Wuan, Hebei]. *Kaogu Xuabao* 3: 339–47.

Zhou, Weijian, et al. 2001. Climate Changes in Northern China since the Late Pleistocene and Its Response to Global Change. *Quaternary International* 83–5: 285–92.

Zhu, Fusheng. 2005. Jiangxi Xingan Niucheng yizhi diaocha [Survey of the Niucheng site, Xingan, Jiangxi Province]. *Nanfang Wenwu* 4: 4–7.

Zhu, Naicheng. 2001. Zhongguo nongzuowu zaipei de qiyuan he yuanshi nongye de xingqi [The Origins of Crop Cultivation in China and the Development of Agriculture]. *Nongye Kaogu* 3: 29–38.

Zhu, Yonggang. 2004. Xiajiadian shangceng wenhua xiang nan de fenbu taishi yu diyu wenhua bianqian [The Spread of the Upper Xiajiadian Culture Southward and the Transformation of Local Cultures], in Jilin Daxue Bianjiang Kaogu Yanjiu Zhongxin (ed.) *Qingzhu Zhang Zhongpei xiansheng qishi sui lunwen ji*. Beijing, Kexue Chubanshe: 422–36.

INDEX